Charles Elliott, Leroy M. Vernon

A History of the M. E. Church in the South-West, from 1844 to 1864

Comprising the Martyrdom of Bewley and Others - Persecutions of the M. E.

Church, and its Reorganization, etc.

Charles Elliott, Leroy M. Vernon

A History of the M. E. Church in the South-West, from 1844 to 1864
Comprising the Martyrdom of Bewley and Others - Persecutions of the M. E. Church, and its Reorganization, etc.

ISBN/EAN: 9783337161699

Printed in Europe, USA, Canada, Australia, Japan

Cover: Foto ©Lupo / pixelio.de

More available books at **www.hansebooks.com**

SOUTH-WESTERN METHODISM.

A HISTORY

OF THE

M. E. CHURCH IN THE SOUTH-WEST,

FROM 1844 TO 1864.

COMPRISING THE MARTYRDOM OF BEWLEY AND OTHERS; PER-
SECUTIONS OF THE M. E. CHURCH, AND ITS
REORGANIZATION, ETC.

BY REV. CHARLES ELLIOTT, D. D., LL. D.,

AUTHOR OF "DELINEATIONS OF ROMANISM," "SINFULNESS OF AMERICAN SLAVERY,"
"THE BIBLE AND SLAVERY," "THE GREAT SECESSION," ETC.

EDITED AND REVISED BY

REV. LEROY M. VERNON, A. M.,

Of the Missouri and Arkansas Conference.

CINCINNATI:
PUBLISHED BY POE & HITCHCOCK,
FOR THE EDITOR.

R. P. THOMPSON, PRINTER.
1868.

PREFACE.

THIS volume professes to be a brief history of the Methodist Episcopal Church in Missouri, and the parts beyond, but especially of Missouri, from the time of the great secession from the Methodist Episcopal Church in 1844–45, to the beginning of the year 1865. From this narrative of facts and events it will be seen that to be a member of the Methodist Episcopal Church in these regions, during the period above specified, was the greatest crime known by the pro-slavery men of the South-West, as membership in that Church was synonymous with *negro thief*, incendiary, insurrectionist, and the like.

Most of the information here presented was collected by the writer from May, 1860, to May, 1864, while he was editor of the Central Christian Advocate. A few of the preachers of our Church in Missouri wrote to us accounts of the persecutions they endured. But most of them did not. Yet we culled from their occasional communications much of the matter of this history. My duties as editor prevented me from furnishing the volume before this time. It is now presented to the public as a part of the history of the Methodist Episcopal Church in the South-West.

CHARLES ELLIOTT.

IOWA WESLEYAN UNIVERSITY, }
April 1, 1865. }

EDITOR'S PREFACE.

THIS volume was prepared while the author was editing, without assistance, the Central Christian Advocate at the close of a long and laborious public and literary career, with the infirmities of age pressing heavily upon him. Otherwise "edited and revised, etc.," on the title-page would be unmeaning or absurd. As it is, the editor has not been without something to do.

The manuscript has been handled reverently and with indisposition to make changes, however trivial, although the partial confidence of the author gave liberty "to abridge, amend, or alter, as seemed best, provided only his sentiments be maintained." Abridgment seemed impracticable. The changes made are such only as the author would doubtless have effected himself, with leisure for their consideration.

Embracing Church history in which "truth is stranger than fiction," as well as much of the general history of Missouri, the book can scarcely fail to interest the general reader. The volume, such as it is, goes forth to a charitable public, with an ardent hope and prayer that it may promote true Christianity, especially in the territory it surveys!

L. M. VERNON.

ST. CHARLES COLLEGE, *Dec.* 5, 1867.

CONTENTS.

10 CONTENTS.

SOUTH-WESTERN METHODISM.

CHAPTER I.

INTRODUCTION.

As preliminary to this volume, we deem it proper to present the views on slavery as they were originally entertained by our leading statesmen, next by the Churches outside of Methodism, and then by the Methodist Episcopal Church and the Methodist Episcopal Church South.

1. We first present the views of our leading American statesmen on this subject:

"It is the most earnest wish of America to see an entire stop forever put to the wicked, cruel, and unnatural trade in slaves." (Meeting at Fairfax, Va., July 18, 1776, presided over by Washington.)

The Declaration of Independence was proclaimed July 4, 1776. Jefferson's original draft of this contains the following:

"The King of Great Britain has waged cruel war against human nature itself, violating its most sacred rights of life and liberty in the persons of a distant people who never offended him, captivating them and carrying them into slavery in another hemisphere, or to incur miserable death in their transportation hither."

In 1776 we have the following in the Declaration of Independence: "All men are created free."

"I tremble for my country when I reflect that God is just." (Jefferson's notes in 1782.)

"The scheme, my dear Marquis, which you propose as a precedent to encourage the black people in this country in a state of bondage in which they are held is a striking evidence of the goodness of your heart." (Washington to Lafayette, 1783.)

"There is not a man living who wishes more sincerely than I do to see a plan adopted for the abolition of slavery." (Washington, April 12, 1786.)

"After the year 1800 of the Christian Era there shall be neither slavery nor involuntary servitude in any of the said States." (Ordinance of 1787, unanimously approved by Congress, and signed by Washington.)

"We have seen the mere distinction of color made in the most enlightened period of time, a ground of the most oppressive dominion ever exercised by man over man." (Madison.)

"We have found that this evil has preyed upon the very vitals of the Union, and has been prejudicial to all the States in which it has existed." (James Monroe.)

"The tariff was only the pretext, and disunion and a Southern Confederacy the real object. The next pretext will be the negro, or slavery question." (Andrew Jackson, in 1833.)

"Sir, I envy not the heart nor the head of that man from the North who rises here to defend slavery from principle." (John Randolph.)

"The people of Carolina form two classes, the rich and the poor. The poor are very poor. The rich, who have slaves to do their work, give them no employment. The little they get is laid out in brandy, not in books and newspapers. Hence they know nothing of the comparative blessings of our country, or of the dangers which threaten it.

Therefore they care nothing about it." (General Marion to Baron de Kalb.)

"So long as God allows the vital current to flow through my veins I will never, *never*, NEVER, by word or thought, by mind or will, aid in admitting one rood of free territory to the everlasting curse of human bondage." (Henry Clay.)

Alluding to the time the above sentiment was uttered, Thomas H. Benton declares: "That was a proud day. I could have wished that I had spoken the same words. I speak them now, telling you they were his, and adopting them as my own."

Similar sentiments were uttered by our statesmen up to the year 1832.

2. In the year 1832 and onward our statesmen began to declare in favor of slavery.

In the year 1832 Professor Dew, of William and Mary College, Virginia, wrote an elaborate essay in favor of slavery, a copy of which we possess; and this seems to be the first open attempt to sustain, by the press, the institution. His essay was designed to counteract the movement being then made by other Virginians to do away slavery in the State as a means of preventing such slave insurrections as that made at Northampton, Va.

The next plea for slavery was made in 1834, by Mr. M'Duffie, Governor of South Carolina, in his inaugural message.

In 1835 Governor Hammond issued a similar pro-slavery message.

Mr. Calhoun was of the same opinion with these—and doubtless there were many then to agree with them—and thus the political heresy progressed till it ended in disunion, bloodshed, and every evil work.

3. The early teachings of most of the American Churches were strongly antislavery.

In 1789 Baptists in Virginia expressed themselves in these terms: "*Resolved*, That slavery is a violent deprivation of the rights of nature, and inconsistent with republican government; and therefore we recommend to our brethren to make use of every measure *to extirpate this horrid evil from our land*," etc.

Most Baptists in the South have since erred much, being rankly pro-slavery.

The General Assembly of the Presbyterian Church, in 1794, adopted a note to the 142d question in the Larger Catechism in the Confession of Faith, in the words following: "1 Tim. i, 10: *The law was made for man-stealers.* This crime, among the Jews, exposed the perpetrators of it to capital punishment—Ex. xxi, 16—and the apostle here classes them with sinners of the first rank. The word he uses, in its original import, comprehends all who are concerned in bringing any of the human race into slavery, or RETAINING THEM IN IT. '*Hominum fures, qui servos vel liberos abducunt, retinent, vendunt, vel emunt.*' Stealers of men are those who bring off slaves or freemen, and KEEP, SELL, OR BUY THEM. To steal a free man, says Grotius, is the highest kind of theft. In other instances we may steal human property, but when we steal or *retain men* in slavery we seize those who, in common with ourselves, are constituted, by the original grant, lords of the earth. (Gen. i, 28.)"

The following resolution was unanimously adopted by the Presbyterian General Assembly, in 1818: "We consider the voluntary enslaving of one part of the human race by another as utterly inconsistent with the law of God, which enjoins that "all things whatsoever ye would that men should do to you, do ye even so to them."

The Presbyterian Synod of Kentucky, in 1835, adopted a report, in much detail, that denounced slavery in terms as strong as John Wesley did, who called it "the sum of all villainies."

Such were the early views on this great subject held by Presbyterians.

4. The Methodists, as all know, have unequivocally uttered the most expressive declarations against slavery, from the organization of their Church down to the present time.

In 1780 the testimony was in the following words, from the Baltimore Conference, which, at that time, was virtually the Methodist Episcopal Church: "This Conference acknowledges that slavery is contrary to the law of God, man, and nature, and hurtful to society; contrary to the dictates of conscience and pure religion, and doing that which we would not that others should do to us and ours. We pass our disapprobation on all our friends who keep slaves, and advise their freedom."

The General Conference of the Methodist Episcopal Church, at its organization in 1784, makes the following declaration: "We view slavery as contrary to the golden law of God, on which hang all the law and the prophets, and the unalienable rights of mankind, as well as every principle of the Revolution, to hold in the deepest debasement, in a more abject slavery than is perhaps to be found in any part of the world except America, so many souls that are all capable of the image of God."

October 2, 1805, the quarterly conference of Livingston circuit, of the Western Conference, then embracing Kentucky, in a memorial signed by W. M'Kendree, President of the Conference, speaks as follows:

"Though we can not assist you with money, at present, to extend the work of the Lord, we can no doubt gladden your hearts by giving you a view of our purifying work at home. Isaiah saith, 'Undo the heavy burdens, let the oppressed go free, break every yoke, . . . and thou shalt be like a watered garden, a spring of water which faileth not; yea, thou shalt be the restorer of the paths to walk in.' This day our official brethren voluntarily submitted all their slaves to the judgment of Conference, whether bought with their money before or after joining the society, given, or born in their house, and we, thereby, had the unspeakable pleasure of decreeing salvation from slavery in favor of twenty-two immortal souls; we did not reprobate one of them. Now, if the grace of God can prompt men to act thus, you may rest assured that the God of grace never designed one immortal soul for eternal burnings. Brother William Cade made a free offering of thirteen; now, eight of these cost him $1,770, bought before joined; the other five were given, or born in his house. Brother Josiah Ramsey offered up six on the altar of love; two of these cost him $850; the rest were born in his house. Brother James T. White one living man, which was his all. Brothers Lewis Barker and Robert Galloway one apiece. All these are to have salvation recorded speedily, and brother Thomas Randolph proposed his for the next quarterly meeting. When this is done we shall, as far as we know, be free from the stain of blood in our official department. Glory! Halleluiah! Praise ye the Lord!

"One thought more. If it be consistent with your authority, and it seemeth good unto you, we should be glad of liberty to exclude buying and selling from our Church, and to require of all slaveholders who may hereafter become members of the Church to submit their slaves to the judgment of Conference, who shall determine the time of servitude upon the same principle, and have a bill of manumission recorded in the same manner as the form of Discipline requires of buying a slave.

"We are, dear fathers, your sons and fellow-laborers in the kingdom and patience of Christ.

"Signed in behalf and by order of Conference.

    "W. M'KENDREE,

    "JAMES T. WHITE."

Such were the doctrines of the Methodist Episcopal Church in 1805, such were they previous to that time, and even down to the present·year of grace, 1868.

The teaching of the Methodist Episcopal Church may be summed up as follows: That slavery is contrary to natural law, to justice, to all the principles of the American Revolution in 1776, and to the law of God, and that it ought to be extirpated.

Yet, in the far South, after 1832, the teachings of some leading preachers seemed to run into the track of the pro-slavery politicians. Rev. Samuel Dunwoody, in 1835, preached a sermon before the South Carolina Conference which was truly pro-slavery, and in 1836 he repeated the same sentiments in Cincinnati, before the General Conference, much to the mortification of the Southern preachers. Even in 1844 the leading Southern preachers denounced slavery on the floor of General Conference.

5. But, after the secession of the Southern Methodists, in · 1845, the pro-slavery elements that had been accumulating in some instances soon became general. In 1854 the Southern Methodists struck out of the Methodist Discipline the chapter against slavery, and in 1858, by the united votes of their General Conference and their Annual Conferences, they struck out of the General Rules the powerful anti-slavery rule that forbid all purchase and sale of human beings. Shortly after, they generally maintained that slavery was supported by Scripture, thus filling up the measure of their apostasy by giving all the aid and comfort in their

power to a direct breach of God's moral law, and then, very
naturally, they became the willing partners of rebels in endeavoring to destroy the Government of the country.

6. The teachings of Scripture on this subject can be presented in a nutshell.

Abraham was an emancipator who bought many slaves
and set them free, of whom the patriarch became the civil
head.   To these emancipated slaves, or freedmen, were
added those *born in the house*, or raised in this free community.   The instances of slavery in the days of the patriarchs were such cases as that of Joseph, which alone condemns slavery in the most decided acts of God's providence.

Among the Jews the fundamental law was, "He that
stealeth a man and selleth him, or if he be found in his
hand, he shall surely be put to death."   Ex. xxi, 16.   This
law was repeated afterward to the Jews; for the bonds-
men of the Jews were not slaves, and, in order to prevent
the extension of the servitude agreed on between the bond-
man and his master, the contract must finally stop at the
year of jubilee.   Such was the Mosaic law, which was followed up by the prophets.

Besides, it was part of the great commission of Christ, as
foretold by Isaiah, and uttered by himself, *to set at liberty
the captives*, thus prohibiting the commencing act of enslaving.   Another part of Christ's mission was *to set at liberty
those that were bruised;* namely, all who were now slaves
should be set free, while the captives taken in war should
not be permitted to become slaves by their sale.   Such were
two of the great objects of Christ's mission; namely, to prevent any from being made slaves, as well as to set free those
already in slavery.

And so does Paul teach, who ranks *man-stealers* with the
worst class of sinners, even with murderers of fathers and
murderers of mothers—1 Tim. i, 9, 10—and, indeed, such

were the teachings and the practice of the first Christians for several hundred years after Christ.

7. The Methodist Episcopal Church, with her strong anti-slavery creed, or, if you will, with her abolition teachings and practice, was the first propagator of religion in the South-West.

In 1818 Missouri was on the Minutes in the Illinois Conference. Jesse Walker was presiding elder, with ten preachers, and 1,482 members. John Scripps was this year on Boonlick circuit, and in 1819 on Cape Girardeau circuit, and David Sharp was on Silver Creek circuit in 1819.

Thomas Drummond, in 1834, and Nelson Henry were transferred to the Missouri Conference. Mr. Drummond died June, 1835, having served to great advantage the Methodist Episcopal Church in St. Louis, and his grave is now in the Wesleyan cemetery near St. Louis. I remember his dying message to the Pittsburg Conference: "Tell my brethren of the Pittsburg Conference that I died at my post."[1] It was, indeed, a time of weeping in the Conference when the chair mentioned the message to the full Conference. Nelson Henry, too, was a man of like spirit, and served the Methodist Episcopal Church faithfully in Missouri till his death. Thus preachers from the North planted the Methodist Episcopal Church in Missouri.

The same remark will apply to Texas. Dr. Ruter, from the Pittsburg Conference, in 1837, was the first superintendent of the then Texas mission. In 1842 Daniel Poe, Homer S. Thrall, John W. Devilbiss, William J. Thurber, William O. Connor, and Richard Walker were transferred to Texas from the Ohio Conference, at its session in Springfield. These, also, were Northern men. Many others whose

[1] These dying words of the heroic Drummond inspired Rev. William Hunter, D. D., to write a beautiful and touching hymn, commencing, "Away from his home and the friends of his youth," etc. It may be found on the 328th page of the "Select Melodies."—EDITOR.

names I do not recollect were pioneer Methodist preachers
in the South-West, as the foregoing names are only specimens.

Thus Northern philanthropy and Christian enterprise
first carried the Gospel into these then remote parts. The
same sources continued to supply laborers for the opened
vineyard, sending them in from time to time as the widen-
ing fields and increased demands required. Those inaugu-
rating this spiritual husbandry in the sunny South-Western
wilds, little dreamed of the vengeful storm that was erelong to assail their "work of faith and labor of love."

How the tempest raged, felling, scattering, and finally
driving in dismay the laborers from the field till recalled
by the voice of God's providence, proclaiming the overthrow
of injustice and oppression and the reëstablishment of law
and liberty, will be unfolded in the following pages.

CHAPTER II.

THE RESTORATION OF THE METHODIST EPISCOPAL CHURCH IN THE SOUTH-WEST.

1. THE period in which the regular ministrations of the Methodist Episcopal Church in the South-West were suspended, or from 1845 to 1848, will now call for consideration. Several persons acted a prominent part in rendering important services at this time, among whom we may name Rev. Anthony Bewley, Rev. Mark Robertson, Rev. Nelson Henry as permanent laborers. Others performed temporary service at this juncture, the principal of whom was Rev. Peter Akers.

Rev. Anthony Bewley must be mentioned with peculiar interest. He was born in Tennessee, May 22, 1804. His parents were Methodists and his father, John Bewley, was a local preacher. He joined the Methodist Episcopal Church in his seventeenth year, and professed religion the year following. At the Holston Conference, held at Abingdon, Va., December 24, 1829, he was admitted on trial into the traveling connection. After traveling five years he located. About this time he was married to Miss Jane Winton. In 1837 he moved to Missouri, and settled in Polk county, about seventy-five miles north of the Arkansas line, and sixty-five miles east of Kansas. At the Missouri Conference, held at Lexington, Mo., October 4, 1843, he was readmitted into the traveling connection, and appointed to Neosho circuit, in the south-western part of the State. In 1844 he was appointed to Sarcoxie circuit, in the Springfield

.district. Such are the early incidents connected with the life of Rev. Anthony Bewley.

2. Another prominent actor in the time of the suspension of the Methodist Episcopal Church in Missouri was Rev. Mark Robertson. He was originally from North Carolina. His parents moved to Tennessee, and subsequently to Gallatin county, Ill., while he was a minor. He was licensed to preach in 1834, and, as a local preacher, was ordained deacon, in 1843, by Bishop Andrew. In 1845, having moved to Missouri, he joined Mr. Bewley in serving the remnants of the Methodist Episcopal Church, after the Missouri Conference had gone South, in 1845.

3. Rev. Nelson Henry was a man of remarkable firmness and self-sacrifice. While the wide-spread and contagious apostasy of the South swept thousands from right principles and a humane practice, he wavered not in devotion to the Church of his fathers, but served her faithful fragments with commendable zeal and fidelity.

4. The Missouri Conference sat in Columbia, Mo., September 24, 1845, at which Bishop Soule presided, and used every effort to carry South the Conference. He made a long and elaborate speech in favor of secession, and took especial pains to confute the positions of Dr. Elliott, at that time editor of the Western Christian Advocate. He was but too successful in wafting over the body of preachers in favor of uniting with the new Church just formed under the name of the Methodist Episcopal Church South.

As the alphabetical list of the Conference was called, and each answered to his name, Mr. Bewley's name was soon reached, and his response was, "The Methodist Episcopal Church of the United States of America." This was an utterance worthy of the purest days of Christian confession and martyrdom, if the circumstances are considered. And from that very hour the demon of persecution went howling upon his track, nor ever ceased till it was glutted with his life-blood.

The Bishop and his allies employed a fiction with which to entangle the memory. It was deceptiously couched in the requirement that each should answer *North* or *South* as his name was called. Brother Jameson objected to the Bishop's mode of putting the question, and replied that he would remain in the Methodist Episcopal Church.

Many of the Missouri preachers, though a minority of the whole, left the State and joined other Conferences of the Methodist Episcopal Church.

Mr. Bewley utterly refused to unite with the Southern Church, and labored in South-Western Missouri from 1845 to 1848, working with his own hands for support, and preaching to those who remained in the Methodist Episcopal Church as he had opportunity. Several of our preachers labored with him as best they could. Rev. Mark Robertson was among the leading associate laborers in connection with Mr. Bewley, and traveled the Sarcoxie circuit for three successive years, or from 1845 to 1848.

5. At the dissolution of the Methodist Episcopal Church in the South-West by the secession of the great body of Methodists, a few only were left to remain by the prostrate altars of their now disrupted Church.

On Spring River, Missouri, a convention of adherents to the Methodist Episcopal Church was held December 25, 1845, at which Mr. Bewley presided, and arrangements were made, in the best way they could, to feed the scattered sheep in the wilderness. George Sly, David Thompson, and Joseph Doughty were the laborers in Missouri, and in Arkansas there were Thomas Norwood, J. K. West, and James Hanen. These, and Messrs. Bewley and Robertson, were the principal laborers.

In St. Louis there was a remnant left who declined joining

the new Southern Church. Indeed, the leading laymen, at first, were much opposed to the Southern measure. Rev. Joseph Boyle at first opposed it, and called in our office at Cincinnati, in the Fall of 1845, advising opposition to it. He also visited Bishop Hamline, then in Cincinnati, for the same object. But at the Louisville Convention, in May, he was fully transformed, and became Southern from that time forth. He and Rev. Wesley Browning, both from the North, became leaders in urging the success of the Southern apostasy from Methodism, and from Scripture as well, when the thing is properly considered.

Rev. Joseph Tabor, however, a local preacher, and a small number of the lay members *remained in* the Methodist Episcopal Church, and erected their small church, which they significantly called Ebenezer; and this small beginning became the seed-bed of the movement in 1862, which purchased and occupied the Union Church, at the corner of Locust and Eleventh streets, a full notice of which will appear in a future page.

6. In 1846 Rev. Mark Robertson attended a camp meeting in Arkansas, where a meeting was organized in which he presided, and there it was agreed that J. K. West should have the Washington circuit, James Hanen the Van Buren circuit, in Arkansas. Mr. Bewley was appointed to the Springfield circuit, as presiding elder, and Mr. Robertson was on the Sarcoxie circuit. The quarterly conference also chose Mr. Bewley as presiding elder.

7. At the General Conference of 1848 the Missouri Conference of the Methodist Episcopal Church was reorganized. The Conference had decided that the South had forfeited, by their unscriptural course, all right to be considered a sound branch of Methodism. They therefore reorganized the Church in the South-West. The Conference met this year—September 13, 1848—in connection with the Illinois

Conference, at Belleville, Ill. There were found 1,538 Church members, and twenty-four local preachers. There were three districts formed, manned by twenty preachers, leaving four appointments to be supplied. One district was in Arkansas, over which was Nelson Henry, presiding elder.

In 1848 Messrs. Bewley and Robertson attended the Illinois Conference, and were recognized members of the Missouri Conference. Mr. Robertson was admitted on trial and ordained a local elder. Mr. Bewley was stationed at Washington mission, Arkansas, and seventy-five dollars were appropriated for him. He received about one hundred dollars from the people, and the rest of his support was provided by the labor of his own hands.

Mr. Robertson was appointed to the Van Buren mission, Arkansas, and seventy-five dollars were appropriated for him by the Missionary Board. He received about the value of seventy-five dollars in produce on his mission, and the rest of his support was furnished by his own manual labor. Mr. Bewley had to travel two hundred miles, from Dade county, Mo., to his field of labor, and Mr. Robertson had to move two hundred and fifty miles, from Jasper county, Mo., to Van Buren, in Arkansas.

Mr. Bewley arrived in September, 1848, on his circuit, and was well received. He had a very good camp meeting. He resided six miles west of Fayetteville, in a parsonage. This was some fifty miles south of the Missouri line. In his labors he had to contend with the Southern Methodists, who considered him and his associates as intruders on their proper fields of labor.

While Mr. Robertson was on the Neosho circuit, previous to the organization of the Methodist Episcopal Church in Missouri, in 1848, a curious incident took place in that region. Rev. Joseph Woods, a Southern Methodist preacher on the Neosho circuit, in a speech addressed to his people for support, said that he had eaten up a negro wench during his labors among them. He had to sell her in order to buy tea, coffee, bread, and butter. Rev. Mr. Robertson was reduced to a somewhat similar necessity. He and his family had to eat up a wagon and two horses in order to subsist. There was, however, this difference in the two cases: Mr. Wood ate up the property of another person—for, before God, the slave woman belonged to herself—but Mr. Robertson expended only that which was his own, namely, the wagon and horses.

Mr. Robertson traveled the Van Buren circuit in 1848. He had thirty-five members who had been collected by Mr. Hanen, his predecessor. He had no difficulties but with the Southern Methodists, who harassed him all they could.

On Van Buren circuit, in 1848, Mr. Bewley attended Mr. Robertson's quarterly meeting, in the absence of the presiding elder, Mr. Henry. Mr. Bewley preached five sermons at the meeting, and while preaching the fifth a man in the congregation rose up and asked, "Are you preaching that sermon to me?" To this Mr. Bewley replied, "I am preaching to the congregation, and if it suits you receive it." The man's mother said, "It does suit him." The result was that this man joined the Church, and became a truly religious man.

8. The Missouri Conference met in St. Louis, August 29, 1849, at which Bishop Janes presided. Mr. Bewley was placed on Sarcoxie circuit this year, and his residence was in Dade county, Mo. W. J. Markham, his colleague, died during the year, and this left him much to do; nevertheless, much prosperity attended his labors.

Mark Robertson was appointed this year—1849—to Batesville mission.

Bishop Janes at this Conference instructed Joseph Tabor that, if any letters came for him to St. Louis, he should open them, and inform him as to the contents. After the Bishop had left St. Louis letters came to the city from Batesville. These were from a public meeting held in Batesville, over which a Southern Methodist presided, warning the Bishop and the Missouri Conference not to send another Methodist preacher North to Batesville, and declaring if they did violence must follow, and they must account for the blood shed. The brethren in St. Louis held a special prayer meeting to intercede for the preservation of Mr. Robertson.

Batesville is on White River, Independence county. Mr. Robertson had to move two hundred miles this year, and did not learn of the threat till he had reached Batesville and stopped with Robert Williams. Nothing daunted, however, he got his appointment circulated, and preached the first Sabbath to a large congregation. On Monday morning the court was in session, and encouraged a public meeting, at which it was resolved that Mark Robertson, a Northern Methodist preacher, should leave immediately—peaceably if he would, forcibly if need be. But Mr. Robertson declined to obey, and his persecutors thought it best to let the matter rest there. He continued to preach to the close of the year. He had a glorious revival, by which one hundred and thirty-two were added to the Church by letter or probation. He had about one hundred at the beginning of the year, and at the close of the year he had two hundred and forty-six.

Rev. A. J. Crandall labored in St. Louis this year with great success, and built up a prosperous Church at Ebenezer, leaving the names of three hundred and twenty-one members on the Church records.

At the close of the year 1849 the statistics gave an increase of 1,901, making, in all, 3,463 members.

9. The year 1850 commenced in the Missouri Conference

with quite an increase of members and preachers. There were five districts, manned with thirty-five preachers stationed, and fourteen places to be supplied, making, in all, forty-nine preachers, as the vacancies were all supplied by the presiding elders with local preachers.

The Conference met this year at Pleasant Green, Cooper county, Mo., August 28th, Bishop Hamline presiding.

Mr. Bewley was this year appointed to Springfield mission. He resided at Ebenezer, ten miles north of Springfield, for the sake of schooling his children at an academy there under the supervision of the Southern Methodists. As among the first persecutions visited upon our people, we may mention the proceedings of a meeting held in Green county, Mo., where the school was located. The account of the meeting was headed, "Proceedings of the Trustees of the South-Western High-School, at Ebenezer, on the second day of October, 1850."

Here are two of the resolutions:

"*Resolved*, That Anthony Bewley shall not be allowed to preach on said forty acres of land.

"*Resolved*, That Rev. A. H. Matthews shall not permit the children of Anthony Bewley to attend the South-Western High-School till a meeting of the curators and a decision be made thereon."

This last resolution served as a precedent for the Missouri Legislature, at a future day, to refuse charters for "Jackson Seminary" and "Jefferson City University," as these were institutions under the patronage of the Methodist Episcopal Church. But Mr. Bewley, though unceasingly persecuted, was too brave a man to ever leave the South-West. He bore it all, and as a minister in a law-abiding Church, he traveled and preached wherever he was appointed.

Mr. Bewley went to see the teacher, and wished him to treat his children as the others were treated. The teacher agreed to this, for the present, and the matter ended there for the time. At this period they were not just prepared to carry out their own resolves, as they did subsequently.

The following incidents will show the outside influences that pressed on Mr. Bewley. His presiding elder, Mr. Bird, preached at Mr. Bewley's house while he resided at Ebenezer. Mrs. Bewley had two sisters residing in the place, but they declined going to their sister's house to hear Mr. Bird preach, though invited by Mrs. Bewley. At Derrick's appointment, this year, some hundred persons signed a paper urging him to cease preaching at that place. When they presented the paper he said that he had dreamed about such a paper the night before, and declared that he considered the paper of no importance. They then jerked it from him, and there the matter ended for the time.

Mr. Robertson, on Batesville mission, had, during the year, an increase of one hundred and one members, despite the constantly chilling and threatening bearing of Southern Methodists toward him and his cause.

At the close of this Conference year there was an increase of 1,868 members in the Missouri Conference.

10. The Missouri Conference sat in Hannibal, Mo., August 27, 1851, Bishop Waugh presiding, and L. B. Dennis being Secretary. Mr. Bewley was on Springfield mission. His family residence was four miles north-east of Springfield, where he resided four years, or till he removed to Texas.

Mr. Robertson was on Greenbriar mission this year, six miles from Batesville. At his first appointment a mob endeavored to break up his meeting by throwing stones on the house while he was preaching on the judgment. Five young men went out after the miscreants, and pursued them half a mile. Nevertheless, two or three were converted that night and added to the Church. The additions for the year numbered sixty-one. The increase in the Conference this year was only two hundred and seventy-seven.

11. In 1852·the Arkansas Conference was formed, and the Missouri and Arkansas Conferences met together in St. Louis, Mo., October 7th, Bishop Janes presiding.

Mr. Bewley was this year on Osage mission, Arkansas Conference, within the bounds of Batesville district, over which Mark Robertson presided.

The Batesville district embraced all South-Western Missouri, reaching among the Ozark Mountains. In-Arkansas it embraced the counties of Marion, Carrol, Izzard, Independence, Van Buren, Sebastian, etc. The town of Batesville, on White River, and Fort Smith, on the Arkansas River, were on this district. Mr. Robertson now had to meet the subject of political secession, as well as ecclesiastical schism. Rev. John Cook, of the Methodist Episcopal Church South, maintained that our political union failed to answer the object of its establishment by Divine providence, and that it would be cut down as a cumberer of the ground, and two new ones would be planted in its place. We had the Church North and the Church South; so it would be, Mr. Cook maintained, in the civil condition of the United States. This was a manifest indication that the elements of secession were then in existence in the South.

Mr. Robertson preached a corresponding sermon on the text, "Cut it down; why cumbereth it the ground?" in answer to a Mr. Wood. He contended that the Methodist Episcopal Church was not cut down, and gave statistics and arguments to prove his points. Mr. Robertson resided at Batesville six years, or till 1854.

The year 1852 presented to the Church at large such encouragement as to induce the organization of the Arkansas Conference. Yet the work of driving our Church from the South-West had already been conceived. Most of its preliminaries were arranged in purposes which afterward culminated in the mobocratic attack on the Arkansas Conference, in 1859, and in various murders, as well as the expulsion of many thousands of the Methodist and Free-soil population by pro-slavery men, and especially by Southern Methodists. The increase in the South-West this year was only two hundred and three, which presaged the dispersion of our people in the succeeding years, till our Church was nearly extinct in this region.

12. The Arkansas Conference met at Fayetteville, Washington county, Ark., October 26, 1853, Bishop Morris presiding. Mr. Bewley labored this year on the Springfield Mission district, while Mr. Robertson was on the Batesville Mission district. He had much hard work, but also numerous conversions. The influence of the pro-slavery party, however, was increasingly pressing against him, urged on by the members and preachers of the Methodist Episcopal Church South. A Mr. Cochran, editor of the Batesville Eagle, published Mr. Robertson as an abolitionist, and as, therefore, engaged in the underground railroad business, of enticing and aiding slaves to run away from their masters. He refused to allow Mr. Robertson the privilege of correcting the misrepresentation in the columns of the Eagle. Mr. Robertson, on this refusal, took the Eagle to his meetings, read the misrepresentations and confuted them in public, in the presence of great multitudes. The enraged editor threatened to whip Mr. Robertson. Shortly after, both happened to meet in a store, and Mr. Robertson broached the subject, and informed the editor that he would not submit to any such treatment, from him or any other man. The editor was satisfied to decline any further attack, by pen or otherwise. But his evil course seemed to follow him with its penalties, for he was sold out, lost his press, and, when last heard from, was employed as a day-laborer.

In St. Louis the crushing influence arrayed against our cause was felt severely, so that Ebenezer and Mound missions had only one hundred and sixty-five members, all told, and the increase for the year in the South-West amounted only to two hundred and fifteen.

In Missouri the pro-slavery rage, with great violence, began the work of murder. Rev. Charles Holliday Kelly was the martyr after whose blood they thirsted. Mr. Kelly was a young man of great promise, but of feeble constitution and health. While holding a quarterly meeting for Chambersburg mission, on Saturday and Sunday, February 12th and 13th, 1853, at the close of the eleven o'clock service on Sabbath morning, a rough-looking man calling himself Trabue came to the stand and entered into conversation with Mr. Kelly, in which he expressed a wish to have him preach in his neighborhood, and, at the same time, laying his hand on Mr. Kelly, said, "You are my prisoner." Rev. J. H. Dennis, who was present, stepped forward and asked what he meant by such conduct in a place of worship. He immediately drew a Colt's revolver, and cried out, "Hands off," falsely calling himself Marshal of the State of Missouri, and ordering his associates to tie Mr. Kelly's hands, threatening to blow a ball through any man that interfered, and, snapping his revolver, cried out, "Stand back; half of this house is mine." After Mr. Kelly's hands had been tied, and his feet had been made secure by a chain and padlock, he asked Trabue if he would permit him to ask one question. To this Trabue roughly answered, "Shut your mouth, or I will blow a ball through you in an instant."

They then placed Mr. Kelly on a rough-gaited lame horse, and started for Fort Madison, Iowa, the seat of the State prison, not allowing him to put on an overcoat, gloves, or wrapper. An unusually cold north-west wind was blowing at the time. Mr. Dennis followed after, and, with much ado, prevailed on his captors to allow him to put on his gloves and overclothes. He was at this time almost ready to sink from exposure and exhaustion. They stopped at Farmington, and obtained there a two-horse wagon, and then proceeded to their destination. At Fort Madison he was placed in the Eagle Hotel, still in chains. When morning came some of the officers of the penitentiary were brought to see him, to ascertain if he were the Charles F. Kelly who had escaped from the prison, and whom Trabue *pretended* to be after. No sooner did they see Mr. Kelly than they declared, "*He is not the, man.*" From the time of his release he lingered till the 17th of September, 1853, when he breathed his last, in consequence of the barbarous severities and exposure of this farcical arrest. Charles F. Kelly had escaped the Iowa State Prison. This man's name was Charles H. Kelly. This partial coincidence in name, since the latter was a talented minister of the hated Methodist Episcopal Church, furnished pretext for his arrest. Arrest and return without forms of law afforded an occasion for violence and slow murder easily explained and excused by prejudice-inspired fabrications. Mr. Kelly's death being the real object of their endeavors, and having no thought of his really being identified as the escaped convict, it became the more necessary to the desired end that their treatment should wound him beyond recovery.

Thus those frenzied, lean, and hungry loons, lying at the gates of slaveocrats, and at their hiss hunting down and destroying the just, leaped upon their victim in the public sanctuary, and, beast-like, worried him till he fell, fainting and dying, at the prison gates, only regretting, as they turned away, that they could not make him die inside the walls, with a convict's stigma upon him.

But, though God suffered his servant to be promoted to martyrdom through the madness of his foes, he took care they should not blot his name with even temporary dishonor. They had "killed the body," but there was no more they could do. Martyred saint! Rather let me share thy sufferings than the retributions of thy destroyers when God's vengeance shall be waking.

13. The Arkansas Conference was held, in 1854, at Peugh's Chapel, Sebastian county, Ark., November 2d, Bishop Ames presiding. Mr. Bewley was still on the Springfield· Mission district. He and Rev. S. H. Carlile had a public debate with two Campbellite preachers. On the second day of the debate one of the Campbellite preachers left the ground on the score that his side was defeated. On the third day the Campbellites made up their lack of argument by pronouncing Messrs. Bewley and Carlile abolitionists. This was resorted to as the last mode of defense for a defeated party. The vile sophistry, of course, had its effect; for at this time, in Arkansas, such a charge was considered an overwhelming argument to confute any thing maintained by a person representing the Methodist Episcopal Church. Members of this Church were regarded as identical with the most vicious men, and it was believed to be their chief work to entice slaves to run away from their masters. Yet nothing could be more false, for neither members nor preachers ever had recourse to this, much as they hated slavery and detested the practice under the Fugitive Slave law. But the mad-dog cry, once uttered against a man, was caught up and sounded around till, in the popular clamor, there was no hearing for reason and truth.

Mr. Robertson was yet on the Batesville Mission district. It then became the policy of Southern Methodists to represent that the Methodist Episcopal Church had no right to plant themselves in the South. Rev. John Cole was the presiding elder of the Methodist Episcopal Church South in that region. Mr. Cole was an Englishman, had belonged to the Indiana Conference, but so apostatized from the principles of Wesley and of the Methodist Episcopal Church as to become a public supporter of slavery. Mr. Cole gave out publicly that in two weeks he would show that the Methodist Episcopal Church, North, was an abolition Church, and had no right to an organization in the South. On the day appointed he employed three hours with his documents to make this appear to three thousand people.

Mr. Robertson listened patiently during the whole performance, at the close of which the audience was hurriedly dismissed with the benediction, so as to cut off any response. But Mr. Robertson called the attention of the people to the consideration that Mr. Cole was an Englishman, had also taken lessons among the Yankees, and, seeing that he was a turn-coat, and probably not sincere in his present declarations, he might justly be regarded as the most dangerous of the abolition ranks. This retort in the place of argument was answering a fool according to his folly, but it had the desired effect. The people dispersed quietly, and were very well pleased with the reply.

Mr. Robertson had several good camp meetings this year, and general prosperity, although there was no general increase. The reason was that many of our members removed from these localities. They saw no prospect of enjoying their religious or civil rights in Arkansas or Texas, and, like the Pilgrim fathers, they emigrated in order to secure their inalienable rights. By this means only remnants of the Methodist Episcopal Church were left in the southwestern slave States. Our people were constantly harassed with persecutions and annoyances on account of their religious sentiments and associations. Thus, at this time, many of our people went to California, Oregon, and Kansas, or returned to the old States from whence they came; and this stampede was only the beginning of what ended, a few

years after, in an almost total emigration of our people from
Arkansas and Texas.

The Kansas-Nebraska bill, that passed Congress in 1854,
became the occasion of developing sentiments that were
then entertained by many in the North, as well as in the
South. The purport of the bill was to revoke the Missouri
Compromise, made in 1820, by which it was guaranteed
that north of thirty-six degrees and thirty minutes there
should be no slavery in the territory formerly called Louisiana west of the Mississippi River, Missouri excepted.
This excluded slavery from Kansas and Nebraska. But
the Kansas-Nebraska bill did away with this compromise.

In consequence of some Church members being forced,
by arbitrary slave laws, to become slaveholders, although
without their act, will, or deed, vehement objections were
made by some against making any missionary appropriations in behalf of Missouri, Arkansas, and Texas. The principal objector was Mr. Hosmer, of the Northern Advocate.
In his issue of April 19, 1854, in an article headed, "The
Methodist Missionary Society and Slavery," he assailed vehemently the Missionary Society for making missionary appropriations for Southern territory, as this tended to support
slavery, and the outcry, "stop the supplies," became the
watchword of Mr. Hosmer and others of like sentiments.
The Missionary Board appointed Dr. Durbin, Dr. Carlton,
and F. Hall to reply to these and similar allegations, a task
they performed with great ability and complete success, si-
lencing the objectors.

This opposition to our suffering brethren in the South-
West was the "unkindest cut of all," inasmuch as the
preachers in that quarter were the most deserving laborers
in the whole missionary field. It was hard, indeed, to be
hunted and persecuted because they were antislavery and
abolitionists of the strongest type, and at the same time

to be branded by the friends of the Methodist Episcopal Church as unworthy of support.

The Southern Methodists, at this time, were rapidly advancing in pro-slavery doctrines. This was manifest from the acts of their General Conference, in May, 1854. For the extirpation of the General Rule on slavery there were sixty-five votes, and forty-three against it. But on the following perversion of that rule there were ninety-eight yeas, and only ten nays:

"*Resolved*, That the General Rule in the Book of Discipline on the buying and selling of men, women, and children, with an intention to enslave them, is understood as referring exclusively to the slave-trade as prohibited by the Constitution and laws of the United States."

In connection with this moral heresy they excluded from their Discipline the entire chapter against slavery.

At this Conference Dr. Smith delivered to the citizens of the place an address which was eulogized by the Southern papers as a most masterly defense of the South and her institutions. He argued that slavery was right, both in the abstract and in the concrete. He ridiculed the idea that "all men were created free." We remember more than once to have heard Dr. Smith contending that slavery was wrong in the abstract and right in the concrete.

The fact is, at this time the Southern Methodists were rapidly advancing to the sentiment that slavery was right and holy; or, in other words, that it was right to steal, rob, commit adultery, and oppress the weak and innocent. Hear the following, from the Memphis Advocate, written about this time:

"What is slavery? It is the providential relation which one man stands in to another as master and servant. Is this providential relation a sin? No, it is not; the sin is not in the providential relation, but in the abuse of that relation. There are many other providential relations which are not sinful till they are abused, when they become evil. The rich and the poor, the wise and the ignorant, the capitalist and laborer, the landlord and tenant, the master and apprentice, lawyer and client, preacher and people, husband and wife, parent and child, all these are providential relations, and all may be and have been abused, and thus become sinful and evil. As to the providential relation of master and servant, as it exists in the South, it is, next to husband and wife, the most sacred. A mysterious Providence has placed one race of men of a different color and of peculiar instincts under the control and command of another race of superior intelligence and foresight. The former, as a race, have always been wild, savage, lawless, improvident, and uncivilized. The latter are civilized, organized into government, and live under religious and political institutions. These two races of men form the population of the Southern States. They sustain to each other the relation of master and servant, and woe be to the powers or combined influences that aim, by undue means, to sever this relation till the same mysterious Providence that permitted it interposes, by unmistakable signs, to abolish it."[1]

The foregoing shows how much the moral views of slavery had corrupted the Southern Methodist press. The acts of their General Conference of 1854 are of the same character, and this was preparatory to the act of 1858, which excluded the General Rule; and this last step prepared the way for the monstrosity which taught that the Scriptures support slavery. Thus step after step was taken in the moral descent till it was practically conceded to be right to murder Bewley and others, and to drive citizens from Texas, Arkansas, and Missouri because they were members of the Methodist Episcopal Church. It may be asked, with

[1] See Western Christian Advocate, vol. xxi, p. 100.

surprise, "Is thy servant a dog, that he should do such things?" And yet history proves that it has been even so.

14. The persecution of Rev. William Sellers, while traveling the Lagrange circuit, will show the growing hostility to the Methodist Episcopal Church in Missouri among all classes of pro-slavery men. In the Fall or early Winter of 1853 fifteen slaves made their escape from Fabius township, Marion county, Mo., and proceeded to Canada. This produced so great a sensation among the slaveholders that they formed an association for self-protection. On the 24th of December, 1853, Thomas L. Anderson made a speech in which he urged the necessity of attending to the "fanatics." Shortly after, the Marion county association sent a committee of five to wait on Rev. Mr. Sellers, to ascertain his views. Mr. Sellers declared, as well he might, that he had no connection with those who had aided the fugitives. Rev. J. H. Dennis, presiding elder, met the men of Fabius township February 18th, and explained the principles and course of the Methodist Episcopal Church. A Colonel Ben. Davis, who was formerly a member of the Baltimore Conference, acted as attorney for the association, and stated that the Northern Methodist preachers in Missouri were abolitionists, that Jacob Gruber was one, and that some of them carried Benton's Free-soil speeches in their pockets. Such were the allegations.

Two public meetings were held by the citizens of Fabius township, Marion county, Mo., for the purpose of carrying out a scheme to expel Rev. Mr. Sellers from the country. At the meeting of February 4th, committees were appointed. At that of February 18, 1854, the following preamble and resolutions were adopted by the meeting unanimously:

"*Whereas*, but a short time since the Methodist Episcopal Church was divided into 'Northern' and 'Southern' divisions; and, *whereas*, this division was created solely by a difference of opinion among the clergy upon the subject of slavery, the clergy of the North taking decided ground against that peculiar institution; and, *whereas*, there is in our community considerable excitement, arising from the belief, upon the part of many of our citizens, that the ministers of the Northern division of said Church, who have for some time past been preaching in Fabius township, are the representatives of a body whose sentiments upon the subject of slavery are decidedly hostile to our interests as slaveholders, and dangerous to our peace, and that the leading object of their mission here is the destruction of slavery by the propagation, in any manner not inconsistent with the safety of their persons, of doctrines calculated to array against the institution the weak-minded and fanatical among us, and to create discontent, dissatisfaction, and insubordination-among our slaves; be it, therefore,

"1. *Resolved*, That the peace and best interests of this community require that the said ministers, from this time and forever hereafter, desist from visiting and preaching among us.

"2. That we regard it as a sacred duty we owe ourselves and our country to take, and that we do now take, high, firm, and positive ground, never to be abandoned, against all abolition influences, no matter whence they emanate, and that we now solemnly declare that, while we shall ever be willing to seek and glad to receive at the hands of the law protection from existing ills, yet, when the law fails to protect, we claim to have the natural right, as a community, to resort to the use of such means as will afford us protection

"3. That the fanatics of the North have forced the question of slavery into all the Churches, and, by their effort to rule or ruin all who refuse to join them in their unholy crusade upon our rights, the division of the original Methodist

Episcopal Church was created, the only point of difference between the two wings being the subject of slavery, the Southern wing claiming, under the constitutions and laws of the slave States, as well as the Constitution and laws of the United States, the right to hold slaves, and to regulate all their own domestic affairs, while the Northern wing declared slavery a great moral evil, and sinful in the sight of God and man, and that there is a law higher than the Constitution and the laws of the land authorizing them to destroy the institution of slavery, and for this purpose to send their emissaries, upon every pretext and under all sorts of covers, into every portion of the slave States.

"4. That, as the tenets and Discipline of the two wings of the Methodist Episcopal Church are identically the same, the ministers of the Northern wing can do no good here, but great harm, and that, with all due respect for the right of religious toleration as furnished and protected by the Constitution and laws of our country, we, the citizens of Fabius and adjoining townships, do solemnly protest against the practice of the said Methodist Episcopal Church, North, in sending ministers among us, and we respectfully request such ministers to make no more appointments in this vicinity.

"5. That, as we are situated contiguous to Quincy, a city containing some of the vilest abolition thieves in the Mississippi Valley, and, as we have already suffered so much at the hands of those incendiaries, we regard it absolutely necessary to the protection of our slave interest that we close our doors against abolition and Free-soil influences of every character and shade, and that we shall, therefore, esteem it highly improper for any citizen hereafter to countenance or encourage the preaching or teaching in this community of any other minister or ministers, person or persons, the representatives of or in any way connected with

4

any Church or Churches, any association or society, whether religious or political, or of any character whatsoever, who have heretofore or shall hereafter take ground, directly or indirectly, expressly or impliedly, against the institution of slavery."

This preamble and resolutions go to say that the Methodist Episcopal Church was considered, at this period, as intolerable in Missouri, and these resolutions show the heart of slavery; for, when there was no law to justify their conduct, they assumed supreme control over all law, truth, and justice in order to maintain the slave system. The resolutions, however, speak for themselves, and need no exposition to show their barbarous and despotic character, as well as their special hostility to the Methodist Episcopal Church.

The quarterly conference of Hannibal station, of the Methodist Episcopal Church, shortly after the Fabius township affair, passed unanimously the following resolutions:

"1. That the proceedings of the citizens of Fabius township against the Methodist Episcopal Church is a base persecution, and can not be regarded by an intelligent community in any other light than an attempt to proscribe their fellow-citizens for opinion's sake; and not only so, but we regard it as an attempt to hunt up the opinions of their fellow-citizens in order that they may have some shadow of a reason for attempting to crush the rights of thought and the rights of speech.

"2. That, while we regard the system of slavery as a great moral, social, and political evil, we do heartily protest against any attempt, directly or indirectly, at producing insubordination among slaves; and, furthermore, we do regard with fidelity the rights of slave-owners to property in their slaves, and declare that it would be inconsistent with our duty as Christians and loyal citizens to dispossess them of their rights; and, furthermore, we do heartily condemn what is usually termed the underground railroad operation, and all other systems of negro stealing.

"3. That our opposers of Fabius township have failed—*utterly failed*—to produce any evidence of guilt against the Church, or any individual member of the Church. We appeal to the justice of enlightened public opinion for redress for our wrongs, and for a just condemnation of all such attempts to gag men for fear that they will dare to speak their sentiments on a great moral and political subject.

"4. That, as citizens of Missouri, and as citizens of the United States, we regard it as a sacred duty we owe ourselves and country, *to take, and that we do now take, high, firm, and positive ground, never to be abandoned*, against all such attempts to destroy the liberties which our fathers have transmitted to us—the religious and political liberties which we claim in common with other citizens, and especially the liberty of worshiping God according to the dictates of our own consciences."

15. Just after the persecution of Sellers, and others of the Methodist Episcopal Church in Missouri, Rev. H. C. Atwater, of the Providence Conference, Phœnix, R. I., wrote two letters to the Missouri Courier, a pro-slavery sheet published in Hannibal, Mo., the one dated June 17th, and the other October 21st, in which he aided the pro-slavery party in their work of persecution by denouncing our preachers in Missouri as untrue to right principles, and urging that no more missionary supplies should be furnished to the Missouri and Arkansas Conferences, till they should become abolitionists of his own stamp; and he seems to have been among the most ultra of the Garrisonian school. He was met in his attacks on the Missouri Conference by Rev. N. Shumate. Mr. Atwater seems to have been an earnest antislavery man, who did not consider

the subject in any other than an entirely impracticable light, and did great injustice to the brethren on the south-western border.[2]

The term abolitionist at this time was very equivocal. In the South-West it was really a raw-head-and-bloody-bones, pregnant with every moral, social, and political iniquity. A law among the Cherokees, passed in 1854, banishing the missionaries of the American Board, declared that "an abolitionist was one who teaches a negro or slave to read, write, or sing, or who sits at meat with him." In short, to such a state of fanaticism had the slaveholders arrived, that every one who could not actually plead and act for slavery and against freedom was considered an enemy to the South, and fit only to be banished from the entire South-West.

[2] See Central Christian Advocate of 1854, pages 34, 38, 42, 46, 54, 58, 122, 126, 157, 162.

CHAPTER III.

EVENTS OF 1855.

1. THE Arkansas Conference convened November 1, 1855, for its annual session at Timber Creek, near Bonham, Fannin county, Texas.

Mr. Bewley was put in charge of the Texas Mission district. He moved from near Springfield, Mo., where his family had resided several years, and after a journey of five hundred miles, settled in Johnson county. The same year he moved thence to Milwood, Collin county.

This year Rev. B. M. Scrivner, on the Bonham mission, abandoned the cause he professed to serve, and joined the Methodist Episcopal Church South. In the Southern Church he was to receive a salary of five hundred dollars, and yet he endeavored to get the missionary money appropriated for the mission of the Methodist Episcopal Church without doing any work on the field to which he had been sent. But Mr. Bewley refused to give him the missionary money. This Mr. Scrivner, as we learned from Mr. Robertson, in the Summer of 1862 raised a company for the rebel army, but was too cowardly to lead them.

Mr. Robertson was reappointed to Batesville Mission district. He and Mr. Bewley as delegates attended the General Conference at Indianapolis in May, 1856.

After General Conference the slavery question was so stirred up in Texas that our members found themselves almost entirely disfranchised, and therefore they emigrated more extensively to Oregon, California, Kansas, and the old free States than in previous years, that they might enjoy their rights as American citizens, which they could not do in Western Missouri, Arkansas, and Texas.

2. At this period the excitement was very great in Missouri, especially on the Missouri River and Western border, where the Kansians and Missourians were engaged in mutual border conflicts, instigated principally by the proslavery men of Missouri, and met by the Kansians with great intrepidity, as the only mode of defense on their part. The Missourians had a secret organization, and all who refused to join it were branded with abolitionism, and their movements watched, even though they were citizens of long standing, and whose integrity was unimpeachable.

Among the objects of this hostility was Rev. W. H. Wiley, an itinerant minister of the Methodist Episcopal Church, of unimpeachable character. We give his case as narrated by himself in the Missouri Democrat, and so corroborated by others as to place the narrative beyond suspicion as to correctness:

"MR. EDITOR,—I wish to present to the public, through the columns of the Democrat, a plain statement of an affair which recently took place in Cass county, Mo. In the providence of God, and the arrangement of the Methodist Episcopal Church, I was called to preach the Gospel in Cass county, Mo., in the Harrisonville circuit. I endeavored to discharge my duty as a Christian minister to the best of my ability, teaching nothing but those truths which make wise unto salvation, and having nothing to do with any of the vexing questions of the day. I had labored thus on the above circuit for a period of seven months, and up to about three weeks ago the blessing of God attending my labors, and nothing occurring to mar the peace between me and my people. About the time named, an article appeared in the Cass County Gazette, written by John A.

Tuggle, a member of the Methodist Episcopal Church South, in which there was an attempt to excite public opposition against me, by alleging that I had said certain things to him in a *private conversation*, respecting the decision of the question of slavery or on slavery and Kansas, and styling me a Northern abolitionist. About a week after the appearance of this article, two negroes attempted to escape from Harrisonville, and a report was immediately circulated that I, together with other residents of the town and county, had instigated them to make the attempt— than which nothing could be more false, as I had not even once spoken to a single negro in Cass county; and the other persons were citizens of long standing whose characters were above suspicion, one of whom had been a resident in the State *forty-seven years.*

"On Thursday, July 26th, while peaceably pursuing my way along the public road, I was overtaken by two men— one of them known as Col. Worley—who addressed me some impudent questions respecting where I was going, etc., and finally informed me that I had been accused of inciting slaves to escape, and of preaching abolition doctrine, and that I must return with them to Harrisonville and have the charges investigated. This conversation they interlarded with the most profane oaths that could fall from human lips. I protested against their right to stop me thus on the public highway, when the aforesaid Col. W. leaped from his horse and began fumbling about his person as if feeling for a pistol. After some further parley, I informed them that, inasmuch as I was entirely innocent of the charges alleged, I did not fear a fair investigation, and would accompany them to Harrisonville for that purpose. Just as we turned to go back, sixteen more men, mounted, made their appearance. We stopped at a cabin in the prairie for supper, where the bottle was freely passed, and

I received the most insulting treatment, being asked to drink, and made the subject of obscene jests and horrid oaths.

"We reached Harrisonville about twelve o'clock at night, and I was taken to a hotel and a guard of three men placed over me during the night, as if I had been the greatest criminal. Next morning I was waited on by three men who informed me that they were appointed a committee to search my effects, in order to ascertain if I had any abolition documents. The committee was composed of Rev. Mr. Allen, a *Baptist preacher*, Mr. Bailey, and the proprietor of the hotel where I was confined. They searched every thing I had, examined my Bible and hymn-book, and read my *private letters*, carefully, but they could find nothing to substantiate their charges. While this examination was in progress, a meeting was called at the court-house, and I could hear some person delivering what seemed to be a very inflammatory speech. After a while, a committee, composed of Dr. Hansbraugh, Col. Worley, and Rev. Mr. Allen, came to inform me that I was wanted at the court-house. I accompanied them, and found about two hundred men, the most of whom were of a low class, for I will do that community the justice to say that very few respectable persons participated in these outrages. A certain Dr. Maxel sat as chairman of the meeting. After a call to order, Dr. Hansbraugh rose and said that I had been accused of aiding some negroes in running off, and had been preaching abolition doctrines and circulating abolition documents, and that it had been resolved as the sense of that meeting that I leave the State in seven days.

"I replied briefly that I protested against their entire proceedings; and that with a fair investigation I could prove all their charges false, and challenged them to such investigation; that if I had done any thing contrary to law, I held myself amenable to it, and was willing to suffer its penalties to the full. I was told by one of the foremost in the matter, that the law was not strict enough, and they intended *to take it into their own hands*, and that if I did not leave, the consequences would be on my own head.

"This, sir, is but a brief statement of the manner in which I have been treated on American soil, by persons calling themselves American citizens. How long these things are to continue I can not tell, but I think it is high time that something was done to put a stop to them. The fair name of Missouri is thus disgraced by bands of outlaws—for certainly men thus acting can be termed nothing else—and as yet no effort has been made by the officers of the law, or the executive of the State, to relieve her from the stains. What a contrast do such proceedings form to the genius of our institutions and the spirit of '76! Can this be called a land of liberty, if such a state of affairs is allowed to continue? I, sir, am a Southern man by birth, and came here from a Southern city; but if Southern institutions are to be protected by such men as have maltreated me, I think I shall seek some spot where at least my dearest rights shall be free from invasion. Let the citizens of Missouri think upon the circumstances which I have endeavored dispassionately to describe—one only of several similar ones which have recently occurred—and let them decide what they will do—whether they will let these fire-eating politicians ride over them rough shod any longer, disgracing the State and bringing contempt upon themselves and their children.

"Hoping that wise and prudent counsels may obtain, I am, yours, etc., W. H. WILEY.

"ST. LOUIS, *August* 8, 1855."

The foregoing presents several facts worthy of observation, and which form part of the history of the times.

5

The principal accuser of Mr. Wiley seems to be Mr. John A. Tuggle, a member of the Methodist Episcopal Church South. This man endeavors to involve Mr. Wiley in consequence of a *private conversation* respecting Kansas. It is likely that Mr. Wiley uttered something against the border ruffianism that was then invading Kansas, as every sensible man would who was not a slavery propagandist. This was cause enough to pronounce him an abolitionist, that is, a stealer of negroes, and therefore guilty of a mortal sin according to the moral creed of many Southern Methodists.

And then the Baptist minister comes in to take part with his pro-slavery Southern Methodist brother. Indeed, a large portion of the Baptists of the South-West, perhaps a majority of them, were pro-slavery, and united with Southern Methodists in their clamor against the Methodist Episcopal Church.

The next thing we remark is, that the low rabble were the mere tools of the respectable Southern Methodists and the devout Baptist ministers and their aids. These ground-lings loved to drink, to swear, to give insults, and the like; yet these professedly religious men used them as their tools to do a foul work, which common self-respect prevented them from doing themselves.

Furthermore, the respectable citizens looked on, if not complacently, at least inactively, and without interference, while the rabble gave laws to citizens after the fashion of real mobocrats.

Another thing is presented, namely, by a kind of common consent of this respectable community, it was agreed that the respectable Southern Methodist and Baptist, and their respectable neighbors, counting in the rabble—which was supposed to be a rather respectable rabble—should *take the law into their own hands*, and make decrees for the occasion, and thus become legislators, judges, and executors in order to consummate speedily the arrest and punishment of an innocent citizen! This was one of the precursors of the rebellion which broke out a few years after, and in Missouri there were many similar instances.

Had Mr. Wiley incited the slaves to run away, he would not have been pitied by the Methodist Episcopal Church in suffering a legitimate penalty, as from the first that body deemed it wrong for any of its members or ministers to perpetrate such an interference, much as they condemned the slave system with its licensed inhumanities and abominations. And the history of the Methodist Episcopal Church, in discipline, administration, and practice, proves the truth of this assertion.

This was publicly declared by the quarterly conference of Hannibal station, held February 18, 1854, in reference to the mobbing of Rev. Mr. Sellers by those of Fabius township, Marion county, Mo. The charge was that Mr. Sellers, and all preachers of the Methodist Episcopal Church, were engaged in inducing and aiding slaves to leave their masters. The conference in its resolutions pronounces this charge a base persecution. In the second resolution the conference boldly says that such a course is not justified by the Methodist Episcopal Church. We refer the reader to the resolutions themselves, as presented in the history of 1854.

3. While expelling Methodist preachers and laymen seems to have been, at this time, according to a "higher law" in Missouri, we need not wonder that unusually summary methods were sometimes employed to catch absconding negroes. The following appears in a Missouri journal, the Lexington Democratic Advocate:

"NEGRO DOGS.—I would inform the citizens of Holmes county that I still have my negro dogs, and that they are

in good training, and ready to attend all calls for hunting
and catching runaway negroes, at the following rates: For
hunting, per day, five dollars; or, if I have to travel any
distance, every day. will be charged for in going and returning, as for hunting, and at the same rates. Not less
than five dollars will be charged in any case, where the
negroes come in before I reach the place. From fifteen to
twenty dollars will be charged for catching, according to
the trouble; if the negro has weapons, the charge will be
made according to the difficulty had in taking him, or in
case he kills some of the dogs, the charge will not be governed by the above rates. I am explicit to prevent any
misunderstanding. The owner of the slave to pay all expenses in all cases. I venture to suggest to any person
having a slave runaway, that the better plan is to send for
the dogs forthwith, when the negro goes off, if they intend
sending at all, and let no person go in the direction, if
they know which way the runaway went, as many persons
having other negroes to hunt over the track, and failing of
success, send for the dogs, and then perhaps fail in consequence to catch their negro, and thus causelessly fault
the dogs. Terms, cash. If the money is not paid at the
time the negro hunted for is caught, he will be held bound
for the money. I can be found at home at all times, five
and a half miles from Lexington, except when hunting
with the dogs.   JOHN LONG.

"*February* 14, 1855."

The service of blood-hounds had been called into requisition in Florida, in 1840, to catch runaway slaves, and the
same method had been resorted to in various other portions
of the South. General Jessup approved of this in a letter
to Col. Harney, in which he instructs him to inform Os-
ceola of this mode of procedure. He says: "Tell him
[Osceola] I am sending to Cuba for blood-hounds to trail

them, [the negroes,] and I intend to hang every one of them who does not come in." By resolution Col. Fitzparick was "authorized to proceed to Havanna and procure a kennel of blood-hounds, noted for tracking and pursuing negroes." Accordingly Mr. Fitzpatrick reached St. Augustine, January 6, 1840, with thirty-three blood-hounds, which cost each one hundred and fifty-one dollars and seventy-two cents, in all the sum of $5,006.76. Also five Spaniards were employed who were trained to the business, and whose language the dogs understood. Mr. Poinsett, of the War Department, December 30, 1839, declared that the "Government had determined to use blood-hounds in the war against the Florida Indians." The officers of the army had urged this measure, and Mr. Z. Taylor, July 28, 1838, agreed "to employ a few dogs with persons who understood their management." Mr. Poinsett, however, was careful to state that the dogs should be employed "to track and discover the Indians, not to worry or destroy them."

These dogs were attached to different regiments, and fed liberally on bloody meat. Young calves were provided and driven with each scouting party to supply food for them. The Spaniards were supplied with a sufficient number of assistants to take care of them. The dogs were blithe and frolicsome, and paid no more attention to the tracks of the Indians than to those of the ponies on which they rode.

Mr. Long, of Lexington, had the example of Government officials in the use of blood-hounds for hunting down human beings. Negro-mongers, therefore, in their descent to this savage plain, easily passed over all former restraints, especially so since these merciless beasts were likely to be so efficient and rapid in recovering and herding their human chattels. Blood-hounds were, therefore, procured and advertised in Missouri for service in catching negroes. Under these circumstances is it surprising that a strong odium should rest on our preachers, who were reputed negro-stealers? It made no difference to state that this charge against them was utterly untrue when the falsehood was fully believed by the public generally. This statement is verified in the case of Mr. Sellers, who, having been pronounced an abolitionist, must suffer banishment from the country, though the allegation was totally false.

4. It is no wonder that Methodist preachers and members should be very obnoxious to the pro-slavery men of the South-West if we view the depravity of morals that tolerates and practices the traffic in slaves, receives the sanction of law, and the constant patronage of slaveholders.

Rev. J. B. Finley, in January, 1855, portrayed it as it existed in New Orleans at that time, and, in a higher or lower degree, in all slave regions. He thus describes a visit to the barracoons, in New Orleans:

"On entering the mart we found something in the shape of a man driving round a room open to the street twenty-two females, and a child six years old, and fourteen men. As soon as we entered they filed off, the men to the left, and the women to the right. We were met with, 'Do you wish to purchase some slaves?' From my appearance, and the size of my corporation, I was taken for some old Southern planter. I told him I had come to look at his stock, and he was most eloquent in their praise. I asked if his females were good field hands. He presented several, but called from the ranks a mulatto girl, handsome and youthful. He said, 'That woman can pick more cotton in a day and stand it longer than any one in the country.'

"I then turned to the men. He presented three fine young men, and said: 'These can not be beat. One is from Maryland, one from Virginia, and one from Kentucky; one is a good carpenter, and not one scar on their backs—you may strip them and see.' I saw one poor fellow down whose temple the blood was trickling from under his·hat—I suppose from a blow by his keeper. I then inquired for a good house-woman. He recommended several, but ordered out the woman with the little girl. 'There, sir, is the best house-wench in the city to cook, wash, or iron. You shall have the child for four hundred dollars, or the woman and child for twelve hundred and fifty.' I said, 'I will not buy the one without the other.' As soon as the woman heard this she came up, leading her child by the hand, saying, 'O, do buy me, master, I want to go with you,' and followed us to the door pleading for us to buy her. Having satisfied myself with respect to this glorious institution of the South, I left with a feeling of indignation and contempt I have no language to express, nor can I have any sympathy with a system that is in direct opposition to every law of God. This is a villainy, morally and socially; if there is one villainy worse than another, the act of brutalizing man made in the image of God, and rearing him as a brute for market, is the worst of all villainies. Yet how·many sympathizers has it in the religious world!

"From this, in passing along, we saw some half dozen well-dressed women, nearly white, sitting in a room open to the street, and something in the shape of a man at the door. I was struck with their appearance, and, thinking that I might be mistaken, I went back to see if they were employed at any thing. I made strict inquiry of one who was conversant with the city for twenty-five years, and he told me this man had purchased these women, and kept them for the accommodation of gentlemen! This is another feature of this glorious Southern institution against which no man must speak, and for which the whole country was agitated last Winter; and here I ask, can or will the citizens of this glorious country, so famous for its religion, and its religious and political liberty, sympathize with and justify such iniquity? But, sir, to give you an idea of some of the feelings of some of those who hold slaves: As we passed up the river we stopped to wood. Here were eleven young women, the most of them mulattoes, with four boys, putting up cord-wood. An old planter, looking on me, said: 'Here is some fine stock. These women are all young. They will have children, and if eleven a year they will be worth two hundred dollars apiece as soon as they are born, and, if mulattoes, more.' " [1]

The low and vicious depravity that would authorize, or even tolerate such barbarism as we find in these barracoons could readily assent to, if it did not even aid in the banishment and persecution of good men, whose principles and practice were a standing reproof to such low immoralities. Who can wonder, therefore, that the attempt was made in Texas, Arkansas, and Missouri to banish from their borders all preachers and members of the Methodist Episcopal Church, and to thrust out of existence its very organization? For such an inquisitorial work recourse to various stratagems, intimidations, banishments, and murder was but natural for people so lapsed into gross abandonment; and the declaration of Bishop Pierce, given in a former chapter, was only the watchword for the deluded rabble, and their work of proscription and bloody violence was the logical sequence of the premises and principles involved in mob-law and the barracoons.

5. Certain ultra sentiments of some earnest and good men in the North provoked extreme views and measures in the South, and were often adduced, though fallaciously, by Southern men as an apology for their high-handed procedure.

Among those of our Church following the views of some

of the Garrisonian school, Rev. William Hosmer, editor of the Northern Advocate, was the principal. We must believe he was a good and earnest man, though much mistaken in his sentiments, and unfortunate in the leaders he followed.

Mr. Hosmer published a book on the subject, in which there is much good antislavery matter, but it is greatly deformed with the then current extreme sentiments of the ultra Garrisonians. The following extracts from his book will give the reader some idea of the character of its discussions:

"That slaveholders can not be Christians is no arbitrary or harsh judgment, provided, simply, that slavery is a sin." (Page 101.)

"He [the master] must execute the horrible purpose of the State. The State has placed the slave among brutes, and it is the owner's business to keep him there. He is bound, as a law-abiding citizen, to see that the design of the Government is not frustrated; he is intrusted with a fearful responsibility of keeping the slave precisely what the law has made him—a thing, a chattel." (Page 103.)

"Slavery . . . compels the owner to stand in the place of God, and exercise a power which does not belong to man." (Page 104).

"The trade in slaves, whether foreign or domestic, is no worse than the simple ownership of slaves." (Page 106.)

" Christians must obey the law of God; therefore slaves can not be Christians." (Page 91.)

"Slaves can not be Christians; because in order to slavery they must part with the humanity which God has given them, and in doing so they commit sin." (Page 89.)

"Slaves may be converted, but they are not converted slaves." (Page 84.)

" However hard it may seem to unchristianize the slave

for remaining a slave after his conversion, there is no other alternative." (Page 97.)

"If slaves cower beneath the lash and refuse to die for their rights, they seal their own doom. Such men refuse liberty on the only terms ever granted to man. They are not worthy of freedom, or they would be willing to pay its price." (Page 81.)

Such sentiments as these were publicly avowed and maintained by many in the North at that time which threatened to subvert the very foundations of the true antislavery doctrines, as taught by the Scriptures and the Discipline of . the Methodist Episcopal Church. To meet this, Dr. Durbin published an article in the Advocate and Journal of July 26, 1855, in the Western Christian Advocate of August 8th, in the Central Christian Advocate of December 27th, and other papers copied it.

The principal points of Dr. Durbin's article were, 1. That the apostles admitted and retained slaveholders in the Churches which they organized and governed; yet under a discipline subversive of slavery. 2. That the Churches which succeeded the apostles admitted slaveholders into their communion under a discipline at variance with slavery, and which gradually destroyed it.

These points were denied by some, and certain intended proofs were adduced to sustain their proposition. But the New Testament sustained the first, and the undoubted testimony of history sustained the last. In denying the truths of the first point, they unwittingly conceded the thing in question. In regard to the second, the proofs on which it is based were not even assailed; and the allegations against it were mere assumptions, wholly unsupported by history; the progeny of ignorance of the subject, or mere credulity.

An opponent in Zion's Herald denies the position of Dr. Durbin, and in the same paragraph agrees with it where he says that the apostles admitted only legal slaveholders. In this he concedes every thing contended for, because there is no other sort of slaveholders than legal ones, as slavery is the creature of law. The opponent says the contrary of Dr. Durbin's position was proved in New England, but he does not say by whom. Such proofs as mentioned could not be found, just because they did not exist, and were only the confident assertions of those who had never studied the subject with any accuracy. Similar declarations were made by the Northern and North-Western Christian Advocates. But these lax denunciations amounted to nothing.

While the preceding views are correct, as we firmly believe, the Pauline code and the discipline of the post-apostolic characters were strongly antislavery and subversive of the system. These points are fully sustained.

The extravagant views referred to above were currently circulated in the South-West, and every antislavery man was popularly held to an indorsement of the idea that every slaveholder was a sinner of the worst sort, and that no slave could be religious. This only fanned the flames of passion and prejudice in the pro-slavery party, and our preachers and people, as a consequence, suffered grave annoyances.

Indeed, these declarations had much truth connected with them, as well as much error. Some were, however, by inheritance or will, made slaveholders without their will, knowledge, or act, and therefore could not be wicked in that respect till they made the matter their own. As it was, our people were much harassed, and their trials greatly increased.[2]

6. The bishops, in their official course, found it necessary to call for missionaries to go to the South-West. As this

[2] See Central Christian Advocate for 1855, pages 201 and 205.

was slave territory, the Southern Methodist press viewed the demonstration with undignified wrath, and therefore gave its readers the benefit of sundry scraps of mob law, and denunciations of freedom.

The Nashville Christian Advocate quotes with approbation the following:

" St. Louis, April 23, [1855.]

"The office of the Luminary, Parksville, which paper was suspected of Free-soilism, was attacked on Saturday by two hundred citizens of Platte county. They destroyed the fixtures, threw the press into the Missouri River, and the editor's absence saved him from a coat of tar and feathers. Resolutions declaring the paper a nuisance, denouncing the editors, and threatening their lives, as well as other Free-soilers, were passed. No Methodist preacher is to be allowed to preach in the county, under a penalty of tar and feathers for the first offense, and hanging for the second."

The editor of the Nashville Christian Advocate thus comments on the foregoing: "The agitation of the slavery question is disastrous to the cause of Christ. We hope Northern bishops will not augment the flame by sending missionaries into slave territory." The outrages of the mobocrats are here passed over, and the Free-soilers, especially Methodists, are singled out as the pests of the earth. It is not marvelous that the rabble proceeded in their cause when stirred up by persons in higher positions.

The Missouri Democrat, commenting on the outrages of Platte county, says: "Passion is an unsafe guide! It leads men into those extremes which oftentimes produce painful rebounds. It has been the guide of the people of Platte county, Mo., till they have got so far as to meet with a re-action which is giving them trouble. They drove Park and Patterson away, and threw their press into the river. They

notified all ministers of the Methodist Church [North] to
cease their preaching in the county; they passed resolutions to take M'Crea from the custody of the law and to
hang him; they countenanced the riding of Phillips, tarred
and feathered, through the streets upon a rail, because he
proclaimed himself a Free-soiler; and finally they have compelled Revs. Woodward and Starr, two estimable ministers
of the Presbyterian Church, to leave the charge of respectable and large congregations because they were suspected
of being unsound on the slavery question."

The better portion of the community endeavored to correct the mistake about the Presbyterian ministers, but the
leaders of the mob had so drilled them that, although several meetings were called to protect the ministers, they
were so interrupted by the mob and its leaders that mobocracy gained the day.

7. The term abolitionist was at first used to designate
one who was in favor of doing away with slavery. In the
North, when the Garrisonian party arose, it was confined
to them especially, because some of them had no scruples
about aiding slaves to flee from their masters. Methodists
of the Methodist Episcopal Church disowned the name; for
although they hated slavery and the Fugitive-Slave law,
they scrupulously avoided aiding or advising slaves to leave
their masters; but because they were antislavery the South
soon began to class them with the most ultra. And then
to make them odious, indeed, they were denounced by the
pro-slavery men as abolitionists, negro thieves, and the
like. The antislavery principles found in the Methodist
Discipline were greatly distorted by them, and made an
occasion for the use of the most degrading terms in denunciation of our people.

A Mr. Atwater, who denounced all men that did not go
in their views to the full length of Garrisonianism, had

been writing to a Southern preacher, and declared that all
the North were of his own type. This stirred up the
due prejudice against the Methodist Episcopal Church in
the South-West. It also elicited the following letter from
Bishop Morris:

"CINCINNATI, OHIO, *May* 17, 1855.

"REV. ISAAC BURNS: *Dear Brother,*—Yours of the 5th
was received yesterday. The recent excitement in Western
Missouri, gotten up by designing partisans, is cause of regret to all lovers of peace and order, especially to all consistent patriots and Christians. They who brought on the
present state of affairs will have finally to answer to God
for the evil done. As to the impression sought to be
made by enemies that the bishops of the Methodist Episcopal Church send preachers to Missouri to carry out
ultra abolition principles, it is false and absurd. Our
bishops are not abolitionists themselves, and of course they
do not seek to make abolitionists of others; neither are we
pro-slavery men. We are Methodists, as we ever have
been, opposed to all sorts of wickedness, but ever loyal
subjects to that civil government under which we are providentially placed in the prosecution of our Gospel mission.
And as for the letter of Rev. Mr. Atwater to a Southern
preacher, which is relied on for proof against us, he alone
is responsible; it was written without our knowledge or
consent. We neither approve the tone of it, nor indorse
its doctrine. It may have been well meant on his part,
but the practical tendency of it is evil, only evil, and that
continually; for it not only hedges up the way of his own
brethren in their efforts to be useful, but influences their enemies with a spirit of persecution. I disclaim any sympathy
with such documents. In 1848, some two or three thousand
Methodists in Missouri and Arkansas who wished to remain
under our jurisdiction, petitioned our General Conference

to have preachers of the Methodist Episcopal Church sent among them, and their request was granted. This was the occasion of sending some preachers to Missouri and Arkansas. The object of sending them was, first, to furnish these destitute brethren and sisters with pastors from the Church of their choice; secondly, to get as many sinners of all sorts converted as possible. This is the whole story in few words, and whoever charges us with sending them for any political or sinister purpose, or to accomplish any object other than to feed the flock of Christ and save the souls of the people, does us great injustice. You are at liberty to make any use you think proper of this letter.

" Yours, in the Gospel of peace,

" T. A. MORRIS."

This was well said by one who always utters the words of soberness and truth.

8. Our brethren in the South-West were constantly annoyed, by either extravagant representations or by a well-meant jealousy, lest the Church on the border should be misled by the pro-slavery views so current there. The editor of the North-Western Christian Advocate, Dr. Watson, a good and zealous man, seems to have entertained fears as to the soundness of the border in its principles.

The North-Western Christian Advocate of May 23, 1855, in an elaborate article on occupying slave territory, says:

" In our view, Providence seems clearly to indicate that the time has fully come when, with so many more inviting fields before her, to tax fully her powers and resources, the Methodist Episcopal Church should not waste her energies by *futile* attempts to *push* her institutions into Missouri, or even Kansas and Texas, at least during the present distracted state of affairs. But especially are we opposed to the pushing of our institutions into these territories under the old regimen of tolerating voluntary slaveholding in the

Church. . . . Morally, numerically, and pecuniarily, we have lost fivefold more than we have ever gained by seeking to push our institutions into Kentucky, Missouri, and Arkansas."

In this connection Mr. Watson goes over the Kelly affair, the Fabius township meeting, the conduct of the Missouri Legislature in reference to Jackson Seminary, and argues that our ministry should be withdrawn from the whole South-West, Kansas included. He states that "martyrdom in Missouri, in the flames of pro-slavery hatred, should be a martyrdom destitute of all honor."

Mr. Conklin, editor of the Central Christian Advocate, quotes from the Western Christian Advocate, then edited by C. Elliott, a response as follows:

"As to the Methodist Episcopal Church in Kentucky, it is small and feeble as to numbers and general influence at present; yet it is pure, aggressive, increasing, and possesses all the elements and constituents necessary to preserve Methodism and pure religion in Kentucky from being swallowed up by pro-slavery contamination. It is feared, hated, and opposed by the leaders of the Methodist Episcopal Church South, in Kentucky, but looked on with interest and hope by multitudes of members of that Church. The high pro-slavery oligarchy hate and oppose it, yet candid men among them confess that it is right. . . . As it is we have much hope and no fear in regard to this matter. The cause is of God and must prevail. Did not our age and prospective infirmities of age forbid, we would certainly volunteer for the Kentucky or Missouri service, especially for the Platte country; and as we do not belong to the Church *North*, but to the Methodist Episcopal Church, their spirited resolutions could not affect us.

"In conclusion, *there is no part of our work so full of promise as that now in the slave States.* Our people and preachers in these conferences, as a whole, are right, and nothing but right; and as to moral wrong among them on the vexed question, as Christians, the moral wrong is not on their side, but on the side of their accusers in the North, who take up the unfounded accusations of their enemies, such as Mr. Sedwick and others, publish the false charges, and then condemn, without 'examination, the supposed offenders; but this mischievous course has had its day, and will be met, and receive the merited rebuke it deserves."

The foregoing declarations were uttered in 1855, and now, February, 1868, thirteen years after, the events justify fully the soundness of our views. 'The just principles of our Church on the border have been, under God, a great blessing to Western Virginia, Missouri, and Kentucky. By God's grace in the heart, and his overruling providence, the services of our Church in these States have been made singularly successful in preserving the purity of religion and the union of these States with the United States of America. What in 1855 was only the clear reason of the thing, is now a matter of history, and our reasonings are fully sustained by the historical facts of the times. Missouri, Western Virginia, and Maryland are now free, principally, under God, by the instrumentality of the Methodist Episcopal Church.

Mr. Watson responded promptly, but kindly, "that he was not for giving up Missouri or Kansas, provided that the policy of our Church in reference to slavery be changed;" but that the policy of the Methodist Episcopal Church *at that time* was founded upon "the same principles of policy that produced the Church South." He also stated that "the day of organizing Conferences and establishing papers in slave territory, on the old obsolete, conservative basis, was gone by."

Mr. Conklin responded, among other things, that in

organizing in the slave States we go to a tried people, who, for four years after the secession, remained scattered and torn rather than go into a pro-slavery Church; that we have the benefit of the experience of the Methodist Episcopal Church South, and her fate is a warning to us; that our guards against being betrayed into error are now greater than they were in the early history of the Church; that there is a radical difference between the two Churches that will forever prevent any close affiliation; the members of the free States will exercise a guardian watch-care over the Church in slave territory.

The Texas Christian Advocate says, "The Methodist Episcopal Church can do nothing but harm by its labors in slave territory, and it would be wisdom in it to cease these labors. It can never prosper in Texas, nor in Arkansas." Such was the general decision at that time by Southern Methodists.

The Central Christian Advocate quotes the editor of the Western Christian Advocate—C. Elliott—who declared, "That the Methodist Episcopal Church had labored eighty or ninety years in the slave States. Up to 1845 her labors extended to all the slave States. That the Methodist Episcopal Church will have work in slave States till God in his providence shall make them free States, and even after that glorious event. They will then be on their *own ground*, as they are *now* on their *own ground* in these States. That there will be slaveholders in the Church, by inheritance and will, is plain, and matter of fact, while slavery is in the State. Some cry out, all slaveholders out of the Church! and in the next sentence they retract this, as they retain the *moral* and exclude only the *wicked* slaveholders. That the Methodist Episcopal Church can apply only *moral* tests, not merely civil ones. And this course never *sanctioned* slavery, and never can. The Church excludes only those who commit *sin*, or refuse admittance on that account, and no other tests can stand."

9. An unpleasant controversy took place between the editor of the Central Christian Advocate and him of the North-Western Christian Advocate on the continuance of the former paper. The position assumed by the editor of the North-Western Christian Advocate was, "That the chapter on slavery be so changed as to admit no *voluntary* slaveholders into the Methodist Episcopal Church." Mr. Conklin contended that the Church in the South-West was correct on the subject. But the difficulty in the case all along was one that Dr. Watson, good and intelligent man as he was, overlooked in his zealous mode of expression. Such is the despotism of slavery that it compels many to become slaveholders without, or even contrary to their will, their knowledge, or their acts in any way. Such is the case with all those who are made slaveholders by process of law, by will, or inheritance. The law makes them slaveholders. And yet a lax phraseology obtained on this subject. Mr. Duncan, a Presbyterian minister, in his admirable Treatise on Slavery, at the close of his discussion, stated "that those who became slaveholders by inheritance were not slaveholders," and in the Winter and Spring of 1855–56 Dr. Watson placed at the head of his paper for months the statement, "Those who are slaveholders by inheritance are not slaveholders." Of course, up to that point, such persons were innocent; but if they received cordially the grant, they became as guilty as though they had gone into the market and purchased them.

Besides, by this very means of becoming slaveholders by inheritance, and by stringent laws at the same time forbidding emancipation, the Church has been tyrannized over from the beginning. Many lax expressions were used on both sides of this question, which gave much occasion of disturbance on the border. The Southern press seized all such, and used them to trammel our brethren in Missouri. Furthermore, amid the views of those desiring new rules, the subject became confused. Many on the border were so sensitive as to be very easily offended, and were reluctant even to use the stereotyped language of the Methodist Episcopal Church, which pronounced slavery a great moral wrong, and fit only to be eradicated instead of being supported, or even tolerated. The phraseology used on both sides was more or less calculated to confuse the subject rather than to develop its real merits.

10. The Missouri Conference was this year to have met at Independence, Mo., October 11th. But the opposition to the Methodist Episcopal Church was so much on the increase as to call forth the vigorous interference of the proslavery portion of the community. Accordingly a meeting was held in Independence, on Monday, August 13th, to remonstrate against the meeting of our Conference. This was the first instance, in the United States or elsewhere, of a public meeting for such an object. Colonel James Chiles was called to the chair, and N. R. M'Murry was chosen Secretary. The following preamble and resolutions were then adopted:

"*Whereas*, it is known that the people of Western Missouri have been and still are greatly excited on the slavery question, owing to their proximity to the territory of Kansas, and various other causes well known to the public; and, *whereas*, it is known that the Methodist Episcopal Church, North, design holding their Annual Conference in this place, in October next; and, *whereas*, we believe that the sitting of said Conference in this place, in view of the state of public opinion here, and the supposed antislavery sentiments and opinions of the ministers and others who will constitute the Conference, may lead to results and acts to be regretted by the citizens of this community, we deem it but an act of justice to notify the Conference of the state of things here, and earnestly requesting them to hold said Conference at some other point where less excitement prevails; therefore,

"*Resolved*, That, for the reasons above stated and set forth, we respectfully remonstrate with the ministers, bishops, and others who will constitute said Conference against the holding of the same at this place in September or October next, and earnestly request them to hold said Conference at some other point, where less excitement prevails upon this vexed subject of slavery.

"*Resolved*, That we deem it but an act of justice to ourselves to ask for peace and repose upon the slavery question, and for this reason, as well as for those already stated, we trust the ministers and others constituting said Conference will hold the same at some other place.

"*Resolved*, That, if the ministers and others constituting said Conference should, after this respectable remonstrance, persist in holding the same here, we shall hold ourselves fully acquitted from any consequences that may result therefrom.

"*Resolved*, That a copy of the proceedings of this meeting be forwarded to the Western Christian Advocate, published at Cincinnati, and the Central Christian Advocate, published at St. Louis, with a request that the same be published in each of said papers."

The proceedings were published in the Western Dispatch, Independence, Mo., August 17th.

In the Western Christian Advocate of September 5th, C. Elliott, the editor, published the proceedings as requested, and made a response to them, from which we select the following:

"I and my readers are not acquainted with any Church, which you designate by the name of 'The Northern Meth-

odist Church,' and 'The Methodist Episcopal Church, North.'
We are total strangers to the 'ministers, bishop, and others
who will constitute said Conference.' Yet, although we are
unacquainted with any Church by either of the two titles
designated, or with any of their bishops, ministers, or members, we publish cordially and gratuitously the proceedings
of the meeting, as requested.

"If it be said that the body intended to be designated is
'The Methodist Episcopal Church of the United States,'
organized in 1784, and existing in Missouri coeval with its
first white settlers, none of its officials, whether its General
Conference, Annual Conferences, bishops, ministers, or members, will respond to the name 'Northern Methodist Church,'
or 'Methodist Episcopal Church, North;' they do not belong to such Church, as their Church is known, in law and
equity, by the name and title of the 'Methodist Episcopal
Church of the United States.' Had our paper been called
by the name of the 'Western Christian,' the Western Christian Advocate would never answer to the call under such a
name."

And it was further added, in regard to the members
of Conference: "It is true they believe, hold, and, by their
Discipline, inculcate that slavery is contrary to natural law,
contrary to the Word of God, and contrary to just human
laws, as the laws which enact it are founded in injustice and
wrong. But, though these laws are bad laws, they submit
to them as far as God's law will allow, and no further, and,
as loyal citizens, they are the supporters of law in general.
It is their right, as citizens, thus to dissent, to alter bad
laws when they are able by a majority of votes, and be the
better class of citizens on this account, because that which
is morally wrong, as slavery is, can never be politically
right. The bishops, ministers, and members of the Methodist Episcopal Church are of the faith of Washington,

Jefferson, and the best American statesmen on this subject, and their rights can not be called in question."[3]

The members of Ebenezer Church, St. Louis, September 4, 1855, passed the following preamble and resolutions in reference to the persecuting edict of the Independence meeting:

"*Whereas*, we have learned from a variety of reliable sources that very strong opposition exists in the city of Independence and surrounding country, to the meeting of the Missouri Annual Conference in that place; and,

"*Whereas*, we would most deeply regret the occurrence of physical and violent collision between the members of our Conference and the enemies of our cause in that section of the country; and,

"*Whereas*, various leading members of the Conference have signified by letter to the editor of the Central Christian Advocate their conviction of the propriety of a change in the place of holding the next session in view of existing circumstances; therefore,

"*Resolved*, That we, the members of Ebenezer Charge, in the city of St. Louis, do sincerely sympathize with our brethren of the border work, and would most cordially invite the Conference, if any change is made, to hold the next session in this city.

"*Resolved*, That in our estimation this change will involve the sacrifice of no principle of Methodism whatever, but that it will be promotive of peace in our borders, and at the same time will be in accordance with the pacific precept of the Great Head of the Church to his first disciples—'If they persecute you in one city, flee to another.'"

For the sake of peace, the Conference met at St. Louis and transacted their business without molestation. And although the wording of the proceedings at Independence

[3] Western Christian Advocate, vol. xxii, p. 142, col. 3.

was more courteous than that in most similar notices, such
a declaration was in the full spirit of intolerance. It was
the common excuse of mobocrats, and is of a piece with
the most bloody edicts of persecution in ancient and medieval times. It was the forerunner of the ukase against
Bishop Janes and the Arkansas Conference, as well as the
murderous decrees authorizing the hanging of innocent
and good men in subsequent years.

11. In the course of the year 1854, the buildings and
grounds of a joint stock company of Jackson, Cape Girardeau county, were offered to the Missouri Conference of the
Methodist Episcopal Church, in consideration of the establishment of a good school at that point. The offer was
accepted, teachers secured, and a school organized under
very encouraging prospects. Wishing to secure permanency and enlargement, the Trustees of the institution applied to the Legislature for a charter. On the 21st of
February, 1855, after considerable discussion in the House,
the bill was rejected by a vote of sixty to thirty-six.

The reasons for rejecting the bill were fully stated during its discussion. Among many other things it was alleged
that the Methodist Episcopal Church was an abolition
Church, that it was opposed to slavery, and labored for its
destruction, and that the object of sending missionaries into
the State was simply the extirpation of slavery.

At this time there were between five and six thousand
members of the Methodist Episcopal Church in Missouri,
and these would favorably compare with any other class of
citizens. But because the Church and its members were
antislavery they could not be countenanced by granting
them a charter for a respectable school or academy. Similar grants were made to all other Churches in the State,
such as Protestant Episcopalians, the Southern Methodists,
Presbyterians, Baptists, Campbellites, Cumberland Presby-

terians, etc. The reasons were, that those Churches in Missouri were, in their majorities, pro-slavery, and their minorities made no marked opposition to it. But the " Northern Methodist Church " was an abolition body, and could not be countenanced.

The Southern Methodists, who by this time were become truly pro-slavery, aimed at expelling from the South-West the Methodist Episcopal Church, and therefore took a leading part in the opposition, as they considered the Methodist Episcopal Church their principal competitor.

This refusal to grant the common rights of citizens to the Methodist Episcopal Church was the more aggravated, since it was in direct opposition to the Constitution of Missouri. This instrument declares "that all men have a natural and indefeasible right to worship Almighty God according to the dictates of their own consciences; that no human authority can control or interfere with the rights of conscience; that no person can ever. be hurt, molested, or restrained in his religious professions or sentiments, if he do not disturb others in their religious worship.'"

The course of the Legislature, in refusing a charter to the Jackson Seminary, was only a prelude to the disabilities thrown in the way of the Methodist Episcopal Church in Missouri, with the manifest design of driving it from the State.[4]

12. The St. Louis Christian Advocate, the organ of the Southern Methodists, at this time was constantly engaged in presenting the Methodist Episcopal Church as an obtruder in Missouri. In its representations it left us no sphere of usefulness; no work of well-doing with which to be busied; no apology for our presence in the South-West, or even for an existence. The constant implication of its language toward us was, that we were about some

[4] Central Christian Advocate, 1855, p. 38.

secret vice, working some clandestine evil, and preparing for open villainy. Our Church was habitually denounced, and its members and ministers were constantly held up to public contempt as negro thieves.

Rev. Andrew Monroe, in a letter dated Kansas Territory, March 14th, and published in the Nashville Christian Advocate of April 12, 1855, makes a strong plea for the occupancy of Kansas by the Southern Methodists. Mr. Monroe was superintendent of the Southern Church in that State. He argues that, although much can not be done immediately, it is the time for the Church to act. Now is the time for the great South to locate and establish her claims, to put her impress upon the institutions of the country, and now is the time to lay deep and wide the foundations of Southern Methodism. So far they had the vantage-grounds, as they were the first in the field, and the sympathies of the Southern people were with them. As the country will be densely populated, now is the time to act. This very season is the time for the Church to act. He says that he had the services of two local preachers, and the promise of two more from Missouri. He urges the preachers of Kentucky and Tennessee to emigrate to Kansas. The South generally, and the Church in particular, has much to win or lose in this matter. His letter concludes thus:

"We hope to see thousands of families here from slaveholding States before six months shall pass. Then let local preachers come and seek a home in this good land, and have a position where their ministry is greatly needed. Our bishops, presiding elders, preachers, and people ought to know that this country will be settled, and furnished with preachers and institutions. If we do not do it, others will. May we not hope for prompt and efficient action on the part of the South, till the men and the vast wealth of the South be called into requisition. The Church, North, is already contemplating the founding of a Methodist University in Kansas Territory, and will spare neither men nor means to accomplish their object. Will the South be behind, dragging at the end? No, never. We have the resources, we have the strong, motive power. I am urged to write this by the wants and pressing demands of a common cause, in which I would interest all Southern hearts, hands, and purses."[5]

From the foregoing it is manifest that the Southern Methodists took an active part in the efforts put forth to make Kansas a slave State.

Like attempts were made in California, by sending men and means to establish a pro-slavery Church in that Territory. Rev. B. T. Crouch, jr., February 18, 1855, gives a doleful account of the Southern Methodist Church in California. It was published in the Memphis Christian Advocate, and copied in the Central Christian Advocate, (May 24, 1855.) Mr. Crouch states that the Southern Methodist Church is a failure in California, and unless new and more energetic means are employed it must soon be extinct. Two years ago he says Bishop Soule promised to send them a supply. Of the preachers in the country he also says eight left and returned home, and two located.

Slaveholders were liberal in contributions for the support of Southern Methodist preachers in California. But notwithstanding all these endeavors, the Southern Methodist Conference there run its race, and now—February, 1868—scarcely a vestige of it remains. So it was in Cincinnati; for a pro-slavery Church in a free State is a monstrosity. Nevertheless, nothing was left undone by Southern Methodists to sustain their Church and establish slavery in California and Kansas.

[5] Central Christian Advocate, 1855, p. 66.

The Memphis Christian Advocate of November 17th was rampant against the sending of our preachers into slave territory.[6]

13. The border war in Missouri was now raging. In Platte county, the pro-slavery men drove Messrs. Park and Patterson away, and threw their press into the river. They notified all ministers of the Methodist Episcopal Church to cease their preaching in the county. They passed resolutions to take a Mr. M'Crea from the custody of the law and to hang him. They countenanced riding a Mr. Phillips on a rail through the streets, tarred and feathered, because he proclaimed himself a Free-soiler. They compelled two excellent Presbyterian ministers, Revs. Messrs. Woodward and Starr, to leave their charges because they were *suspected* of being unsound on the slavery question.[7]

14. But the Missouri and Western Virginia Conferences gave full proof of their soundness, by adhering to the true principles of Scripture and of Methodism.

Dr. Durbin, who attended the Western Virginia Conference, held at Wheeling this year, reports its condition. After stating that they voted unanimously against the change of the General Rule, he remarks:

"We visited this Conference, and was much gratified at its growth in numbers, influence, and wealth. Without relinquishing, in any degree, the position the Methodist Episcopal Church has occupied on the subject of slavery, this Conference makes progress in the midst of a slaveholding population, and in the face of the Methodist Episcopal Church South, which is pro-slavery. Thus the Methodist Episcopal Church in Western Virginia is a living protest against the evils of slavery, and uses her authority, by way of discipline, to ameliorate the condition of the slave, and

---

[6] See Central Christian Advocate, 1855, p. 190.
[7] Central Christian Advocate, 1855, p. 91.

to prepare, as far as she may, both master and slave for emancipation."[8]

The Missouri Conference was in more difficult circumstances, but retained its principles, and did not abandon its practice.

The Arkansas Conference still existed, but, through the persecutions of the slave power, it became in time extinct.

15. Such was the sympathy felt for the Missouri Conference, by our brethren generally, that the late Dr. Bond, sen., this year editor of the Christian Advocate and Journal, urged the appointment of a day of fasting and prayer on behalf of the Conference. We here quote the words of this venerable man:

" But the strangest thing in this whole business is the position in which the outrageous proceedings of a part of the citizens of Missouri have placed the Methodist Episcopal Church.

" We have an Annual Conference whose operations are chiefly confined to that State. The pro-slavery patriots have denounced our preachers, and threaten all ministers of the 'Church, North,' as they are pleased to call it, with ' tar and feathers,' if they dare to bring the message of salvation, with which they are charged by their Lord and Master, into Missouri. The patriots of the French Revolution commenced by voting that ' there is no God.' The patriots of Missouri begin with the declaration that God shall not send any to preach his Gospel but such as they approve, only those ministers who, like themselves, hold ultra pro-slavery opinions. On the other hand, our ultra-abolitionists denounce our preachers in Missouri and other slaveholding territories as pro-slavery men, pandering to the prejudices of the 'sum of all villainies,' and denounce our Missionary Board for making any appropriations for the

---

[8] Central Christian Advocate, 1855, p. 102.

support of the missions under the care of such Conferences. Our suffering brethren are thus placed between two fires. 'But they trust in God, and know in whom they trust.' All we can recommend in this time of unusual peril and distress is founded on this trust. Let our bishops appoint and proclaim a fast—a day of fasting, humiliation, and prayer, to be observed throughout all our charges. Let us all make the condition of our southern border-conferences a subject of earnest supplication. Let us pray for their deliverance from the threatened persecution, or that they who may be called to suffer may endure as seeing Him who is invisible, but is ever present to those who are faithful in his cause. Brethren, shall we have such a fast—such an opportunity of uniting in supplication at the throne of heavenly grace, in favor of our suffering brethren? We really hope so; and that in our prayers we will not forget to ask mercy for our enemies and persecutors."

CHAPTER IV.

EVENTS OF 1856.

1. The Arkansas Conference for the year 1856 was held, November 6th, at Cave Spring, near Sarcoxie, Mo., Bishop Baker presiding. Mr. Bewley was on the Texas Mission district. Mr. Robertson was on the Fayetteville district, but moved his family to Mound City, Kansas, and called his residence *Pleasant Garden*. His design in moving was to leave his family in a free State, and to have a burial place for them on free soil. Notwithstanding the remoteness of his family residence, he attended faithfully to his work in Arkansas and Missouri.

We have already seen how Rev. Wm. Sellers had been mobbed in 1854 by the inhabitants of Fabius township, Marion county, Mo. This year we have a similar instance while he traveled Rochester circuit, Andrew county, Mo. We find this occurrence noted in the Central Christian Advocate of June 26, 1856. The notice is quoted as follows, from the St. Joseph Gazette, which may speak for itself as to this matter:

" Difficulties at Rochester, Andrew county, Mo.— On the outside of to-day's paper will be found the proceedings of a public meeting at Rochester, which gave rise to the recent tragical events in that town. The proceedings of that meeting will explain themselves, as their only object was to rid the community of what is universally considered in Southern States a dangerous class of preachers, a Church which, on account of its Discipline and doctrines on slavery, is a nuisance—a stench in the nostrils of our people; we mean the *Northern Methodist Church.* There can be no good or satisfactory reason offered why a Southern community should tolerate the existence of a Church in their midst which declares that its members can not hold slaves—that the institution of slavery is against the spirit of religion. At the time of holding this meeting a difficulty occurred between a pro-slavery man, Samuel Simcox, and an abolitionist, one Hardesty. A few days afterward they met again, when angry words passed again between them, which ended in a fight, and the shooting of Simcox, the ball taking effect on the back of his head.

"In defiance of the will of the community, as appears by the resolutions which we published on last Saturday, the *Northern Methodist preacher* proceeded to hold his meeting. He was asked to desist, but would not, and, as the penalty of his temerity, was 'tarred and feathered.' In the difficulty which occurred, in consequence, another man—Holland, we believe, was his name, an abolitionist—was killed. We have not, however, the particulars of this last affair, and may be in error in regard to the real facts. Much excitement exists in that section, and a fixed determination on the part of the citizens to tolerate no more preachers of the above obnoxious school to preach or hold meetings in that neighborhood. The denomination of preachers would consult their safety by leaving Southern soil, where they are looked on with suspicion, and do no one any possible good. They are not wanted here."

Mr. Holland, referred to above, was a man of "threescore years and ten," whose only offense was that he was a member of the Methodist Episcopal Church, and a friend to its preachers. He died breathing the spirit of a martyr. One of our older preachers, in a private note, writes as follows in reference to him: "I have long been acquainted

with old brother and sister Holland and their children; I
have often eaten at their table and rested on their beds.
He was a great friend to old Methodist preachers, and
therefore mobocrats wanted him out of the way. He was
a devoted Christian, and has died a faithful martyr to the
cause of God."

But let us hear Mrs. Holland's letter of June 24, 1856,
directed to Mr. Conklin, of the Central Christian Advocate,
and inserted in its issue of July 10th:

"BROTHER CONKLIN,—With great sorrow of heart I
communicate to you an account of the murder of my dear
husband, Benjamin Holland, which took place in a mob
which was raised against Rev. Wm. Sellers, of the Methodist Episcopal Church in Rochester, Andrew county, Missouri. I merely state what came under my own knowledge.
Brother Sellers was to have commenced a protracted meeting in Rochester, on Saturday, 14th inst. He came to our
house on Thursday evening before, and remained till Saturday morning. He and my husband were in doubt about
going to the meeting, as there was great excitement in the
place, a man having been lately killed there; but they concluded to go and see if there could be a chance to hold
the meeting peaceably. They asked me to go with them,
but I concluded not to go. They went, and after some
time two men came and informed me that my husband was
shot and mortally wounded, and wished me to be sent for
in haste; before I got started, another friend came in a
carriage for me. When I got to the place, brother Strack
and wife, and other friends, met me at the door, weeping,
and informed me that he was dead; this so affected me
that I partially fainted, and when I came to myself I was
lying on a bed where I had been taken while powerless.
As I lay on the bed I got a sight of my murdered husband, where he was laid out. The sight so affected me

that I fainted again, but by the attention of kind friends I recovered again. Here I wish to express my thanks to brother Strack and wife, and sister Dillard, for their kind attention to my husband till he breathed his last, and for preparing for his burial. But there were others that I saw sauntering about on Saturday evening and Sunday, with sticks in their hands, and, as I was told, they were using abusive language. My husband was in the seventieth year of his age. He has been a member of the Methodist Episcopal Church twenty-five or thirty years, and for that time and longer our house has been a home for Methodist preachers, and we were always glad to see them come. The murder took place, I am told, while the mob had hold of brother Sellers, and was abusing him; but I am told that my husband was not interfering or saying any thing at the time.

"The first words he spoke, after he received the shot, were, 'Lord, have mercy upon the wicked!' which showed that he possessed the meek and lowly spirit of his Lord and Master.   LYDIA HOLLAND.

"P. S. Since writing the above, we have just heard that it is reported that my husband stood with a revolver in his hand, and presented it and threatened to shoot. This report is utterly false.   L. H."

The foregoing will show very clearly that to belong to the Methodist Episcopal Church, as a member, preacher, or friend, was to incur the character of an abolitionist; and an abolitionist was, in the popular view, a stealer of negroes, and could not be permitted to live in Missouri; and if such they must be banished from the State; they might be tarred or feathered, rode on a rail, or put to death in the most summary way, without judge or jury, or any law process, save that of mob-law, in defiance of constitutional and statute law. Such was the dilemma in which the

members, preachers, and friends of the Methodist Episcopal
Church in Missouri at that time were placed. It is true a
portion of the community disapproved of this course. But
the pro-slavery leaders had the rabble under their control,
and this governed, while the others looked on in silence,
and thus gave consent.

2. The pro-slavery men in Missouri, among the various
expedients to support the institution, instituted "Pro-Slavery Aid Societies." In the Western Weekly Platte Argus,
of February 15, 1862, we find an account of one which the
citizens of Jackson county had formed. The object of this
society was to assist persons from that county who desired
to move to Kansas, and who were friendly to making the
same a slave State. From all we can ascertain these, or
similar organizations, were formed in all the slave States,
in order to encourage poor white people to emigrate to
Kansas, under leaders, and thus prevent it from becoming
a free State. Subsequently, antislavery men in the free
States formed aid societies to encourage emigrants who
would go for freedom. The slaveholders of Missouri could
not be behind others, and so coöperated in money and
mobocratic assaults on the Kansas Free-soil men. All the
administrative aid of the ruling presidents, in appointing
officials, was used to aid the pro-slavery cause, and to crush
the Free-soil men. Of course, this produced efforts, on the
defensive side, to resist the murderous assaults of the
propagandists.

3. The raids on Kansas by Missourians were of the most
savage description. As a specimen of their spirit, we give
below an appeal made to the citizens of Lafayette county,
Mo., in the Fall of 1856:

"Now is the time for ACTION. *We must have men to go
to the Territory immediately, or all will be lost.* The intention of the abolitionists is to drive us from the Territory

and carry the next election, and GET POSSESSION OF THE
REINS OF GOVERNMENT. This we *must not submit to.* If we
do, *Kansas is lost to the South forever,* and our slaves in
upper Missouri will be useless to us, and our homes must
be given up to the abolition enemy. *Come, men, to the rescue! Up, men of Lafayette!*

"Meet at Lexington on WEDNESDAY, at 12 o'clock.
BRING YOUR HORSES WITH YOU, YOUR GUNS, AND YOUR
CLOTHING, all ready to go to Kansas. Let every man who
can possibly leave home go now to save the lives of his
friends. Let those who can not go hitch up their wagons
and throw in a few provisions, and get more as they come
along by their neighbors, and bring it to Lexington on
Wednesday. Let others bring horses and mules, and sad-
dles and guns—all to come on Wednesday. There is no
time to spare, *and no one must hold back.* Let all do a little, and the work will be light. We want two hundred to
three hundred men from this county. Jackson, Johnson,
Platte, Clay, Ray, Saline, Carroll, and other counties are
now acting in this matter. All of them will send up a
company of men, and there will be a concert of action.
NEW SANTA FE, Jackson county, will be the place of rendezvous for the whole crowd, and our motto this time will
be 'no quarter.'"

Similar appeals were made in all the border counties, so
that between two and three thousand men were soon ready
to enter the Kansas Territory. Colonel Doniphan was in
command of the Missourians.[1]

These repeated attacks on Kansas were made with great
vigor and savage fierceness.

A committee of the National Kansas Society waited upon
and addressed President Pierce, about the last of August,
and the following is the account of the interview:

[1] See Central Christian Advocate for 1856, pp. 351, 353, 354, 367.

"Mr. President, during the eighteen months or more that executive power has been exerted, as is alleged, to preserve peace in Kansas—and vainly exerted, it would seem, from admissions here made—the disorders of that Territory have grown only worse. At this moment they are more threatening than ever. A peaceful solution of its troubles seems still more uncertain than at any period of its former history. The President affirms that he has exhausted all his Constitutional powers; and yet order is not restored. Under such circumstances may it not be worth while to inquire *whether the germ of the evils is not to be found in the Territorial laws themselves?*

"*President*—This question I do not propose to discuss at the present time.

"*Committee*—From whatever source, then, sir, the difficulties in Kansas have originated, this one thing is patent to the country and to the world, that, notwithstanding all the efforts of the Government, disorders of the most frightful character have prevailed, disorders that would shame the worst despotisms of the worst ages, disorders so widespread and so atrocious, so bloody and so infernal, so deeply damning and inhuman that, to escape them, the wretched inhabitants would make a gain if transferred to the despotic governments of Russia, Austria, or of France. During this dark reign of blood and terror, during this fearful tempest of violence and anarchy, these poor unshielded victims of plotted vengeance have broken no law and committed no crime. For hating slavery, because they loved liberty, all these things have come upon them."

The Committee then continued:

"Such, sir, is the nature and character of the events which have transpired in Kansas during the past eighteen months' policy of the Government. As representatives of the National Kansas Committee, we are here to-day to ask *whether any change in this policy of the Administration is to be expected?*

"*President—No, sirs!* THERE WILL BE NONE!"

A correspondent of the Missouri Republican of August 27th states: "The acting Governor at Lecompton on yesterday issued his proclamation declaring the Territory in a state of insurrection, calls upon all law-abiding citizens to aid the legal authorities, and to endeavor to preserve the peace, to protect property and person from injury, and secure the innocent and unoffending in the rights guaranteed to them by the Constitution. He will ask aid of Colonel Coffer and General Smith, but it is understood they have no orders to give assistance, and the militia of the country must attend to the matter themselves."

This proclamation was of a piece with the treasonable response of the President; and thus the loyal men of Kansas were left to the tender mercies of their invaders.

These principles and assaults of Missouri slaveholders were readily made to act on the members and ministers of the Methodist Episcopal Church in the State and Territory above named, as the historical narrative in these chapters fully demonstrates.

4. The tyranny of slavery, recruited by the Georgians and other extreme Southern men, passed from Missouri to Kansas by acts nothing less sanguinary than those practiced by the African slave-traders. Rev. William Butt, September 2, 1856, writes thus from Fort Leavenworth: "I am informed this morning that one Free State store and several law-offices are in ashes. The only terms upon which Free-State men can remain in this city are to insert their names in the pro-slavery list, and enter their ranks. On last Sabbath I had a span of horses worth three hundred dollars taken before my eyes." September 6th, Mr. Butt writes: "The pro-slavery men are fortifying the city, making a

breastwork of wagons. A majority of the Free-State men have fled from the city; of the balance, some have been murdered, some forced off on boats, with their families, on ten minutes' notice, leaving all their goods in the hands of the enemy, some are kept prisoners, and others forced into the ranks of their enemies. The bodies of Free-State men are frequently found scattered upon the prairies and along the roads."

The foregoing are mere specimens of what loyal and anti-slavery men had to suffer in those times and places. Indeed, the pro-slavery power, supported, or, at least, not restrained by the General Government, had undertaken to make every thing bow to the despotism of its favorite institution. This was peculiarly so in regard to Methodists, as they were considered the most active and aggressive element of the antislavery power.

5. The Kansas difficulties during this year were in their hight of violence. The President of the United States, Mr. Pierce, and his subalterns seem to have espoused the side of the slaveholders without remorse and without reason. I can, for want of space, give only an instance or two. The following is gathered from a communication by Rev. L. B. Dennis, dated Lawrence, Kan., August 29th, and found in the Central Christian Advocate of September 11th:

"The pro-slavery men, reënforced and supported by the Government, had formed forts, well armed and provisioned, in different places, in order to attack the Free-State men, as well as to protect themselves from retaliation. The town of Franklin was thus occupied with men, provisions, and United States arms. On the 10th of August Major Hoyt was selected by the Free-State men to examine one of these forts. He was apparently kindly received, but the next day he was found buried in a shallow grave under some brush, having been assassinated by the pro-slavery men. This excited the Free-State men, and they determined to break up one of these forts. They made the attack, and the pro-slavery men ran away. Over one hundred United States muskets were found in the fort. Thus, as mere specimens, we mention that Hoyt was murdered, Hoppy was scalped, Jennison was murdered in a cowardly manner.

"But the case of Mrs. Cantner was most atrocious. On the night of August 22d, near midnight, she had occasion to leave her bed a few moments, and proceeded a few steps from the house, when she was violently seized by the throat and dragged away by a party of men. After going some distance they stopped, took out her tongue, tied a string tightly around it, and then around her neck. Then four men, in their turn, gratified their brutal lust on the woman, then, kicking her and otherwise maltreating her, left her, and supposed she was dead. However, early next morning she revived, and with difficulty made her way to the house. Being a widow, and living with another family, she was not missed during the night. The string was cut from her tongue, which was then so swollen that she could not get it into her mouth. As soon as she could speak she gave the particulars. Whether she ever recovered the narrative does not say."

Slaveholders are so accustomed to compel, if they do not succeed in persuading the colored women to gratify their lusts, that the brutal treatment of the widow is only an instance of what often occurs.

The course of pro-slavery men on the border gave full proof of what was, in the course of events, to take place in after times. We see the results of this violence in the slaughter now crimsoning the South-West. Retributive justice, in part, at least, is falling upon slaveholders in the war now raging. They have sown to the wind; they now reap the whirlwind. Yet they follow their bloody appetites, for "returned rebels," while we write—August 10, 1864—are reported as having indiscriminately murdered some five hundred Union men, within the last few weeks, in Missouri.

6. Although retribution for the terrible wrongs above alluded to as yet has come but in part, there are indications that its measure will be full at last, and the mind of society be so revolutionized that universal public opinion will stamp them with deserved condemnation. After the lapse of eight years, precisely, the martyrdom of Mr. Benjamin Holland is now celebrated, as of old times in other cases, by an annual commemoration. Rev. Alfred H. Powell, under date of June 14th, has the following article in the Central Christian Advocate of June 30, 1864, giving an account of the "Martyr Celebration at Rochester, Mo.:" "It has been truly said that the 'blood of the martyrs is the seed of the Church.' For some time past it has been contemplated by the loyal Unionists of Rochester, Andrew county, to commemorate the death of Benjamin Holland, who was murdered in that place eight years ago on this day—June 14th. On the morning of the day a large number of persons, some in wagons, some in carriages, others on horseback, and others on foot, were seen going to Rochester to pay a tribute of respect to the memory of the sainted Holland, the proto-martyr of Methodism in Andrew county, Mo. Rev. L. V. Morton, of the Methodist Episcopal Church, opened the services by preaching from Matthew xxiv, 16—'And this Gospel of the kingdom shall be preached in all the world for a witness unto all nations; and then shall the end come.' The preacher stood in the door of the old deserted store where father Holland was murdered. The crowds without, as well as those within, listened with great attention. The preacher remarked that 'in that very door father Holland was shot, and his friends

8

determined to have the discourse commemorative of his death delivered upon the very spot upon which he fell.' During the sermon the stars and stripes were seen waving in various places of the vast assembly, while at the left hand of the preacher the National flag stood draped in mourning.

"After the sermon was over the people repaired to a grove, where seats were prepared and a stand erected. Colonel Bonham called the people to order. The hymn commencing,

'Servant of God, well done,'

was then sung, and Rev. Mr. Young, of the Presbyterian Church, led in prayer in patriotic style. Rev. Mr. Schofield, of the Baptist Church, then preached an hour and a half. Judge Heron made appropriate remarks, and the congregation united in singing,

'Together let us sweetly live,' etc.,

and they were then dismissed, and retired peaceably to their respective homes.

"What a change has taken place in Missouri in the course of eight years! Mr. Holland was murdered because he was a member of what they called, in derision, 'The Northern Methodist Church.' The preacher Sellers was tarred and feathered and otherwise abused on the occasion, and warned, and even forced to leave the country. Now the incumbent Methodist preacher preaches the anniversary sermon, while the Presbyterian and Baptist preachers join in the service. Truly the proverb is fulfilled which says, 'The blood of the martyrs is the seed of the Church.'"

CHAPTER V.

EVENTS OF 1857.

1. THE Arkansas Conference sat at Rocky Bayou, Izzard county, March 2, 1857; Bishop Ames presiding. Mr. Bewley was presiding elder on Texas district, as well as preacher in charge of Denton circuit. Thomas M. Willet was in his district, on Clear Fork circuit. They had a good camp meeting, but we can furnish no particulars. Mr. Robertson was on the Springfield district.

Persecution made its appearance with increased violence, and the emigration to California, Kansas, and Oregon continued.

Disunion seems now to have become the watchword of several leading journals in the South, both religious and political, but especially the latter. They seemed to cast behind them the sober judgments of Jefferson, Jackson, Clay, and Benton.

The Richmond Enquirer entered on the year 1857 with increased vigor in its well-known nullification career. The following extract from the Enquirer will speak for the others on this occasion:

"Liberated from the illegal restrictions and unjust operations of the Federal Government, and left free in the development of its splendid resources and the expansion of its vigorous institutions, the South would march forward in the career of glory with a firmer and faster step than was ever witnessed among nations. Oppressed by the burdens of unequal taxation, discouraged in the cultivation of its

commercial and manufacturing interests, and dwarfed in its
territorial expansion, the South will soon become the help-
less dependency of the antislavery power. This is the
alternative before us—a grandeur without a parallel in
history, or an ignominy which one shudders to contem-
plate in the bare conception. Will the South choose the
career to which interest, honor, and every manly motive
beckons it, or be content with the lot of the craven and
the slave? The timid fool may whisper that the expansion
of our institutions is an impracticable achievement; but
nothing is impossible with the people of the South. If the
North resists, upon what stronger ground could we stand
than upon this issue of the extension or restriction of
slavery? If the struggle is to come, let it come now, while
yet we have the spirit and the power to defend our rights.
If we are to fight, let us fight for the principle which is
essential to our equality in the Union, or our independence
out of the Union. Henceforth, let the free expansion of
its institutions be the ultimatum of the South."[1]

The religious press in the South, though more guarded,
was not less bold in uttering sentiments corresponding with
the above. Wayland's Moral Science, and text-books of
the same sort, were denounced, and largely excluded from
the Southern schools and colleges. The declaration that
" all men were born free and equal " was denounced by the
religious and political press as absurd. The retiring Governor of Missouri denounced St. Louis on account of its
antislavery character. Col. Benton was nominated by the
Benton democracy in the Missouri Legislature for election
to the United States Senate; but the opposing candidate
was chosen. Thus, for a time, the pro-slavery party had
the dominance, and thrust Mr. Benton aside.

2. As was said above, the religious denominations of the

---

[1] Central Christian Advocate, 1857, p. 7.

South, with some circumspection, were in full harmony with the political press. Bishop Pierce, in his third letter from Kansas, describing his Western tour, says: "Very likely it will appear that if the South loses Kansas, she will be more to blame than those, with all their faults—I may add crimes—who have warred on our institutions." The Bishop considers Kansas lost to the South, should it be admitted with a free constitution. So here is a fixed hatred of and opposition to freedom by a professed Christian Bishop; and this associated with a love and support of slavery.[2]

The Texas Christian Advocate, early in this year, writes as follows:

"Kansas, after all that has been said to the contrary, is proved to be as much fitted for slave labor as any other part of the South; and if, during the current year, a steady tide of emigration is kept up from the South, it will yet be free from abolition domination. The Southern settlers there have by no means given up the question, but are actively preparing for the convention which is to form the State Constitution. We learn from the Columbus (Ga.) Times and Sentinel, that Captain Clayton, of Clayton, Ala., who so successfully emigrated a prosperous colony to Kansas, last Fall, and located them near Tecumseh, Kansas Territory, will take out in the Spring a much larger and more imposing colony. Other patriotic citizens from other portions of the South will doubtless follow his example, and Western Missouri will literally empty her population upon the Territory.

The common and piously avowed professions of these papers were "a total disconnection with politics." "Such a position is both Scriptural and politic." "Non-intervention." "Letting it alone." "Neutrality on the subject of slavery." These were their chosen forms of expression.

[2] Central Christian Advocate, 1857, p. 62.

The politicians of the South decided beforehand that the Bible sustains slavery; and many ministers aided them with their approval of this teaching. Hence, they imposed silence on the ministry, as it was a political question with which the Gospel ministry had nothing to do. The ministers in the South, in general, as by a strong delusion to believe the lie, took up the hackneyed expression, "we have nothing to do with politics."[3]

3. The Southern Methodist press seems to have been very much grieved that the Methodist Episcopal Church should send her ministers into slave States. Bishop Pierce is reported as follows in his speech, delivered before the Western Virginia Conference, for the current year, and it is indorsed and copied by the Memphis and Nashville Christian Advocates:

"He [Bishop Pierce] thought that all the denominations of Protestant Evangelical Christians ought to-prosper; but he did not think that those whose affinities were for and whose affiliations were with those who constantly sought by all means to subvert our interests and overthrow our institutions, ought to prosper in Virginia, Kentucky, Arkansas, Missouri, etc., when their peculiar notions of moral and religious obligations led them directly to oppose the civil institutions, and local rights and interests of the community. The Bishop very clearly intimated that there was room enough for our Northern brethren to work where they were wanted and their labors needed, and where they could carry the news of salvation without sacrificing their honor, violating their own solemn contract, and imposing themselves upon those who did not want them. The wonder was, how a Methodist preacher, acquainted with the history of Methodism, whose affiliations were with the North, the leading object of whose life and labors was to meddle

[3] Central Christian Advocate, 1857, p. 92.

with other people's business, instead of minding his own, and preaching Christ crucified, could rest in peace and keep his conscience quiet before God." •

The Charleston editor gives the following position of the Church South, which is indorsed and enforced by Dr. Lee, of the Richmond Christian Advocate:

"We therefore hope the time is not far distant when every religious denomination *in Virginia* and the entire South will hold and entertain the same views of the institution of slavery as are now held and maintained by the Methodist Church South. And this should be so. What an anomaly does it present, and in what a contradiction does it place the people of the slaveholding States to have in their midst and to be supporting any religious sect whose doctrines are that African slavery is a sin, or that it is a moral, social, or political evil! We repeat that such a state of things is an anomaly, is a contradiction. And Virginia people in some portions of the State are doing *but little* to correct public opinion in this respect. The time, however, will come, and we sincerely hope it will come *very soon*, when every religious denomination in Virginia will hold upon this subject views in accordance with the rights and interests of the South. The signs of the times clearly indicate that the Methodist Church *South* is to be, erelong, the most powerful and influential denomination in Virginia and the entire South. The times plainly show that the masses of the people, outside of the Church, feel a deep interest in the success and welfare of the Church *South*. · The people regard it as a *Virginia* Church, as a *Southern* Church. · Its preachers are Virginians and Southerners. They are men who are devotedly attached to the cherished institutions of the South; they are men who are satisfied that their sacred duty is performed by 'preaching Christ and him crucified,' and who have no sympathy for nor hold any communion with Free-soilers and abolitionists.' " [4]

We extract from one of Bishop Pierce's letters on Kansas the following:

" It is, however, beyond all controversy that the North, in their blind zeal to make Kansas a free State, provoked all the troubles that followed by picking up and forwarding a population to serve their purpose; and the abolitionists were the aggressors, by their violence and rebellion, and lawless intrusions on the rights of others: still the South erred in imitating a bad example. She ought to have sent citizens, not soldiers, and to have left these abolition knights to the law and the troops of the General Government. This plan would have saved the Territory to the South, and a quiet, *bona fide* emigration would do it yet. Not that I think the climate, soil, and productions favorable to slavery, but it might be recognized in her constitution, when the time for her admission as a State shall come, and there would be slaves enough, along with this, to identify Kansas with the Southern States in the councils of the country. No physical law bars-the institution. *It is there, and there it might remain.* Nevertheless, I think the South will lose it, by her own fault rather than by the contrivance of her enemies."

The Bishop then annexes an extract of a letter from Kansas to himself, written in December previous, from which we select the following:

" As a Church, the Methodist Episcopal Church South in this country, in the affections and confidence of the community, has the vantage-ground; but in reference to number of preachers, the Northern Church has the advantage of us considerably. We stand as to numbers as we were at the formation—two transferred from us, and one super-

4 Central Christian Advocate, 1857, p. 166.

annuated, and three transferred to us. We have been
anxiously looking for transfers, but in vain. We need
them—we must have them or give up the field. I believe
if this is made a slave State we shall have peace and quiet,
with law-abiding citizens; otherwise, confusion and disorder, with a law-defiant community." [5]

Thus we see a Bishop of the Methodist Episcopal Church
South, and the preachers under his superintendence, joining
with the Southern pro-slavery men in extending this system over free territory. Who can wonder that Bishop
Pierce wrote as he did in 1859, urging that all Methodists
in slave territory should be forcibly driven from the soil?
And this teaching was an exhortation, in effect, to murder
Bewley and others: and we may here ask the question that
we asked in 1860, " Was he Bewley's hangman ?"

The sentiments uttered in the previous declarations of
Bishop Pierce, the Southern Methodist press, and the pro-
slavery Southern people generally, were, that no ministers
of the Methodist Episcopal Church should be allowed to
exercise their ministry on slave territory. In short, neither
a minister nor layman of the Methodist Episcopal Church
should be tolerated as such where slavery existed. The
obvious reason was that a fundamental principle in the
moral code of Methodism was that slavery was a moral
wrong, that it ought to be extirpated, and every member
and minister of the Methodist Episcopal Church was bound
to endeavor to secure its extirpation, as far as in them
lay. This change would have excluded the first Methodist
preachers from the United States, for all the States were
then slave States, and all the preachers and members were
antislavery, and they then—in 1784—avowed their purpose
of *extirpating slavery.* They disavowed using any unlawful
means; they never did use any. And now we may record

[5] See Central Christian Advocate, 1857, p. 54.

the result, that these endeavors of the Methodist Episcopal
Church, seconded by those of like minds, by God's blessing, have finally accomplished the object always kept in
view by the official teachings of our Church—we mean the
extirpation of slavery.

4. Rev. Dr. W. A. Smith, President of Randolph Macon
College, at this time, wrote an elaborate book in favor of
slavery. It had been delivered to his students previously,
in the form of collegiate lectures. In this book he asserted
"that slavery *per se* was right; or that the great abstract
principle of slavery was right, because it was a fundamental principle of the social state; and that domestic slavery,
as an *institution*, is fully justified by the condition and circumstances—essential and relative—of the African race in
this country, and therefore equally right."

He then complains that, in the early history of the country, "Thomas Jefferson denounced slavery as sinful, *per se,*
and declared that 'there was no attribute in the Divine
mind which could take sides with the whites in a controversy between the races,' thus assuming in this remark that
the providence as well as the attributes of the Deity are
against the slaveholder." After thus denouncing Jefferson,
he states that as early as 1780 the Methodists declared that
"slavery is contrary to the laws of God, man, and nature,
and hurtful to society; contrary to the dictates of conscience and pure religion; doing that which we would not
that others should do to us and ours; and that we pass our
disapprobation upon all our friends who keep slaves and
advise freedom." He also complains that this doctrine was
reasserted at the organization of the Church in 1784, and
that the same doctrines have been maintained to the present time by the Methodist Episcopal Church, without any
material alteration. He further asserts that these sentiments pervade our literature, our politics, and our theology,

so that it has become a kind of National belief, as it has long been the conviction of the leading Churches.

He then states that the teachings of Jefferson, of the Methodist Episcopal Church, and the Declaration of Independence are false. Dr. Smith proceeds with abstract reasoning, in order to prove his new doctrines. It would puzzle him to do away the wrongs in the following characteristics of the slave system, which makes property of man, and thus subjects him to the accidents of property. It deprives him of the right of acquiring property, or of inheriting it, or receiving it from others. It deprives him of the inalienable rights of liberty and the pursuit of happiness. It deprives him of the right of bringing a suit, and strips him of his wife and children, without redress. Add to these the long list of other wrongs, to say nothing of its bastardy, its degradation, etc.

Dr. Smith[6] also allows that slaves must not be educated, and gives his reasons for that position.

Alas, what is man! We remember the time, and heard him make the declaration that we of the North knew little of the evils of slavery, but that they of the South were aware of its wrongs. This we heard him say in General Conference, in 1844, and privately at other times.[7]

5. The decision of what is called the Dred Scott case at that time was in keeping with the growing and exacting claims of the pro-slavery party. The case is thus stated:

Dred Scott commenced a suit in the District Court of Missouri against Mr. Sandford, to whom himself and wife and two children had been sold by Dr. Emerson, claiming that they were free by virtue of having been taken by Dr. Emerson into a free State—Illinois—and kept there two years, and then into a free territory north of the State of

---

[6] This hoary perverter of "the right ways of the Lord" is now in Missouri finishing up his unenviable career.—EDITOR.

[7] Western Christian Advocate for 1857, pp. 74, 78.

Missouri, and kept two years more. The case was tried in 1852, before Chief Justice Gamble, of Missouri, and two associate judges. The Chief Justice totally differed from the others, but they being a majority ruled. Their decision was, that the constitutions and laws of other States and Territories could not govern in Missouri.

Judge Gamble decided that the master, by choosing to make the free State the residence of his slave, came under the operation of the laws of the State to which he brought his slaves, and that the act, in this case, was equal to an emancipation.

The case thus decided against Dred Scott, in Missouri, was, five years after, brought before the Supreme Court of the United States, March 6, 1857.

The following among other points were decided: That persons of the African race are not citizens of the United States, according to the Constitution.

That the ordinance of 1787 had no force after the adoption of the Constitution.

The Missouri Compromise of 1820, exceeding the power of Congress, had no legal force.

Among the strange things which Judge Taney said in his decision, we select the following: "That persons of African descent were not recognized in the Declaration of Independence; that they were beings of an inferior order, and unfit, socially or politically, as associates for white people; and the black man had no rights which the white man was bound to respect; that he might be reduced to slavery, bought and sold, and treated as an ordinary article of merchandise; and that these sentiments were public opinion when the Constitution was formed." The conclusion of Judge Taney was:

"The right of property in a slave is expressly conferred in the Constitution, and guaranteed to every State.

"It is, therefore, the opinion of the Court, that the act of Congress which prohibits citizens from holding property of this character, north of a certain line, is not warranted by the Constitution, and is therefore void; and neither Dred Scott nor any of his family were made free by their residence in Illinois. The plaintiff was not a citizen of Missouri, but was still a slave, and therefore had no right to sue in a court of the United States."

Judge M'Lean's opinion and that of Judge Curtis were the opposite of that of Mr. Taney.

Judge M'Lean showed that the civil laws of the continent of Europe decided that slavery could exist only in the territory where it was established by law; and that in America it existed only by the authority of the State, or that it was a State institution.

The logical effect of the decision of Judge Taney would be to introduce slavery into all the free States, as well as the Territories, and thus fully barbarize the entire United States.

Our Chief Justice seems to have been utterly stultified—by what influences we can not decide, except that they could not be good. In 1819 the Judge seems to have been of quite a different judgment from that which he entertained in 1857, or thirty-eight years after. In his plea for Gruber, in 1819, he uses the following language—and this was uttered in Frederick county, Md., a slave State:

"Any man has a right to publish his opinions on that subject whenever he pleases. It is a subject of National concern, and may at all times be freely discussed. Mr. Gruber did quote the language of our great act of National independence, and insisted on the principle contained in that venerated instrument. He did rebuke those masters who, in the exercise of power, are deaf to the calls of humanity, and he warned them of the evils they bring upon themselves.

He did speak with abhorrence of those reptiles who live by
trading in human flesh, and enrich themselves by tearing
the husband from the wife, the infant from the bosom of
the mother; and this, I am instructed, was the head and
front of his offending. Shall I content myself with saying
he had a right to say this—that there is no law to punish
him? So far is he from being the object in any form of
proceedings that we are prepared to maintain the same principles, and to use, if necessary, the same language here in
the temple of justice, and in the presence of those who are
the ministers of the law. *A hard necessity, indeed, compels
us to endure the evil of slavery for a time. Yet, while it continues, it is a blot on our National character,* and every real
lover of liberty confidently hopes that it will be effectually,
though it must be gradually wiped away, and earnestly looks
for the means by which this necessary object may be best
obtained; and till it shall be accomplished, till the time
shall come when we can point without a blush to the language held in the Declaration of Independence, every friend
of humanity will seek to lighten the galling chain of slavery, and better, to the utmost of his power, the wretched
condition of the slave."[8]

It is an unfounded assumption in Judge Taney to assert
that it was a common sentiment in America, at the forming
of the Constitution, that slavery was right. The history of
the case is that Mr. Taney himself, in 1819, denounced it,
as his own words show, as quoted above; that it was only in
1832 that the very first plea, or rather *apology*, was made for
it by Professor Dew, of William and Mary College, and
after this the Southern governors fell into the ranks of apologists, and finally the preachers of the South, Catholics
especially, and then Protestants, followed the current of evil
teaching.

[8] Central Christian Advocate of 1857, p. 100.

The decision on the Dred Scott case gave a new impulse to the already strong opposition in the South-West to the members and ministers of the Methodist Episcopal Church, and was an encouragement to the pro-slavery persecution which, in 1859, mobbed the Methodist Conference in Texas, and later led to various murders, and to the expulsion of half the members of our Church from Missouri, and the utter expatriation of them from .Texas and Arkansas.

6. The attempt to establish a university at Jefferson City, Mo., by the Methodist Episcopal Church, became the occasion of developing the pro-slavery spirit and opposition to the Methodist Episcopal Church which Bishop Pierce and the slavery propagandists endeavored to promote. The Land Company, of Jefferson City, in order to improve their property and secure the best educational advantages, made handsome appropriations to the trustees of the university. Mr. Green, a pro-slavery member of Congress, opposed this with great vehemence. Mr. James B. Gardenhire, President of the Jefferson City Land Company, on October 28, 1857, delivered an able address in favor of the company. The object of the company was to improve their property, establish manufactories, and promote education, and any and all were invited to coöperate who saw fit, whether from the North or the South. Mr. Green's position was that slavery agitation and the evils resulting from it were attributable to the enemies of negro slavery, and in this description he included abolitionists, Free-soilers, emancipationists—all who do not believe slavery a moral, religious, and political blessing.

Mr. Gardenhire goes on to show, as follows:

First. That the British king, before the Revolution, was the supporter of slavery in the colonies. This he substantiated by several proofs that can not be refuted.

Secondly. That the early colonists were the enemies of slavery. As proofs he adduces the fact that the Provincial

Government of Georgia, January 18, 1775, after denouncing
the slave-trade, declared, "That we will neither import nor
purchase any slaves imported from Africa or elsewhere, after
the 15th of March next."

In Virginia a similar complaint was made against Great
Britain, and like purposes declared to discountenance it by
the introduction or purchase of any more Africans. Mr.
Gardenhire quotes several decisions of the colonists, both
against the importation of any more slaves, or holding as
slaves those then in the country, and remarks, with great
truth, that, as the trade was wrong, slavery itself was wrong.

Thirdly. Mr. Gardenhire proved, by quoting their opinions, that the most eminent men of the Revolution were the
enemies of slavery. As proof of this he quotes Washington, Jefferson, Franklin, and others.

Fourthly. He shows that the authorities of the Federal
and State governments were the enemies of slavery. As
proof he mentions the ordinance of 1787, which excluded
slavery from the North-Western Territory.

Fifthly. He also proves that the framers of the Constitution of Missouri considered slavery as an evil to be removed,
in time, in enacting that slavery might be done away by
paying their masters for them, as well as prohibiting others
from entering the State.

To Mr. Green's position that slavery was a moral, religious, and political good Mr. Gardenhire gave a scathing
correction, and, among the most forcible strokes, adduced
the celebrated plea of the Mohammedans, in 1815, for enslaving Christians.

He then points out the injustice of the treatment of the
members and ministers of the Methodist Episcopal Church
in disfranchising them from the common privileges of
citizens.

The city authorities of Jefferson City at this time passed

resolutions denouncing the course pursued by the opponents of the university and of the Methodist Episcopal Church.[8]

7. As to the state of the Methodist Episcopal Church in Missouri, we may note the following:

It had been complained that during the last five years the increase of members in the Methodist Episcopal Church in Missouri had been small. This is really accounted for by the following considerations: Two Annual Conferences, since its organization, had been set off from the Missouri Conference. In 1852 the Arkansas Conference was set off, and, in 1856, both the Kansas and Nebraska Conferences. These, to be sure, were small Conferences, but they, in part, account for the small number in the Missouri Conference.

Our people and cause were constantly proscribed by the pro-slavery portion of the South-West so as to impede our progress to a considerable extent. Our names were constantly cast out as evil. Many of our own members who migrated to the State withheld their certificates or united with other Churches. Hundreds and thousands, within the last five years, have been lost to our Church on this account. The new-comers were hunted up and told that the Northern Church had no reputation in Missouri, that the public would not patronize them did they unite with so disreputable a Church. In short, the political and the social influences, the Church influences of other denominations, the commercial and business patronage was all against us. All these tended to prevent many thousands from uniting with us in Missouri who had been good members of our Church where they came from. Also, some of our own members and ministers, visitors from other States, took up these unfounded reports against us and reported them to our disadvantage to our people in other States.

The Iowa Conference that sat this year in Mt. Pleasant,

[8] See Central Christian Advocate for 1857, pp. 178, 182, 185.

took up this subject, and in an able report represented the
case of Missouri as it really was. In the preamble, they
state that the preachers in Missouri and other slave States
of the South-West, have been subjected to relentless persecutions, suffering the loss of social position and property,
assaults of personal violence, and in several instances even
death, because of their adherence to the doctrines and discipline of the Methodist Episcopal Church. And many of
our brethren at a distance were misled by false representations, so as to question the fidelity of our preachers, and
in consequence, proposed to cut off our supplies, and even
to disband the Conference. But, as the providence of God
pointed out that our Church had a great work to do in the
South-West, the following conclusions were drawn from the
whole: 1. That they had unshaken confidence in the antislavery character of the brethren in Missouri and Arkansas.
2. That they express their cordial sympathy for them, and
consider them worthy of support. 3. That there are multitudes in the South-West that have no sympathy with the
opposition to religious liberty and the mob violence which
has applied tar, feathers, and hemp ropes to our suffering
brethren. 4. That missionary aid should be afforded to
our brethren in the South-West, and we offer them our
sympathy, support, and prayers.[*]

* Central Christian Advocate of 1857, p. 6.

CHAPTER VI.

EVENTS OF 1858.

1. THE Arkansas Conference was held March 25, 1858, at Fayetteville, Washington county, Arkansas. Anthony Bewley presided, no bishop being present. Mr. Bewley was on Hamilton's Valley district, Texas. He resided at Johnson, about sixteen miles from Fort Worth. He labored as best he could, held prayer meetings, etc., but could do very little besides. Mr. Robertson was on Carthage district.

Rev. Mr. Butt was this year transferred from the Arkansas to the Kansas and Nebraska Conference.

This year opens with a continuance of the pro-slavery teachings and of the deep hatred and opposition to the Methodist Episcopal Church, the ministers of which were, in consequence, able to do but little.

We adduce a few specimen declarations, and these speak the general language employed.

The Lynchburg (Va.) Republican utters the following in February:

"The ministers of the Baltimore Conference are the most deadly foes to our domestic institutions, and they should be expelled from the State as soon as possible. They dare not take open ground against slavery, but they insinuate their antislavery doctrines into the minds of the ignorant and uninformed, and thus they do more harm than they would do were they outspoken in their pernicious views.

We are extremely gratified that the Church South has made a permanent lodgment in Fincastle, Lexington, and Lewisburg, and other important points hitherto held by the Northern branch. Let the good work commenced continue till the whole valley and Western portion of Virginia are cleansed of the foul leprosy of antislavery Methodism. The God of Abraham and of Isaac is not their God any more than he is the God of Giddings."

The Memphis Appeal, in reference to the Mississippi Conference, says: "During the session of the Mississippi Conference, at Brandon, Bishop Early presented the resolutions of the Alabama Conference recommending the striking out of the General Rule against 'selling men, women, and children, etc.' The Conference concurred in the amendment by a vote of seventy to seven. A correspondent of the Mississippian wishes to know who were the seven dissenting."

The Oxford Mercury also speaks out, and says: "We join the correspondent of the Mississippian in asking who were the seven dissenting. We want to know the names of the seven *abolition* preachers who live and fatten on the people of Mississippi. It is due to the high standing and character of the Methodist Church that the seven negro worshipers should be exposed, and held up to the scorn and indignation of every honest man. We have no use for abolitionists in our State; there is no room for them, and their presence should and will not be tolerated. If we can get the names of the immortal seven, we will promise to give them an advertisement free of cost, which will make them known all over the country. We have fully determined to show no favor to any abolitionist, no matter what position he may hold, and we should always denounce in unmeasured terms such characters as vile reptiles, who ought to be driven from the land. We ask our brethren of the press throughout the State to join with us in calling for the names of the seven dissenters."

The Panola (Miss.) Star responds: "We add our feeble voice to yours, brother Mercury, and would like to see the seven names in full, 'bold-face.' Ferret them out and expose them, that the people may know who are opposed to buying and selling slaves in Mississippi."

Such are the utterances of the fanaticism which at this time maddened the minds of the leaders of the Southern people. This prepared the way for driving Methodists out of Texas and Arkansas, and taught the people to murder Bewley and others, under this moral insanity.

2. The line of distinction between the two Churches at the time of separation in 1844, as far as their respective Disciplines were concerned, had not been drawn; but now the line is made clear, the Southern Church renounces, we may say, dogmatically, her antislavery character, and condemns the Methodist Episcopal Church for the very teachings of their common Discipline up to May, 1858. The Southern General Conference of 1854 decided that the General Rule on slavery had reference to the slave-trade only. But now, as this seems to have been a manifest sophism, it is purposed to erase the whole from the book of Discipline.

The subject of slavery came up first before their General Conference by a petition from the Southern Church in Washington, asking assistance to their cause in that city. A committee on this subject, whose report was adopted, among other things, declare "the little band of Southern Methodists in Washington City have been, for the last eight years, manfully stemming the tide of opposition from the thousands in that city who hold connection with an avowedly abolition Church, and are served by the members of a Conference openly declared to be antislavery. They might have suppressed their convictions of duty, and remained in the Northern Church, but they could not sacrifice principle. Thus, the charge against the Baltimore Conference and the Methodist Episcopal Church was, that they were antislavery and not pro-slavery, as the Southern Methodist Church was.

But the General Conference entirely struck out the General Rule by a vote of one hundred and forty for, and eight against; absentees, three. In the preamble to this report it is said that the rule is "ambiguous in phraseology, and liable to be construed antagonistic to the institution of slavery, in regard to which the Church has no right to meddle, *except in enforcing the duties of masters and servants*[1] as set forth in the Holy Scriptures." The two following resolutions express their decision :

"*Resolved*, By the delegates of the Annual Conferences of the Methodist Episcopal Church South, in General Conference assembled, that the rule forbidding 'the buying and selling men, women, and children with an intention to enslave them' be expunged from the General Rules of the Methodist Episcopal Church South.

"*Resolved*, That, in adopting the foregoing resolutions, this Conference express no opinion in regard to the African slave-trade, to which the rule in question has been 'understood to refer.'"[2]

In view of this decision Rev. Joseph Brooks, then editor of the Central Christian Advocate, declares, concerning the Methodist Episcopal Church South, that they have

---

[1] We have italicized this clause that special attention might be called to the sentiment here expressed. These resolving ministers are thus so happily on the way of fulfilling the part of the pious parson in Whittier's "*Sabbath Scene*," and so forcibly call up the sentiments of that poem, that we can not refrain from this method of advising the reader to procure and read it, as the most natural and happy illustration and exposition of the above resolution and theory we remember ever to have seen in print.—EDITOR.

[2] Central Christian Advocate for 1858, p. 90. See also pp. 94, 98, Western Christian Advocate.

"placed themselves beyond the pale of the great Methodist world. They are not acknowledged by deputation or official intercourse by any Methodist Conference worthy the name on the face of the earth."

Dr. E. O. Haven, then editor of Zion's Herald, after quoting the action of the Southern General Conference, most justly says: "Thus ended the Conference. Their sad action on slavery, unparalleled in Christendom, casts a baleful shadow on all their proceedings."[3]

But the Richmond Whig asks: "When a whole Christian denomination sees nothing wrong, or immoral, or improper in the buying and selling of men, women, and children with an intention to enslave them, why should mere politicians presume to pronounce as wicked and atrocious the reopening of the African slave-trade?[4] Indeed, the last Southern General Conference considered it as referring to the African trade. Dr. Capers and many Southern preachers did so interpret it. No language was more unequivocal than the rule, as applying to any purchase or sale of slaves, and requiring freedom as the end always in view. No man ever could mistake its meaning who considered the force of language and the object in view; namely, *freedom* in any purchase or sale made. That is what it means, and never meant any thing else except as perverted by the glaring sophisms of pro-slavery interpreters.

Bishop Soule's opinion may here be considered, as it is a very strange one indeed. After the session of the Conference the Bishop revised his speech, and published it in the Southern Christian Advocate, from which it was copied into the Advocate and Journal of 1858, page 120. We select a portion of this marvelous speech. He says: "I

[3] Zion's Herald of 1858 p. 96.
[4] Central Christian Advocate for 1858, p. 106.

recollect that at the General Conference in St. Louis [1854] when it was proposed to take out of the Discipline the section on slavery, that although I had always regarded that section as evil, and only evil; and although the Conference desired that it should be put out, yet I doubted whether the time had come, and I now believe that if the General Conference had voted to put out that section it would have produced an unhappy state of things. But at the next General Conference it did go out peaceably, and without injury to the Church any where."

He says further: "This rule is ambiguous in its phraseology, and liable to be misunderstood, and on this account, as well as for other reasons, brethren strongly desire to remove it from the book."

From the conclusion of his elaborate essay on the rule we make the following extracts: "I know not that this rule ever did us any good; but I am sure that it never did us a hundredth part of the harm that the legislation of the Church on the subject of slavery has done. From the very first, the legislation of the Church on slavery has been evil, only evil, and that continually. I have always been opposed to that legislation. If slavery be an evil, it is impossible for the Church to remedy that evil. What does the legislation of the Church propose? Nothing more nor less than the extirpation of the evil of slavery. Did it ever enter into the minds of these legislators that their acts could extirpate slavery? But, sir, that section is gone from the Discipline of the Methodist Episcopal Church South, and I bless God that it is. . . . O, brethren, be united. Cling to the great elementary principles of the Gospel as embodied in the Wesleyan system. Keep to the old landmarks of primitive Methodism."

In 1854 the General Rule on slavery was interpreted as referring to the African slave-trade; now, as it is expunged, therefore, to enter on this trade would be admissible, according to this exposition.

3. The presence of the ministers of the Methodist Episcopal Church in Missouri, after 1848, was exceedingly offensive to the ministers of the Methodist Episcopal Church South and their pro-slavery political friends. Dr. M'Anally, editor of the St. Louis Christian Advocate, pronounced our members covenant-breakers, and the most vituperative language was employed in their denunciation. In his paper of January 14, 1858, he says:

"It is true that Northern preachers are here in our midst—right where the General Conference of 1844 solemnly promised they never should be; and it is also true, as we believe, they can never do much good here. God's blessings rest on covenant-*keepers*, not on covenant-breakers. Honorable, God-fearing men *keep* covenants—dishonorable men break them. *Our* side has kept the covenant, and stands where true Methodism ever stood." Such were the general charges uttered at this time by the organs of the Methodist Episcopal Church South, and great exertions were put forth to enlist on their side the pro-slavery portion of the community. And this was one of the reasons put forth for ridding Missouri and the South-West of the presence of the members and preachers of the Methodist Episcopal Church, who would not be induced to unite with the Southern Church.

Rev. Samuel Huffman answered these and the like allegations, in a series of letters in the Central Christian Advocate for 1858,[5] and these letters were published again in pamphlet form, and did good service to the cause of truth against the unfounded charges of Dr. M'Anally and his associates in the opposition.

Indeed, the report of the General Conference of the

[5] See pp. 21, 29, 33, 40, 41, 45, 49, 57.

10

Methodist Episcopal Church of 1848 showed very plainly that the Methodist Episcopal Church South failed in keeping the covenant comprised in the adjustment of 1844. There were conditions in the arrangement of 1844 which the Southern Church *never complied with;* and for want of fulfilling their .part of the covenant they were justly deprived of its advantages. It was stipulated that such a state of things as was feared should be ascertained. In the place of this, steps were taken to produce what did not then exist, such as the decision of the Southern delegates in the city of New York to secede, before they could know the state of things in the Church. Next, the modes subsequently pursued in the South to inflame the public mind; and then there were several conditions of the plan of the General Conference with which they never conformed, such as the three-fourth vote of the Annual Conferences.⁶ The report of the General Conference of 1848 sets forth in full these points.

And, as many of our members were moving to Missouri and the South-West, the Methodist Episcopal Church owed to them the ministry of the Word, as many of these refused to unite with the Methodist Episcopal Church South in consequence of its pro-slavery character.

4. But the change of opinion which had been in progress in the South in favor of slavery since 1832, when Professor Dew first became its defender, seems now to have come to be the settled creed of the Southern people.

The Texas Christian Advocate of this year confesses that the general opinion in the South was, that slavery was a good institution, and that the former opinions of the South were erroneous. It says: "We do not deny that the South

---

⁶ Allowing for the moment that both parties fulfilled all conditions in the plan of separation, the fact is that the Church South was the first to violate that "covenant" by an endeavor to build up and maintain a pastoral charge of the Methodist Episcopal Church South in the city of Cincinnati.—EDITOR.

has changed its opinion on the subject of slavery. Once she thought it an evil; she now thinks differently."

We find in the New Orleans Christian Advocate, early in this year, a letter from a Mr. Cartwright, M. D., of New Orleans, to Dr. Cartwright, of Illinois, which declares as follows:

"But why class slavery among the sins at all, considering it is not so classed in the Bible? Why look for it to fall under the preaching of the Gospel, considering that it is not denounced as a sin in Holy Writ, and stands on the same footing as the institution of marriage? You did not derive your belief in the sinfulness of slavery from any thing you read in the Bible, and I am sure you did not derive it from the writings, lectures, or preaching of the modern abolitionists. You brought the belief with you from Virginia and the South. In former times a great many people in the slaveholding States regarded negro slavery as a social, moral, and political evil. They were led to this belief principally from abstract or theoretical reasoning founded on the assumption that the negro was a being like themselves, except in the color of the skin. My father and a great many others fell into this error, and emancipated their slaves. But experience proved, not only in Virginia, but in other States, that emancipation, so far from bettering the condition of the negro, almost invariably made it worse."

Such views led them to consider negroes as beasts, and to treat them accordingly. A candidate for high office this very year, in his stump speeches, expresses himself as follows:

"Slaves are property. A man is as much entitled to the increase of his property, as to the property itself. It is not competent for the Legislature to declare that the *colts* and *calves*, born on your farm one year hence, shall belong to me, or shall become the property of the State, or shall belong to no body. The *mares* and the *cows* being yours, the colts and calves are yours also, and the Legislature has no more right to confiscate the one than the other. If Fanny is a slave and my property, Fanny's children belong to me also, and the Legislature can no more take Fanny's children from me than it can take Fanny herself."

This sentiment is from the old heathen Roman law, whose maxim is, "*Partus sequitur ventrem.*" "The child follows the condition of the mother." As this can not, in modesty, be translated except as above, a paraphrase will be necessary to explain it. As slavery entirely excludes marriage, and therefore establishes promiscuous intercourse of the sexes, the father is never a known person, in law or in social society, and the mother is a mere productrix and a nurse, and the child, after that, is not the mother's, but the master's, just as his colts and calves are his. Of this class of persons, doubtless, was Melchisedeck, who was without father or mother. That is, he was originally a slave, but, providentially, he arose to be king over a freed colony, who, like himself, had been freed, and who chose him as their chief or king.

But the maxim does not apply to negroes alone, as many white persons now, in consequence of this principle, become slaves. There is a remarkable technical expression on this in the English law, in very clumsy and unclassical Latin, to the import that the colt of a mare belongs to the owner of its dam, and not to the owner of its sire. The Roman and English laws agreed precisely with the American laws when slavery existed in these countries. These English and Roman laws were coeval with slavery, and we find in the convention of Virginia, about 1832, when emancipation was discussed, that an old Virginian broached and referred to the same principle that governed pro-slavery England and Rome, and enlarged the range of argument, remarking that it was just and proper to transfer the reasons for the ownership of colts and calves to the young Fannies, for when men even cultivated fields they were entitled to the crops raised.

Such are the low and corrupt teachings of the slave system in every land where it prevails. There being no marriage, bastardy follows, and manners so corrupt as even to shame heathendom, in many cases.

5. At this time there was considerable discussion respecting the state of our Church in the border Conferences, that is, those in whole or in part in slave territory, such as the Philadelphia, Baltimore, West Virginia, Kentucky, and Missouri Conferences. There is no need of indorsing much that was said on both sides; but our brethren in these Conferences were assailed with much censure by those further North. Even where emancipation was greatly impeded by State laws the influence of the Methodist Episcopal Church was great in promoting emancipation, and in elevating the condition of slaves. Without allowing ourselves to be misled by partisan views, let us look to the facts in the case. In the State of Delaware, in 1790, there were 8,887 slaves, and in 1850 only 2,290. The laws in this State were favorable to freedom, and, as the State was largely composed of Methodists, their course and influence were on the side of freedom, and the result is manifest from the decrease of slaves and the increase of free persons.

In Maryland, in 1790, the free colored population amounted to only 8,043, while the slaves were 103,036. In 1850 the free colored were 74,728, and the slaves 90,308. In Baltimore city, in 1850, the free colored people were 25,442, against a slave population of 2,946.

At this writing—August, 1863—we need scarcely state that the antislavery character of the Methodist Episcopal Church, with which its loyalty is associated, has had a powerful moral influence in promoting freedom in all the border States, as well as in sustaining the Government by their undivided and open, active loyalty.

That there have been individual cases of pro-slavery character in the Methodist Episcopal Church needs not be denied any more than we need deny the apostasy of Judas. But, on the whole, the Methodist Episcopal Church proper has, from its organization up to this day, been consistently antislavery, in theory and practice, and the result of this is now made clear by the events of the present war. In 1844, though at the expense of her unity, the real pro-slavery portion of the Church sought a pro-slavery position because they could not secure it in the Methodist Episcopal Church. In Missouri, small as has been the number of her members, and much as they have been diminished in numbers and depressed by the pro-slavery element, they have preserved their principles, and have been and are now the most reliable portion of the State in behalf of freedom.

And even in the far South the labors of the Methodist Episcopal Church, till she was thrust out, have left a salutary influence behind her among the many thousands of truly religious colored people who were gathered into her fold. Those now scattered and peeled remnants of their former numbers will be found to form the nuclei of the numerous Methodist Churches that will yet flourish in the South.

6. In the tide of Northern immigration to Missouri were many members of the Methodist Episcopal Church, and, owing to the circumstances, very many of these cast in their lot with the Southern Methodists, and were thus lost to the Methodist Episcopal Church at a time when their numbers and influence were greatly needed for sustaining it. The circumstances were peculiar, and these peculiarities misled many.

Many were not aware of, or were poorly informed as to the existence of two Methodist Churches in Missouri, and hence they could scarcely be informed as to the true character of the Southern Church, that it was a pro-slavery Church in principle and practice. The Southern Methodists would say to these Northern immigrants that they were neither for nor against slavery, and while in one breath they said it was a civil institution, in the next it would be said that it is authorized by Scripture. Thus, with various sophistries, the new immigrants were led into the snare which was laid for them. The periodical press of the South also sustained slavery to the utmost. Dr. Smith's book was generally circulated, as was also Baldwin's "Trinity of Races."

Some, on their arrival in Missouri, have been met with the statement that they belonged to the Church, *North*, or to the Northern Methodist Church. This term has been employed with great address by those illy disposed toward the Methodist Episcopal Church, and very many have been seduced from their proper Church connections by the sophistry connected with its use. Southern Methodists were accustomed, when it would give effect to their representations, to omit the word *South* from the name of their Church, and to speak of it in such a way as to ignore the existence of any other Methodist Church. But, when it suited them to speak directly of our Church, they invariably spoke of it as the Methodist Episcopal Church, *North*, or The *Northern* Methodist Church, uttering the word North or Northern with a derisive emphasis which must be heard to be appreciated, and which is inimitable by those not burdened with their sectional prejudices. The Southern preachers began this misnaming of the Methodist Episcopal Church. They taught it to their people. Preachers and people taught it to other Churches and the outside world. It is a strange spectacle to see grave divines—by a hateful misnomer—catering to seething prejudices which they themselves have fostered, if not, indeed, planted. Such a course, persisted in toward the uninformed, can only be adjudged, by the broadest charity, to lie so near a habit of falsehood as to be poisoned throughout by its grossness. Well, we give them joy in their fond prevarication. It will, at least, afford us amusement, since it reminds of the fabled fox, who, falling upon a steel-trap and thereby losing his tail, called a council of his comrades, and labored long and hard to persuade them that, after all, the tail was a useless and cumbrous appendage, and that they had better adopt his style. Our friends, in an evil day, attached the unhappy, ill-fated appendage *South* to their name, and now the only consolation and relief to them in their dilemma seems to lie in a persistent effort to drum their innocent neighbors into the same fashion.

Another plea has been very successful in leading our members into the Church South. The resident Southern Methodists were numerous, influential, and wealthy. The immigrants, at least many of them, were poor, and relied on their business or trade for a livelihood. It was represented to them that, if they united with the Northern abolition Church, they could never be respected by reputable society, nor could they engage successfully in business. This was a powerful argument with too many, as the history shows, and misled numbers from the Church of their better choice.

So serious was this evil that the Missouri Conference of this year passed the following resolution:

"That we hereby earnestly and affectionately request our brethren of other Conferences, in dismissing from their charges by letter members who intend migrating to Missouri, that they be at the pains to inform them that, under the blessing of the Great Head of the Church, the Methodist Episcopal Church in this State is living and thriving, and urge upon them the propriety of attaching themselves to our Church here immediately upon their arrival."

The quarterly conference of Ridgely circuit, Platte county, took up this subject early in the Spring, and passed a preamble and resolutions on the subject. They state that very many of our members remain out of the Church altogether; that many have backslidden, waiting to see what the surroundings of the Church would be. Some wandered into the communion of other Churches, where they were less happy and useful than they would be in the Church of their choice.

Moreover, several preachers of the Methodist Episcopal Church saw fit to unite with the Southern Church, and thus strengthen their cause and weaken the Methodist Episcopal Church. Some of these came to serve the Methodist Episcopal Church, and united, afterward, with the Southern Church. As an instance, we may mention Rev. Mr. Barrett, who came from the Pittsburg Conference, was stationed in St. Louis, but subsequently joined the Southern Church, and now edits a disloyal paper in Missouri. Mr. White, who came also from Pittsburg, and was subsequently in the Illinois, then in the Rock River Conference, came to Missouri and united with the Southern Church, and at the beginning of the war, in consequence of his Union sentiments, was compelled to flee from his pastoral charge in Lexington. Quite a number of cases of this kind occurred, which we have not time or space to notice.

On the whole, we suffered greatly in temporary force and effect, on society at least, from the combined influences of both preachers and members who abandoned our cause and threw all their influence into the scale of the Methodist Episcopal Church South. Besides, the political influence

11

was against our Church, as our people were considered as
in opposition to the ruling power, whether this was the case
or not. The social influences of the various localities were
against the Methodist Episcopal Church, and were used to
throw into the shade every thing respecting it. The commercial and business portions of the communities were in
the opposition, so that our people, either as partners or
employés, were denied the usual influences arising from
their number and qualifications. The religious bodies of
Missouri had no welcome for us. The Churches of the
State were, in the main, on the side of slavery, in their
several aggregates, and our real character was an objection.
We had the odium of being abolitionists, and this was an
insufferable stench under their exquisitely sensitive olfacto-
ries, cultivated and long soothed by the odoriferous offices
and relations of African vassalage.

Such is a brief survey of the situation at that time. Our
cause in Missouri suffered much more than can well be estimated from the many transfers to the Southern Church
of our members emigrating to this State, who thus, instead
of strengthening their once-cherished Church, weakened it
by uniting with its principal opposer. The true men of
those times remember even now the unprincipled desertions
of many of these persons with a feeling of pity, if nothing
more. One, not observant of the effect, could scarcely cal-
culate the force of the adverse influences encountered by
our denomination. These, as mentioned above, may be
classed as the political, the business and commercial, the
social, and the ecclesiastical. They are both a direct and
indirect sway over the condition of those against whom
they were exercised.

7. As the reënslavement of free colored persons had been
proposed and attempted by some Southern States, for several years prior, the movement was renewed this year in

Maryland, and threatened to spread over all the border States. And as the Methodist Episcopal Church had stood in firm opposition to it in Maryland, it cast an odium on the Church in Missouri and the South-West, and occasioned great opposition to her from the slaveholders. A similar attempt was made in 1841–2 in Maryland, a brief survey of which may be proper.

A convention met in Maryland, in 1841, in order to induce the Legislature to pass "an act for the better security of negro slaves, and for promoting industry and honesty among the free people of color." Such was the plea; but the mature design was to reduce the free colored people to slavery or expel them from the State. The Methodist Episcopal and the Methodist Protestant Churches interposed by petition. Memorials were signed and forwarded by them to the General Assembly, expressing strong opposition to the contemplated measure. Bishop Waugh and Rev. Robert Emory bore the memorials from Baltimore to Annapolis. Public meetings were held in the principal Methodist Churches in Baltimore, and speeches were delivered in opposition to the movement. Judge Hopper, of the Methodist Episcopal Church, a slaveholder, drew up the paper which was read at the Baltimore meetings, and made appropriate comments. This opposition, principally by the Methodists, aided by others, arrested the enactment of the contemplated law.

A meeting, similar to the convention above alluded to, was held at the court-house at Cambridge, Md., at which a preamble and resolutions were adopted. They stated that, considering the present laws, it was impossible to control and regulate the negro community in a proper manner; that the free negroes were idle and dissipated, and their example made the slaves dissatisfied and worthless, and that they aided the slaves to make their escape. They concluded in their resolutions, that free and slave labor were incompatible, and that prompt and effective legislation was absolutely necessary in order to secure the interests of the people. Such were the brief points in this endeavor to reënslave the free negroes. The members and ministers of the Methodist Episcopal Church took an active part in defeating this step of cruel despotism and injustice.

In the discussion on this subject it was shown that out of 20,000 colored people in Baltimore, a large number paid taxes; that upward of 500 were owners of real estate; that they had then over $16,000 in the treasuries of their benevolent societies for the relief of their own people.[7]

The odium of this opposition to slavery in Maryland was readily transferred along the border by slaveholders, and reached Missouri and the South-West. And this was one of those causes that led subsequently to the opposition to, and persecution of, the members and ministers of the Methodist Episcopal Church in Missouri, Arkansas, and Texas.

[7] See Central Christian Advocate, p. 186.

CHAPTER VII.

EVENTS OF 1859.

1. As a historical decision on the profligacy of Southern Methodists, we adduce the recorded testimony of the Richmond Christian Advocate to the soundness of Dr. Smith's book on the subject of slavery. The Advocate fully indorses it, and says:

"The treatise contains the component elements of sound public opinion, which need only to be understood to become universally popular, and to be applied properly to elevate our political and social conditions. It would be counteractive of the process of abolitionism, which can not advance without producing immense mischief; and would that that already caused could be forgiven and forgotten! It would invigorate the life-tide of our National character, and animate the American Churches with healthy spirits. The position the Doctor takes in social, political, and moral science is impregnable, and furnishes the only true and permanent basis of domestic slavery and civil government of any land."

Dr. Smith was the first, or among the first, who contended that slavery is right *per se*, and is a normal and divine institution. This principle overthrows the foundation of all true morals. This book was issued, and the repeal of the General Rule on slavery in the Church South took place at the time that Southern opinion became most profligate. The false position of Southern Methodists greatly promoted the degeneracy of Southern politics on the question. But God and man will hold these errorists accountable for these gross moral heresies. We need not wonder that mobs, murders, and expatriations took place when such views as these were proclaimed and indorsed.

2. The storm thus raised by the false teachings of the South began to spread with great fury in the South-West, especially in Texas. The Central Christian Advocate was withheld or destroyed by postmasters and their hirelings, and the Methodist Episcopal Church was especially regarded as a dangerous intruder into slave territory. A long list of principles and deeds were attributed to her which she never believed or practiced, such as stealing negroes, inducing them to leave their masters, as well as direct political interference, none of which had any foundation in fact. Certainly our Church aimed at *extirpating* slavery, but it was to be done only by *moral* means, and sound religious teaching and discipline; and the course of the Church, pursued from its organization in 1784 up to 1859, a space of seventy-five years, never, in any instance, disturbed the civil laws, and it was notorious that in no instance did any of our preachers engage in inducing slaves to leave their masters, much as they hated the institution. The secret of the matter is, notwithstanding the bluster of slaveholders, they feared the proclamation of the truth, not in its inducing slaves to run away, but in its impressing the consciences of slaveholders and others with the conviction that it was sinful to support such a system.

Accordingly we find on the 4th of March, 1859, at Millwood, Collin county, Texas, a meeting was held in which it was complained that certain sentiments were entertained by Northern Methodists in regard to slavery, and that, while they profess to be for peace, such principles are eminently calculated to excite the deepest alarm, and are in violation of the laws of their country. The proceedings were pub-

lished in the Bonham Independent, which editorially says:
"We kindly warn these people to beware, lest, in an hour
when they least expect it, they will be visited by citizens entertaining adverse sentiments." The meeting also appointed
a committee of twenty-five or thirty who should, *as spies*,
ascertain the sentiments of our people by attending our
preaching and other places.

Matters stood thus when the Arkansas Conference convened, near Bonham, on Friday, 11th of March. During
the session of the 11th two preachers of the Methodist
Episcopal Church South, Messrs. Dickson and Porter, attended as observers, spies, or reporters, which of these we
say not.

On Saturday, 12th inst., a town and county meeting was
held in Bonham, Fannin county, in reference to the Conference.

A General Green stated the object of the meeting, remarking that it was known that there was an organization
of the Northern Methodists in that region, and that it was
increasing, by accessions of members and preachers from
the Northern States, so as to endanger the security of slave
property—that the avowed object of the Church was its extirpation. As proof of this he called on a Missouri border
ruffian to read resolutions from official documents of the
Northern Conferences, adopted at their annual meetings of
1858, and Mr. Green argued that they could not be engaged
in putting down a greater evil than the Northern Methodists, and that such was the object of the present meeting.

Judge Roberts, a Southern Methodist, said that the Methodist Episcopal Church South differed from the Northern
Church only on the slavery question, and that this organization, coming here from the North and presided over by
Northern men, should not be tolerated by the people. He
said he was not in favor of mob law, but it was necessary

the people should take decisive measures. Let them act mildly, but firmly.

A committee of three, namely, Mr. Green, Judge Roberts, and John M. Crane, was appointed to draw up resolutions. In their absence several addressed the meeting in a strain similar to that of Mr. Green and Roberts. Rev. A. W. Brown, of the Methodist Episcopal Church South, said that "he was gratified to see that decisive measures were to be taken at last against that organization. He had watched its growth from the first, and could see nothing to do but what was being done for the destruction of those injuries to our cause. He was in possession of the resolutions adopted by the Conferences of the North, proving this Church to be abolition to the core."

We transcribe the preamble and resolutions adopted by the meeting. They are as follows:

"*Whereas*, a secret foe lurks in our midst, known as the Northern Methodist Church, entertaining sentiments antagonistic to the institution of slavery, and the manifest intention of whose Northern coadjutors is to do away with slavery in these United States; and, *whereas*, the further growth of this enemy would be likely to endanger the perpetuity of that institution in Texas; and, *whereas*, sentiments diametrically opposed to the interests of the South have this day been publicly proclaimed upon our streets by a minister of said Northern Methodist Church; therefore, be it

"1. *Resolved*, That, the Methodist Church having separated into divisions, North and South, the organization of a Northern branch of that Church in our State as a screen behind which to hide the emissaries of a Northern political faction known as abolitionists is dangerous to our interests, and ought not, therefore, to be tolerated by the people of Texas.

"2. That the public denunciation of the institution of

slavery, and the public action, by a minister of their Church, to the effect that the Northern Methodists designed the extirpation of that institution in our land, heard in our streets this day, was a gross insult to our people, and should be boldly and summarily resented.

"3. That the teaching and preaching of the ministers of that Church do not meet the views of the people of Fannin county, and must therefore be stopped.

"4. That a committee be appointed to memorialize the Legislature to pass laws to punish the utterance of such' seditious sentiments as are mentioned in resolution second, and that other counties be earnestly called on to consider the matter.

"5. That a suitable committee be appointed to wait on the bishop and ministers now in Conference assembled, on Timber Creek, in this county, and warn them to withhold the further prosecution of said Conference, as its continuance will be well calculated to endanger the peace of this community.

"6. That our motto be, Peaceably if we can, forcibly if we must.

"7. That we hereby bind ourselves to coöperate in the future to do all we can to suppress abolitionism in our midst, and that henceforth we will suffer no public expression of abolition doctrines or sentiments in our streets or county to go unpunished."

A committee of fifty persons was then appointed to visit the Conference on Sunday, and to meet on Monday again and report. Among the committee we find Rev. A. W. Brown, of the Southern Methodist Church, and Rev. Samuel M'Kee, of the Cumberland Presbyterian Church.

The Conference, as usual, had their love-feast on Sunday, and at the conclusion of it the sacrament of the Lord's Supper. At 11 o'clock Bishop Janes commenced the public

service, the house not being full. While he was reading
the Scripture lessons the committee were advancing toward
the house, with their associates, amounting to some two
hundred, on horseback, marching in order, and armed with
revolvers and bowie-knives. During prayer they gathered
around the house. While the congregation was singing the
second hymn, as many as could crowded into the house.
When the Bishop began to give out his text, the spokes-
man of the mob, Judge Roberts, standing half-way up the
aisle, said, "Do I address the Bishop?" The Bishop continued giving out his text. He repeated, "Do I address
the Bishop?" The Bishop replied, "I am a bishop of the
Methodist Episcopal Church." He then said, "I have an
unpleasant duty to perform, and I presume it will be equally
unpleasant to you." He then described the meeting which
sent him, looked around and referred to the committee, his
associates, and called on one of them to read the proceedings of the meeting.

When the reading was ended, he resumed his remarks,
commenting on and sustaining the resolutions, and concluded his harangue by saying that, unless our Church
should cease to operate in Texas, blood would be shed, and
the responsibility would be on the Bishop and Conference.
He would not allow of any discussion, but two hours would
be given them to form an answer. The Judge was excited,
and his address inflammatory. As he began to withdraw,
Bishop Janes asked his name. He stopped, and said his
name was Roberts. The Bishop then remarked that the
time was too short, that the topic was not just one for Sabbath consideration, that the Conference was not then in
session, etc. But the Judge said no longer time could be
given, and left the house.

After the Bishop had preached, and the ordination services were finished, the Bishop, and preachers, and the lay

brethren had an informal meeting, at which it was concluded that, as the laity were concerned, the next quarterly
conference should be consulted as to this occasion, and the
preachers present agreed to suspend their services till the
mind of the laity could be consulted and obtained, and that
was to decide their course. This information was conveyed
to the mob, and they dispersed for the time being.

On Monday another meeting was held at the court-house,
when the committee before named reported, and many
speeches were made. Taking into view the whole, the
great sin of our people was that the Methodist Episcopal
Church was antislavery, and the Southern Methodists were
pro-slavery. Judge Roberts said, "They differed from the
Methodist Episcopal Church South only on the subject of
slavery. Holding connection with the Methodist Episcopal
Church, and being prospered and increasing in numbers,
was the cause of the abusive treatment which the Conference received." This was the "head and front of their
offending."

On Monday, 14th, the Conference reassembled, according
to adjournment, finished its business, united in devotion,
and adjourned *sine die*.

3. The defense of the outrage on the Arkansas Conference, by Judge Roberts, only confirms the opinion, that to
be a member or minister of the Methodist Episcopal Church
in Texas, was crime enough to call forth the aid of mobs
to drive one out of the country, without the authority of
civil law. The Bonham Weekly Era, of July 23d, contains
the statement of Bishop Janes and the answer of Judge
Roberts to it. Without noticing the carping of the Judge,
on some expressions of the Bishop, we find in his reply the
following declarations still adhered to: "We demanded a
categorical answer to the resolutions requiring the ministers
of his Church henceforth to cease their ministerial functions

in our country. I begged the Bishop would not allow himself to be cheated into the belief that this was the movement of a few idle, dissolute malcontents, but assured him that the wealth, the talent, and the best elements of our society were in it, with a unanimity unprecedented. . . . The Northern and Southern Methodists differ on *nothing* except on the slavery question. We know the position of the Northern Church on that subject. No one living in the South need adhere to the Northern branch of the Church, then, upon *conscientious* scruples, save on that one point alone, there being no other difference. He must be conscientiously opposed to the institution of slavery, or an imbecile, to persist in his adherence to the North, while living in the South. He must mean to teach the *eradication*, or, in other words, the abolition of slavery; and, therefore, a Church, claiming such privileges, could not, and would not be tolerated among us; that we were not disposed to sit quietly by till they had located themselves firmly in our midst, when it would be too late to help ourselves; that we thought we knew our rights, and intended to maintain them." Such are the points insisted on by Judge Roberts, and they are the same as those which the mob assumed, whose leader and expositor he condescended to be, without considering, it seems, how greatly he defiled the ermine of his profession by doing so.

Such is the defense of the mob by its leader, and it is the best he could give of this disgraceful act. In none but slave States is it necessary to resort to violence, rob the mail, interfere with assemblies worshiping God, etc., in order to guard securely their institutions. But freedom of speech, of the press, or of worship can not exist along side of slavery. Every thing inconsistent with the interests of slaveholders must be suppressed at once and at any cost. The Church itself is a chattel, and its ministers must be dumb unless they choose to speak as their masters dictate.

Hence it became the settled policy in Texas that no minister or member of the Methodist Episcopal Church should reside in the country, unless they renounced the doctrines of their Church, and as proof of this united with the Methodist Episcopal Church South. Some did so. Many refused; and most of these emigrated to Kansas, California, or Oregon, or fled to the free States from whence they removed. This was fully exemplified in thousands of cases, and the violence of the next year was the crowning proof of the prevalence of these unscriptural and unpatriotic principles.

Alas, how are the mighty fallen! Up to 1844 the Southern Methodists generally avowed themselves to be anti-slavery. In 1835 Rev. Samuel Dunwoody first openly quoted Scripture to support the institution. In 1836 in Cincinnati, in our hearing, he repeated his pro-slavery argument, on which the Southern preachers hung down their heads with shame. But after their severance from the Methodist Episcopal Church in 1845, there seems to have been a general departure from first principles. In 1854 they struck out of their Discipline the chapter on slavery, which declared the Church determined on its extirpation or abolition, by the use of all moral and lawful means. In 1856 or 1857 Dr. Smith attempted to prove that slavery was, *per se*, agreeable to Christianity. In 1858 the Southern Church, by a two-thirds vote of her General Conference, and a three-fourths vote of her Annual Conferences, abandoned the previous Scriptural testimony of the Church against a moral wrong. And such was the nature of the decision as, by a kind of tacit recognition, allows of the African slave-trade. And now, in 1859, the general maxim becomes a ruling principle, and no member or minister of the Methodist Episcopal Church can enjoy their Church principles in the South; and if they attempt it the mob is ready to rob and beat them, or drive them out of the country, by intimidation, harassment, or main force. But there was one other way by which they could remain in the country, namely, if, Judas-like, they would join the Southern pro-slavery, mobocratic Church,[1] and renounce their Scriptural principles. Such was the state of things in the South-West in the year of grace 1859.[2]

4. Bishop Janes, in his modest and truthful account of this mob, goes on to state, that he does not attribute this mobocratic outrage to the Methodist Episcopal Church South, but only so far as she or her people have indorsed it. He adds, "When editors or others apologize for such lawlessness and wrong, or speak of them approvingly, they become morally *participes criminis*, and show that they only need the opportunity to do the like themselves. Surely

---

[1] As corroborative of this surprising statement we give, of many cases, one which came to our personal knowledge: Rev. Hiram Hess, a member of the Arkansas Conference during its entire existence, informed us, in 1864, that in the Summer of 1860 an armed mob of sixty men came to his house in Arkansas, and reviled and abused him for being a Northern Methodist preacher and an abolitionist, etc.; and said they had come either to make him join the Methodist Episcopal Church South, or to tar and feather him, and drive him out of the country. He remonstrated with them against their violent and summary measures, and besought time for consideration. He told them if they would spare him any injury he would report to them at the approaching session of the Southern Conference as to what course he would adopt. They finally yielded to his requests, and suspended their inhumanities in view of his pledge to report his conclusion at the Conference, and departed, most positively assuring him, with profane emphasis, that if he did not unite with the Southern Methodist Church, they would tar and feather him, ride him on a rail, and then give him twenty-four hours to leave the country in, and if he did not go they would hang him! But, said Mr. Hess, by the time the Southern Conference met, I had left that locality, and put myself beyond their reach, and supposed no further report was necessary. He also stated that in this select company were a considerable number of Southern Methodists. Mr. Hess made these statements when upon the very verge of the grave, from the abuses and persecutions of the enemies of our people in Arkansas, and we believe them reliable.— EDITOR.

[2] For the Judge's answer, see Central Christian Advocate for 1859, p. 357.

they will do themselves, in like circumstances, what they commend in others. Or if position or policy should restrain them from the actual outrage, they would at least hold the clothes of those who throw the stones." This is truthfully said. But the following is said nobly and magnanimously, as if uttered by one of the old martyrs:

"In conclusion, I wish to express my thankfulness, that when the Methodist Church South has sent her ministers to the free States to take the pastoral charge of such as *preferred her ministry*, they have never been mobbed. I pray they never may be."

Let us see what testimony we have on this point:

In the *first place*, we find that in no instance has this mobocratic course in reference to the Methodist Episcopal Church been condemned or protested against by any of the officials of the Methodist Episcopal Church South, or their pro-slavery allies. If such protest exists we have not seen it, or it has not been published to the world. In the absence of any condemnation of this course by them, under all the circumstances, we are compelled to adopt the adage, "Silence gives consent."

Secondly, Judge Roberts virtually, but evasively, justifies the mobocratic course of the Southern Methodists by stating that they took no greater part in this than the Baptists and Presbyterians did. In his answer to Bishop Janes, of July 23d, several months after he led the mob, he says:

"The accidental circumstances that two or three members of the committee were of the Church would no more prove it a Methodist Church movement than the presence of Baptists and Presbyterians would prove it a Baptist or Presbyterian movement, for there were fully as many members of the two latter Churches as of the former of the committee."

The excuse or apology that Southern Methodists were no worse mobocrats than Baptists and Presbyterians goes to say they were all alike in guilt and in sin as to the acts. But he forgot that it was a mere Southern Methodist mob, got up for their benefit, and supported by their regular aids, the pro-slavery Baptists, Presbyterians, and other respectable people, whose police was the lowest portions of depraved Southern society. The object was not to drive away Baptists and Presbyterians, but Northern Methodists, for the Southern members of other Churches, at this time, were as pro-slavery as need be, for we find there was no active anti-slavery element among the other Churches in the South-West.

The Texas Christian Advocate, in an elaborate article, indorses the mob in the following words:

"We hope the meeting will insure the end designed in a manner at once thorough and immediate. *Thorough*, because, however fondly the Northern Church may cherish the delusion that it is her mission to *extirpate* slavery in the South, there can be nothing better for her and for us than that she should, if possible, be at once radically cured of this benevolent folly; *immediate*, because it is evident that the citizens of Fannin county, and all other Southern people similarly beset and outraged by this pestilent overplus of Northern ingenuity or fanaticism, do not desire to be troubled with taking measures to rid themselves of it further than to give a plain intimation that its absence is desirable. This should be enough, and we hope the Northern *missionaries* will not force any additional action upon the Southern people. It is quite evident that the South is determined not to be converted in the Northern way, and we do not think it prudent that the imported method should be insisted upon any longer. Whether our Northern friends have been led into their present position by mistake or design is of less consequence than that they should get out of it at their earliest and comfortable convenience. They should not stand on the order of their going, but go at once. Let them shake off the dust of their feet, if they choose, and consign us to any fate which their nutmeg genius may deem pungent enough for our iniquities."[3]

The Nashville Christian Advocate, under the heading, "Bishop Janes's Statement," makes light of the matter thus:

"From all he states, we suppose there could not have been much sign of violence. The Bishop was but slightly interrupted in his public exercises, and was permitted, unmolested, to proceed to the close of his sermon and the ordination services. We are not in favor of mobs, regret to hear of any rashness or violence, but really our friends at the North seem to be trying to make a great ado about a matter in which they are but slightly interested. If, however, our brethren persist in sending abolition preachers into slave territory, they can not expect any thing less than excitement among slaveholders, and men excited do not always act with strict prudence. We judge that the Bishop's statement will likely call forth a rejoinder from the citizens of Fannin county. We really think his publication had better have been suppressed; it will only serve to inflame the people, North and South."[4]

This was no slight affair. A mob of two hundred persons, armed with bowie-knives and revolvers, headed by a Southern Methodist, a judge of the bench, interrupted the public exercises of religion by stopping them, reading denunciatory resolutions, and making a speech on them. Two hours only were given for an answer, and that time would be necessary to complete the religious service; and the decision of the mobocrats was that a whole Conference of loyal citizens must leave their flocks and their fields of labor and never return. But the Nashville paper regards all this as quite

[3] Central Christian Advocate for 1859, p. 274.
[4] Western Christian Advocate for 1859, p. 106.

trivial. Glittering bowie-knives, swinging revolvers, and threatening crowds menacing worshipers in the public sanctuary are inconsiderable circumstances; in other words, it indorses the doings of the mob.

Many more quotations could be given to show that the officials of the Methodist Episcopal Church South sanctioned mob measures, and the expulsion thereby of our preachers and people from all slave territory.

5. The state of things in the South-West at that time called forth a plea for this region from the pen of C. Elliott. It was published in the Christian Advocate and Journal, September 1, 1859, and is now inserted here, in substance:

In answer to the objection that this territory is already occupied by the Methodist Episcopal Church South, and there is, therefore, no need of any other Methodist agency there, it was responded: 1. The principles and course of this Church disqualify them for evangelizing Missouri, Arkansas, and Texas. They have gone away from the principles of Methodism and the Bible in regard to slavery, and have had recourse to mobs, and other antiscriptural means. They are not, therefore, the people to evangelize slave territory. 2. There are many of our people in the South-West who call for our ministrations; we are, therefore, bound to hear their call, and send them preachers and organize Churches.

In connection with this view the following considerations were then presented:

Let the South-West be supplied with preachers with equal or greater liberality than Oregon, California, or other new countries. The Ohio Conference, some forty years ago, and for many years after, reënforced the Missouri Conference with preachers who rendered eminent service. So did the Pittsburg Conference, as it sent Drummond and Henry to Missouri, and Dr. Ruter to Texas. Great numbers of

preachers were always sent from the more Eastern Conferences to the Western.

Let our Missionary Society be as liberal to these regions
as to any other missionary field, so that Texas, Arkansas,
Missouri, and Kansas may be well reënforced, and the ordinances of our Church be furnished to all who are willing
and properly, disposed to receive them.

Let the press in St. Louis be fully sustained. This center
will, in time, be as important a point for circulating weekly
sheets as Cincinnati or Chicago.

One of our newly elected bishops should make his residence in St. Louis after May next. While he does his work
in common with others, he can especially attend to the South-
West, and provide for all the nooks and corners among the
slopes of the Rocky Mountains.

The principles of the Methodist Episcopal Church, its
Discipline and influence, are much needed in the South-
West. Its moral principles on slavery are needed there.
These principles are eternal and immutable, being based on,
or portions of, the unchangeable morals of the Decalogue, as
indorsed by Jesus Christ. Our Discipline in practice is
needed in this region. It is needed to teach Christian masters and slaves their duties respectively till the slave becomes
a free man, with the least possible delay, on the principles
of right and justice, and the law of love and Christian
brotherhood. The salutary influence of the Methodist Episcopal Church here is needed for the promotion of religion,
the suppression of mobs, the advancement of education, and
its indirect moral influence on civil institutions; although
the first and principal work of the Church is the salvation'
of souls, and then, after that, every good work and word,
in all godliness and sincerity.

Notice the extent of these vast regions. Already there
are six Conferences in the South-West. Soon their num-

ber will be doubled. At no distant time there will be
twenty Conferences in this region.

The ministers of the Methodist Episcopal Church are the
men to do this great work, if they are faithful to their
trust. If they will not do it, there are no others in the
field at present to accomplish this work. Here is a great
mission indeed, on which great interests depend.

The Southern editors took fire at the foregoing representation of the religious state of the South-West, and
wrote many hard things respecting it.

The Texas Advocate, after preliminary remarks, proceeds
as follows:

"Here it is distinctly charged that the Southern Methodists are unfit for doing Christian work on slave territory,
because they are unsound on the subject of slavery. Their
position is, that a slaveholder may be as good a Christian
as any other man, and they receive such in their communion on the same terms on which they receive the slave
or any one else. They leave the question of slavery with
the Government, to which it belongs, and persistently refuse
to meddle with it in any way. If this proves that they
'are *not* the people to evangelize slave territory,' the Northern folks must be the people to do that work, for the sole
reason that they are more enlightened than we upon the
subject of slavery; or, to speak to the point, because they
are unmitigated abolitionists, however they may choose to
disguise the fact, on prudential considerations, under certain
circumstances. If they are determined on the crusade ad-
vocated by Dr. Elliott, the issue is not between them and
the Southern Methodists, but between them and the Southern people."

"The charge that Southern Methodists 'have had recourse to mobs' is so gross a slander that nothing but inveterate prejudice could have deceived a man of Mr. Elliott's

good sense into its employment. It is untrue, and has been proved to be false by the most incontestable evidence. The only shadow of ground for it is, that the Texas Advocate, a paper of the Methodist Episcopal Church South, sustained the action of a Southern committee in warning a Northern Conference, which was actually at its antislavery work in Texas, of the dangerous impracticability of its proceedings. We did do it, and should do it again; if that was mobocracy, all concerned are welcome to make the most of it."

"The Northern Methodists are bitterly wrong in this thing; we sincerely regret their pertinacity in a cause fraught with no possible good to themselves, and with positive evil to others. We had hoped that they would see their error in time to avert any very serious consequences; but as they seem to wax more determined, and as their most prominent men and papers have assumed the ultra ground on the subject of Northern religious interference with Southern civil institutions, we have lost all expectation that they will stop short of the unenviable glory of being the cause of civil conflict. That such will be the result of taking Mr. Elliott's advice is beyond question with any one who is competent to form an opinion on the subject."[*]

The St. Louis Christian Advocate publishes the foregoing with approbation, and among other things says: "If the Texas brother knew the *status* of Northern Methodism in Missouri as we do, he would not be particularly concerned as to its future. . . . Such ecclesiastico-filibustering meets poor encouragement among the sober-minded people of the West. The cry of mobs has become too stale to be seriously regarded by any one, and is only repeated by such as are pitiably ignorant of the facts in the case, or

* See Central Christian Advocate, 1859, p. 355, col. 1.

too much prejudiced or corrupt to tell the truth. The Church South has never instigated, and we have no idea ever will instigate, a mob."

We admit that there has been no *official* indorsement, in terms, of mobs by the General Conference, or Annual Conferences, of the Southern Methodist Church. But there are examples enough of the ministers and members of that Church instigating mobs against our people, and also partaking with them. And this has been with the full knowledge of the authorities of their Church, and that not only without any remonstrance, but evidently with their approval. The Texas mob is only one example; many more exist equally outrageous, as the pages of this volume will fully show.

So true is the declaration of Bishop Janes, in his account of the Fannin county mob, that we recite and apply it to the editors of the Texas and St. Louis Advocates: " When editors or others apologize for such lawlessness and wrong, or speak of them approvingly, they become morally *partic-ipes criminis*, and show that they only need the opportunity to do the same themselves. Surely they will do themselves, in like circumstances, what they commend in others. Or if position or policy should restrain them from the actual outrage, they would at least hold the clothes of those who throw the stones."

The editor of the Texas paper virtually confesses that he is a mobocrat, as he says he approves of the action of the mob, which he calls a committee, that attacked Bishop Janes and the Conference in Texas, and then boldly says, " We did do it, and should do so again; if that is mobocracy, all concerned are welcome to make the most of it." The editor of the St. Louis Advocate is in the same category with his brethren in Texas. " What men do by others, they do themselves."

6. The raid of John Brown on Harper's Ferry was one of those unusual events which tended to stir up the pro-slavery and the antislavery elements of the country, both North and South. The reasons for the raid are given by the Washington Republic as follows:

"The leader of the assailants was John Brown, who had lost two sons in the Kansas contest, under the most harrowing circumstances, induced by the slaveholding interest. Brown and his associates had been obliged to practice, upon the border counties of Missouri, the system of defending themselves by assailing their assailants. What happened at Harper's Ferry was directly caused by the invasion of Kansas. The assailants at the Ferry were those who had been fighting in defense in Kansas, and whose passions had been there aroused. The raid of Brown, in itself, was wicked, and, in regard to Brown, it was most foolish."

"The insurrectionists had a constitution called the 'Constitution of the Provisional Government,' the general drift of which was the emancipation of the slaves in Virginia and the whole South. For months past those who had known Brown best had pronounced him insane. On Sunday, October 15, 1859, he and a gang of some twenty whites and five blacks took possession of the arsenal and Government pay-house, cut the telegraph wires, stopped the trains on the railway, and commenced to force every person they met in town to join their ranks. The insurgents were mostly killed, and Brown was taken prisoner, and, after a trial, was hung for his rash crime."

The course of Brown was condemned by the general voice of the free States, although most considered that he ought to be treated as a crazy man or lunatic. The South were forward to consider it the work of the abolitionists, and made much capital of it in stirring up the spirit of pro-slavery men. The Southern Methodist press was not behind

in sounding, we may say, the war-cry, which was well calculated to stir up evil passions. In short, the civil, political,
and religious departments of the South were stirred up as
though an earthquake were shaking the country and ruin
was coming from all quarters.

We subjoin a few sample extracts from Southern Methodist papers on this occasion:

The New Orleans Christian Advocate exclaimed: "Read
the astonishing account of the Harper's Ferry insurrection, on our third page. The devil is surely let loose for a
season."

The Richmond Christian Advocate says: "Abolitionism,
that has already devised and executed so many profound
schemes and originated so much evil in Church and State,
is not wanting in minds capable of the conception and enterprise. Disclosure and retribution may not be remote.
With Brown was the execution and the failure; we must
look elsewhere for the infamy of origination. The disclo-
sures of correspondence are startling, and another Arnold
may yet be discovered, to the disgrace of humanity and the
reproach of the American character. The extent of complicity in this sanguinary conspiracy is yet to be revealed.
A mystery shrouds this event whose solution may involve
the country in serious and lamentable evils. We can not
repress our fears." He continues: "Abolitionism is the concentration of infidelity, skepticism, hypocrisy, fanaticism, and
treason, and consequently no law or interest, human or divine, can restrain its frenzy beyond the moment favorable
to involve the country in overwhelming confusion."

The Nashville Christian Advocate says: "Abolition and
Black Republican schemes are blowing up prematurely and
disastrously, as will be seen by an account of the Harper's
Ferry insurrection, published elsewhere."

The St. Louis Christian Advocate comes forward as

follows: "The outbreak is but the legitimate result of the incendiary doctrines which, for some years past, have been so fervently urged from a portion of the secular and religious press, and from a number of the pulpits of the country. There is no difficulty whatever in tracing such things back to their true origin. The everlasting writing, and preaching, and praying, and whining, and sniffling about the great evil of slavery, the insane and demoniac spirit of abolitionism, the senseless shrieking for freedom—to these, and to these only, are we to attribute the bloody affair at Harper's Ferry. It was but the legitimate result of such unscriptural, ungodly, mischievous, and wicked proceedings, and while 'professed ministers of the Gospel and entire bodies of Christian people will keep the public mind agitated by their continual reiterations of such unsocial and unscriptural doctrines we may look for further practical developments of their folly."

We are surprised at the blindness which has happened to these Southern editors. They do not even hint at the theft, violence, and gross injustice of the system which they defend in all its unscriptural grossness; nor do they hint at the maddening influences brought to bear on this now insane John Brown. For five years the invasion of pro-slavery men was at work to force the antiscriptural, immoral, and corrupt system on Kansas, and John Brown's family were especial sufferers from the savage barbarities thus visited, in a general way, on thousands of others. We do not now wonder that these editors were up to the foremost in the vile rebellion of 1861, and encouraged and supported it up to the last.

7. The rejection of the charter of the Methodist university at Jefferson City, by the Missouri Legislature, was an occasion for showing how the pro-slavery influence was exercised against the Methodist Episcopal Church.

13

In the year 1857 the Jefferson City Land Company proffered to any religious denomination which should coöperate with them in building a university twenty-five thousand dollars of the stock of the company. Rev. Joseph Brooks, Dr. L. W. Berry, and other members of, the Methodist Episcopal Church took up the proffer, trustees were appointed, and preliminary arrangements made to establish the university. Steps were taken to procure a charter, but the proposition failed, being voted down by a large majority, because it was to be under the patronage of the Methodist Episcopal Church.

Charters had been granted to the Catholics, the Southern Methodists, the Baptists, the Presbyterians, the Reformers, etc., but to the Methodist Episcopal Church none could be given, and the refusal of the charter to our Church stands alone on the journals, a solitary act of proscription in the legislation of forty years. This refusal was a punishment on good citizens, and contrary to the very Constitution of Missouri, which states "that no preference can ever be given by law to any sect or mode of worship." In 1837 St. Charles College was chartered, then tacitly under the patronage of the Methodist Episcopal Church, whose principles on slavery were the same as they are now. In 1847 this college, by an amendment to its charter since declared unconstitutional, passed under the especial patronage of the Methodist Episcopal Church South.

In 1859 application was again made for the university charter, and December 19th it was discussed and rejected in the House by a vote of eighty-eight against it, and twenty-two for it. Such expressions as the following were uttered in the House while the subject was pending: Mr. Cordell "hoped this would be indefinitely postponed, as it was an effort to establish a Northern Methodist Church." Mr. Anthony asked "how many nigger-thieves there were among the communicants of this Northern Methodist Church." Mr. Ferry said "it was an effort to build up a monster Methodist Church that had for its object the overturning of the institution of slavery." Such are samples of the sentiments which governed four-fifths of the legislators of the House in 1859, and they are similar to those uttered two years previously. In short, as the other Churches were entirely, or chiefly, at least, pro-slavery, they could readily receive legislative protection. But not so with the Methodist Episcopal Church—it could have no college or seminary in the State; and, although its ministers and people were the patrons of its first college—that of St. Charles, chartered in 1837—as well as the pioneers of religion, civilization, and education, they were proscribed in 1859. Yet the Methodist Episcopal Church had not changed its sentiments, for they were the same in 1859 as they were in 1837, or twenty-two years previous. But the people and other Churches in Missouri had changed, and not the Methodist Episcopal Church.

The storm of opposition in the Legislature was barely an expression of what existed among the Southern Methodists, the other Churches of Missouri, and the pro-slavery party in general, and these events only presaged what occurred in 1860, when antislavery ministers were murdered, or what happened in 1861, when the pro-slavery people and Churches were enlisted on the side of rebellion.[6]

8. We may here very reasonably present a few facts vindicating the genuine antislavery character of our Churches in the border Conferences, while we may allow there was some laxity of expression on their part, as well as some cases of unsoundness.

There has been, since the defection of Southern Methodists, a pro-slavery Methodist Church along the line, but our

[6] Central Christian Advocate for 1859, pp. 413, 414.

people chose our communion, with its antislavery Discipline. They have done more for the slave and colored man than all the rest of the Churches put together. They have stood for nearly a century in the midst of slavery with the protest of our antislavery Discipline against it. Emancipation has been promoted by this means to a very great extent. They have stood up as the protectors of the colored people: instance in Maryland. They have, to a very considerable extent, prevented slaveholders from entering the ministry. They were foremost, in 1844, in opposition to slaveholders entering the Episcopacy.

Rev. W. S. Harlow, Principal of Mt. Morris Seminary, formerly of the Providence Conference, having visited the West in 1859, expresses himself thus in Zion's Herald, in reference to Missouri Methodists: "We regretted to learn that some, professing to occupy high antislavery ground while in the East, should, in coming to Missouri, not have more principle than to identify themselves with an ecclesiastical organization whose members buy and sell human beings without restraint, and which already begins to *glory* in its pro-slavery character. Against such inhuman proclivities our brethren here have taken the right stand, and in the position which they occupy there is much of the moral sublime. They have planted the battlements of freedom in the presence of its enemies, and are working out the great battle of fighting the sum of all villainies on its own soil. A braver and more self-sacrificing band is not to be found in the annals of Methodism. They surely deserve the sympathy, prayers, and support of the Church."

CHAPTER VIII.

CAPTURE AND MURDER OF BEWLEY.

1. THE circumstances that induced Mr. Bewley to leave Texas may be stated as follows:

In 1860 the Legislature of Texas authorized the people to take the law into their own hands, and run out all suspicious persons, or punish them as they saw fit, were it even with death.

Northern Methodists were especially obnoxious to the pro-slavery men of Texas. They were known to be anti-slavery; but the name of abolitionist was usually attached to them, and this name, in the view of the Texans, comprised all manner and degrees of wrong. Indeed, for several years previous, the members and preachers of the Methodist Episcopal Church were so harassed and annoyed that they gradually left the country and emigrated to California, Kansas, and Oregon, or returned to the Northern States from whence they came.

Bishop Pierce, of the Methodist Episcopal Church South, in his letters from the Pacific, in the Summer and Fall of 1860, greatly tended to keep up the excitement in Texas against the members and ministers of the Methodist Episcopal Church. These letters were published in all the Southern Methodist papers, being copied from the one to the others. On the 4th of October, one appeared in the Southern Christian Advocate, which is the mere echo of the teachings of the Southern Methodist press, their bishops, their preachers, and members. We give an extract from Bishop Pierce's letter:

"Alas! the very 'principles of Northern Methodists are local, sectional, and beyond their proper geographical limits they become *suspicious*. If they are honest and consistent, their avowed doctrines constitute them disturbers of the peace. They come into the slave States as open, declared enemies of the institutions of the people. On their own theory, they can not be faithful to God without aiding and abetting runaway slaves. They must sympathize with arson, blood, and murder, insurrection and carnage. Recent developments in Texas, and editorials and articles in the papers of the Northern Church, justify the logic of these conclusions. For these reasons, *abolitionists* can not and ought not to be tolerated in the Southern States. No quarantine will justify their admission, no fumigation can disinfect them. Rank, rotten with the foul virus of an incurable disease, foes of God and man, spies and traitors to their country and their kind, let them stay where they belong!"

Such are the spirit and sentiments inculcated by the leading Southern Methodist authorities toward the members and preachers of the Methodist Episcopal Church. For years previous to the murder of Bewley, such was the teaching; and though this letter appeared, October 4th, in the Southern Christian Advocate, it was written weeks before that, while Bishop Pierce was traveling in California, and it was but the echo of voices which had been sounding in his Church and other pro-slavery bodies for years previous.

Besides, it was circulated extensively in Texas, that the members of the Methodist Episcopal Church, Mr. Bewley and Mr. Willet in particular, had been engaged in burning houses through the State, and therefore their presence in the country could not be tolerated. These reports were without the semblance of a foundation, but it was all the same with the infuriated enemies of the Methodist Episcopal Church. About July 17, 1860, it was thus circulated that Mr. Bewley and those of his class had burned several towns.

Furthermore, a forged letter attributed to one W. H. Bailey, dated Denton Creek, Texas, July 3, 1860, and addressed to Mr. Bewley, as an accomplice in the work of raising insurrections in Texas, was another means of stirring up public indignation against Mr. Bewley. And this forged letter was sworn to as genuine, August 10th, before a magistrate in Tarrant county, Texas.

2. As to Mr. Bewley's appointment to Texas, in the Spring of 1860, it has been stated, without foundation, however, that Bishop Ames used unusual persuasion to induce him to go to Texas. This is incorrect, as will appear from the following from Rev. James Hanan, of Sarcoxie, Jasper county, Mo., under date of November 20, 1860. He says, "I was present in Bishop Ames's cabinet, or, if you please, council-room, when brother Bewley and the Bishop met in their first interview at the Conference referred to, which was held at Pleasant Hill Church, in Franklin county, Arkansas, and the following is the conversation, after the common salutation and inquiry after each other's health. The Bishop took his seat at the table and said, 'Brother Bewley, now tell us about Texas.' Brother Bewley then stated how they had got along there. The Bishop then asked 'if he thought that we could do any good there?' He replied, 'It is not likely,' and then gave his reasons; but said 'there were large German settlements on the Nueces, west of the Colorado, and they wanted our preaching.' The Bishop then asked him if he was willing to go back to Texas. Brother Bewley then said, 'I told them that if the Conference said "Go back" I

was coming back; but if not, I was going wherever they sent me.' The Bishop asked him 'how much it would take to support his family on the Nueces.' Brother Bewley said 'he thought $400 would do it.' He set it down for him. The Bishop then asked 'what he thought would support brother Willet's family? if $300 would do it?' Brother Bewley answered, 'Yes.' It was set down for him. The Bishop then instructed Bewley, as superintendent of the Mission, 'for him and Willet to go to the Nueces and get them homes, and preach where they wanted them; but that it was not best to organize societies next Summer, but to correspond with the Missionary Board.' I was present at every interview between them at that Conference."

3. From the time of the secession of the Southern Methodists from the Methodist Episcopal Church, the Southern people were very much averse to having any intercourse with Methodists in the North. This was especially so after 1848, when our General Conference pronounced the Southern organization an unscriptural secession. And this aversion was greatly increased when the Methodist Episcopal Church was organized in Missouri and the South-West. Opposition to our Church was manifested in a great variety of ways, from 1848 onward. Passing over many proofs of this, we mention only two in this place.

We refer to the outrage, March 11, 1859, on the session of the Arkansas Conference at Bonham, Fannin county, Texas, under the presidency of Bishop Janes. We need not here enter into particulars, as this occurrence has been noticed in a previous chapter.

We mention especially the expulsion of Rev. Wm. Sellers, from Missouri, in 1854. A meeting of citizens of Fabius township, Marion county, Mo., on the 4th of February, 1854, passed some five resolutions, in which they, in mobocratic spirit, declare that no ministers of the Methodist Episcopal Church can be allowed to remain in Missouri. In the preamble to their five resolutions they say, respecting the ministers of the Methodist Episcopal Church, that they are the "representatives of a body whose sentiments on the subject of slavery are decidedly hostile to our interests as slaveholders, and dangerous to our peace, and that the leading object of their mission here is the destruction of slavery by the propagation, in any manner not inconsistent with the safety of their persons, of doctrines calculated to array against the institution the weak-minded and fanatical among us, and to create discontent, dissatisfaction, and insubordination among our slaves; be it therefore resolved, "That the peace and best interests of this community require that the said ministers, from this time and forever hereafter, desist from visiting and preaching among us."[1]

The ministers of the Methodist Episcopal Church, as a matter of conscience, never engaged in inducing slaves to leave their masters, or in making them discontented with their condition. The Church, however, professed to do what they could, as Christians, to extirpate slavery. But, in attempting this, they never disturbed the peace of society. The Methodist Episcopal Church has a clean record on this subject, in two respects. First, she never allowed the ministry or her members to engage in opposition to law. Secondly, she has always taught her ministers and members to use their influence against slavery.

The Committee of Fabius township declare that they will make law, where there is none, and execute it, too, by mob violence against peaceable citizens and ministers, who believe that slavery is wrong and ought to be done away by the power which established it.

These Fabius township resolutions, issued February 4,

[1] See the resolutions in full in Chapter II, for 1854.

1854, contain mere specimens of the sentiments inculcated by the Methodist Episcopal Church South, and their pro-slavery allies in the South-West, from 1848 down to the famous declarations of Bishop Pierce in 1860. And the zealous and headlong Bishop only repeated in 1860 what he and his Church, its press and preachers, and their coadjutors, have been proclaiming and practicing, when convenient, from 1848 up to the day that Bewley was murdered, without crime, or trial, by the hands of a mob which carried out practically what the Bishop had taught. The resolvers of Fabius township carried out the same also in practice, for they drove Mr. Sellers, by mob law, out of the country, and he barely escaped with his life. This was only a prelude to the persecutions and slaughter which followed.

4. When Mr. Bewley was first appointed to Texas in 1858, he resided in Johnson county, about sixteen miles from Fort Worth. In consequence of the opposition to him, he could not do much, although he held his ground till after his appointment at the close of February, 1860. It was 575 miles from his residence, in Johnson county, Texas, to Barry county, Mo., where he was seized by the mob.

Mr. Bewley, in view of the clamor about the Bailey letter, forged and addressed to him, and in consequence of the allegations brought against him, of burning houses, poisoning wells, and many other such unfounded charges, concluded to leave the country, and repair to Cassville, Barry county, Mo., where his former friends resided.

Rev. James H. Vaughan, September 14, 1860, Barry county, Mo., wrote as follows to us:

"*Mr. Editor,*—It is with considerable excitement that I take this opportunity of addressing your readers on a subject about which they are doubtless eager to hear something, namely, Brother Bewley, and his difficulties with the Texas and Arkansas outlaws, or mobs. Brother Bewley was coming in from Texas, having learned that he was accused of the burning of towns, and inciting others to do so. Knowing the prejudices that existed against him, he thought it best, for the present, to leave. He was insulted frequently in Arkansas, as he came along, but was permitted to pass, till he got into Barry county, Mo., near Cassville, when a company of eight men came upon him, saying that they had news from Texas; that there was one thousand dollars offered for him. I learn from his daughter, that our brethren in Arkansas are being threatened with violence, if they do not stop preaching. The above is what I have learned from sister Roper, brother Bewley's daughter."

Rev. H. Harryman, under date of September 25, 1860, writes that he received the following account from Mrs. Bewley, on the 17th of September, 1860, on the Neosho River, six miles below Humboldt, in Kansas Territory:

"Brother A. Bewley, having repaired to the field of labor assigned him, and finding the outrage and persecution so violent, that it would be impossible for him to labor to any advantage in the ministry, he therefore notified them of his intention to give up the field and retire, which he did, and proceeded into Missouri, where, halting for a few days to rest and recruit his team, he was overtaken by a mob on Monday, the 3d of September, and was taken back to Fayetteville. He was visited on the 7th by his son-in-law, Mr. Garoot; he was then alive, and in the hands of a mob consisting of about three hundred. They stated their intention to take him back to Texas, and of starting that evening with him. But the settled opinion of Mr. Garoot is, that they will kill him, the excitement being exceedingly high. They gave Mr. Garoot his orders to leave for

Illinois, or some of the Northern free States, or they would attend to him in the same way, believing him to be as grand a rascal as Bewley. The only real charge against these people is, they belong to the Methodist Episcopal Church. Injustice, persecution, and cruelty can find their counterparts among the slaveocrats of Missouri. The above is the last account we have of brother Bewley, and his family are left in awful suspense to await the result."

It is stated respecting him, but from an unreliable source, that, in the Winter of 1859–60, he promised that, should they permit him to leave Texas unmolested, he would not return. It is also said, though contrary to the testimony already adduced, that Bishop Ames over-persuaded him to return. After Conference, in 1860, he and family came to Missouri to see their friends, and take with them their two sons-in-law, one of whom lived in Kansas and the other in Missouri. And while in Missouri, his friends persuaded him, his wife joining with them, not to go back to Texas. But his reply was the same to all: " Let them hang or burn me on my return, if they choose; hundreds will rise up out of my ashes."

He and his family went back, and after staying about a month, increased excitement broke out, and he was threatened by the people. Then he proceeded to leave Texas, believing he could do no good there.

Rev. Mark Robertson gives the following extract of a letter to him from Arkansas: "There is so much confusion here, I hardly know what to write. I do not know what the North is doing, but it seems to me the South has gone crazy. They have run Mr. Bewley from Texas. He stopped at Elm Spring, to rest his team awhile. A company of men, headed by a Southern Methodist preacher, went out and ordered him to leave; he started on for Missouri. The other day there came a company of men from

Texas, with a thousand dollars reward for him. They said he had been the cause of burning five or six towns, but no one who knows him here believes it; but I expect they will hang him. A company came out and told Mr. Bewley to leave. He told them 'he would die first.' They said they intended to drive every Northern Methodist out of Texas."

A traveler in Texas states "that during his travels in Texas he met with Bewley, who told him that the mob were then in pursuit of him, and that he expected to be taken, carried back, and hung. Upon inquiring of Bewley what he had been doing, he replied that he had done nothing, but was a law-abiding man, and the only crime with which he was charged was that of being a member of the Methodist Episcopal Church." A great crime, indeed! After some other conversation, our friend and Bewley parted.

5. When Mr. Bewley, after attending Conference and paying a visit to his friends in Missouri, returned to his field of labor in Texas, he found the public mind very much excited against him, and, as mob-law had been established in Texas by their Legislature, he saw there was no prospect of his serving the Church, and that his life was in imminent danger, as threats of assault in various ways had been made in terms and in a manner that he could not mistake. He remembered the injunction of our Lord, "When they persecute you in one city, flee to another."

Accordingly in July, about the 17th, he left his residence in Texas. He left, also, all the property he had, besides the team and carriage by which he and his family traveled, and it was lost to them forever. He had no time to dispose of it, and if he had had the storm raised by his persecutors would have prevented any adjustment. No one would have dared to act as his agent, and, indeed, purchasers might have exposed themselves to suspicion first, then accusation, and then summary vengeance, in pursuance of the newly recognized mob-law. It was practically in force before that period, for special cases; now mob outrages became part and parcel of the law of the land.

About 10 o'clock in the day, near the middle of July, 1860, Mr. Bewley, Mrs. Bewley, and their son George, then eleven years old, quit their Texan home, and, traveling in a spring-wagon, came on to the Indian Territory. There they remained eleven days, waiting for the rest of the family. The first two or three nights of their journey Mrs. Bewley kept watch, and then they drove and watched alternately. Mrs. Bewley often drove while Mr. Bewley slept. They pursued their journey often at night, and mostly through byways, to shun exposure.

The part of the family left behind were Mrs. Roper, Mrs. Garoot, William, aged nineteen, John, sixteen, Sarah, fourteen, and Robert, aged nine years. These at length followed the rest of the family, and joined them in the Indian Territory. Here they all rejoiced together that they had thus far escaped the bloody hands of those who sought the life of their beloved parent and head, who was persecuted for the testimony he bore, on the one hand, to the purity of religion, and, on the other, against a great moral wrong.

6. The whole company then came on to Benton county, Arkansas, where Mr. Bewley was acquainted. There they remained and rested a few days in the Brickey neighborhood. One of his sons-in-law, Mr. Garoot, went on ahead to Missouri, between Keetsville and Cassville, in Barry county.

7. The day they left the Brickey settlement a mob of Arkansans followed, and overtook them about 12 o'clock, at a place where they had stopped to get dinner. This was on September 3d. The pursuers rode up, armed with bowie-knives and six-shooters, and having a bottle of whisky. One

was leading a horse blind in one eye, while all the others were well mounted.

As they rode up, two by two, the leader asked Mr. B. if his name was Bewley. He answered in the affirmative. They then questioned him as to his views on slavery. He proposed to give them an address on that subject, but they declined, so he could only make some brief statements to them on the subject. They then threatened to hang him, and cursed him bitterly. Sometimes they would ask him to leave, and then they would stop him, and thus endeavor to provoke him. One of them, in taunt, offered him a negro.

Mr. Bewley's sons, William and John, were armed, and ready to defend and protect their parent, but the circumstances prevented the use of their weapons.

One of the mob, a Mr. Smith, questioned Mr. Bewley as to whether one of his sons had not been killed in coalition with two negroes. To this Mr. Bewley replied that all their sons were with them except the one who had died in Texas. This Mr. Smith had often heard Mr. Bewley preach, and when Mrs. Bewley observed to him that it was hard to be treated thus, the response was that they must stand up for Southern rights.

Finally they suffered Mr. Bewley to set out on his journey. The whole ten of them sometimes went before, and sometimes behind, while some mostly went along beside him. While proceeding thus they seemed to be on the lookout for a suitable tree and place to hang him.

At last they all dropped off but two, who proceeded a little ahead. They afterward turned back, toward evening, and said to Mr. Bewley, should he proceed to Illinois or Indiana, they would allow him to go unmolested; but, should they go to Kansas, they should find them out and seize him. Then they left.

The Patriot of September 15, 1860, published at Sherman,

Grayson county, Texas, says that "Bewley was pursued from Texas, by A. G. Brayman and Joe Johnson, to Cassville, Mo., captured, and brought back on the overland stage on Monday evening"—probably September 10th. The editor adds that he saw him, and proceeds to describe his personal appearance, and conversation with him, in which he assured Bewley that "if any thing whatever was substantiated to show his guilt, $40,000,000 would not save him." He accused Bewley of being one of "the Timber Creek Conference, presided over by Bishop Janes," all of whom fled but Bewley, and adds, "Long before this notice reaches Bishop Janes his soul will be before the God that gave it, if he has any." He says further, "Bewley was saved, while under arrest in Fayetteville, Arkansas, only by the Sheriff of Washington county. There were eleven of these wretches in company, but all escaped but Bewley."

8. Mr. Bewley then came on to where Mr. Garoot had stopped, in Barry county, Missouri, between Cassville and Keetsville, and there rested a few days. He thought he would be safe in remaining there for some time. In this view he was encouraged by one of his friends from Tennessee, who assured him there would be no danger in doing so. This, as the sequel will show, was a great mistake on the part of the good Tennessean, as well as on the part of Mr. Bewley, for his pursuers were even then on his track, and the reward of one thousand dollars for his capture and return to Fort Worth was proclaimed throughout the South-West.

9. A camp meeting of Southern Methodists was being held at that time at no great distance from where Mr. Bewley then was, and there were placarded advertisements in or near the camp-ground offering a reward of a thousand dollars for the apprehension of Bewley and his return to Fort Worth. This award was offered by the Fort Worth

Committee on Mobs, and one-half was to be paid by
the Fort Worth Committee, and the other half by the
Sherman Committee, of Grayson county, Texas. Observe,
too, that the new mob-laws of Texas authorized this cruel
process.

10. On Sabbath, while Mr. Bewley was delaying, two
men came and conversed with him, and wanted him to go
on Monday to a certain place and trade with them. This
he refused to do. On Monday morning he was remarkably
lively, and, having finished his breakfast, he stepped out
without his coat and vest, as it was very warm. He then
went to a house not far distant, where they were getting
corn to feed their horses.

While thus engaged, a mob rode up, and surrounding
him told him he was their prisoner, and must go with them
to Fayetteville, Arkansas. Two of those of the first mob
were a part of this. These were likely those named by
the Sherman Patriot, as pursuing him from Texas, namely,
A. G. Brayman and Joe Johnson.

The correspondent of Mr. Robertson, from Arkansas,
writes thus under date of September 5th: "In the first
part of my letter I told you a company had gone after Mr.
Bewley. They brought him into Fayetteville yesterday—
September 4th. He says he would not mind going back to
Texas if he could have a fair trial; but such is the state
of excitement, he knows they will hang him. They have
him locked in a room up stairs in the tavern. I have no
idea they will let him bid his dear family farewell; and
now he does not ever expect to see them again."•

When they surrounded him at first, they were about to
tie him; but, at the expostulation of Mr. Garoot, they
did not.

11. When Mr. Bewley and Mr. Garoot urged that he
might be permitted to go to the house where his clothes

14

were, they utterly refused. They did not want to see the
women, Mrs. Bewley and her two daughters. They were
also evidently afraid of Mr. Bewley's sons, and did not
want to come in contact with them. Mrs. Bewley sent
clothing after him with Mr. Garoot, but they would listen
to no expostulation, and hurried on.

Mr. Garoot, however, proceeded with the clothes to Keetsville, a distance of five miles, where they allowed him to
put them on.

12. As the mob proceeded from Keetsville to Fayetteville, they talked as if he would have a fair trial, and said
Mr. Garoot and his wife might come and witness the whole
process. They said Mr. Bewley was not the man they had
taken him to be. He was a gentleman, and should be
treated well. But all this, as the events showed, was only
to save appearances, and prevent his rescue by his sons
and others who might be disposed to interfere in his behalf. They kept out of view the taking him to Texas.
This prevented Mrs. Bewley from attempting to see him
then, a circumstance she greatly regrets; but she could not
believe that he would come to a tragic end. For if they
had not hurried him off, a *habeas corpus* could have been
obtained, which they greatly feared, as Mr. Bewley had
many friends in Fayetteville and other places not far from
the scene of these disgraceful offenses.

13. From Missouri they hurried him on into Arkansas.
They conveyed him on a horse, telling those they met
that they were breaking a young colt. In this way they
brought him to Fayetteville. There they suffered the mob
to curse him and call him an abolitionist, negro thief, and
every other offensive name they could think of, so that he
was moved to tears. They kept him there a few days,
abusing shamefully any of his friends who came to see him,
and sending out word that they had started, or were about

to start that evening, or next morning, all the time they kept him at Fayetteville.

After all the ignominious treatment they could heap upon him, they set out from Fayetteville, our best accounts say in the overland stage, others say in a hack. It is also said he was tied or chained to a post in the stage.

As he passed through Van Buren, he addressed the people on the street, from the stage, while making a temporary stay. Many citizens here, as well as friends, we learn afterward regretted they had not rescued him from the hands of the mob.

At his last supper, he was heard saying that he would never see another sun, but would die an innocent man.

14. We may here notice the letter which Mr. Bewley wrote to his wife and family. Mrs. Bewley, as we have seen, was left on the road with her children, when her husband was seized by the mob, not knowing what to do, or where to go. Her blind daughter Catherine was left at Springfield, Mo., when the family went to Texas, and remained there till after the death of her father.

We give the letter as published in the Central Christian Advocate of January 9, 1861. As the letter shows, it was furnished us by Rev. M. Robertson, presiding elder in the Kansas Conference; but formerly the faithful fellow-laborer with Bewley in Arkansas, Missouri, and Texas.

"*Sept.* 5, 1860, FAYETTEVILLE, ARK.

"DEAR WIFE AND CHILDREN,—I never took up my pen under such circumstances before. After I left there that day, I was hurried on, and the next day, about nine or ten o'clock, we got to Fayetteville. I am here yet. They have not put me in jail, but keep me under guard. At night I am chained fast to some person, and in the day I have liberty to walk about with the guard. I have been in the general tolerable, though my company in *general* has not been as desirable as some. They are now after Tom Willet. So soon as they succeed in getting him, I suppose they will set out with us to Texas in the overland stage, and if so, hand us over to the Fort Worth Committee, and receive the reward. Then we will, I suppose, be under their supervision, to do with us as seemeth them good. And if that takes place, *dear* and *much beloved wife and loving* children, I shall never in this life expect to see you; but I shall *look* to meet you all, with our little babe that has already gone to that blessed heaven of repose. The reason why I so speak, in these times of *heated* excitement, mole-hills are raised mountain-high, and where there are none, it is frequently imagined they see something. That being the case, it seems it is enough to know that we are 'North Methodists,' as they are called; and from what we learned in Texas about that Fort Worth Committee, they had sworn vengeance against *all such folks.* I expect when they get us we will go the trip. But, dear wife and children, who are big enough to know about these things, know that, so far as I am concerned, all these things are *false.* You have been with me, and you know as well as I do that none of these things have ever been countenanced about our house, but that we have repudiated such to the last. So you see that I am innocent, and you, my love, will have the lasting satisfaction to know that your husband was innocent, for you have been with me for some twenty-six years, and your constitution is emaciated and gone down to feebleness. You will have to spend the remaining part of your life as a bereaved widow, with your orphan children, *with one blind daughter.* Now my feelings I can not describe, but I know there is a God that doeth right. As I was taken away, and was not even permitted to see you, that I might bid you and the children farewell, I have to do it in this way, and would say to all to try to continue your way onward to heaven. Tell George and baby, when they get old enough, they must seek religion and be good boys, and meet pa in heaven. I want William and John, as they are the oldest, to be good to their mother and their blind sister.

"Do with your scant means as you think best. I have feelings—I can not tell you *how* I feel for you. There on the road, in your wagons, we thought ourselves at home. But I can only leave you in the hands of Him in whom I put my trust. I know you will not forget me in your prayers; you have mine—shall have while I have breath. I believe much in prayer. I feel no guilt, from the fact that I have done nothing to cause that feeling. Dear Jane, I can not tell you what is the best course for you to pursue, but I want you to get somewhere that the children can have a chance at school. Keep as clear of these one-horse towns as you can. Frequently, at such places, boys are early led astray. I do hope that the good Lord will comfort you and guide you to the best conclusions.

"I would be glad you would tell Henry M'Cary to write to Capt. Daget, at Fort Worth, my standing since he was first acquainted with me, and when you write to your friends, tell them to do so too, or as they choose. I now close by subscribing myself your affectionate husband and father, ANTHONY BEWLEY.

"You will doubtless preserve this imperfect scroll.

"A. B.

"This is September 6th, 1860.

"CITY OF FAYETTEVILLE, ARK.

"I, with a portion of the vigilance committee, will leave Fayetteville to-night sometime. The committee has returned without Willet, and have given up hunting him any more. A. BEWLEY."

"BROTHER ELLIOTT,—The above is a *fac-simile* of brother B.'s letter to his wife, seven days before his execution. I have not changed one word in it. I send it to the *Central* for publication, as many will be glad to know any facts concerning his last days. We have delayed to do this, hoping that news of his release would reach us, for we were not prepared to believe that all traces of humanity were blotted out in Texas. But in this it seems we were mistaken.   M. ROBERTSON.

"Mrs. Bewley's post-office address is Humboldt, Kansas Territory. As Mrs. Bewley is in want, any thing addressed to David Reese or myself, at Mound City, will be conveyed carefully to her, till different arrangements can be made. As several letters of inquiry have been addressed to me, I would say, she has one horse, five pony colts, one cow and calf, and about one month's provision. She is well worthy the MATERIAL sympathy of all. Inducements have recently been held out to her to leave this Territory to join the Church South; but she prefers rather to suffer affliction with the people of God than to enjoy the pleasures of sin for a season.   M. ROBERTSON, P. E.,
" Ottumwa District, Kansas Conference."

15. When the mob had reached Fort Worth, Texas, with Mr. Bewley, they put him in charge of a hotel-keeper. He was much fatigued, and was suffered to retire early, uninformed of the gloomy fate hovering so near him.

A little slave showed him to his room up stairs. His ardent prayer offered, a good conscience united with tired nature quickly to lull the venerable man into a sweet and quiet sleep. About eleven o'clock he was taken from his bed by three men, and when they reached the street, they were joined by a crowd there assembled. They took him a few hundred yards away, and there, amid vile ribaldry and horrid oaths, that made midnight hideous, they hung

the unblemished man of God. But the bravest soul that
listened to the violent throbbings of that feverish and
eventful night, was the man who died. He ascended to his
native place, his long-sought destiny. They retreated, as
cowering hounds from a neighboring fold, with overcast
visages and theft-glutted greed, yet ill at ease, to seek repose, but, alas, only to find themselves tossed by appari-
tions in disquiet slumber. Mr. Bewley was suspended upon
the same limb and tree upon which several negroes and a
Northern man named Crawford had been hung.

This gallows had been called "the Crawford limb;" after
this, however, the people called it "the Bewley limb."

Such an event must of course be somewhat variously
reported, but the above may be regarded as reliable beyond
a doubt.

The *Arkansan*, a paper published at Fayetteville, says:
"Bewley was taken to Fort Worth, where he was tried,
condemned, and hung. There was enough evidence against
him to hang twenty men. Bewley expected to be hung,
said so here, said so along the road, whenever the people of
Fort Worth got him. The history of his trial will furnish
our readers with the proofs and circumstances of his guilt.
Bewley made no confession; he said if he made a confession
they would hang him, and if he did not make a confession
they would hang him any how, and he was not going to
make one for the world to blow about. He could have
made one, and it would serve the ends of justice. There is
no doubt of the guilt of other parties, whose names are
mentioned in Bailey's letter, and they are all under watch
and will get their meeds, if ever they see Texas."

There are some true statements in the foregoing, such as
that Bewley was taken to Fort Worth, was condemned,
made no confession, and was hung. There are also manifest falsehoods in the above narrative, such as that Mr.

Bewley was tried, that there was testimony enough against him to hang twenty persons, etc.

The Rev. H. W. South, in a letter dated Waxahachie, Texas, October 4, 1860, published in the Nashville Christian Advocate of October 31, 1860, states, among other things, that Mr. Bewley was followed to the vicinity of Springfield, Mo., taken and brought back to Fort Worth, and, on the 13th of September, 1860, was hung on the same limb of the same tree on which Mr. Crawford had been hung before.

The following letter from Mr. D. O. Hoover relates to these events, and deserves a place here:

"STOCKWELL, IND., *December* 4, 1860.

"BROTHER ELLIOTT,—My family has at last arrived from the bloody land of mobocracy, North-Western Texas, from which I was cruelly driven in July last. My family says the mob stopped near my house at a Mr. Penn's, and took dinner, while taking brother Bewley back to Fort Worth. While there, the good old man, pointing to the sun, remarked, that was the last setting sun he should ever see.

"Shortly after dinner they marched him off to Fort Worth. At the regular hour for supper he went to the tavern and ate his last meal with a set of bloodthirsty assassins of the South. He was then taken a short distance from town by a party of those demons, and there, with a rope entwined around his neck, he was suspended between the heavens and the earth like a dog, to die by the hands of his fellow-men. After letting him remain all night in this position, a hole was dug by two negro men. The dead victim was then taken down by these two Africans and thrown in without coffin or box, the dirt then thrown upon him scarcely covering his body. They report they found him in a field helping to gather corn. He desired before being marched away to return to the house and take leave of his friends. This privilege they denied him. He was then in possession of one dollar, which he wished to be sent to his wife. This request was also hooted at, and the poor defenseless prisoner driven away by his merciless enemies.

"While living in Texas, brother Bewley preached at my house time and again, during a period of four years, and many are the times I have accompanied this good man from one appointment to another, but never did I hear him hint any thing that would prejudice the negro against his master, nor did I ever hear him preach an abolition discourse. But the whole matter was, he was a member of the old Church, and that was all they could say against him. One of the clan, Julius Smith, remarked, that the time had come that ninety-nine innocent had better suffer than let one guilty escape. Thus, my friends, lived and died a valiant soldier of the Lord and Savior Jesus Christ.

"There is not now in Texas a member of the old Methodist Episcopal Church that dare own his membership."

But the scene of Bewley's murder does not end with his unlawful arrest, his treatment on the long journey from Missouri to Fort Worth, over five hundred miles, and the shameless act of brutal execution. His burial the next day corresponded with his death. Not even a decent grave was opened for his reception. A very shallow opening was made in the ground, the rope by which he was hanging was cut, and without shroud or coffin the remains of the martyred man were then deposited, with scarcely a covering of mother earth. It is said, too, that when the interment was finished, his bare knees were seen protruding above the scanty soil that but half covered the corpse, while the length of the shallow grave was too scant to permit his

15

lifeless remains to be placed horizontally, and his limbs to be extended in the usual natural posture of interment.

Hon. Ellis G. Evans, of Rolla, Mo., addressed a communication to the Central Christian Advocate, September 7, 1867, relative to this martyrdom and the burial of its victim, in which he says:

"The next day the body was taken down and put under the ground, but in about three weeks was taken up, and the bones were stripped of their flesh and put upon the roof of the storehouse of 'Captain' Eph. Daggett, who still resides at that place in affluence. The bones seemed to be in the care of Dr. Peak, who occasionally went up and turned them about. The boys, making that a play-place, would set up the bones in a variety of attitudes by bending the joints of the arms and legs, and further mocked these remains of this humble Christian by crying, 'old Bewley,' 'old abolitionist,' etc."

Thus the last stroke of abusive ignominy is laid upon the wasting bones of him they "hated without a cause." Exhausting their own capacities for insult and injury, they teach and commission the lips of innocent childhood to deepen, if possible, and perpetuate their work of shame, and to be its defenders in after years, when the perpetrators of the iniquity are dead and gone. The bones of the martyr, disallowed the quiet of even a barbarous grave, are held by a hate-sealed lease, in the face of the refined and pious community of Fort Worth, as a relic of a former and now sometimes lamented civilization. One of these days a trumpet call will annul their lease, and persecutors and persecuted will stand face to face in judgment.

The editor of the St. Louis Christian Advocate gives the following account of the case of Bewley, from a reliable source, as he says, although it has his own image and superscription upon it.

" 1. Mr. Bewley was carried to Fort Worth, after his arrest, by the men from Arkansas, and there, at or near Fort Worth, he was tried by the civil authorities, and required to give bail to appear for trial before a higher court. This he could not or did not do, and was ordered to prison.

" 2. On the way to prison a mob overpowered the sheriff and his posse, took Bewley and hung him. Our informant did not *see* these things, but heard them in Texas, from what he regarded as reliable authority, and believed them to be true.

. " 3. The evidence on which Bewley was sent on for further trial, consisted partly in what sundry persons testified they had heard him say, and partly in statements made by others who had been arrested and punished. These statements implicated him as one of the party organized to carry out the purposes expressed in the Bailey letter; but the evidence consisted mainly in the fact that the original Bailey letter was produced at the trial, and Bewley acknowledged *he had received and subsequently lost it.*"

Allow, for the moment, that Mr. Bewley, according to the above, had a trial; Dr. M'Anally here acknowledges that the main proof against him was " the Bailey letter," which has all the internal marks of a forgery or an imposition. Any man may have such a letter addressed to him through the post-office, without any participation whatever in its contents.

Dr. M'Anally then utters the following: " The cry in several papers that he—Bewley—was charged with nothing except being a Northern Methodist preacher is *utterly and wholly false.* Whether he was or was not guilty of the charges brought against him we do not know. He was naturally of a self-willed, stubborn disposition, and remarkably persistent in efforts to carry out what he undertook. But, if ever so guilty, he ought to have had a fair trial, and ought not to have been mobbed; and it is all so much the worse if he were innocent."[2]

Whoever considers the purport of the resolutions of the Fabius township meetings, and hundreds of other such declarations, as well as the declarations of Bishop Pierce, finds it is strictly and literally true, that to be a decided minister of the Methodist Episcopal Church, or a member, professing the antislavery principles of the Methodist Episcopal Church, is the highest crime known in the moral code of the pro-slavery Methodist Episcopal Church South. Or to be a *Northern* Methodist in the South-West, till recently, was the same as being guilty of the highest crime, worthy of death, banishment, or any other penalty.

Bishop Morris, in a letter written to Rev. B. N. Brown, which was published November 17, 1860, thus represents the crime of being a member or preacher of the Methodist Episcopal Church in slave territory. He says: "Look at it. Our Missouri Conference was, a few years since, prevented by threats of violence from meeting at Independence; Arkansas Conference was mobbed off from Texas; Kentucky Conference was warned not to meet at Germantown last Spring, though it did meet. An effort was seriously contemplated recently in the Virginia Legislature, to drive all our ministers out of the State. Still more recently, one of our godly and inoffensive ministers, A. Bewley, was hung by a Texan mob for no crime but connection with the Methodist Episcopal Church. All which outrages, and many more, the papers of the Church South either indorsed or winked at. Very many of her preachers have publicly warned the people against us as dangerous incendiaries."[3]

Although one thousand dollars was offered for the seizure and delivery of Bewley at Fort Worth, one half to

[2] St. Louis Christian Advocate, November 8, 1860, p. 54.

[3] Central Christian Advocate, November 21, 1860, p. 59.

be paid by the Fort Worth Committee on Mobs, and the other half by the Sherman Committee of Grayson county, Texas, the advertisers for innocent blood thought it no crime to withhold three-fourths of the price for the murder. Five men took him back, and received only two hundred and fifty dollars, or fifty dollars apiece. It was said that this pittance was "not enough to pay their liquor bills," if they drank as much as when at home. They expected, according to the public pledge, to receive one thousand dollars, but were put off with one-fourth of the sum. The brethren of Joseph sold him for a certain sum, but they received the whole amount promised, even from these traders in human flesh and blood. The Jews, who bought the Savior of the world for thirty pieces of silver, were honorable men compared with these Texan advertisers; for they did not cheat even the traitor Judas out of seven and a half pieces, or one-fourth of the stipulated price of blood, much less three-fourths of the whole sum. Nay, they refused to receive back the price of blood from the penitent betrayer, and bought a burying-place for strangers; while these Texan murderers would not afford one poor uncoffined grave, of generous depth and length, for their martyred victim. They gave him short measure in length, and even grudged enough of mother earth to cover the naked remains of one of her noblest and best sons.

16. Let us now survey the life and acts of Bewley, and note his proper character.

He was admitted into the traveling connection in the Holston Conference, at Abingdon, Va., December 24th, the same year with Dr. M'Anally and others; and previous to his admission, as well as during his five years of ministerial service, and after his location, he maintained an unblemished character; and this, too, in the very country where he was born and grew up to maturity. It was also in a slaveholding country, Tennessee. So far, we have a sufficient guarantee, certainly for good character, so that the charge of incendiarism could not be made against him while in his native State.

When he lived in Missouri, before he recommenced pastoral duties, no allegations were brought against him by his neighbors or others for any thing contrary to the character of a law-abiding citizen, in all respects, whether in regard to slavery or any thing else.

While a member of the Missouri Conference, from October 4, 1843, to 1848, and then of the Arkansas Conference till his death in 1860, no just charge could be brought against him by those outside the Methodist Episcopal Church, or those in it. The Methodist Episcopal Church authorities, whether Conferences or bishops, would not tolerate a preacher who would engage in seducing slaves to leave their masters. This never was tolerated among the members or preachers, in slave territory, by the rules or authorities of the Methodist Episcopal Church, whether the thing in itself is right or wrong.

Dr. M'Anally, under date of September 13, 1860, says in the St. Louis Christian Advocate: "In regard to Rev. A. Bewley, we have yet to be satisfied that he met the fate reported; but if it be true that he was hung by a mob in Texas, few men will regret it more, or condemn the act more heartily or honestly than we will. He was one of our classmates in the Holston Conference; was admitted into the Conference at the same time; ordained deacon by Bishop Hedding at the same time; ordained elder by Bishop Roberts at the same time; and as we labored together for some years, in the same Conference, it is fair to presume we would deeply regret he could meet a fate so untimely, cruel, and merciless. Still, if such a fate he really met, it by no means follows that it grew out of what the editor calls 'the enormity of the system of slavery.' It might have occurred from various causes other than this."

Hon. E. G. Evans, who was well acquainted with him for many years, speaks thus, October 6, 1860: "I knew the man. He was a cautious, deliberate man, born, I believe, in Tennessee. He was no abolitionist, though an antislavery man of the Washington and Jefferson school. Modest and peaceful, he never asserted all the rights mentioned by the author of the Dred Scott decision. He was twice chosen a delegate to our highest ecclesiastical council, and was esteemed for his unobtrusive but genuine piety. A large family, one member of which was a blind daughter, was dependent on him. Yet, without a fair trial, without a sworn jury, without counsel, without forms of law, it seems this brave, this good, gray-haired man is murdered by a mob. Tell not this country, that American citizenship is a prouder boast than to be a Roman. We of the Methodist Episcopal Church, who refuse a sectional affix, are almost compelled to say it is a cheat, a sham—something we pay dearly for, but which brings us no protection."

Rev. M. Robertson, who was very intimate with him, writes thus: "Brother Bewley was a man of more than ordinary talent in the pulpit, of strong faith, able in prayer, and one of the sweet singers of Israel."

Bishop Morris, who knew him well, in his letter to Rev. B. N. Brown, writes thus concerning him: "One of our godly and inoffensive ministers, A. Bewley, was hung by a Texan mob, for no other crime but connection with the Methodist Episcopal Church." In his letter on this case, of November 7, 1860, the Bishop says: "He was a good man, one of a meek and quiet spirit, and for thirty years enjoyed the full confidence and fellowship of his brethren. He was antislavery in the conservative Methodist sense; but no unprejudiced man, knowing his character, believes that he sympathized with any insurrectionary movement, either in principle or action."

Rev. Joshua Monroe, a very aged minister of the Methodist Episcopal Church, Pittsburg Conference, and a Virginian by birth and education, writes thus, December 5, 1860: "In this country we generally believe that all who participated in the execution of A. Bewley are guilty of one of the most brutal and atrocious murders that was ever committed in our land, and we think but little better of those editors who have become the apologists for these murderers."

Rev. Dr. Cartwright, in a letter to us, December 12, 1860, says: "Brother Bewley I knew long and well, and a better man hardly ever lived. He was no ultra-abolitionist. He was a peaceable, law-abiding citizen. I know some of his murderers, and if they had had justice meted out to them, they would have been hung long before they went to Texas. The Lord pity our country! It seems to me that all law is to be outraged, the Constitution to be overthrown, the day of anarchy and bloodshed to be inaugurated, and instead of enjoying the right of private judgment and liberty of speech, for which our fathers fought and bled, we are not to be allowed to preach the Gospel to our dying fellow-men. Nevertheless God reigns."

The foregoing is the testimony of a few who were acquainted with Mr. Bewley. The number could be increased indefinitely, but the above will suffice.

Mr. Bewley bore an excellent character with all impartial men, wherever he was known, and maintained an admirable standing among his brethren. He was decidedly opposed to slavery when his sentiments were asked, although he was not accustomed to obtrude his opinions on others, whether in public or private. He never directly or indirectly induced slaves to leave their masters, nor did he ever employ any arguments to render them discontented with their condition, either in Tennessee, Missouri, Arkansas, or Texas, in all of which States he lived as a citizen and labored as a pastor. He was a law-abiding man in all respects, and in every place where he lived. As to his being associated with John Brownites, or any others of that class, there was nothing of it. No such charge was ever sustained against him, nor could it be, unless by false witnesses. The whole and only charge against him was, that he was a sound member of the Methodist Episcopal Church, and antislavery according to her principles and the teachings of Holy Scripture. He was also a minister in slave territory, and a promoter of the Methodist Episcopal Church in Missouri, Arkansas, and Texas. This was his only crime, and all the allegations brought against him were founded on this alone, and nothing else. While unobtrusive, as to his antislavery principles, he never declined uttering his opinions, or professing them, so that all who knew him were fully aware of his views.

He was a man of settled principles, and so honest was he in following them, that no worldly consideration could induce him to abandon, or modify, or evade them. Dr. M'Anally says of him, that "he was naturally of a self-willed, stubborn disposition, and remarkably persistent in efforts to carry out what he undertook." This is a high eulogium, coming from a Southern Methodist preacher. The truth is, that Mr. Bewley retained the views held by all Methodists in the South when he was young. He was born in 1804, joined the Church in 1821, and commenced to travel in 1829. And up to that time all Methodists asked, "What shall we do for the extirpation of the great evil of slavery?" In 1835, in South Carolina, the gifts of a Methodist preacher, for the first time in the history of the Church, were perverted and prostituted by a plea for slavery. If any of them were pro-slavery before, they kept their minds to themselves, and did not utter in public their moral heresy. Rev. Anthony Bewley, in his maturity, retained the genuine Methodistic and Scriptural doctrines on slavery which he imbibed in the true Methodist school while a youth, and continued in that faith, without swerving, till at last he sealed his testimony with his blood, shed by the influence, if not the hands indeed, of Southern Methodists, who abandoned the teachings of their better days and of the Bible, and who drank in the vicious sophistries of the Calhoun school of politicians. Happy, noble man! He was thus "self-willed," and "remarkably persistent in efforts" to carry out his principles. And now he wears the martyr's crown.

17. Let us now return to the desolate Mrs. Bewley. Amid constant and fearful apprehensions of violence, she, with her cherished ones, had wound her way through by-paths from Texas across the Indian country, and into South-West Missouri, where she had acquaintances. Under the harrowing solicitude and wearing watchings and road-services of the journey, her already shattered constitution quite gave way, and she almost sank down with exhaustion as her feet struck the threshold of her friend's dwelling. Not even here could she find rest. Bribed assassins were even then lingering on their footsteps. Their cowardly strategy soon enables them to seize her husband when defenseless.

Denying him the privilege of seeing again his family, caressing his children, or bidding them a final farewell, they hurry their victim away as an ox to the slaughter. Covering their black, murderous, and covetous designs with hypocritical pretenses, they hasten the innocent man, half-clad, toward the place of butchery, looking forward for the reward of iniquity, the promised thousand dollars. Under such circumstances was Mrs. Bewley left with her family on the road, almost destitute of means of support. What to do, whither to go she knew not. In this perplexing exigency, she and her family proceeded to Southern Kansas, Allen county, five miles below Humboldt, where Mr. Garoot, her son-in-law, lived.

The blind daughter, Catherine, was still at Springfield, Mo., with relatives, where she had been left on their departure for Texas.

At Humboldt Mrs. Bewley had much affliction with pneumonia, and was near dying. Her oldest son, William, was sick at the same time with the same disease. There they remained till March, 1861, when they removed to Baldwin City, Kansas. She was scarcely able to get into the buggy when she set out on this journey with her five children.

After reaching her destination, she had another severe attack of pneumonia, from which she did not recover till midsummer.

When the family arrived in Baldwin City, a two-horse team and wagon, with a little bedding, constituted about all their possessions.

The proprietors of the college located at that place gave her six lots, and she bought another, all together making about an acre and a half.

She succeeded in negotiating for a small house of two rooms, which was moved upon her lots and somewhat enlarged and improved, and again she rejoiced in a home, humble certainly, but secure, and situated in a community where civilization was cherished, law reverenced and obeyed, and the flag of the country honored, and where she could not be plundered and despoiled with impunity.

She received also some contributions of money from friends and persons moved by her misfortunes. These donations afforded her temporary relief, and enabled her to visit St. Louis with her blind daughter, where Dr. J. W. Birge had the benevolence to treat them both professionally without any charge whatever.

CHAPTER IX.

OBSERVATIONS ON THE MURDER OF BEWLEY.

1. As the celebrated forged letter, attributed to Wm. II. Bailey, and purporting to be addressed to Rev. Wm. Bewley, was one of the stratagems to lead to the murder of Rev. A. Bewley, we may properly place it before our readers. It was dated Denton Creek, Texas, July 3, 1860. It was copied from the New Orleans Delta by the Missouri Republican of October 2, 1860. The date of the Delta is not given, but its preface to the letter is given by the Republican as follows:

"THE JOHN BROWNITES IN TEXAS.—The following well-authenticated and clearly proved document has been sent to us from Texas, by a gentleman of this city, who assures us that there can not be a particle of doubt as to its genuineness. It is a startling and fiendish document, which is quite worthy of the perusal of those credulous, easy-going citizens who have no anxieties about the South—no fear of any real design to interfere with our institutions by Northern emissaries."

The Delta then states, from the Fort Smith Herald, that Rev. W. II. Bailey was caught, and arrived in Fort Smith on Sunday last, in the overland stage, under the charge of Mr. Johnson, an officer from Texas; that Bailey is one of the disciples of the John Brown school, and has been engaged in burning, stealing, etc., in a sister State; and that a reward of three thousand dollars had been offered for his delivery at Fort Worth.

The following is the celebrated letter, concerning which so much has been said:

"DENTON CREEK, *July* 3, 1860.

"*Dear Sir,*—A painful abscess in my right thumb is my apology for not writing to you from Anderson. Our glorious cause is prospering finely as far south as Brenham. There I parted with brother Wampler; he went still further south; he will do good wherever he goes. I traveled up through the frontier counties—a part of the time under a fictitious name. I found many friends who had been initiated, and understood the mystic red. I met a number of our friends near Georgetown. We had a consultation, and were unanimously of the opinion that we should be cautious of our new associates; most of them are desperate characters, and may betray us, as there are some slaveholders among them, and they value the poor negro much higher than horses. The only good they will do us will be destroying towns, mills, etc., which is our only hope in Texas at present. If we can break Southern merchants and millers, and have their places filled by honest Republicans, Texas will be all easy prey, if we only do our duty. All wanted for the time being is control of trade. Trade, assisted by preaching and teaching, will soon control public opinion. Public opinion is mighty, and will prevail. Lincoln will certainly be elected; we will then have the Indian nation, cost what it will. Squatter sovereignty will prevail there as it has in Kansas. That accomplished, we have at least one more step to take, but one more struggle to make; that is, free Texas. We will then have a connected link from the Lakes to the Gulf. Slavery will then be surrounded, by land and by water, and will soon sting itself to death. I repeat, Texas we must have, and our only chance is to break up the present inhabitants, in whatever way we can, and it must be done. Some of us will most assuredly suffer in accomplishing our object, but our Heavenly Father will reward us in assisting him in blotting out the greatest curse on earth. It would be impossible for us to do an act that is as blasphemous in the sight of God as holding slaves. We must have frequent consultations with our colored friends. (Let our meetings be in the night.) Impress upon their clouded intellects the blessings of freedom; induce all to leave you can. Our arrangements for their accommodation to go North are better than they have been, but not as good as I would like.

"We need more agents, both local and traveling. I will send out traveling agents when I get home. We must appoint a local agent in every neighborhood in your district. I will recommend a few I know it will do to rely upon; namely, brothers Leake, Wood, Evans, Mr. Daniel Vicry, Cole, Nugent, Shaw, White, Gilford, Ashley, Drake, Meeks, Shultz, and Newman. Brother Leake, the bearer of this, will take a circuitous route, and see as many of our colored friends as he can; he also recommends a different material to be used about town, etc. Our friends sent a very inferior article—they emit too much smoke, and do not contain enough camphene. They are calculated to get some of our friends hurt. I will send a supply when I get home.

"I will have to reprove you and your co-workers for your negligence in sending funds for our agents. But few have been compensated for their trouble. Our faithful correspondent, brother Webber, has received but a trifle—not so much as apprentice's wages; neither have brothers Willet, Mangum, and others. You must call upon our colored friends for more money. They must not expect us to do all; they certainly will give every cent if they knew how soon their shackles will be broken. My hand is very painful, and I close.

"Yours truly,   W. H. BAILEY.

"N. B. Brother Leake will give you what few numbers of the Impending Crisis I have; also, Mr. Sumner's speech, and brother Beecher's letter, etc. Farewell."

Such is the clumsy forgery which was used as an occasion to murder an innocent man, whose character, from his youth up, had been above suspicion.

The Rev. J. R. Burk, in a letter to Dr. M'Anally, both of the Methodist Episcopal Church South, dated Weston, Texas, September 17, 1860, says: "Brother J. R. Bellamy furnished me with the inclosed document—that is, Bailey's letter—which he has read in manuscript, and we wish you to publish it in the Advocate, that our friends in Missouri may see how abolitiondom is doing here, and what it aims at accomplishing. The letter was directed to Mr. Bewley, a Northern Methodist preacher, who has since fled to Kansas or Missouri, for whose arrest five hundred dollars reward was offered. I think there is no fiction in the letter, merely to run Bewley from Texas, as a few days before it was found, this town of Henderson was burned, over one hundred miles from the place where it was found; and the man in that letter, as the Corresponding Secretary of this State, was taken at Henderson, acknowledged himself to be acting in that capacity, and was hanged. Many others have shared the same fate, both black and white, and others will soon go the same way."

Dr. M'Anally, in publishing the above, says: "Mr. Bellamy and Mr. Burk are both ministers of the Gospel, men good and true, and would no more favor a wrong than any other person."

The Fayetteville Arkansian stated that "Mr. Bewley confessed that he wrote the famous letter, addressed to one Bailey, which was picked up near Denton Creek, Texas, and published generally in the Southern papers." The letter itself declares that W. H. Bailey wrote it. Again, it said his conviction resulted from the letter's identification by witnesses under oath, but as whose is no where stated. Any of Mr. Bewley's writing would have satisfied his enemies he did not write it._ Such a man as Bailey was not known to exist, and it could not be identified as his. Of the accusers of Bewley it may be said, as was said of the false witnesses who accused our Savior: "But neither so did their witnesses agree together." Mark xiv, 59.

The most reasonable construction of the matter is, that the writer of this letter, whether Mr. Bailey or some one else, addressed it to Mr. Bewley, in order to accuse him falsely, or to make him an accomplice in a nefarious work.

There is a manifest anachronism and lack of certainty in the matter. The letter of Bailey is dated July 3d, and now, September 17th, it comes to light by Mr. Burk. In short, the letter attributed to Mr. Bailey has the leading marks of a forgery, and a false direction. It seems to have been forged by some pro-slavery zealot, in order to drive out the ministry of the Methodist Episcopal Church from Texas. For, at this very time, it became the settled policy of the pro-slavery party, with which the periodicals of the Methodist Episcopal Church South, without exception, and their preachers in general coöperated to persecute the ministry of the Methodist Episcopal Church, and drive them from the slave territory of the South-West. And this course has been avowed by the leaders of the Methodist Episcopal Church South, from 1848 down to the present time.

2. But as suitably answering the famous forgery, we adduce the letter of Bishop Morris on the subject. It would be difficult to find a man of more moderation and impartiality than the Bishop. We therefore give his letter, which settles the question with every unbiased mind. The Bishop, under date of November 7, 1860, Springfield, Ohio, says: "Much is said of a certain letter, written by Bailey,

16

which was found six miles from the place of execution, directed to Rev. Wm. Buley. I have read it in print. It details the plan of insurrection, and the names of the conspirators, but the name of Anthony Bewley is not in it, on it, or about it. Mrs. A. G. Fowler, a correspondent of the Galveston News, says, October 8, 1860: 'None of the published copies of this letter has ever contained the address upon the back, which is thus: "REV. WM. BULEY?"' The same writer further says: 'The original of the Bailey letter is still in the hands of the Vigilance Committee of this place,' [Fort Worth.] I am glad it is. There is some difference between Buley and Bewley, and still more between William and Anthony. Texas logic seems to be thus: Any man to whom an incendiary letter may be addressed—whether with or without his consent—deserves to die; but such a letter was addressed Wm. Buley; therefore *Anthony Bewley deserved to die!* Now, if A. Bewley had united with others to raise an insurrection, his associates in crime would have known his name, and so directed the letter as to prevent it falling into other hands. Besides, how easily could unprincipled men, such as thirsted for the blood of Bewley, have gotten up such a letter on purpose to insnare him! As to the statement that Anthony Bewley confessed, under the gallows, that he had lost the Bailey letter, directed to Wm. Buley, I regard it as one of the many falsehoods manufactured by his persecutors to mitigate their own crime. All executions by mobs are murders; that of Bewley was willful, deliberate murder, not claiming even the excuse of haste, from the heat of passion suddenly excited. After he had left the State to avoid trouble to himself or others, his enemies pursued him to Missouri and Arkansas, brought him back without legal process, and hung him. Will these monsters of cruelty be indicted? Will any Criminal Court try and punish them for murder as the law directs? Perhaps not. But they may rely on a future reckoning, when 'every one of us shall give an account of himself to God.' How changed the scene from Fort Worth to the general judgment, where the murderers of this innocent man shall be confronted by him and his injured family, under the withering eye of a just and holy God! The case of Anthony Bewley will then appear infinitely desirable compared with that of his murderers and their apologists. To that tribunal his friends appeal the case for final adjudication."

Thus, Bishop Morris establishes Bewley's innocence, and exposes the gross forgeries and false accusations invented against him, and circulated in the Texas Christian Advocate, the St. Louis Christian Advocate, and other papers, laboring in the interests of human bondage.

3. We may now consider what the Southern Methodist papers say of this murder.

The Southern Christian Advocate of November 29, 1860, censures Bishop Morris, in no measured terms, in consequence of his letter directed to Rev. Mr. Brown. The editor says: "Of course, Bishop Morris does not read our papers. He certainly is a good, though blinded man, and honestly believes what he says; but for all that, he is retailing a falsehood at second-hand, which he has accepted as truth from some abolition editor." Such is the disparaging language uttered in Charleston, the seat of the Southern conspiracy against liberty and human rights.

On the case itself the editor waxes truly warm. He says: "As to the last case, the hanging of Bewley, we defy the production of a sentiment from a Southern Methodist paper, that either indorses or winks at his execution by a mob, without judicial sentence—or one in which the act is not condemned, if there was no charge but that which Bishop Morris alleges."

After this declaration he proceeds to quote what he wrote, when this case first came up, in answer to the editor of the Advocate and Journal. "Some of his [Bewley's] brethren believe it lawful to help slaves to run away from their masters, taking whatever is necessary to help them. This *we* call abetting theft. This man may have thought this right." Thus he proceeds, and then declares as follows: " Then, what is our crime? We have warned the Northern Church that our fellow-citizens would not allow the enemies of our institutions, incendiaries and slave-stealers, to come into our midst breeding mischief; that such criminals would be dealt with as their crimes deserved; and when we counseled legal proceedings we have told them what they well knew without telling, that it was not wonderful if an exasperated people would not wait on law—we have counseled no violence. We have advised obedience to law. What more could we have done, unless it were to applaud incendiaries, and hail them as martyrs? Because we do not this we are classed with mobists and murderers, by the Senior Bishop of the Methodist Episcopal Church, North—the representative of more than a million of our fellow-countrymen. How we Northern and Southern Christians are likely to love one another!"

On the foregoing we remark: 1. That the ministers, principles, or authorities of the Methodist Episcopal Church never countenanced nor practiced enticing or even aiding slaves to leave their masters. 2. That neither Mr. Bewley nor any Methodist preacher of our Church in the South-West, whether in Missouri, Arkansas, or Texas, ever took a part in such acts as the editor charges. 3. The evil lies in the system of slavery, which is one of theft, robbery, injustice, and wrong, in the worst forms of these crimes; and now, when reprisals are made on it in consequence of its gross immorality, although it has the sanction of law, mobs must be resorted to as a defense, as no regular legal proceedings can meet the case. 4. The Methodist Episcopal Church has a clear record in this matter; although antislavery, in the strictest sense of the term, her course is according to law and the ten commandments. 5. Our Southern friends have sown the wind, and they reap the whirlwind. 6. The whole United States have been participants in this, and they are now visited, in the providence of God, for the wrongs done to the slaves.

4. We come next to the Texas Christian Advocate. This paper, in its issue of September 13, 1860, has over a column on the Bewley catastrophe, in the spirit of a mobocrat, or one of the old inquisitors, who would, according to his creed, put a heretic to death for God's sake. This reminds us of the declaration of the wealthy Methodist, Harry Hill, of Nashville, Tennessee, who, in 1844, wished to have the opportunity of pulling the rope to hang Dr. Bond, sen., and ourself. The Texan editor says: "We published in our News column a paragraph of four lines, stating that a Rev. Mr. Bewley, of the Northern Church, had been hung at Veal's station, after having been condemned by a jury of three hundred men. . . . There are cases in which Lynch-law is expedient, necessary, just. We are not now prepared to declare that Mr. Bewley's was one of these cases, nor that it was not. He fell a victim to his lawlessness, which he and others of his kind have, for some time, been laboring to inaugurate and promote in Texas. He was a member of the Timber Creek Conference, and was calmly warned by a large committee of Southern men that antislavery missionary operations among us would certainly result in bloodshed, and that if he persisted, he would be regarded as an aggressor, and treated accordingly. When that Conference was asked, categorically, whether it intended to continue its efforts to build up an

antislavery Church organization in Texas, it managed to
get off, as Bishop Janes afterward boasted, with an uncate-
gorical answer—a Delphic response." He next states the
untruth, " That preachers of the Northern Church had
been detected in some subterranean efforts to further the
mission of slavery extirpation in the State." He adds:
" Timber Creek was involved; and Bewley is reported to
have been hung. If this report prove true, we shall regret
that he did not take the good advice of the committee in
March, 1859, and leave the State." He concludes by giving his pro-slavery creed in these words: " We argued that
the South could not abolish slavery if she would, and that
therefore the introduction of an antislavery Church must
produce evils instead of progress; that she would not abolish slavery if she could."

We remark, that the verdict of this Texan jury of *three
hundred men, acting as a mob,* would make a singular example to be incorporated into the decided cases of supreme
courts, and to be reconciled by Blackstone, Kent, or Story,
in their arguments, with other decided cases of the supreme
courts of Britain and America.

Indeed, if the above is written in sobriety, what a spectacle we have! Here is an editor of a Southern religious
journal, representing a large body of professed Christians,
bound by all considerations to conform to law, both divine
and human. He looks upon a heterogeneous gathering of
three hundred ill-sorted, frantic, and blaspheming men with
daggers, bludgeons, and halters, rushing their victim to the
slaughter, and crying, as they go, " Hang him, hang him!"
and fancies this bloodthirsty pack of slave-hounds a jury
of his fellow-countrymen administering justice!

This editor, rising from his evening prayers, in the so-
lemnity of his sanctum, and going forth, lays his holy
hands upon the bloody heads of this shrieking mob on the

field of its deeds, and baptizes it a "*jury*," dignifies it with all the sanctity of the ermine-clad court, and turning, records his holy service in the columns of his own journal! Alas! for the Texas Christian Advocate and the Southern Methodist Church, if this is the civilization and Christianity they inculcate and promote.

But if the editor calls this mob "a jury of three hundred men," in sneering irony, then is his offense not lessened, and his influence is equally vicious, and promotive of lawlessness and murder.

He apologizes for lewdness by calling it chastity, praises vice by calling it virtue, and pleads for murder by making it the occasion of merriment and jocoseness, and by covering up its offensive carnage with roses of rhetoric.

5. Another source of information respecting this case is a letter from Rev. H. W. South, dated Waxahachie, Texas, October 4, 1860, and published in the Southern Methodist Itinerant of October 31, 1860, with approbation. He says: "The letter found near Fort Worth was certainly addressed to Rev. Mr. Bewley. It is further said here, that the son-in-law of Mr. Bewley, Rev. Mr. Willet, has been taken in Missouri, and is now on his way back to Fort Worth, where he will hang on the same limb. The information in reference to Mr. Bewley is true. I regret that the thing has got into confusion."

In commenting on the letter of Mr. South, the editor of the Texas Christian Advocate of October 31, 1860, says: "The most charitable construction we can put upon Bishop Ames's conduct in the matter is that he acted under authority from his Church, which has constantly avowed, through its organs, its intention to force an antislavery Church organization into Texas. The Brownism of Bewley's spirit, as herein manifested, is too evident to be mistaken."

6. Dr. Hamilton, a distinguished member of the Alabama

Conference, is introduced into the Texas Christian Advocate of October 11, 1860, as follows:

"But all danger is not passed," says Dr. Hamilton; "what was aimed at by the real authors of the late plots will be attempted again, and perhaps *again*, and in widely different ways. All that has transpired was but the partial development of a purpose formed years since by men far removed from the scene of action, and still entertained by those widely separated through the country, and from which they will not desist so long as there is the least prospect of success. That purpose is simply this, to prevent the admission of any more slave States into the Union; to accomplish this the plan is to make a large portion of Texas free territory. Of this purpose I have been fully convinced for years; I was made aware of its existence by various facts that came to my knowledge—by hints and inuendoes thrown out by Northern wire-workers from time to time. If any man supposes that what has been already done will put an end to their attempts, he knows less of Yankee character and abolition hate and malignity than I do. I prophesy that Northern and North-Western Texas will be *the* battle-ground between slavery and abolitionism for the next twenty years."

7. It was not the press of the Southern Methodists alone that gave countenance and aid to the persecution and murder of Bewley. We find the same manifested in the Cumberland Presbyterian Church in Missouri and the South-West. This we gather from the St. Louis Observer, edited at that time by Mr. Cox, a truly loyal and good man, with whom we were well acquainted for many years. Mr. Cox had said that Mr. Bewley was "a man and a minister above suspicion." One of his correspondents from South-West Missouri, November 8, 1860, thus calls Mr. Cox to account:

"You say in the Observer, that the said Rev. A. Bewley

is '*a man and a minister above suspicion*,' etc. Now surely in this you speak unadvisedly, and I say this is the first time I ever heard him indorsed. His antecedents from Tennessee to Texas were those of an intermeddler and disturber of the peace; and I am credibly informed by one of our ministers that his father-in-law offered him one thousand dollars if he would go to a free State and remain; and, finally, that they made South-West Missouri too hot for him to remain there; so he came to Texas, where he has long been known as a most hateful intermeddler, and more than once has been ordered to leave camp-grounds."

To the foregoing the editor of the Observer replies, " We did not 'speak unadvisedly;' but it now appears that we were *misinformed*. Brethren who knew the said Rev. A. Bewley for years, concur in saying to us that he was a busy intermeddler and a dangerous man to the community in which he lived."

Another correspondent of the Observer of October 20, 1860, from South-West Missouri, says: " Mr. Bewley resided in this neighborhood for quite a number of years, and was known by friends and foes to be a decided abolitionist. It may be that he was wickedly and cruelly murdered; but as to his being above suspicion, it surely is not among his own neighbors. And the number here who believed him to be a good man is very few." This is quoted, with approbation, by the Texas Christian Advocate of November 8, 1860.

The Cumberland Presbyterians, in the slave States, are generally pro-slavery, and, in the free States, are strong sympathizers, in general, with pro-slavery men. Of course, they condemned Bewley, just as they would any minister of the Methodist Episcopal Church, for being antislavery. And the name abolitionist would be as freely bestowed on any of our ministers as upon Garrison, or any other.

17

Hence the influence of his pro-slavery associates on Mr. Cox, then editor of the Observer, who is both loyal to the country. and truly antislavery. And indeed Mr. Cox, like Mr. Bewley, but in another way, has suffered for his loyalty and his antislavery principles, for his people in general forsook his paper because he was antislavery, and have patronized a neutral paper, printed in Alton, Illinois. And we can not locate or classify these neutral papers and persons, except by ranking them with the enemies of the country. "He that is not for me is against me."

The denunciations of Mr. Bewley by the Cumberlands of the South-West we place among the well-deserved eulogies which he has received from those who knew him best, and were well qualified to represent his character, such as Bishop Morris, Dr. Cartwright, Mark Robertson, and a host of others.

8. The preachers' meeting of the Methodist Episcopal Church in Pittsburg, consisting of twelve members, passed unanimously the following preamble and resolutions, which were published in the Pittsburg Christian Advocate of November 20, 1860, and in the city dailies:

"Whereas, the fate of Rev. A. Bewley is regarded no longer as in a state of uncertainty, but it is now ascertained that he was actually hung at Fort Worth, on the 13th of September, 1860; *therefore, resolved:*

"1. That we regard the death of Mr. Bewley as the murder of an innocent man.

"2. That we sympathize with the bereaved family, and, regarding their claims on our denomination as strong, request the authorities of the Church to make known their condition, and we will bear our part in the support of the widow, and education and comfort of the orphans.

"3. That we regard the action of mob-law, under any circumstances, as wrong, and worthy of denunciation by Christian ministers.

"4. That we regard the course of Bishop Pierce and the papers of Southern Methodism, in attempting to vindicate the action of the mob in the case of Mr. Bewley, as altogether unworthy of Christian men.

"5. That these resolutions be published in the Pittsburg Christian Advocate and the city papers."

On the foregoing the St. Louis Christian Advocate of November 29, 1860, comments as follows: "The names appended to the resolutions are the names of Methodist preachers in that city. It is really singular, that men occupying the position they do, should make such thrusts as contained in the fourth resolution above, when there is no ground for or justice in them. When, where, to whom, in what way did Bishop Pierce attempt, in any way whatever, to vindicate the action in the case of the unfortunate man, Bewley? When, or in what way, was it vindicated by the papers of Southern Methodism? Did these men, these Christian ministers know what they were talking about? Were they in possession of the *facts* in the case? If so, how shall we excuse them for attempting to make the impression the above resolution evidently does? Alas! we have indeed fallen upon evil times. Law and order are disregarded by some, and truth and justice equally disregarded by others."

The foregoing is strange language indeed, when we consider the letter of Bishop Pierce, the usual style of the Southern papers, the proceedings of the mob of March, 1859, that assaulted and mobbed the Arkansas Conference, the resolutions passed, February 4, 1854, by the meeting of Timber Creek township, and the general temper of slaveholders, as manifested by the press and in speeches. The quotations already given in these pages show very plainly that the resolutions of the Pittsburg preachers are fully sustained, and they fully and explicitly answer the very innocent interrogatories and statements of the St. Louis Christian Advocate. Read an extract from Bishop Pierce's letter, and then judge whether the Pittsburg preachers have stepped beyond the bounds of Christian charity.

Bishop Pierce proposes to qualify his strong denouncement of the Methodist Episcopal Church by the following effort to palliate the severity of his anathema. And yet it only aggravates the maranathas of the original curses. He says:

"Understand me, I speak of the *out and out* abolitionists. There are sound, good men in the Northern Church, preachers and people, but they are in bad company, in the midst of evil advisers, maintaining unscriptural opinions, and must share the opprobrium of their association. Sorry for it, but we can not help it. Let them come out and stand with us upon the Bible, and Methodism, purged and clean, may once more be a unit, a grand unity, filling the whole country."

9. When the intelligence of the murder of Bewley reached us, and the letter of Bishop Pierce, with scores of such declarations teeming from the Southern press, we asked the question, in a heading to a short article in the Central Christian Advocate, in regard to Bishop Pierce: "WAS HE BEWLEY'S HANGMAN?" The Southern Christian Advocate of November 28, 1860, takes fire, assumes this heading, and says: "The question is asked by the notorious Rev. Charles Elliott, D. D., an abolition editor of the Methodist Episcopal Church, North, known personally, or by character, to very many of our readers, was 'he'—who? George F. Pierce, one of the Bishops of the Methodist Episcopal Church South, known and loved by thousands, as one of the most amiable of men, and as one of the most devoted, laborious, spiritual, and self-sacrificing preachers of Christ on this continent?—Charles Elliott wishes to know if George F. Pierce was the hangman of Anthony Bewley!"

Our castigator goes on to quote the declaration in Bishop Pierce's letter, denouncing all Methodists of the Methodist Episcopal Church, who believed in their Discipline, that calls on the Church to use Scriptural and lawful means to extirpate slavery. And to palliate the matter he quotes the intended exception of his pious Bishop, which amounts to no exception, as the curse of Bishop Pierce rests on all true Methodists, who are such, as he himself once was in profession, to our knowledge, while he was a preacher in the Methodist Episcopal Church.

We now—January 21, 1863—recite and renew what we then said. "With the spirit and principles exhibited in this extract—from Bishop Pierce's letter—we were led to ask, did Bishop Pierce act the hangman for the mob when they hanged the martyr? Or did this sanctimonious Southern Methodist Bishop serve as chaplain for the murderers who assassinated the innocent man? Such inquiries are forced on us by the murderous teachings and assassin-like declarations of the Bishop. Alas! what will Southern Methodism come to under such evil teachings as these? The heart sickens at the sight. And their vast resources of men and means are now put forth to propagate this form of Methodism in free Kansas, California, and Oregon, and over Missouri, Arkansas, and Texas. We see in this the verification of the aphorism, 'Evil communications corrupt good morals.' We now cease to marvel on reading of the persecutions of Christians by Christians. Yet the time is come—a day we never expected to see—when a Methodist Bishop cries out with the mob, it is right to hang the man because he is not in favor of enslaving his fellow-man."

And now, after the lapse of more than four years since the paragraph was written, we are compelled to conclude that our protest against the course of Bishop Pierce is no exaggeration of the matter. The Southern Christian Advo-

cate was in a manifest rage at what we then said, and we
grieve that the events of the last few years give us no room
to modify the first declarations on this unhappy affair.

10. The Cumberland Presbyterians in Missouri, who were
mostly secessionists, gave a very bad character of Mr. Bewley, as a desperado and an outlaw. The Evening News of
September 27, 1860, misled by pro-slavery misrepresentation,
had the following in reference to him: "He is somewhat
notorious in the Southern part of Missouri, where he has
been regarded as an outlaw and desperado." Under date
of October 6th, Mr. E. G. Evans made a very pertinent reply
to the News, the substance of which is as follows: Senator
Evans states that he was born in South Missouri, and has
lived there ever since, and that no man could be found who
could sustain such charges against Mr. Bewley. For he
was early a preacher in Missouri, and all went on well till
1845, when a Church "South" was organized. Mr. Bewley
refused to unite with it, and retained his early principles
and Church relation. Among the first persecutions of the
Church South may be mentioned their refusal to allow
Mr. Bewley's children to attend the Southern Methodist
school at Ebenezer, South Missouri. Although unceasingly
persecuted, he was too brave to leave the South-West. He
was sent as a missionary to the benighted inhabitants of
Texas, where he fell into the hands of ruffians who once
figured in Kansas, but were driven to Texas for their ruffianism. A Texas preacher, who is also lately from Missouri, sends back to the St. Louis Christian Advocate for
publication a letter purporting to be a copy of one written
to Mr. Bewley—signed W. H. Bailey. This letter was
extensively circulated, in order to convict Rev. Anthony
Bewley, when any sensible person can see that it is a forgery gotten up by some one who was seeking the blood of
Bewley. Why did they not forge a letter, and sign

Anthony Bewley's name to it? Just because so much of his handwriting is in reach, that they could not successfully counterfeit it, while no one knows such a man as W. H. Bailey. So far Hon. Mr. Evans, who is as reliable as any other man.

CHAPTER X.

ANTECEDENTS TO 1861.

1. THE pro-slavery men of the South became so incensed at the Methodist Episcopal Church, on account of her anti-slavery principles, that they took occasion from every incident to denounce our Church. Our Kentucky Conference was denounced in the most pointed manner. Mr. A. J. Morey, editor of the Cynthiana News, in Harrison county, Ky., uses the following language, in speaking of his correspondent "Kentucky:"

"It should attract the attention of every Southern man, and the people of Germantown and surrounding country especially. Will they permit a band of incendiaries to hold a convocation in their midst, for the purpose of perfecting their plans of abolitionism? We would as soon believe that the people of Germantown would permit a convention of horse-thieves to be held there, as allow men entertaining such unconstitutional and traitorous principles, as those who belong to the Conference spoken of in the communication. The people in that section have driven others out, and we hope they will give a cold reception to this Northern Conference, which is headed by Bishop Simpson."

The correspondent "Kentucky" writes thus in the same paper:

"ABOLITIONISM IN KENTUCKY.—I was pleased with your remarks on expelling persons of abolition opinions and aims from our State, as you gave them in your last issue,

and suffer me to add, that an editor who will advocate and
defend the interests of his fellow-citizens ought to be sustained. The Methodist Episcopal Church NORTH has an
Annual Conference in this State, with 24 traveling preachers
from Ohio, and 31 local preachers, and 2,496 laymen scattered along the Ohio River, and from one end of the State
to the other; and are moving the border back in this
direction, and declaring in their papers that this will erelong
be a free State. This abolition Conference is to meet on
the 9th of next month, at Germantown, Ky., and Bishop
Simpson to preside. These men in 1850 urged the negroes
to "organize with the whites" who would do so, and resist
the laws of Congress to the utmost ability God had given
them. And they did so at Harper's Ferry, and will do so
again when the opportunity will serve.

"Kentucky is now exposed, and these twenty-four
agents, with Bishop Simpson at their head, aided by their
friends on the other side of the river, can run out all the
slaves in the State in a few years. I say, we should desist
in driving out such small fries as Fee and Co., while we
can manage one of the most powerful abolition associations
in the world in our midst! I have no hope for the union
of these States, while the Methodist Church in the North
can supply the slave States with their abolition preachers.
In his late visit to England, Bishop Simpson made a flaming
speech, and expressed himself with bitterness against the
South."[1]

On the whole the people of their State did not see fit to
take part with the incendiary editor, Mr. Morey, and his
furious correspondent "Kentucky."

2. Mr. Bledsoe wrote a work on "Liberty and Slavery,"
maintaining the new Southern pro-slavery doctrine. We
were acquainted with this gentleman in Cincinnati, for he was

---

[1] Western Christian Advocate of 1860, p. 34, col. 2.

a Northern man, and professedly antislavery at that time. After he went to the South and joined the Southern Methodist Church—so we think—he became fully Southern. In his work on behalf of slavery, he undertakes to criticise our work against it. Dr. Bledsoe says, speaking of the passage, "Be ye not the servants of men:"

"Be the meaning of this passage what it may, it is not an exhortation to slaves to burst their bands in sunder. Yet, in direct opposition to the plain words of the apostle, he is made to teach that slaves should throw off the authority of their masters. Lest such a thing should be deemed impossible, we quote the words of the author by whom this outrage has been perpetrated." He then quotes us as follows: "The command of the twenty-third verse, 'Be ye not the servants of men,' is equally plain; there are no such commands uttered in regard to the relations of husband and wife, parent and child, as are here given in regard to slavery. No one is thus urged to dissolve the marriage relation. No such commands are given to relieve children from obedience to their parents."[2]

Mr. Bledsoe greatly misrepresented us, as is plain from the following in our book (vol. 1, p. 295): "It is the duty of the slave to aim at freedom. 'Art thou called being a servant, care not for it, but if thou mayest be free, use it rather.' Here it is declared that freedom is preferable to slavery, and yet, that the deliverance of the soul from sin is of greater importance than civil freedom. Yet the command is clear: *if* thou mayest, or rather, if thou CANST, if thou ART ABLE to become free—that if it was IN THE POWER of the slave to become free, he was to avail himself of the privilege. If the laws, or if his master set him free, if he could purchase his freedom, if some one would purchase his freedom for him, if in *any way not sinful* he could become free, he was to avail himself of the advantage."

Such was our position, for no slave could be free by fleeing from his master. As the Roman law then governed the world, seeing the scepter departed from Judah, there was not found a free country on earth to which the runaway could flee, and therefore he might be recovered and his state of slavery continued. But the apostle must mean that the slave should endeavor to obtain such freedom as could not be wrested from him.

Mr. Bledsoe, having learned his Southern lessons in favor of practical theft, robbery, and man-stealing, expresses himself thus: "If such violence to Scripture had been done by an obscure scribbler, or by an infidel quoting the Word of God merely for a purpose, it would not have been matter of such profound astonishment. But is it not unspeakingly shocking that a Christian man—nay, that a Christian minister and doctor of divinity should thus set at naught the clearest, the most unequivocal, and the most universally received teachings of the Gospel? If he had merely accused the Christian men of the South, as he has so often done in his two stupid volumes on slavery, of the crimes of swindling, of theft, of robbery, and of man-stealing, we could have borne with him well, and, as we have hitherto done, continue to pass by his labors with silent contempt. But we have deemed it important to show in what manner and to what extent the spirit of abolition can wrest the pure Word of God to its antichristian purpose."

As to the actual theft, swindling, and robbery, these crimes are common to some of the stages of slavery. But as to man-stealing, according to St. Paul, that crime continues to be committed in all the stages of the system, till its extinction, although man-stealing, that is, buying, selling, or dealing in slaves, is of the same criminality with parricide and matricide. See 1 Tim. i, 10.[1]

We barely referred to Mr. Bledsoe to show how far the South had deviated from the principles of the Revolution, of the Bible, and of Methodism.

3. The action of the Baltimore Conference in March of this year shows how far they had departed from the principles of their fathers, the Scriptures, and the Methodist Discipline. This action also shows how far they had advanced toward the pro-slavery sentiments and spirit of the Southern Methodists. They deprecate the discussion of the slavery question in Church or State, especially in our periodicals, and with these they pass the following resolutions:

"That the Conference disclaims having the least sympathy with abolitionism. On the contrary, we are determined not to hold connection with any ecclesiastical body that makes non-slaveholding a condition of membership in the Church, and that we are opposed to any inquisition upon the motives underlying the relations of master and slave.

"That no action of the General Conference can influence us to violate our principles and practices, as indicated in the foregoing declarations; but that we will stand by the rights and interests of our people to the last extremity.

"That our mission, as ministers of the New Testament, is to preach the Gospel of the Son of God, both to master and slave, and to devote ourselves to our appropriate work of winning souls to Christ."

We can readily conceive of the supreme inconsistency of allowing no slaveholders to be in the Church, when so many, by the despotism of the system, are made slaveholders by law, without their knowledge, will, or act. This

[1] Western Christian Advocate of 1860, p. 53.

is a plain case, and can not be called in question. But not to call these afterward to account, for making this act of the law their own act, by consent, will, or deed, is quite another matter. And, that no inquisition upon the motives of slaveholders should be made, is unscriptural, unmethodistic, and contrary to the usage of our fathers in the Baltimore Conference.[4]

Dr. Bond, jr., in the Baltimore Advocate of April 14th, considers the subject acted on by the Conference, and says their action was received with intense and almost universal satisfaction. He also states that emancipation in the British settlements resulted very unfavorably; in Hayti, disastrously. He might as well have said that the deliverance of the Israelites from Egypt was a failure, or that the elevation of the Saxons from low serfdom to civilization was a crime.

He makes one unwilling concession, however, which amounts to a confession. In this article he says: "There was a time when the religious feeling of the South inclined masters to emancipate, and preachers to advise emancipation. Under that influence, hundreds of thousands were made free. Some did well; but the greater number were not benefited by the change."[5] In 1780 the Baltimore Conference pronounced slavery to be contrary to the laws of God and nature. In 1784 a similar decision was made, and onward the moral evil of the system has been recognized and reasserted in the Discipline up to this day, and such was the case of the Baltimoreans up to 1844, when they were the principal prosecutors of Bishop Andrew, because he refused to emancipate or allow his wife to do so.

In 1844 we heard the following declarations from the mouths of Southern Methodist preachers in New York, on

[4] Western Christian Advocate of 1860, p. 46.
[5] Western Christian Advocate, p. 66, col. 1.

the floor of the General Conference, and those utterances
are on record as noted below in the Journals of that body.

Rev. Samuel Dunwoody, of South Carolina, said: "The
Southern men are generally charged with being pro-slavery
men—it is not so. They are opposed to the principle, and
will be as long as they live. I believe slavery to be a
great moral evil."[6]

Dr. Wm. A. Smith, in the same General Conference, said:
"We of the South take both sides of the question; it is a
great evil; it is not necessarily a sin. Now, on this broad
platform the Southern Church stands. We must quietly
submit to a necessity."[7]

Dr. Smith also says: "In 1831, so rife was the popular
feeling and the popular sentiment on this subject that there
is no doubt, so sorely did we in Virginia feel this evil, that
long before this day some act of gradual emancipation would
have passed but for the interference of the Northern abolitionists. We felt the evils, and groaned under them, that,
from the debates in 1831, in the Virginia Legislature and
the popular sentiment expressed in the pulpit and through
the press, no doubts were expressed that the State was
about to adopt immediate measures for its gradual emancipation."[8]

4. The Southern clergy seem to have been carried away
with the political sentiments of the South. The Methodists
at this time had gradually given up their antislavery teachings; in 1854 they perverted the general rule that prohibited all purchases and sales of slaves except to free them,
to refer to the African slave-trade, and therefore allowed it
no reference to the worse than African trade that existed
in the United States.

The South Carolina Christian Advocate, of August 2,

[6] Debates, General Conference, 1844, pp. 184, 186.
[7] Idem, p. 30.
[8] Idem, p. 27. See Central Christian Advocate, p. 166.

1860, speaks out unequivocally on this point, and says: "An antislavery Church can have no practical existence on slave territory—and we may add, that now that the foundations of the old Church are unsettled, and organization is begun anew, hereafter the principles adopted will conform precisely to the only ecclesiastical practice respecting slavery that is possible in such territory. This is to leave the question of the *relation* alone, and to address itself to enforcing the observance of the duties that arise *in* the relation of master and slave."

The editor adds: "Slavery is not contrary to the law of God. Such law can not be formed. Under the Mosaic dispensation it was allowed. Christ and the apostles dwelt in the midst of it, and uttered no word against it. Christ healed the slave of a Roman soldier, and left him a slave. The apostle gave rules for regulating the morals of the relation. Paul returned a fugitive slave to his master."

He further states, in the usual fallacious sophistry of those who plead for sin: "Are not all our duties *relative* duties, and is it not the sole business of the Church to point out, and explain, and enforce these duties—not to attempt a cure of the incidental evils by dissolving the relations? So we understand its duties as to every relation, not itself clearly prohibited by Divine law."

It will be instructive to note what the distinguished Henry Clay declared on the subject of secession recently before his death. In the presence of some leading Methodist ministers and others, who observed that there were few who would be mad enough to rush into disunion, he shook his head ominously and said, "Gentlemen, if I have studied any thing, it is the genius and spirit of the American people, both in the North and in the South, and I tell you there is danger. There is a spirit rising up in both sections of this Republic, which, if not speedily quelled, will bring about a severance of the union of these States, not in two, but into half a dozen little petty republics or despotisms, as the case may be." It was said to him, that at former times there were like threats of division. "Ah!" said he, "that was before the rise of modern abolitionism— fanaticism can not be controlled, and especially religious fanaticism. The Churches of the country then stood together, and in their great annual assemblies they drew the bonds of union and brotherhood together. Now, most of them have been rent asunder, and they are acting as dividers, rather than to bind the country. Gentlemen, you are both of you ministers of the Gospel, and I tell you this sundering the religious ties, which have hitherto bound our people together, I consider the greatest source of danger to our country. If our religious men can not live together in peace, what can be expected of us politicians, very few of whom profess to be governed by the great principles of love? If all the Churches divide on the subject of slavery, there will be nothing left to bind our people together but trade and commerce. That is a powerful band I admit; but when the people of these States become thoroughly alienated from each other, and get their passions aroused, they are not apt to stop and consider what is to their interest. So men will fight if they consider their rights trampled upon, even if you show them that ruin to themselves and families will be the probable result. Besides, in times of high excitement, the violent men on both sides get the control of matters, and moderate men are thrown into the background, and their counsels go unheeded. If you preachers will only keep the Churches from running into excesses and fanaticism, I think the politicians can control the masses. But yours is the hardest task, and if you do not perform it we will not be able to do our part. That I consider the greatest source of danger to our country."

The pro-slavery teaching of the Southern Christian Advocate is most unsound. According to the law of Moses, he that stole a man and sold him, or held him as a stolen man or a slave, was to be put to death. God never instituted the relation, but enjoins its dissolution. The case of Joseph is a clear example of the acts of enslavers; and the man-stealer—that is, the buyer or seller, or dealer in slaves—is placed in the same list with murderers of fathers and murderers of mothers. The Southern clergy were bewitched into the doctrines of the pro-slavery politicians, and thus were decoyed away from the truth of Holy Scripture, which, in the patriarchal age, in the Mosaic law, in the prophets, and the New Testament, condemned most plainly the system of slavery. It is at least the implied office of Christianity, among other things, to elevate politics and other civilizing agencies to its own lofty plain. How sad, then, is the spectacle when the Church prostituted truckles low at the heels of a corrupt State!

It is the peculiar part of God's ministers to sway, impress, fashion mankind, and girt with truth, to lead the van of the world's benefactors. But how pitiably is their cause betrayed when they, seduced and entrapped, come to be swayed, impressed, fashioned by the cunning craft of men, and finally fall to performing an enemy's service in the King's armor!

Mr. Clay seems to have been much misled himself as to the true Scriptural teaching on slavery, like most others who allowed themselves to hold slaves. It was not abolitionism that was first or principally in error, many or serious though their errors might be; it was enslaving human beings, and thus depriving them of the fruits of their labor, denying them education, and brutalizing them by absolutely prohibiting the marriage relation, and reducing them to a state of degradation. The charge of Mr. Clay, that

18

abolitionism would be the cause of disunion, was incorrect, as the history of the present war fully testifies. Not abolitionism, but slavery drew the sword for disunion, and by the sword it perished.

5. The sentiment of disunion became very general among the leading Southern politicians. The same spirit was caught by the Southern religious press. The indications were that, on the division of the Democratic party, Mr. Lincoln would be elected President. And, indeed, the violent Southern men were even disposed to divide the Democratic party in order to have a plea for their cause.

The Richmond Christian Advocate of January 19, 1860, says: "The whole South is arming. Non-intercourse with the North, which would be fraught with ruin to the North, is becoming the popular idea of the South. Strong men regard disunion as inevitable. The South is grappling existing facts with a giant hand. The Southern mind is deeply roused, and tranquillity and confidence can be restored only by protection of its constitutional rights, and not by compromises of any sort, or speeches however eloquent, or resolutions however sound. The entire South is concentrating on the single principle of self-preservation and separate independence, for Southern conservatism is fast settling on this principle. Northern conservatism alone can save the Union. The contest now is between national conservatism and abolitionism. If Northern conservatism quails in the present crisis, a darkness comes down upon us in which we can not even see our hand before us."

The St. Louis Christian Advocate of February 9th, after stating that there has been a constant increase of free States from the Revolution down to the present, says, there need not be any fears on the part of slaveholders for want of room, as the slave States have much unoccupied country. The argument on this was to the effect that the slave power was not increasing. But this was a manifest fallacy, as it had been constantly increasing its power, and by the Dred Scott decision might cover all the free States. The Memphis Christian Advocate of the same date seems to be hopeful as to the Union. But the South-West was not, at that time, fully imbued with the disunion doctrines. They deemed it enough to harass Union men in Texas, Arkansas, and Missouri, and to control them by mob-law and intimidation, till they would either adopt the pro-slavery platform or leave the country for Kansas, California, Oregon, or the old free States. Indeed, the Methodist population of Missouri, previous to 1863, must have been 20,000 less, in consequence of this persecution, than it would have been under ordinary circumstances. And most if not all of the Methodists of Arkansas and Texas were driven out of these States.

6. The case of David A. Hoover, as given by himself in a letter dated October 23, 1860, and published in an Indiana paper, will show the state of affairs in Texas. This narrative was copied in the Central Christian Advocate of December 19, 1860. His departure from Texas occurred in July, 1860. He says:

"Some eighteen years ago I moved from Lafayette, Indiana, to Cape Girardeau county, Missouri, where I resided about eleven years. From thence I moved to North-Western Texas, where I purchased six hundred and forty acres of land, to which, in a short time, I added one hundred and sixty more, and soon had fifty acres under cultivation.

"I attended to my own business, working on my farm, and hiring white men exclusively to assist me in my labor. This was noticed by a friend of the slave oligarchy, and I was asked by some of them if I never hired negroes to work for me. I told them that when I lived in Missouri I had hired negroes to work for me, but had never done so in Texas. They asked me the reason. I told them I preferred hiring white men for two reasons: First, because I could hire them cheaper; secondly, because I could get a great deal more work out of them than I could out of negroes. They asked my opinion in regard to slavery. I answered frankly that I thought it was wrong, but that it was a matter I did not wish to meddle with—the laws of the State tolerated slavery, and I felt no disposition to rebel against the laws of my adopted State; that while I was opposed to the further extension of slavery, and to the reopening of the slave-trade, I was equally opposed to meddling with it in the States where it already existed by law. I was cautious and temperate in my language, and was careful never to speak against slavery in the presence of negroes. It was whispered around the neighborhood that I was a 'Black Republican, and a Methodist, North,' meaning of the Northern Conference.

"At the Presidential election, four years ago, myself and another man in the neighborhood voted for Fremont. The fat was then in the fire. Whispers gave way to audible curses, and I was openly denounced as a 'd—d abolitionist,' in proof of which triumphant allusion was made to the reception by me at the post-office of one number of the Lafayette Daily Courier, and two numbers of Greeley's New York Tribune, which they considered 'confirmation strong as Holy Writ.'

"My nephew heard them plotting a mob to lynch me, or, in less classic phrase, to 'black-jack' me, which simply meant to tie my arms round a rough black-jack tree, strip me, and whip me with a raw hide as long as they pleased. I eluded all their ambuscades, if any were laid for me.

"About this time Rev. Anthony Bewley—since sacrificed to the moloch of slavery—James Hanan, and —— Willet commenced preaching at my house. Soon the slaveocrats

sent me word that if I let them preach any more in my
house, they would attend to me and them too; in other
words, would make me hug the ' black-jack;' the rest was
understood.   A few days were generally given after the
' black-jack' ordeal for the obnoxious individual to leave
the State.   If they refused to go after being warned, they
were hung without judge or jury.

"Insults like the following were frequently thrown in my
teeth: ' In the free States where you came from, black
men walked locked arms with white women to church.' I
did not deign to answer their jibes and nonsense.

"I purposely refrain from mentioning many indignities
and wrongs practiced upon me and others hailing from the
free States, the lynchings and murders of Free State men,
expulsions of Methodist ministers, etc., as the columns of
our public journals have teemed for months with the sick-
ening details of murders, lynchings, banishments, etc., not
only in Texas, but throughout the entire slaveocracy of the
land.   The writer of these lines was compelled but a few
months ago to fly from his Texas home and his family,
some of whom were sick, to save his life from being sacrificed at the hands of a brutal mob, simply because he. believed that slavery was wrong—that it was wrong to part
husband and wife, parent and child—wrong to withhold the
Gospel from those in bonds, or prayers that the oppressed
might go free—wrong for man to seize upon his brother
and compel him to labor for him without his consent and
without compensation.

"When driven from home I had but fifty-five cents in my
pocket, and dared not stay a moment to prepare for a long
journey of about eleven hundred miles, and take leave of
my dear afflicted family, from whom I have been unable to
obtain any tidings since I left, it being the policy of the
slave-demon to open and intercept all letters and documents

that do not shout hosannas to this mad Nessus, whose shirt
is burning him to death.   Reader, had you been compelled
to fly for your life, to skulk along by-paths like a culprit
to avoid detection, to sleep in the woods at nights without shelter and often without food, as I had to do while
passing through the country of the Philistines—would you
not have come to the conclusion that there was an 'irrepressible conflict' going on in this country between slavery
and freedom? and that bleeding, retreating freedom was in
danger of being crushed out of the land, if possible, and
slavery declared *national*, and freedom *sectional?*   Already
the mouths of patriots and presses have been gagged.   Men
no longer dare to speak or write their sentiments in the
South.   The National mail is rifled by those sworn to protect it from lawless hands.   What a humiliating picture for
a free government, which we are wont to hold up at our
Fourth of July jubilees as the paragon of political perfec-
tion! as the

' Land of the free and the home of the brave,'   .

inviting transatlantic nations to light their torches at freedom's altar fires, which burn brightly on every hill and in
every valley!   But we are careful to say not a word about
the foul blot upon our National escutcheon—that debasing
slavery that would be denounced even by semi-savages.

" Before I close, permit me to say that in Texas and Missouri I found many honorable exceptions who never bowed
the knee to Baal, who assisted and sympathized with me in
my greatest extremity, many of whom were among those
who owned slaves.

" If my family can safely return to a land of free speech,
where there is a free press, even at the sacrifice of my
ample property there, I shall be happy."

In a letter dated December 4, 1860, he says: "My

family has at last arrived from the bloody land of mobocracy, North-Western Texas, from which I was cruelly driven July last." The expulsion of Mr. Hoover was in July, and that of Mr. Bewley in October, 1860.

In a letter dated Stockwell, Ind., January 28, 1861, and published in the Central Christian Advocate of February, 1861, we gather the following further account of Mr. Hoover, and his escape from Texas:

"Soon after this—that is, 1858—I moved to Birdville, Tarrant county, Texas. There being no members of the Methodist Episcopal Church in that place, and the Methodist Episcopal Church South promising us protection, we joined that Church. Previous to that time, I had frequently been urged by preachers of other denominations to join the South, saying then I would have friends, and might be useful to the Church. I was a member of this Church about one year, during which time I have frequently heard the preachers and official members say, that the Northern abolition preachers were sent here to sow the seed of discord among the blacks. After living in Birdville about a year, I moved back to my farm. About this time, I had some relations come to see me from Indiana; this created some excitement. They wanted to know of me what their business was. I told them they had come to look for homes. About the middle of July my brother came to see me and to settle in Texas.

"On the 25th of July, 1860, I left for Fort Worth on business, in company with my brother. When I got home next morning, my family told me that, soon after leaving the morning previous for Fort Worth, a couple of men who hitherto professed to be my friends, came to let me know that the Fort Worth Committee were coming to see me. That week the Committee heard that I was a Northern Methodist; that I thought John Brown was a Christian;

and if they proved such things, I was to be hung. If I had any business to fix up, I had better improve the time. Some of the Committee told my wife that I had too many strangers about me. She told them that we were members of the Church South. They said if the Committee knew that, they might not hang me. This was soon after they hung Crawford and others. After deliberation, I concluded to leave the God-forsaken country, let the sacrifice be what it might, and go to some free State where I could live in peace.

"I started about eleven o'clock the same day, sick and feeble. We expected them to follow us. The second day we missed our way, a man giving us wrong directions, and we did not strike the road for a hundred miles. On the third day, being weary in body and mind, I fell asleep on the saddle, and lost my coat, pocket-book, papers, notes, etc.

"While I told my brother to proceed to where the horses might obtain water, I traveled back five miles in search of my coat, etc., and had to return without finding them. Here we were in a strange land, and not knowing what minute we would be taken and hung. It was then I cried: 'O Lord of hosts! thou who preservest man and beast; if I have given no just cause for this persecution, then do thou deliver me from bloody and deceitful men.' It was midnight when I returned. I lay down and slept till morning. The fourth day I felt that the Lord was with us. This day we heard of some people being run out of the State. On the fifth day a friend gave me a coat and vest. Another gave me thirteen dollars. On the sixth day we rested. On the seventh day we saw three families fleeing to a free State. On the eighth day, in the afternoon, we passed through Clarksville. While there, we learned that a couple of men had arrived from Fort Worth, whom we eluded, and escaped unobserved. I learned that the Texans followed us for eight days. On the ninth day we crossed Red River, and saw a man leaving for Illinois on horseback, intending to send back for his family. The Fort Worth Committee did not follow us, but another did, one at a time."

7. Although the action of the General Conference was less stringent on the subject of slavery than any of its predecessors, nevertheless the antislavery sentiment of the Methodist Episcopal Church, apart from the written expressions of the new chapter, was as deep and as stringent as at any time previous to 1844. But the pro-slavery element had deeply imbued the Baltimore Conference, and hence their opposition to any thing that would give a sound Methodist check to the encroachments of human bondage. The Baltimore Christian Advocate was the mouthpiece of the pro-slavery malcontents. Dr. Bond, jr., the editor, was unmindful of his early teachings, and in close affinity with the Richmond editor, both of whom attended the General Conference, and reported in their papers such material as would tend to throw the Baltimore Conference into the Methodist Episcopal Church South, or to form a new border Church. Portions of the Philadelphia Conference were inoculated with the same virus, but the war cured it. The Western Virginia Conference was partially infected, but this was only temporary. Our Kentucky Conference showed signs of this disorder. A few lay members of the Missouri Conference, who read the Baltimore Christian Advocate, by this sophistical sheet were lost to religion, patriotism, and the Church. But the preachers of the Missouri Conference were entirely free from the contagion. I pass over, however, the anomalies of the more eastern Conferences, and confine our attention to the South-West as the field of our narrative. Yet the prestige of these old Conferences, in the place of aiding the

South-West by their mixed course, was a barrier, for a time, to South-Western Methodist interests; but all this passed away as a morning cloud when the pro-slavery war invaded Missouri.

8. That Southern Methodists entered fully into the interests of the rebels, and labored to draw border Methodists into their measures, we have the fullest proofs.

The Rev. J. B. M'Ferrin wrote for the Richmond Christian Advocate with this special design. In a second letter, headed THE BORDER ONCE MORE, dated July 3, 1860, he even lays down the plan of transferring the border Conferences to the South, or if this did not succeed, to encourage a border Church, which would in the issue be prepared to go South. He sets forth three measures for the Baltimore Conference, one of which they must take, in his estimation.

"1. They have to submit to the action of the General Conference, and subject themselves to a degradation beneath their real position; or,

"2. They must set up an independent organization, and constitute a Church of their own; or,

"3. They must adhere South, and become one with their brethren of the Southern Church."

Mr. M'Ferrin then argued: "The first, Virginians and Marylanders will never do; the second will hardly be practicable, unless they can bring into their organization several neighboring Conferences; the third is the only practicable method."

Such was the plan which he elaborated on true pro-slavery and Southern principles, and maintained would strengthen the Methodist Episcopal Church South by the addition of all the border Conferences, Missouri included, by omitting every thing about slavery in profession. Nevertheless, such a combination, like the Methodist Episcopal

Church South, would have thrown all its influence to extend it, though professing the contrary. The Southern Methodist press was very zealous to carry the border with them, and claiming that nothing should be said against slavery, they persisted in saying nothing against it, except that it was merely a political or civil affair with which the Church had nothing to do. This is absurd enough. As if the Church had nothing to do with theft, robbery, oppression, and disfranchisement of natural rights, such as life, liberty, and happiness. Let us cite a few of their sayings as specimens of a great many.

The St. Louis Christian Advocate of May 17th, in urging such a union as Mr. M'Ferrin proposes, and condemning any antislavery utterance of our General Conference, says:

"And what change do they need? Why, simply such a change as will put them right where the Church South is—a striking of every thing relating to that subject from their book of Discipline; that is what they need. Let that be done, and then each individual be allowed freely to enjoy his own opinion on this as on all other political questions. If they do this, Methodists will again be united from one extremity of the country to the other, but not otherwise. The South is right on this question, and can never recede."

The Richmond Christian Advocate of July 19th declares, "No antislavery Church can flourish or even long exist in Virginia. Why?" The editor then proceeds to give his reasons.

It says, August 2d, in reference to the absorption of the Baltimore Conference by the South: "But how may this most desirable union be effected? We propose the following plan, *and this we do by authority:* Let preachers, circuits, stations, and even a Conference inform the bishops, or any one of them, that they desire to unite with the Southern Methodist Church, and by episcopal authority union will be at once effected. The relation between a pastor and his charge will not be disturbed. For example, in a station or circuit where now there are Baltimore and Virginia churches and preachers, both can remain unmolested, for both will be under the same ecclesiastical jurisdiction. In a word, the Southern bishops, or any one of them, can and will suitably arrange any case of proposed union with the Southern Church. We repeat, this is suggested on high authority, and if accepted, trouble on the border will at once end." From the foregoing it appears that the plan of breaking up, schismatically, the charges of the Methodist Episcopal Church on the border had been adopted by the Southern bishops and the leaders of the Southern Church. The editors of the Baltimore and Richmond Advocates, who had been in close united deliberation at the General Conference, seem to have matured this plan and secured its approbation and indorsement by the bishops and other leaders of the Southern Church.

. The New Orleans Christian Advocate of August 29th is rampant on the subject. On the conspiracy in Texas, referring to his abolition brethren, religious and political, he says: "Their abolition doctrine has been the direct cause of both the John Brown and the Texas conspiracies, together with all similar disturbances." He raves on, and referring to the discolored misrepresentations of the proslavery men, which he ascribes to the abolitionists, he says: "The men, the old women, and the children were all to be killed, and the young women to be devoted to a far more horrible fate. And this is the fruit of abolitionism—of antislaveryism—of the teaching of the antislavery press, and pulpit, and rostrum! Can any man candidly and conscientiously deny it? And this is the forlorn hope of the Black

Republican army which is now seeking the control of the Government. These conspirators are the advance guard of the Black Republican party to which Dr. Abel Stevens professes to belong, and which the majority of Northern Methodists, it is said, will support in the ensuing Presidential election! This is the doctrine taught by the entire Northern Methodist press, edited by such men as Drs. Thomson, Kingsley, Haven, and Elliott, the latter in slaveholding territory. This is what is meant by that freedom of speech." He then laments that "Bishop Janes fills the ear of the country with his complaints against that accomplished gentlemen and patriot, Judge Roberts, and his associates. This is the fruit of the Gospel the Northern Methodist preachers wish to preach in Texas. The blood of the revolution of San Domingo, of Kansas, of Harper's Ferry, and of this Texas infamy, rests on the head of these modern Tories and incendiaries."

He raves on about the "logical responsibility of Black Republicans and abolitionists for these results." He proceeds: "How a man can teach abolition doctrines, or support the Black Republican party, and not be a villain, our casuistry does not enable us to determine. Such a man is logically an incendiary and a murderer, whatever he may be in purpose."

Of slavery he says: "Southern slavery, as a rule, is the mildest and most benevolent system of labor in the world, and the slaves, without abolition temptation, are the most contented and happy laborers."

Of abolition he says: "It is the life of modern politics, the falsehood of modern philosophy, the apostasy of modern Christianity, and the curse of modern civilization. If ever men deserved the doom which Benedict Arnold escaped, Wm. H. Seward, Horace Greeley, Charles Sumner, Wendell Phillips, and their abettors, political and clerical,

are the men." Such were the sentiments uttered by the
Southern Methodist press, and for extravagance they scarcely
find an equal any where. It is not marvelous that Bewley
was murdered by Texans, to whom such teachings were uttered by a professedly religious paper. It would be rather
a marvel if the people at large had been better than their
teachers.

Rev. N. J. B. Morgan, of the Baltimore Conference, in
the Baltimore Christian Advocate of September 29th, under the heading of "The tendency of the movement among
us for immediate separation is to carry us to the Church
South," shows very plainly that the result of the cause
argued by the Advocate would be to transfer the Baltimore
Conference to the South.

At this date, August, 1864, the matter is clear, that the
design of the malcontents was to unite with Southern
Methodists.

9. During this year, Bishop G. F. Pierce, of the Methodist Episcopal Church South, wrote a great number of
letters from California to the Southern Christian Advocate,
and they were copied in all the papers of his Church. In
Letter XIV, dated Sunshine, September 7, 1860, he argues
that his Church should be an occupant of all lands. Hear
him:

"I hope the day will come when we shall be numerously
represented in every State and Territory of the American
continent, in every nation and province, every continent and
island of this round earth."

After this exceedingly zealous and hopeful prognostic of
the future influence of his Church, and after stating that
he had traveled through California, he presents the following methodical programme:

"1. The Methodist Episcopal Church South is a necessity and a blessing in California.

"2. The Pacific ought to be vigorously maintained by means and men.

"3. If our Church authorities would send strong, wise, experienced ministers here, the Methodist Episcopal Church South in five years would outnumber all other denominations combined. The Church, North, would rival us in the cities and in the mines; in the rural districts we should soon count five to their one, and in a short time, as far as Methodism is concerned, would be well-nigh the sole occupants of the land. I put these opinions on record here. Time will test their soundness."

Full of self-confidence, the zealous and fanatical Pierce says: "While we hold to the Bible, and Christ the Head, we can not, dare not change our position. The North, deluded by a false idea, will not change. So we must leave them with Reuben and Gad, and the half tribe of Manasseh, on this side of Jordan, while we go up to possess the land." He then adds: "We have a Conference of sixty odd preachers in California, but they are mostly young men without experience and not adapted to portions of the work." Toward the end of his long letter, he boasts that "we are not obtruders on free soil, as some think."

In his XVIth Letter, in the Southern Christian Advocate of October 18, 1860, the Bishop assumes quite a missionary attitude. He says: "Our division of Methodism is free to go any where and every-where, because our sole aim and policy is to preach the Gospel, and nothing but the Gospel, to bond and free."

He waxes warm in glorying. He says: "We came out from abolition Babylon a persecuted people. We have taken the dead fly out of the pot of ointment; we have got our division of Zion back upon the old apostolic platform. . . . . The great commission ought to be the motto on our banner. The Methodist Episcopal Church South is just as much at home in California as in Georgia. . . She knows no North, or South, or East, or West, but is free to go wherever there are souls to save over this broad earth. Sooner or later, if faithful to her high and holy calling, she will be welcome every-where."

Our missionary Bishop then proceeds to state that he sent four preachers to Oregon, for the people were hungry for the bread of life, and were tired of abolition lectures. He promises, during the current year, to send to Oregon at least *ten* more preachers, and concludes thus about Oregon: "Already they have gathered more than *three hundred members*, have had camp meetings, great revivals, and the fields are white unto the harvest. By 1862 I expect the General Conference to set off the Oregon Conference, and perhaps include the Washington Territory."

Such is the vain boasting of this apostle of slavery. The year 1862 passed away, and their General Conference, which was to have convened in New Orleans, could not meet, because it was composed of traitors. Their Kansas Conference is dead. And even Bishop Pierce, in the place of preaching the Gospel, has become a traitor to his country, and has been engaged in supporting the wicked cause of Southern rebellion. Lord, what is man! What confidence can be placed in princes!

But the worse portion of this same letter of Bishop George F. Pierce is his palpably false caricature of the Methodist Episcopal Church, which we had occasion to quote in our narrative about Bewley.

10. So exceedingly sensitive were the Southern people, and Southern Methodists, as well as others, that they considered the election of Mr. Lincoln as the sign for the disruption of the Union. The Southern politicians led the way, and the clergy had now so learned the lesson of re-echoing only what the politicians did and said, that the

Southern religious press seemed prepared to go all lengths in this false step.

The North Carolina Christian Advocate of August 30th furnishes the following:

"If the present aspect of parties continue till November, Lincoln will be elected by the popular vote.

"If Lincoln be elected, a dissolution of the Union, within twelve months, is inevitable.

"A dissolution of this Union can not be peaceful. It will be followed by a civil war, the most inveterate and horrible.

"The South will not submit to the rule of a Black Republican President."

After these statements, the editor deplores the dissolution of the Union. But he says nothing of the duty of submitting to the choice of the people, whether the elected person belongs to the one or the other school of politics.

The New Orleans Christian Advocate of October 31st utters a similar prognostication.

The same paper, of November 21st, thinks that secession will follow the Presidential election.

Dr. A. B. Longstreet, of Charleston, S. C., on November 12th, the last day of the special session that went for secession, in his prayer as chaplain of the House, gives us the following, connected with general confessions. Referring to the slaves in his prayer, he asks:

"*Have we given to them that which is just and equal, forbearing threatening?* Have we granted to them Gospel and Sabbath-day privileges? Have we made them easily accessible to God's ministers? Have we made no unreasonable exactions of them? imposed on them no unnecessary burdens? Have we ministered to them in sickness and distress? Have we fed and clothed them well? If we have, then we may say, We have nothing to fear from their professed champions.   Our servants shall be to us as Abraham's were to him: auxiliaries in war, and household friends and confidents in peace."   Dr. Longstreet, before he was a Methodist preacher, was a warm politician, and ever since has been, at least, as enthusiastic in politics as in the Gospel.   But the South Carolinians did not heed him, when he warned them, in one of his political harangues, "not to fire the first gun."   They fired on Sumter, and opened the war.

The editor of the Nashville Christian Advocate, in writing from Baton Rouge, December 6th, in his paper of December 20th, sounds the tocsin of revolt throughout the South-West, and represents the whole country as ready for it, and the Methodists especially.

The South Carolina Conference, which sat from the 13th to the 18th of December, Bishop Paine presiding, adopted a report, submitted by eight of their leading men, which declared that " they would act in harmony with the South in resisting Northern domination."   And further, "that this Conference tender the State of South Carolina their encouragement, their sympathies, their affections, their intercession with Heaven, their all—subject only to the paramount claims of God upon them."   This act of the Conference was prior to the act of secession of South Carolina.

Thus, the political press of the South was seconded by the religious press in favoring secession.   And all prepared the way for the events that followed in the South-West, with which our narrative is especially concerned, and the occurrences elsewhere were intimately connected with those of the South-West.

CHAPTER XI.

EVENTS PRECEDING THE CAPTURE OF CAMP JACKSON.

1. IN 1860 the leaders in the South, both in Church and State, as we have seen in the preceding pages, were anticipating and preparing for the premeditated secession.

Before the election of Mr. Lincoln, the political leaders declared that should he be elected secession must follow. Similar utterances were heard from the religious press, with scarcely a dissent from the headlong politicians. Of these we have given specimens.

But when Mr. Lincoln was elected there was a perfect outburst of indignation, accompanied with unscrupulous declarations that secession and rebellion must follow the selection of such a President.

The work of secession, indeed, actually began at the close of 1860. South Carolina seceded December 20, 1860. Mississippi, January 9, Alabama, January 11, Georgia, January 19, and Louisiana, January 26, 1861, declared for secession. In the one month of January, five States joined South Carolina. February 1st, Texas followed; April 17th, Virginia; May 6th, Arkansas and Tennessee; and May 13th, North Carolina. Three States only, namely, Louisiana, Texas, and Tennessee, submitted the ordinance of secession to the people. The eight other rebel States seceded without any regard to the will of the people. They proclaimed their action with all boldness, and called on the other slave States, Delaware, Maryland, Kentucky, and Missouri, to follow their example.

2. The Southern Methodist Conferences seem to have anticipated the rebellion of the South, and were in haste to proclaim themselves the partners of the politicians in the work of rebellion.

The South Carolina Conference, on the 15th of December, 1860, five days before the secession of the State, proclaimed themselves on the side of rebellion. While the State Convention was in session, December 17th, the Conference met for prayer on their behalf, and the chairman, Rev. H. A. C. Walker, declared "the interests of the Southern States are identical, and we must *hang together or hang by ourselves.*" The report of the Conference went to say, that "they can never forget the high allegiance which they owe to the claims of their country, the land of their birth. That while they deplore the necessity that exists for separation from the Federal Union, yet in view of all the history of the past, the perils of the present, and the threatened wrongs of the future, they felt in honor and duty bound to move in harmony with the South, in resisting Northern domination. . . . And that this Conference tender to the State of South Carolina their encouragement, their sympathy, their affections, their intercessions with Heaven in her behalf, their all—subject only to the paramount claims of God upon them."

The Alabama Conference, as a preface to their resolutions, passed December 19th, utter the following moral heresies:

"That we believe African slavery, as it exists in the Southern States of this Republic, to be a wise, humane, and righteous institution, approved of God, and calculated to promote to the highest possible degree the welfare of the slave."

"That the inauguration of any political measures which look to the overthrow of this institution, or provide in any manner or at any time, however distant, for the removal of this servile class out of a dependent relation, which is their true and normal state, into one of whose duties and responsibilities they are incapable, can only be dictated by a blind fanaticism, which will not listen to reason, but madly destroy those whom it attempts to aid."

"That as, in the providence of God, several millions of the African race have been committed to our care as a people, we should be recreant to that trust if we did not defend our right to their service against any and all enemies now and forever."

After uttering these unscriptural and inhuman declarations, the Conference declares that the election of Mr. Lincoln was a declaration of hostility to the people of the South, and in fact, if not in form, dissolves the Union, and forces the South to defend themselves. They then pledge themselves most solemnly to sustain the States of Alabama, Mississippi, and Florida, as their Conference embraced parts of these three States within its bounds.

The Virginia Conference, at its session in December, expresses itself in equally strong terms.

The Georgia Conference was of the same mind with the Alabama, for after their adjournment, of ninety-six preachers in the cars, where a ballot was taken, eighty-seven voted for secession, and nine against it.

Thus, the leading Southern Conferences were fully prepared to encourage rebellion, in its incipient steps, instead of uttering, as they ought, solemn protests against it.

The New Orleans Christian Advocate of January 9, 1861, with the heading, "Let us Separate Peaceably," argues vehemently for the irrepressible conflict, and spurns the very idea of submission by the South. Rev. A. B. Longstreet, in the Southern Christian Advocate, urges secession, and concludes that "any man should be excused for desiring to flee from the dangers of abolition rule."

Mr. M'Tyeire, editor of the Nashville Christian Advocate, in two letters published early in January, while he was attending Southern Conferences in Georgia, Alabama, Mississippi, and Louisiana, very graphically portrays with exultation the spirit of secession which he argues as an event to be looked for with certainty in all the South; and although it was not then an accomplished fact, all the elements that would make it so were then in active existence and efficient operation.

Thus we see secession was now the order of the day in the slave States. But as we are to consider how this affected the Methodist Episcopal Church in Missouri, we turn to the South-West for information.

3. In Missouri, at this time, there was more caution and secrecy used than further South, by secessionists. It is now well known, that for many months the conspirators were stealthily preparing for the revolt.

In St. Louis, the leaders, under Gov. Claiborne F. Jackson, were secretly preparing the way for actual insurrection. It was resolved by them to take away all the money in the Sub-Treasury, and seize the arms in the Arsenal. A steamboat lay at anchor in the river the first week in January, which was to take the money in the Treasury to New Orleans. The prevention was as follows: Although the secrecy of the scheme in St. Louis was complete, one of those privy to it happened to be on a visit to Newport, Kentucky, and while there observed to an acquaintance, that soon the Sub-Treasury in St. Louis would be seized. The person to whom the intelligence was thus accidentally conveyed was a loyal citizen, and informed the military commander at Newport of the purposed robbery. The commander at Newport sent two or more companies of regular soldiers, to guard the Sub-Treasury and Arsenal at St. Louis. By this means the proposed seizure of the money and arms was frustrated, although the rebels had stealthily commenced arming and preparing for the attack. They had even collected ten thousand stands of arms in a tobacco warehouse, and had brought cannon and musketry from the South-West.

4. But another movement was set on foot in favor of rebellion. On the first Saturday of January, 1861, what was intended to be a joint resolution of the Legislature passed the Senate, and was sent to the House for its passage there. But owing to the formalities of the House it was delayed, and, by the exertion of the loyal members, was defeated. The resolution provided that the Mayor, Council, and police of St. Louis should be placed under the entire control of the Governor, thus disfranchising the city, and preparing the way for crushing out its loyalty, as subsequent events fully showed, although none but the initiated were aware of the conspiracy at the time.

The incipient steps thus taken in revolution were for the time frustrated; yet the Legislature labored incessantly to arrange the military affairs of the State, so as to bring the militia to the aid of rebellion, and thus deliver the State to the Southern Confederacy. Several important events took place from January to the capture of Camp Jackson, May 10th, a notice of which will be important to our narrative.

5. When, on December 20th, South Carolina declared her secession from the Union, she threw out a blazing invitation to the people of the slaveholding States to join her in forming a confederacy of such States.

On the 30th of December, the Legislature of Missouri met in regular session. Up to that day no outward response was made to the invitation of South Carolina, although the knowing ones were just waiting for a favorable opportunity to unite with the Palmetto State.

The next day, January 31st, the mouthpiece of secession in Missouri at that time, the Missouri Republican, in a covert way, declared editorially that Missouri would follow South Carolina. The Republican declared that there was no great number of persons in Missouri who desired secession. But should the grievances of the South not be redressed, they would be justified in taking such steps as would secure the coöperation of the slave States, in some definite plan .of action, and then in carrying out resolutely what was agreed upon. And should not the grievances of the South be redressed before March 4, 1861, it would be necessary "then to declare a separation from the United States." He further states, that in case the grievances of the South were not redressed, " the fifteen States would be justified in the eyes of the world IN DECLARING SEPARATION FOREVER."

6. On the 4th of January, 1861, Claiborne F. Jackson was installed Governor, and in his inaugural address, uttered the following disloyal sentiments: "The destiny of the slaveholding States of this Union is one and the same. So long as a State continues to maintain slavery within her limits, it is impossible to separate her fate from that of her sister States, who have the same social organization." He then argued that Missouri would *stand by the South.*

7. January 21st, the Legislature provided for calling a convention, its members to be elected February 18th, and to convene February 28th. But in the mean time, by a seditious and treacherous Governor, Lieutenant-Governor, and Legislature, schemes which led to outward treason were carried on in secret.

The Convention met in Jefferson City, February 28th, and adjourned to meet in St. Louis, March 4th. Mr. Glenn, a delegate from Georgia, appeared before the Convention, read the articles of secession adopted by Georgia, and urged Missouri to follow the example. But the Convention declined to follow Georgia, and declared against secession.

March 27th, the Legislature passed the following joint resolution, by a vote of 62 to 42:

"*Resolved*, That it is inexpedient for the General Assembly to take any steps for a National Convention to propose any amendments to the Constitution, as recommended by the State Convention."

8. On the 14th of April Fort Sumter was taken. This event the conspirators in Missouri regarded as an important signal to carry on their dark designs with caution. And yet it was viewed as ominous of the success that would crown their clandestine schemes when the day for action came.

9. That the conspirators in Missouri were proceeding with their designs of open rebellion vigorously, and as soon as possible, there is ample proof from their private correspondence that came to light afterward. On the 15th of April, 1861, General D. M. Frost wrote an elaborate letter to Governor Jackson, suggesting various expedients for maturing the movement. Among these we name the following: 1. To call the Legislature together in order to gain their coöperation. 2. To send an agent to the Governor of Louisiana, in order to obtain arms from Baton Rouge. 3. To send an agent to Liberty, in order to arrange for seizing the armory there. Several other items of like sort were contained in this letter. Such was the programme of General Frost, who had *taken the oath* to accomplish the work of taking Missouri out of the Union.

When President Lincoln called on the several governors, April 15th, for aid to suppress the rebellion, Governor Jackson replied: "Your requisition is illegal, unconstitutional, and revolutionary in its object, inhuman and diabolical, and can not be complied with. Not one man will the State of Missouri furnish to carry on any such unholy crusade."

April 28th, 1861, Governor Jackson wrote to J. W.

20

Tucker, the editor of a secession paper in St. Louis: "I do not think Missouri should secede to-day or to-morrow, but I do not think it good policy that I should so openly declare. I want a little time to arm the State, and I am assuming every responsibility to do it with all possible dispatch." Again he says: "We should keep our own counsels. Every body in the State is in favor of arming the State; then let it be done. All are opposed to furnishing Mr. Lincoln with soldiers. Time will settle the balance. Nothing should be said about the time that Missouri should go out. That she ought to go, and will go, at the proper time, I have no doubt. She ought to have gone last Winter, when she could have seized the public arms and public property and defended herself."

The Lieutenant-Governor, Thomas C. Reynolds, went to Arkansas and other Southern States, in order to secure aid in taking Missouri out of the Union.

Here we have the fixed determination of the Governor to take his State out of the Union. His correspondence, above recited, occurred at a time when there was no interference by soldiers of the United States with any of the citizens, or with the peace of the State. Thus, before the taking of Camp Jackson, May 10th, a plot was secretly laid and maturing for the secession of Missouri.

10. Governor Jackson and his fellow-conspirators so arranged matters that, April 20th, the Arsenal at Liberty, Missouri, was seized and garrisoned by one hundred men. The arms and cannon were distributed in the county. Yet the Governor declared that his policy was in favor of peace, and that he convened the Legislature for the purpose of organizing the militia, and putting the State in a proper attitude for defense. In short, the entire course of Governor Jackson, from his inauguration, was designed to identify Missouri with the Southern Confederacy.

11. On the 20th of April the Massachusetts soldiers were massacred in the streets of Baltimore. On this the Republican of St. Louis, then in the service of the conspirators, remarks, under the heading, "*Keep Cool:*"

"The time has now come for Missouri *to take* sides on an issue about which she has never been consulted, and in which she has *no direct interest.* All the border States agree in this, that no hostile army shall march over their territory to engage in war. The border States will meet in convention next month, and such measures may come up as will restore peace. It is worth a trial, and we counsel the people of this State, while *preparing for the worst*, to take no steps which would interfere with so desirable a result. We are in no condition to go to war." Such was the utterance of the Republican, the adviser of the rebel Jackson and his intimate associate in the work of the incipient rebellion in Missouri.

12. According to the hint of the Republican, Governor Jackson issued, April 22d, his order for arming and drilling the State forces.

At this time there was much alarm for the safety of the Arsenal at St. Louis. There was only a small garrison in it, under the brave, patriotic Lyon; while the "minutemen," a body of traitors under the special care of the Republican and the Governor, were secretly drilling in their quarters, and even displaying their rebel flag at the corner of Fifth and Pine streets. Their design to seize the Arsenal was openly avowed in the streets. This was also declared in private letters, which subsequently saw the light. Yet the Republican said, April 24th: "There never has been, so far as we can find out, any concerted plan to take the St. Louis Arsenal. The public are opposed to such a course, at least as long as Missouri remains in the Union."

On the 25th the Republican declared: "We do not

believe that any step should be taken now, which admits of secession, or the possibility of any ultimate connection with the North on any terms. The defenseless condition of the State, without an organized military force, without arms, ammunition, artillery, or a solitary appliance of war, constitutes the best ground for neutrality." On the 29th of April the same paper declared that, whether the people be in favor of "neutrality or secession, all will agree that Missouri should arm herself, and be prepared for all contingencies of a turbulent future." Thus the Republican played the part of right-hand hired lackey to the traitorous Executive in the work of promoting public treachery and revolt.

13. The theme of arming the State was dwelt upon and urged daily by the Missouri Republican. An extra session of the Legislature was called for this purpose. Governor Jackson, in his message, says:

"The great and patriotic State of Virginia, after having failed in all her efforts to readjust the Union, has at last yielded in despair, and has seceded from the old Federal Union. North Carolina, Tennessee, and Arkansas, it is believed, will rapidly follow in the footsteps of Virginia, and Kentucky is profoundly moved on this great question. Our interests and sympathies are identical with those of the slaveholding States, and necessarily unite our destinies with them. . . In the mean time, in my judgment, it is indispensable to our safety that we should emulate the policy of all the other States in arming our people and placing our State in a proper attitude of defense."

The Legislature provided for arming the State, robbing the School Fund and the Lunatic Asylum for that purpose; and in order to seize the Arsenal, the Governor directed the formation of a camp at St. Louis for military instruction, for the county and adjoining counties.

This camp, named *Camp Jackson*, was formed May 1st. The minute-men formed part of it. The streets of the camp were named after Jeff. Davis, Beauregard, and other rebel leaders; and one of the publishers of the Republican was an officer in that camp. On the 8th of May, by night, a portion of the *cannon*, and other arms, stolen from Baton Rouge, was secretly conveyed to the camp of the State troops, as they were called. And this was done by the secret agent of Governor Jackson.

14. The *minute-men* of St. Louis were an organized body who, from the beginning of 1861, had their head-quarters at the corner of Fifth and Pine streets, opposite the Southern Methodist Book-Room. They had their rebel flag hoisted from early in January to May 15th, when General Harney ordered it to be taken down. The roll of the minute-men, seized by General Farrar, a year after, contains the following principles:

"1. That if any State or States of this Union, aggrieved by the hostile and unconstitutional acts of the Black Republican party, shall exercise the right to secede from the present Confederacy, and the Federal Government shall thereupon attempt to coerce such State or States back into the Union, Missouri ought to resist such attempt, by arms, if need be.

"2. That on the event of a disruption of this Union, the honor and safety of Missouri impel her to espouse the cause of the Southern States, and in such case, we should endeavor to unite the slaveholding States in one Confederacy."

To this "basis of principles" two hundred and seven names of citizens of St. Louis were subscribed. This association seems to have been formed on or before the election of Lincoln. The basis showed beyond a doubt that the organization existed before the actual secession of a single State.

15. Let us now recapitulate the movements of the rebels as it concerns Missouri, previous to the taking of Camp Jackson, May 10th.

It is now a matter of history, that secession was openly threatened before the election of Lincoln, should this take place. As soon as the election was over, a determination to secede became general in the South. Before the actual secession took place, the minute-men of St. Louis encouraged and promoted its development, were foremost to hail its birth, and to the last they were its supporters, in full communion with Governor Jackson. The Southern States advanced rapidly to open hostility. In January, 1861, the Arsenal at St. Louis was to be taken, the Sub-Treasury was to be robbed, the civil and municipal powers of the Mayor and Council of St. Louis were to be transferred to the recreant Governor. The militia was to be organized to aid the rebellion, under the plea of protecting the State from invasion.

On January 4th, Jackson, as Governor, declared the destiny of Missouri identical with that of the slaveholding States, revolted or about to revolt. The State Convention in February opposed secession. The Legislature, March 27th, in indirect terms, disapproved the taking of any steps favoring the National Convention recommended by the State Convention. April 14th, Sumter was taken. On the 15th of April Frost wrote his treasonable letter to the Governor, laying down the proper course to be followed in taking the State out of the Union. To President Lincoln's call for troops, April 15th, it was replied promptly that neither men nor means could be furnished to preserve the Union. At the same time, all possible aid was given the enemies of the Union. April 28th, Governor Jackson's letter to the conspirator Tucker added another link to the chain of rebellion. The Arsenal at Liberty was seized by the executive, and his men were substituted for the garrison of United States troops. When the Massachusetts troops were assailed in Baltimore, April 20th, the Governor exulted, and concluded it was about time for Missouri to espouse the "Confederacy." The order for arming the militia was issued, and the camp established at St. Louis, May 1st. Thus, the magazine of revolution was ready for the match.

16. In connection with the foregoing, the religious press of the South, especially that of the Southern Methodist Church, was, as a unit, favoring and aiding the work of rebellion. The Southern Churches, the Quakers alone excepted, were one in effort with the leading politicians. In Missouri, the majorities of all the Churches, the Methodist Episcopal Church excepted, were in full agreement and coöperation with the rebel Governor.

The St. Louis Christian Advocate, the organ of the Methodist Episcopal Church South, in St. Louis, edited by Dr. M'Anally, was, in every respect, the promoter of rebellion, and in consequence, he was the bosom ally of Mr. Tucker, editor of that rebel sheet, the Missouri State Journal, subsequently suppressed as an open foe to the Union, and a supporter of the Southern rebellion. Indeed, Mr. Tucker, in 1864, in a letter published in the South, praises Mr. M'Anally as a true man—using the term *true* in the sense of being faithful on the side of rebellion.

Thus, in Missouri, the weight of the religious element was in federation with the conspirators, the small number of the Methodist Episcopal Church alone excepted, which had to bear the whole weight of the opposition and persecution of all rebels and sympathizers with treason.

17. This leads us to the consideration of the Methodist Episcopal Church in the South-West. The original principles, still retained, comprised a decided protest against buying or selling human beings, to be retained as slaves. Not

only so, but its uniform, unrepealed moral creed considered slavery a great moral evil, deserving to be *extirpated* or *rooted* up.

Furthermore, the Church, first and last, impliedly vows to use all lawful means for its extirpation, at the same time exercising the most loyal submission to the Government of the country. This avowal, and the course pursued in consequence, never disturbed the peace of the land. But a class of Methodists and others arose, who, practically denying the freedom of speech and opinion, even lawfully exercised, denounced most bitterly the above-named principles and their just and dispassionate practice.

This heathenish and impassioned illiberality became abusive, and awakened fever and excitement in communities, grew into persecution and bloody violence, and rocked and convulsed commonwealths, matured into treason against law that would not prostitute at its will, and so finally involved the Union in terrible war, covering the land with slaughter and flame. During this course of events—to be a member or minister of the old Methodist Episcopal Church, in the South-West, was to deserve, in the popular esteem, banishment from the country, if not, indeed, hanging at midnight, by "a jury of three hundred," "without benefit of clergy." Of this we have given sufficient proofs already.

That the foregoing is no exaggeration of the wildness of the pro-slavery men, we here present an extract from an article in the Washita Conference Journal of February 16th, by W. C. Hazlip, dated Monticello, Ark., January 18th, and quoted in the Central Christian Advocate of February 17th. Mr. Hazlip says, in proving that the Methodist Episcopal Church South is a pro-slavery Church, "The Latin prefix *pro*, means *for* or *in favor of* slavery. The Methodist Episcopal Church South stands on the Bible platform, for it is straight out in favor of slavery. . . . The Hamite bondage or slavery is one of the important doctrines of Christianity, and taught in the Bible. . . . Without it Christianity would prove a failure."

The editor of the Journal comments on the foregoing, and among other wild things utters the following: "The Methodist, and other Northern religious papers are saturating the religious mind with the fatal, wicked theories of abolitionism, that spasm of satanic fanaticism. . . . We do pray God, and shall pray God, in mercy, to deliver them from these doctrines of devils. . . . Dear brethren, the devil has beclouded you. . . . You are wrong, as the Lord liveth, you are wrong. . . . Proclaim a solemn fast, and pray over your past course. . . . That is what the Church wants. Is it not so, Dr. Elliott, Drs. Crooks, Stevens, and Thomson? is it not so?" [1]

Before the secession of Southern Methodists, their principles were those of the Methodist Episcopal Church. After this they avowed they were neither pro-slavery nor antislavery. Subsequently they proclaim themselves pro-slavery. Then they struck from their Discipline the antislavery chapter. Finally, they erased the old antislavery General Rule. Thus they prepared the way, by foul apostasy, for raising their arms against the Government of the country.

For the Central Christian Advocate of February 27, 1861, we wrote the following in the city of St. Louis, having had full knowledge of what we said:

"A strong secession element of as dark a type as that in the worst cotton States exists in Missouri. About the first week in January, strong indications existed that an attempt would be made to seize the Sub-Treasury of this city, and the arms. But the appearance of the United States military on the 7th of January, guarding the United States property, prevented this act of rebellion. The bill of Mr.

[1] See Central Christian Advocate of February, 1861, p. 34.

21

Johnson, in the Senate, on Saturday, 5th of January, which would transfer the power of the Mayor of St. Louis to the Governor, was a manifest act of treason to the State of Missouri, and to the United States.

"Then the military bill was a part of the same scheme, by which the State should be placed under a military control, worse than ever existed before in the world, and all the civil rights of the citizens and the control of the Courts put under the arbitrary sway of military, ignorant, bloodthirsty, upstart officers, who know little and care less for the great moral and political principles that underlie just civil government. The moral protest of the public, and the noble band of good men in the House, alone prevented the execution of this Catilinian conspiracy against the Constitution of the State and of the United States. And to crown all the attempted joint resolution of Saturday, 16th of February, passed in the Senate, by eighteen for and four against, by which, on the 18th, the elections in St. Louis should be frustrated by the armed force under the control of a revolutionary Governor, put a climax on the treasonable spirit of a band of ultra secessionists, who manifested a recklessness unknown to Keitt and Yancey, and the infuriated fire-eaters of the far South. Through the good providence of God, these morally insane men were prevented from making our streets run with blood on Monday, 18th of February, the election day. Had the plan of the Governor and Senate carried, supported by the Republican of this city, election day would have been a day of blood. Of this we have no doubt, and proof enough could be adduced of this result were it necessary; but we forbear. Thus, through the good hand of God on us, the civil war, in its bloody character, did not commence with St. Louis."

Secession in Church and State are very much alike. That in the Methodist Episcopal Church was without cause, except that of the pro-slavery element in the South. Calhoun, Webster, and Clay so declared. They spoke as mere politicians, considering unity better than purity. Had the Southern Methodists been retained in our Church with their pro-slavery principles, though but recently adopted, the Methodist Episcopal Church would not have been the great barrier to secession in the State it has proved to be, during the war.

18. We may here mention that the Missouri Conference which was to meet at Jefferson City, changed its sitting to St. Louis. The reasons were these: the State Convention was then in session at the capital; our Church members were few at best, but now were much diminished in numbers. Therefore it was concluded best to have the session in St. Louis. The Conference met, March 7th, Bishop Morris presiding.

19. In the Spring of 1861 the affairs of Missouri were such that we considered it our duty to advise the General Government of them. We had abundant reason to believe there was much studied concealment of the plans and calculations of the secessionists in the State. With this conviction we wrote the two following letters, the one to Mr. Chase, and the other to Mr. Cameron:

(COPY.)

St. Louis, Mo., *April 17, 1861.*

Hon. S. P. Chase, Secretary of the Treasury.

MY DEAR SIR,—I thank you for your kind attention to my few lines about Indian agents.

I inclose a letter to the Secretary of War, which you will please read and transfer to him. We, here, are on the eve of a revolution indeed, and much bloodshed, unless the General Government will take the Union men of Missouri under its protection. I have recently visited Kansas. There are now 1,000 men in Southern Kansas, refugees from Texas and Arkansas, whose friends have been murdered, and they themselves expatriated. Kansas will fight to the death before Missouri enters the Southern Confederacy, and thus shuts up their thoroughfares to the free States east of the Missouri. I deemed it my duty to write as I did, as a loyal citizen. I have never troubled our statesmen for any office for any one. Remember me to my esteemed friend, Mr. Whittlesey. I take great liberties with you. I do it for the sake of the best of governments.

Yours,   CHARLES ELLIOTT.

(*COPY.*)

St. Louis, Mo., *April* 17, 1861.

To THE HON. SIMON CAMERON, SECRETARY OF WAR.

DEAR SIR,—I beg to call your attention to a few facts, and offer some suggestions on the crisis approaching in Missouri. We have an avowed secessionist as Governor. We have a Legislature largely of secessionists too. There is a formidable military organization—the minute-men—here, numbering now some 2,800, besides those who have as a cloak been taken into the service of the State, but who still are at the call of the Missouri executive for any treasonable purpose. These men are a standing menace upon the Union men in the city and in the State, and the repeated insults to them and the late city government, by hoisting the secession flag at their head-quarters, tend to produce disorder and bloodshed.

It is a common belief that an overt act of aggression and resistance to Federal authority will soon be attempted, such as the seizure of the Arsenal and the Sub-Treasury, if there be no resistance. As the Governor of Missouri will not respect the call of the President for troops, let me suggest the enrollment of all Union men in the city, and perhaps elsewhere in the State.

There is no more loyal people in the Union than the

members of the Methodist Episcopal Church. I say nothing of the Methodist Episcopal Church South. In the
State of Missouri there are now some 10,000 members of
the Methodist Episcopal Church who are exposed to ecclesiastical and political hostility, and who, were the State to
be forced out of the Union, would be persecuted even unto
death, confiscation, or banishment. There are now nearly
a million of members of the Methodist Episcopal Church
who have a strong sympathy for their brethren of Missouri,
and have spent $20,000 in sustaining their paper, of which
I have been editor since last June. The Methodists of the
free States, as citizens, will remain, to the last, sustainers
of their brethren in Missouri, who have already been dealt
with so rudely by secessionists.

As many as 5,000 sound Union men, they say, are in St.
Louis—Americans, Germans, English, Irish, of all denominations and politics—and are ready to enroll themselves in
a home corps. And if this movement be inaugurated and
supported by the Federal executive, a strong body of Union
men can be organized. The same will hold good of other
places in Missouri.

It should not be forgotten that this body of Union men
can not be raised except by the Federal Government. The
military bill of the last Missouri Legislature takes away
from the people the power of organizing for self-defense,
except under the sanction of the State, or as State militia.
The question shortly to be determined in the South-West
may be, Shall Memphis or St. Louis be head-quarters of
the revolted States? Immediate measures I am persuaded
are necessary to check the evil. I am a stranger to you;
but I will introduce myself, and refer you to my friends
Secretary Chase and Controller Whittlesey for information.
I am an itinerant preacher of the Methodist Episcopal
Church, and have served for forty-three years in the West.

For almost twenty years I have been principal editor of this Church in Pittsburg and Cincinnati; and since last May, in St. Louis, where I was placed by our General Conference in last May, in order to sustain their press in the South-West. I am now in my sixty-ninth year. I will enroll myself in the Union company, as I want to die under the Stars and Stripes, and never succumb to a foreign flag, especially the rebel Palmetto one. Let me add, that unless the General Government will sustain the Union men of Missouri, Kansas, and Iowa, and Illinois will come to the rescue. I have performed what I deemed a duty in writing thus.

Your obedient servant,   CHARLES ELLIOTT,
Editor Central Christian Advocate.

CHAPTER XII.

CAPTURE OF CAMP JACKSON.

1. A BRIEF resurvey of Missouri affairs will naturally preface our consideration of the capture of Camp Jackson. The Governor was a secessionist of the deepest dye, and in close alliance with the Southern Confederacy. The Atlanta Commonwealth, of May 3d, says: "A messenger of Governor Jackson, of Missouri, to President Davis, of Montgomery, passed through Atlanta this forenoon, for the purpose of soliciting aid in taking the Arsenal at St. Louis." The same paper said, "Cannon, from Fort Sumter, passed through Atlanta, to-day, on their way to Memphis, Tenn. Final destination not known to us." These cannon, as after events showed, were for the rebel army to be raised by Governor Jackson. The Legislature, with the Executive at their head, were earnestly laboring to bind the State to the South. On the 8th of May, a resolution of both Houses suspended the appropriation bill for the schools, and appropriated the funds to arm troops for rebellion. The money to pay the interest on the State debt was also appropriated in the same way. Large reënforcements of men and means were expected from Arkansas and Tennessee. The military organizations of the State, under the new bill, were to encamp in four different places, in order to resist the General Government. The force just west of St. Louis was to be enlarged sufficiently to seize the Arsenal and crush out the Union men of the city. The secessionists were harassing

and driving the loyalists out of the State, and thus weakening the power of the Union cause.

On the other hand, the body of the people were for the Union. The Kansans were on the west, the Union men of Iowa on the north, and Illinois on the east. To these must be added the resources of the great North-West, as well as those of the General Government. The Germans, too, in Missouri, were, as a body, true to the United States. But the best of all was, that God, justice, liberty, and the Bible were for the Union.

2. The capture of Camp Jackson took place Friday, May 10, 1861. Captain Lyon commanding at the Arsenal in St. Louis, under instructions, moved with about five thousand men in four columns toward the camp. On his arrival he demanded an unconditional surrender from General Frost, who had about one thousand, one hundred well-armed men in the garrison.

General Frost, after a hurried consultation, surrendered. The march from the camp was attended with an assault by secessionists. As Lyon's soldiers filed out to Olive-street, the secessionists threw stones, brickbats, etc., at them, and several pistols were discharged by the mob, killing some, and wounding others, among them a Captain, who, when he was wounded in the leg, gave orders to fire. Some six shots were fired. How many were killed by this fire is not known.

The second and most destructive fire was from the rear of the column guarding the prisoners. The secession mob was very abusive, and one of them, when expostulated with, drew his revolver and fired at Lieutenant Saxton, of the regular army, three times, the secessionists cheering him, and many of them drawing their revolvers and firing on the United States troops. The man who fired the first shot, while taking aim anew at Lieutenant Saxton, was thrust through with a bayonet, and fired on at the same time, being instantly killed. The mob still persisted in their attack, and several of the soldiers were shot, when they halted and fired with fatal effect. The mob in retreating from both sides of the line, returned the fire, and the troops replied again. Captain Lyon then ordered his men to cease firing, and the order was obeyed as rapidly as it could be passed along the line.

Mr. Lyon makes the following observation on the subject in his official report:

"The sad results are much to be lamented. The killing of innocent men, women, and children is deplorable. There was no intention to fire upon peaceable citizens. The regular troops were over in the camp, beyond the mob, and in range of the firing. The troops manifested every forbearance, and at last discharged their guns, simply obeying the impulse natural to us all, of self-defense. If innocent men, women, and children, whose curiosity placed them in a dangerous position, suffered with the guilty, it is no fault of the troops."

Some twenty-two were killed, four mortally wounded, and many wounded slightly. This result is largely to be attributed to the intense antipathy to the German citizens, who came forward nobly to enroll themselves as home guards and volunteers, in support of the General Government. To the Germans may be attributed, in a great degree, the deliverance of the city from a scene of carnage. Here is an account, from a contemporary, of some of the provocations:

"Language is utterly unable to describe the goading, harrowing, and outrageous insults that were heaped, with the most diabolical malice, upon the United States troops, and which, together with the hurling of dirt and stones, was long borne by them with a forbearance which seemed like abjectness itself. - Fists were shaken in their faces, they were spit upon, caught hold of and jerked from the ranks, and this in addition to taunts most shameful, and abuse too shocking for repetition. The throwing of rocks was only a further step in that desperate work of irritation which was crowned by actually firing into the troops."

On Saturday, May 11th, about 1,100 citizens from the Ninth and Tenth Wards were ordered to the Arsenal to be sworn in as home guards, and to receive their arms. On their return in the evening, at the corner of Fifth and Walnut streets, as they were turning up Walnut-street, the rear company was fired on by a mob. An eye-witness says, a mob of some two hundred occupied the steps and portico in front of the church at the corner of Fifth and Walnut streets, and uttered jeers and bawls as the soldiers approached. The leader of the mob fired a revolver in quick succession at the troops, and several of his associates did the same. Two of the soldiers fell dead, whereupon the rear column turned and fired at the mob. This was followed by more or less firing on both sides.

General Harney, who arrived in St. Louis on Saturday morning, the 11th, issued a proclamation on the 12th, to the people of Missouri, in which he exhorted all to keep the peace, and stated that it MUST BE PRESERVED.

Attempts were made, on Friday evening, to destroy the office of the Democrat; but the firmness of the police force, and the armed hands of the office, prevented this result. The printers, publishers, and editors, and their friends in the buildings, were well armed to protect themselves within, while the police outside were faithful to their duty.

As to ourself, we happened to be out of town on this occasion, attending a quarterly meeting in Carlinville, Ill., some sixty miles distant, by previous arrangement of several weeks' standing. On Friday, 10th, in the afternoon, as

we were leaving our office, No. 97 Fourth-street, to take
the boat for Alton at four, P. M., it was said Lyon was out
with his men. We did not suspect the forthcoming events,
but went to the boat, and read the evening papers till we
reached Alton, about seven o'clock. Then a dispatch gave
some information of the occurrence. Next morning the
papers of the city, with full reports, reached us. We
proceeded, however, to the quarterly meeting, spent the
Sabbath in comfort, and returned to the city, Monday, 13th,
and found our office all safe. Had we anticipated what was
to happen, we would have remained, to watch our office,
however unavailing that might have been. The Anseiger
and the Central Christian Advocate would, no doubt, have
shared the fate of the Democrat, had that paper been destroyed. We thanked God for his protection over us, our
office and cause, and went on, as usual, supporting the
Union, religion, and the morals of citizens, without let or
hinderance.

The St. Louis Advocate was much exasperated by the
doings of the 10th of May, and defended the assault of the
mob against the United States Army. He calls the acts of
Lyon's army " the shooting down in cold blood unoffending
and defenseless men, women, and children." Other like
expressions were uttered against the army for doing its
duty. Similar language in reference to this affair was
used by other traitors as well as by Dr. M'Anally.

3. On May 21st, a truce was agreed upon between General Harney and General Price, the former of the United
States Army, and the latter of the State militia. The
agreement was that the organized State or secession troops
should be disbanded, and that the United States troops
should avoid any collision with the State authorities. This
truce, although of good intent on the part of General Harney, was manifestly a mere ruse on the part of General

Price and Governor Jackson, in order to gain time and new advantages. It seemed to be a mere ambush at Jefferson City for extirpating Unionism out of the capital first, and then out of the State. The result only proved the whole to be a mere feint in the interest of treason. It was only another link in that chain of conspiracies first begun to compass the Sub-Treasury and Arsenal.

4. In the Central Christian Advocate of May 15, 1861, owing to the persecutions of our members and preachers, and their expulsion in many cases from the State, with the view among secessionists of weakening the Union cause and strengthening their own, we wrote the following editorial, which we copy, as it gives a just view of the state of things as then existing:

" *To the ministers and members of the Methodist Episcopal Church in Missouri:*

" It is known to you that recently there has been, and now especially there seems to be, a purpose and effort, on the part of many members and preachers of the Methodist Episcopal Church South, especially by means of mobs and other expedients, to drive you out of the State. Some of our preachers have been assaulted, others warned to remain at their peril. And we find it is deemed necessary for some, on account of the present distress, to suspend their regular public exercises. The great disturbances they meet with, and the small prospect of doing good, render such a course advisable, since the interferences are such as to defeat, for the present, the ends of public preaching and religious exercises. As the members and ministers of the Methodist Episcopal Church South, generally, as far as we can learn, are warmly enlisted on the side of secession, and our people unanimously are decided for the Union, and opposed to secession, the difficulty threatens to remain till the secession element subsides or is exhausted. How soon that will be we know not, although we are fully persuaded that the cause of the Union will finally prevail in Missouri. We would this week, as we did before, beseech all our brethren, as far as is safe and proper, to keep their ground. This we know will be difficult to all, and even impossible to some. Let even life be sacrificed sooner than surrender our cause!

"But while this suspension of public worship must be submitted to in many cases, we trust that all our classes and Churches, however small, will keep up public worship as far as they can, though their preachers may be driven off. Let some one read a sermon, others exhort, and all sing and pray. Where prayer and class meetings can not be maintained, let family devotion be the next chosen means. And, at any rate, let secret prayer be made, and ejaculatory devotion offered while engaged in the various avocations of life. Let prayer, in all its forms, be made by all without ceasing.

"We are persuaded that God will grant us relief in due season, although it may not come as soon as we could wish, and we may be called to experience great privation and suffering in the mean time. The war, too, will make heavy demands on the resources of our friends, so that our assistance for the present may be small, and even precarious.

"While the shepherds may be smitten or driven away, the sheep may be scattered. Then let all, like those dispersed after the death of Stephen, preach the Word, or propagate their religion wherever they go or whatever they do. Your purses, too, are exhausted, and means of replenishing them are uncertain. The only help is in God, whose providence may raise up unexpected means. We pray that the grace of God may sustain us all. We propose to remain at our post to the last extremity."

5. At the same time, May 15, 1861, we penned the

following "*Remonstrance to the ministers and members of the Methodist Episcopal Church South in Missouri:*"

"As far as we can reach you, we would earnestly address you on this important crisis in the history of our country. You are doubtless aware that a very general persecution is now on foot in Missouri, against the ministers and members of the Methodist Episcopal Church. Their persons are assaulted, their religious services are interfered with, notices threatening violence are sent to them with the view of driving them out of their fields of labor, and of expelling them from the State. This, too, is actually done by mob-violence, not only without, but against the forms and provisions of law and the Constitution. It is also known to you that these things are done at the instigation, connivance, and approval of members and ministers of the Methodist Episcopal Church South. These things can not be denied with any show of truth, as the public generally are well aware. A leading politician in Missouri, not of the Republican party, declares, 'I know of none in Missouri who are disposed to interrupt your ministers, except the members of the Methodist Episcopal Church South, and those under their influence.' This answer was given to the following question: 'Why have our ministers been so severely persecuted in Missouri?' We have had no interference from the members or ministers of other Churches, whether Protestant or Catholic. The opposition has come solely from members of the Methodist Episcopal Church South, or from their influence. This, to the best of our knowledge, is the true state of the matter.

"We do not know, or in this case desire to say any thing about the unhappy circumstances connected with the organization or membership of the Methodist Episcopal Church South in Missouri. Suffice it to say, that many of our members and ministers, in 1849, called on the Methodist

Episcopal Church to attend to her scattered flocks in Missouri. The Methodist Episcopal Church, as was her duty, listened to this call and answered it affirmatively. Many of our members, in other States and countries, who moved to Missouri, besought our Church to minister to them. Besides, there are multitudes in Missouri whose spiritual wants require our services, and unless they are furnished, they are as sheep without a shepherd. Thus, those members who remained in our Church after 1845, and members who emigrated to Missouri, and the needy multitude of citizens who depend on our ministrations, call on the Methodist Episcopal Church to supply them with pastors, and give them the ordinances of religion as administered by the ministry of the Methodist Episcopal Church. This Macedonian cry was heard by our Church, as was right it should be.

"Now, we would earnestly remonstrate with those of the Methodist Episcopal Church South to cease to interrupt and interfere with our preachers and members in Missouri. We would beseech you to let them alone. This is all we ask—the right to worship according to the privileges of the Constitution of the State of Missouri and of the United States. Is it courteous, Christian, or proper for one Methodist or Christian sect to annoy, disturb, or hinder another such sect while they are peaceably exercising the rights of citizens? The answer to this question is very plain indeed. The influence of these petty or graver molestations is poorly calculated to impress the public favorably in behalf of the Christian religion. We again entreat you to let our people alone, that they may perform their duty as other Christians in Missouri. We urge you to cease countenancing these assaults on their persons, those notices to leave their fields of labor, and the other interruptions of like sort.

"We are bound, however, to acknowledge, and we are glad

to do it, that many members and preachers of the Methodist Episcopal Church South are averse to the proceedings of their brethren who lend their influence to annoy our Church. And we must further believe that the course deprecated will seriously divide the Methodist Episcopal Church South in Missouri, if persisted in. Let it therefore cease for the future, we implore you, and let the past be forgotten, except in the record of history.

"And yet there is a duty to be performed by you who are opposed to disturbing us. It is this, that you should not only disapprove and discountenance the course referred to, but also *protest against it*, if need be, and even *defend* us in the exercise of our State rights.

"Had we the means of communication with all the members and ministers of the Methodist Episcopal Church South in Missouri, we trust this our humble and honest plea would have the effect we desire. And should our appeal be rejected, we must suffer on to the utmost verge of forbearance before our final appeal shall be presented to the highest tribunal on earth. After this our cause is with God, either to smite or release us as may be right in his eyes. We conclude by asking our common Father in heaven to grant to all of us such dispositions of heart as he will approve of at the last reckoning."

6. The foregoing remonstrance will not be considered out of place, if the real state of things be presented as they existed before the capture of Camp Jackson. This will be seen from the following by Mr. E. G. Evans, a Missourian by birth, a member of the Methodist Episcopal Church, both before and since 1845. He writes from Steelville, Crawford county, Mo., May 4, 1861 : [1]

"All persecutions that we have endured can be traced to that new religion called Southern Methodism. . . .

[1] Central Christian Advocate, May 15, 1861, p. 78.

Their Church is now kicking hard for secession. The common talk is that it is 'a unit for secession;' but I know some stanch men who intend leaving the Church, saying that their eyes are now opened. That Church receives the curses of the wicked, yet loyal people throughout the State. Last week was Court week here. The first secession speech was made on Monday by a Southern Methodist. Two other secession speeches were made by other Southern Methodists. All the male Southern Methodists in town are secessionists, and there are not half a dozen other secessionists in town. A member of the Legislature told me that they were at the root of Missouri secession, and were at the capital in crowds urging the policy."

Mr. Evans calls on Dr. M'Anally to produce evidence of the allegations made against the members of the Methodist Episcopal Church, namely, that they were abolitionists, negro thieves, and that no person of the Methodist Episcopal Church should be allowed to live in Missouri, or the South-West. He refers to the mobbing of the Conference in 1859, in Texas, as only a mere specimen. The editor of the St. Louis Christian Advocate considered these persecutions as a small matter, and resorted to this mode of evasion and misrepresentation, instead of publishing proofs of his charges.

And here, although a little out of date, we may make an extract from a letter found on the person of a secessionist, dated Camp Jackson, St. Louis, May 9th, and addressed to his brother, residing in Natchez:

"Since I last wrote you, we have had accessions to our minute-men, making in all about eighteen hundred men, including the minute-men. Ours, that is the minute-men, have daily accessions. Our rendezvous, corner of Fifth and Pine, is kept busy recruiting. In a short time we shall have enough to bring the Union men or Black Republicans to our terms, or force them to leave the State. We have a Governor who is true blue. He is trying to get a bill through the Legislature that will bring them to terms. When we get, say, from four to five thousand minute-men, well armed, we shall be all ready for them. We pulled the wool over their eyes by making them think we only intended to stay in camp six days. We intend to stay here till the Governor gets all things right at Jefferson City. By that time we shall have all the men we want. We shall force them into measures to suit us or to leave the State. We are for the South.

"I have just received news that Captain Lyon intends to attack us to-morrow. We shall whip the damned United States forces. Our flag flies at the corner of Fifth and Pine, and we shall conquer, and expect hot work. We will make these Union men cry for quarters yet. Hurrah for the Southern Confederacy and Jeff. Davis, and damn Lincoln and the Stars and Stripes. . . . Will finish after the battle is won, and tell you how we have whipped them.

"G. W.

"P. S. I shall mail this on Saturday, when I can give you all the particulars of our glorious victory."

It were endless to enumerate the persecutions of loyal persons, and the outrages of secessionists, about the time of the capture of Camp Jackson. Volumes could easily be filled with the details.

At the village of Fenton, Mo., about eighteen miles west of St. Louis, where a week before a minister of the Methodist Episcopal Church was mobbed, the secessionists were assembled, May 12th, at the dedication of a new church of the Methodist Episcopal Church South. The neighboring secessionists did much in building the church. While assembled in the afternoon, two unarmed soldiers were seen coming along the road. Women shrieked, men trembled, and a general stampede of minister and congregation closed the services. "A guilty conscience needs no accuser." [2]

On the evening of May 13th, several families arrived in St. Louis from the towns of Tipton, California, Sedalia, and other places west of Jefferson City. A reign of terror existed in these regions. They were waited on and ordered to leave in twenty-four hours. Many of those who were unable to get away were compelled to join the rebel army. To declare for the Union was to put life in danger.

A great Southern "love-feast," so called, was to be held, May 16th, as we gather from the De Soto Herald, which headed the programme by "Flag Raising and State Rights' Meeting." The Union men of the county—Washington— having been threatened with extermination, and some of them driven from Potosi, the county seat, complained to Captain Lyon. Lyon sent Captain Cole and one hundred and fifty men, who seized the rebel flag, took several

[2] A somewhat similar but more fatal trepidation occurred to a Rev. Mr. Whaley, several years a presiding elder in the Methodist Episcopal Church South. At the commencement of the rebellion he espoused it, and went down into the Confederacy. As there was more protection and safety, however, for an unpolitical spiritual divine in Missouri, although under the Stars and Stripes, and Union military sway, than in the lawless, rebel wastes of Arkansas and Texas, after a time, he returned to South-West Missouri, the scene of his former labors. Some days after his arrival, while walking along the public road, not far from Neosho, he saw several mounted Federal soldiers in the distance, on the road, coming to meet him. He at once set out on a line at right angles with the road, toward a forest. As the soldiers drew near the point where he left the road, they observed him starting and running. This they took as evidence that he was a guilty rebel, flying some deserved judgment from the avengers of an outraged Government. They put their horses to their speed, and so came near enough to fire upon him just as he reached the foot of a hill thickly overgrown with trees and underbrush. Not earing to pursue the unknown man through these difficulties, they resumed their journey. At this time Union men were being robbed and shot daily by "bushwhackers," who sought their victims with the stealth and fierceness of panthers and these soldiers were their only defense. Their fire at the wood's edge had fatally wounded Mr. Whaley, and he only reached the hill-top, to die there, solitary and alone, the following night. He had taken sides with and become the aider and abettor of indiscriminate murderers, highway robbers, and assassins, and so naturally fulfilled the proverb: "The wicked flee when no man pursueth."— EDITOR.

prisoners, and thus broke up the rebel "love-feast" of the Southern Methodists.

We learn from the Quincy Whig of May 14th, that a reign of terror prevailed in Northern Missouri. Sixty families were driven from Macon City, in two weeks. Secret councils of the secessionists were being held over Missouri, and they were adopting Claib. Jackson's "armed neutrality." On the Hannibal and St. Joseph Railroad many were armed and ready to commit any depredations. `

The Governor's Camp at Jefferson City, was reënforced on the 16th of May, by some two hundred and twenty men from Warsaw and Pettis county. The Warsaw company bore the secession flag, and threatened to shoot down Union men.

Several suburban forts were erected around St. Louis, and three regiments were distributed at these posts, so as to protect the city from threatened occupancy by the rebels.

In South-East Missouri the secessionists were organized, and were parading and marching from county to county, bullying and browbeating Union men, especially Germans, and the members of the Methodist Episcopal Church.

On the 17th the United States troops, by warrant, seized the rebel armaments, deposited in the State Tobacco Warehouse, and the Police Head-Quarters. Large stores of warlike material were found and captured.

The foregoing are only a few of the many instances in which rebellion had organized its dark conspiracies. But on viewing the whole we were led to make the following declaration in our editorial columns, May 22, 1861:

"MISSOURI IS NOW ONE OF THE UNITED STATES, AND WILL REMAIN SO, AND WILL NEVER BECOME A MEMBER OF THE PRESENT REBELLIOUS SOUTHERN CONFEDERACY."

Such was then our firm conviction. On the 10th the rebel mob was dispersed, and though some lives were lost, the act of Captain Lyon was one of mercy, and saved thousands of lives. The Governor acted the traitor, was in combination with the Southern rebels. General Frost's camp was one of rebellion, and hoisting the United States flag was only a feint to shelter the hidden treason in the camp.

But the *coup' de main* of the noble Lyon was a saving act. The expression, "The sword of the Lord and of Gideon," may be applied to this timely act. Generations unborn will sing new and improved editions of "Yankee Doodle," and the "Star-Spangled Banner," "Down with the Traitors, and up with the Stars," etc.

Yet Lyon did not accomplish what he intended. His purpose was to proceed Friday night, May 10th, to Jefferson City, and seize as prisoners the rebel Governor and his disloyal Legislature. But as the secessionists had the control of the telegraph office in St. Louis, they sent a dispatch to the Governor, notifying him of his danger. To prevent his capture, he caused the bridge over the Osage river to be burned, and thus prevented the well-deserved capture of himself and his fellow-traitors.

7. In support of the good cause of the Union we wrote a brief editorial, May 15th, on this heading, "Missouri and the Stripes and Stars, one and inseparable." The purport of our remarks went to say:

There is an unchangeable partnership between Missouri, Illinois, Iowa, and Kansas, consisting of National highways that can not be maintained in any other way than under the flag of the Union. Should Missouri secede, the common river between Illinois and Missouri would be a scene of continual warfare. The mendacity of the Confederate Government would be no guarantee for peace.

The Missouri is the great National water course for Kansas, Nebraska, Colorado, and Dacotah on the west, and for Iowa and Minnesota east of it.

The Pacific Railroad, running through Missouri, from east to west, from the seaboard, must not cross a foreign country in its passage through Missouri.

And then the Lower Mississippi, from Cairo to the mouth, must not be in a foreign country.

Other considerations go to the same amount.

8. Rev. Z. S. Weller, pastor of the Methodist Episcopal Church in Jefferson City, under date of May 14, 1861, wrote for the Central Christian Advocate of May 22d, an account of the persecutions of the Methodist Episcopal Church in the region where he exercised his ministry.

The church building of the Methodist Episcopal Church had been attacked by a mob, made up principally of drunken rowdies and others of like sort, at the instigation of leading men of the Southern Methodist Church and other pro-slavery and disloyal persons. So manifest was it that the work was done by the Southern Methodist Church, or at their instigation, that Rev. Mr. Deitzler and others of that Church, to save appearances, promised to repair the damages on the church. This offer, however, was in pretense, as the subsequent history fully showed. Nothing was ever done by them to repair the church. From Mr. Weller we collect the following items, similar to many other occurrences in Missouri, in reference to the Methodist Episcopal Church.

Although boys and the rabble, says Mr. Weller, were engaged in injuring the church, the mischief was done principally by others who were leaders. The former charges were urged; that the Methodist Episcopal Church had no right to occupy Missouri; that her people were abolitionists, negro thieves, and the like; that they ought to be banished from Missouri, or deprived of all the rights of citizens till they left the country. Such were the events as stated by Mr. Weller, and which other testimonies fully confirm.

A reliable person writing from Jefferson City, May 19th, states that a few days previous two companies of Jackson's militia boasted that they had taken twenty or thirty guns from the Union men. For they went from house to house of Union men, and took from them their guns and pistols, and threatened to hang their owners if they said any thing about it, breaking up trunks and boxes searching for arms. And this was a common occurrence in the entire region about Jefferson City. A spoliation somewhat similar to this has been going on since 1849, with more or less publicity, for the legislative and executive powers since then have been on the side of rebellion. Company after company was organized, bearing the secession flag. No United States flags were there to be seen. One on the Osage bridge was hewn down by order of the Governor. More than one hundred human families were driven from Macon county in two weeks. Macon City was nearly depopulated, and many other parts of Northern Missouri were in like condition. And the members and ministers of the Methodist Episcopal Church were always the first to suffer. The *Northern Methodists*, as our people were called, under this mobocratic rule, were allowed only the right to be rapidly damned in such way as the caprice and passion of traitors dictated.

Rev. Isaac Martin, of the Methodist Episcopal Church, preacher on Shelbyville circuit, North Missouri, under date of May 20th, writes that he could no longer exercise his ministry on his circuit. He was warned to leave one township by a written notice left at his house, signed by forty persons. The document forbade his preaching and presence under penalty of being tarred and feathered, and then set on fire. He confined his services to Shelbyville alone, Union citizens there offering him protection. Many good Union men advised him for the time to desist from further services, which he did. By this persecution he was sorely embarrassed in the support of himself and family.

At St. Joseph, May 22d, the Stars and Stripes were hoisted over the post-office. The secessionists cut down the pole, tore the flag in pieces, threw the pole into the river, and raised the rebel flag in its stead. The American flag which was over Turner's Hall was taken down by the crowd of secessionists. Thus the State was rapidly passing from under the jurisdiction of the United States, under the truce of Harney and Price.

A company of about one hundred and thirty persons, composed of Union men, mostly members of the Methodist Episcopal Church, were driven out of Miller county. They left property worth $100,000, making their way to St. Louis as best they could through danger of assault or assassination, as the temper of the rebels might dictate.

At Fairmount, Clark county, North-East Missouri, Union men, in April and May, were greatly harassed with the view of banishing them from the State. They were compelled to lie in the woods and secluded places to preserve their lives. But as stated in a letter, dated May 21st, the Union men organized into military companies, received arms from the General Government, and by this means stood on the defensive.

The following from *E Pluribus Unum*, in the Methodist, is a just portrait of Methodism in Missouri at this time:

"The enemies of Methodism are more bold and confident than they have been for years. They did not hesitate to say that the time was near when Methodist preachers will have to leave. Intimations are given when their personal safety is endangered. The Methodist Episcopal Church is now passing through the fire, perhaps to come out more pure and bright than ever. I do not know half a dozen of men who are connected with the Methodist Episcopal

Church that are disunionists. We preach in favor of Union. We pray for it, and we talk for it, and defend it among the people. If Western Virginia is saved, she will owe her salvation more to Methodism, under God, than to any other agency. The enemies of the Government are the enemies of the Methodist Episcopal Church."

9. At this juncture.in the affairs of our Church in Missouri, in connection with State affairs, we were led in the Central Christian Advocate, of May 22d, to proclaim OUR DERNIER RESORT, seeing our Church and people were, beyond all others, made the objects of the special opposition and attacks of pro-slavery and disunion men.

In the preface to this declaration we stated that the Almighty, in fostering his gentle and long-suffering people, has appointed ways and means for their relief. To the civil magistrate he has given the sword to protect the innocent. To his witnessing people he has furnished his providential care.

The Methodist Episcopal Church was the first to propagate Christianity in Missouri. When the great secession took place in 1845, only a small remnant of witnesses was left. The great body of our Church was seduced from the maternal fold by pro-slavery politicians, to the great injury of religion and the scandal of Methodism. The pro-slavery party in Missouri, especially Southern Methodists, used many ways of annoyance, in view of driving our people out of Missouri, as they had successfully done in Texas and Arkansas. These persecutions amounted to murders, assault and battery, expatriations, insults, and the denial of equal rights before the legislature, the judiciary, and the executive of the State, and, the last four years especially, even before the United States marshals, and other Government officials. Recently, these embarrassments were increased. In the absence of any declaration of any ecclesiastical body

23

in our Church, we uttered our protest against these invasions of our Federal and State rights. And we now quote verbatim what we penned May 21, 1861, to meet the exigency of our position and that of our people:

" We PROTEST, as a substitute for our rights, the offer of the members of the Methodist Episcopal Church South, in Jefferson City, to pay for the injury done to our church edifice. If this assault has been made by their influence, as seems probable, then we throw back with just indignation the judaic price of the cruel wrong. Or if this proffer has been made in view of sustaining our rights, we reject it as inadequate, while our legal rights as citizens of Missouri and of the United States, are withheld and even trampled on. The crisis is now come, and we want to meet it fearlessly. We spurn these aids, whether well or insidiously meant, as the price of our natural and legal rights.

" We further *protest*, as an equivalent or substitute for our just rights, the proffered aid of General S. Price, in any other form than our just rights as citizens. It will be too late to furnish redress to save life after the murderer has done his work, or the wrong be such that no redress is possible from the nature of the injuries inflicted. Wooden arms and legs are poor substitutes for the natural members.

" *First.* We APPEAL to the constituted authorities of the State of Missouri for redress of grievances. We appeal to the *legislative* power to give us the same benefit of legislation as that given to other citizens of the State. We appeal to the *judiciary* of Missouri, that we may have the privilege of the true interpretation of law, and the accordance of our rights. We appeal to the *executive* powers of the State, and the corporate officers of towns and cities for protection in our own persons, property, right of worship, and their connected rights. And as these have been denied us,

"*Secondly.* We APPEAL to the Government of the United States to sustain us in the enjoyment of our lawful rights as citizens of the United States, and of Missouri. We ask, instead of being assailed and maltreated, a regular process of law and trial before we are condemned and punished by mob law. And if the common civil tribunals continue to assail us, so that we can not have the benefit of a civil process, we ask for the protection of martial law, till we shall have the privilege of enjoying the free exercise of our rights by the civil power of the country.

"*Thirdly.* We appeal, for the justice of our cause, to our loyal fellow-citizens of the United States. We ask them, is it not hazardous to the stability of our civil institutions to allow the law to be frustrated, and the rights of the American Magna Charter to be violated, and thus to encourage mobs and misrule of all sorts?

"*Fourthly.* Should we fail in the foregoing process, for the recovery of the rights of the Methodist Episcopal Church in Missouri, we leave our cause in the hands of Almighty God, beseeching him to grant to our persecutors better dispositions of heart, and to our suffering brethren grace to bear whatever, in his all-wise providence, he sees fit to permit."

10. In the course of the month of May, the religious services of our Church in Missouri were quite suspended, outside of St. Louis. Most of our preachers were either compelled to leave the State or to confine themselves to one single place. Their members were in a like condition. Mr. Weller was compelled to flee to St. Louis to save his life. His wife and children were at Jefferson City, in terror of death, and she could not, with safety, get away to join her husband in St. Louis. This was the state of things, May 24th.

The Spring and Summer of 1861 was truly a reign of

terror in Missouri. In St. Louis, every one was armed, and slept with fire-arms within reach. Our office was also our bedroom. Mr. S. M. Kennedy, now a book publisher, and editor of the elegant "Chicago Home Circle," who slept with us, had his revolver within reach every night. Another who slept in an adjoining room, was armed in like manner. We slept in the third story, and these two were ready to defend the passage, should an assault be made. We, on our part, did not feel the necessity of being armed at all. We slept soundly, and never lost any rest in consequence of the surrounding alarms.

After the capture of Camp Jackson, perhaps one-fourth of the population left St. Louis for a time.

11. At this critical juncture, May 17th, Bishop Morris wrote an admirable letter for the Central Christian Advocate, to encourage consistent loyalty. We here give it to our readers. It appeared in the Central Christian Advocate of May 29th:

"OBEDIENCE TO LAW.—Law is a rule of action prescribed by the supreme authority of a State or Nation, and obedience is compliance with its requirements. The importance of these is apparent to all. Without them all is anarchy. Might claims to be right, brute force holds dominion, and mob violence pours its desolating flood over the land. Without wholesome law, properly enforced, we have no security that our domestic, social, civil, or religious liberties will be safe for one day or hour. Any law, even martial law, is preferable to anarchy. It would be better to live in a conquered province, where law is respected, than to live under the best theoretical form of government, in name only, where insubordination is openly avowed, and mob violence prevails.

"Any combination or association of men—call it a vigilance committee, or what you please—to supersede the law, and take the administration into their own hands, is a mob, an irresponsible, lawless mob, and the peace and safety of the country depend on a successful resistance to all such.

"All party strife about republicanism and democracy, about abolition and pro-slaveryism, etc., should be suspended. The question before the American is, Government or no Government? It has but two sides, and we can employ but two parties. Let all the friends of God and their country take the affirmative side of the question, and the rest may take the negative side or no side at all, as they like. He that is not for us is against us. There is no middle ground. Every friend to his country can render her some aid. Some can take the field, and others can contribute toward defraying the expenses, and they who can neither fight nor give, can pray.

"'God is the judge: he putteth down one, and setteth up another.' Ps. lxxv, 7. This he does by his providential interference with the affairs of men for his own glory and their good. The Supreme Ruler of the universe has much to do with the government of nations. Paul says: 'Let every soul be subject unto the higher powers. For there is no power but of God: the powers that be are ordained of God. Whosoever, therefore, resisteth the power, resisteth the ordinance of God: and they that resist shall receive to themselves damnation.' Rom. xiii, 1, 2.

"This testimony of an inspired apostle fully sustains the propositions: that God is the primary source of civil authority; that he ordains civil government; that he requires all men to obey it; that resistance to lawful authority is rebellion, not only against the Government, but against God who ordains it, and that he will hold the rebels to a fearful account.

"To deny either of these propositions is virtually to deny the truth of God's Word. It may be asked, is there any exception to the rule, 'Let every soul be subject unto the higher powers?' I answer, yes. When a government becomes so corrupt as to deprive its citizens of their natural and acquired rights, in an unconstitutional and reckless way, the Government may be changed, by constitutional means, if practicable, or by force, if necessary.

"But this exception is not applicable to the case now pending. No attempt is or has been made by the Federal Government to deprive the secessionists of any rights secured to them by the Constitution of the United States. On the contrary, the favors of the Government have been lavished upon them in undue proportion. Secession, therefore, is rebellion, without any plausible excuse, and will result in the destruction of its authors and leaders, and many of those engaged in it. One thing is cause of deep regret, that is, many innocent persons will suffer with the guilty. This is unavoidable, from their involuntary relation to the revolutionary movement. As for us who adhere to the Union, we have little to fear, and can say with David, 'Though a host should encamp against me, my heart shall not fear; though war should rise up against me, in this I will be confident.' Ps. xxvii, 8. It remains for Christians to watch, pray, and trust in God to save the country, and calmly wait for the result. May all end well!

"T. A. MORRIS.

"SPRINGFIELD, OHIO, *May* 17, 1861."

12. At this time, in behalf of the good cause in which we were engaged, especially in support of the glorious Stars and Stripes, we deemed it proper to mention some encouragements we met, in the trying circumstances in which we were placed. More particularly did we value the judgment of our Bishops, who are men of large experience, and in the exercise of their functions, are schooled to habits of impartiality, as no other class of men in the Church. In

some incidental communications, on Church matters, from our Bishops, they felt free to express themselves in a private way, as to the Central Christian Advocate, and other matters.

Bishop Morris is noted for his sober judgment and safe opinions on all points within the sphere of his observations. He has never, in our opinion, given an unwise or even doubtful decision. And then his pure English style is so correct that it can not be misunderstood, nor can a single word be added, diminished, or changed in his writing. In a detached note accompanying his admirable and timely article on obedience to law, he says:

"If my scrap will help you, print it; if not, burn it. The concentration of our troops at all exposed points, from Kansas to the Atlantic, along our border, and the blockading of Southern ports, are exerting a great influence. The rebels are confused and fear defeat. I trust God is on our side, and if he is we are safe. The Central is at the right place for us in this crisis. Long may it flourish! Yours as ever and forever."

Bishop Ames, as most are aware, is a man of statesman-like views, has never been a partisan in politics, nor a candidate for office. Had he been he would have long since been a United States Senator. But he held to his ministerial work, and God has greatly blessed him in it. On the fifth of May, the Bishop, having occasion to write to us, speaks as follows:

"I thank God that you are doing so nobly with the Central. May you continue to prosper more and more in your noble work for God and humanity! Madness rules the hour in the South; but God, I am persuaded, will bring great good out of all these great commotions. I have more hope for our country now than I have had at any time for ten years past."

We have received similar encouraging words from Bishops Janes, Scott, and Baker. From many other sources, too, we were cheered, in our most trying circumstances.

At the time Camp Jackson was taken, it was under consideration by the Agents to send the Sunday school books at St. Louis to Cincinnati or Chicago. On reflection this was not done, as it would seem to be a sign of giving up the South-West. It was also considered, whether the Central Christian Advocate should not be published in Illinois, should our office in St. Louis be torn down—a catastrophe which some feared. But the storm passed away, and the Central Christian Advocate still lives, although five religious papers in St. Louis perished under the pressure of the times.

CHAPTER XIII.

EVENTS IN JUNE, 1861.

1. THE case of Rev. S. Ing deserves notice here. In January, 1861, while traveling the Rolla circuit, he visited Salem to attend a quarterly meeting in the place of the presiding elder, Rev. R. R. Witten being preacher in charge. A band of slaveholders warned him to leave, under the general charge of his meddling with slaves; if he disobeyed their demand he was to be "black-jacked," tarred, hung, or something of the sort. On Sabbath they came forward in the congregation and read a paper, with the heading, "State of Missouri, County of Dent, January 18, 1861. To Rev. Ing, minister of the Gospel in the Methodist Episcopal Church. Respected Sir, etc." This document asked several questions about slavery. Mr. Ing made a reply, which decided the question for the time, and covered the interrogators with confusion.[1]

A private letter, sent to Illinois, stated that Mr. Ing had been hung by a mob. To this he replies, May 16, 1861, that he is still alive, but threatened every day with mob violence. He was waited on by two men, who commanded him to stop preaching at one of his appointments, swearing they would violently interfere. Two Southern Methodist preachers assisted in raising the excitement as high as possible. These sectional divines have almost invariably instigated and aided the persecutions we have had to suffer in Missouri. Without them and their influence there would

[1] Central Christian Advocate, February 20, 1861.

have been little of it. In a controversy with Mr. Ing, one of these preachers said we ought to be "driven out," "scouted out," "kicked out of the country." He then had the rabble standing around him. Mr. Ing then said, "I am sorry to see our preachers leaving the State. If they can not continue to preach, the most of them could stay in the State till the difficulty is over, and then resume their work; for by the grace of God we will hold on to Missouri. Let us preach as long as we can, and then if we must be stopped, let us fight in the defense of our rights, and fight in the same way we preached, and the God of battles will help us."

Such was the heroic counsel Mr. Ing gave the other preachers. He also followed out in practice the purpose he expressed; for he continued to preach till no congregations could assemble in any safety for the uprising of the secessionists. He evaded his pursuers, and when no other way was left, joined the Union army, and was commissioned to raise a company of cavalry. This he did among the mixed population of rebels and loyalists. Chosen to the Captaincy, as a courageous soldier, he led his company through many perilous scenes; and when the condition of the State allowed it, he went to his former work of preaching, praying, and exhorting, his piety being much replenished while he served his country as a good soldier and performed gratuitous services as chaplain.

When the commander had learned the true character of Mr. Ing, he gave him in charge a sufficient number of men to range the country. They brought several secessionists to camp, and a number of horses and mules. Mr. Ing showed his company three several places where gallows had been erected for hanging himself. Although waylaid and pursued, he eluded his pursuers, who mostly thought it the better part of valor to avoid coming in contact with a man fully armed for his defense, with revolvers and other weapons necessary to meet the assaults of sworn assassins.

Rev. Mr. Wood, whose circuit was in the same region, made out to take his family to Illinois. He then returned to join the cavalry company of the heroic Ing, in support of the Stripes and Stars. With these two men there was no need of any other chaplain in the command.

2. The persecution that followed Bewley, and put him to death, seemed still abroad in Texas at this time, driving Union men from the country. Most of the members of our Church had been driven out before this. While they were especially obnoxious to slaveholders, much the same spirit was manifest toward other Unionists. Rev. J. H. Hawley, from Kansas, May 13, 1861,[2] wrote us as follows:

"For the last four weeks the roads leading into Kansas, by the way of Fort Scott, from Arkansas and Texas, have been literally lined with emigrants, with their families and large herds of cattle. They look well, but the emigrants tell a sad tale. 'Truth is turned away backward, and justice is fallen in the streets.' Liberty of conscience is entirely out of the question. To be a Free-State man is crime enough for the halter or gibbet. A Baptist preacher (missionary) had resided eight years in Austin, Texas, where he, under God, had built up a good Church, and they were all obliged to leave and abandon their property, if they could not rent or sell it, and that was out of the question. He left a farm there that he could not sell. Many of these emigrants stop with us, others pass still further North."

3. Rev. A. J. Gaither, of Mt. Vernon circuit, comprising parts of Lawrence, Barry, Stone, Taney, and Christian counties, South-West Missouri, June 5th, writes that a large majority of preachers and people of the Southern

[2] Central Christian Advocate, June 5th.

Methodist Church were for secession; while some of their best members and one of their preachers were loyal, some of whom were expelled from the Church on that account.

In a letter from Rev. R. R. Witten, dated Kansas, June 20, 1861, we learn the following: His appointment was Salem circuit, near Rolla. He went to Rolla to see brother ' Sellers, who, on the previous morning, set out for Kansas, seeing his life was in danger and his way to success in preaching hedged up. Mr. Witten was immediately notified by the secessionists to leave, under peril of attack. While the mob was hunting for him, he made out to get his horse, and proceeded to Rev. N. Shumate's, about three o'clock, A. M., a distance of eight miles. When he returned to his circuit he found several of his members and others had been warned to leave the country. Father Cook, a member of the Church, about seventy years of age, had been pelted with stones, badly hurt, and ordered to leave the country within a few days. Dr. Archer, a local preacher, was ordered to leave immediately. An organized mob was in readiness at every appointment to assail the preacher. On consulting his people, Mr. Witten and they concluded that religious meetings could no longer be held. Hence, on Friday, May 17th, in a two-horse wagon, he and his wife set out for Kansas. On reaching the eastern part of Cedar county he found the secession element very strong; but getting into a Union neighborhood he stopped a few days. Here the Southern Methodist members were Union men. While prosecuting his journey, he was at one place pursued by rebels, but as he missed his contemplated road, his pursuers missed him, and thus, by the good providence of God, he escaped and arrived at his destination in safety.

Rev. J. W. Prince, on Kirksville circuit, June 10th, writes, that in Kirksville there were three secession preachers, belonging respectively to the Presbyterian, Baptist, and Southern Methodist Churches. They exerted their influence for the Southern Confederacy. The Southern Methodist preacher used his influence especially against the Methodist Episcopal Church. Mr. Prince was met by mobs at his appointments, but, as it were by an overruling Providence awing them, they did not violently attack him, though collected for that purpose. His people were too poor and few to support him, under these untoward circumstances, the small amount of missionary money did not reach him, so that he suffered much pecuniary embarrassment.

4. The outbreaking of the rebellion received great encouragement from the ministry and press of the Methodist Episcopal Church South in Missouri. Of this there are more proofs than we have room to notice. But we will abbreviate as much as possible.

The Missouri State Journal, a secession paper edited by Mr. Tucker, worked hard to destroy the Constitution of Missouri, and to place the State under a foreign jurisdiction, on the platform of South Carolina. Mr. Tucker was from South Carolina, and a zealous Southern Methodist in St. Louis. He was the familiar friend of Dr. M'Anally, and the leading Southern Methodists of St. Louis. In his day he advertised runaway negroes, using the common cuts for that purpose, those of negroes and negresses running with their bundles in hand or on their shoulders. This man Tucker was very zealous in the Southern Methodist Churches in St. Louis, and labored with great earnestness in the rebel cause, till his rebel sheet was suppressed as an incendiary paper.

From Fayette, Missouri, June 5, 1861, Rev. Andrew Monroe addresses the members and ministers of the St. Louis Conference of the Methodist Episcopal Church South, urging July 3d as a day of fasting and prayer, that all might deplore National sins, and pray for peace. In this he is joined by the signatures of the leading preachers of St. Louis; namely, Messrs. Boyle, Marvin, Watts, and Pinkard.

Mr. Monroe, May 28th, writes a general letter to his brethren, made up of generalities, and yet sufficiently plain to show he was identified with the rebels. He says:

"Then my earnest advice to all our preachers and editors is, to maintain STRICT NEUTRALITY in regard to the partisan strife of the country." June 5th Mr. Monroe writes another letter of generalities. Indeed, the style of these two circulars, and the call for a day of fasting and prayer, is that of the non-committal secessionists, who used this language to keep up appearances, while their entire influence was for the rebellion.

The editor of the St. Louis Christian Advocate, June 27th, has a long article on "News of the Week," in which by evasive declarations he indorses the rebels, although, in passing, he disavows the very thing he indirectly and covertly maintains. We cull the following paragraph from the article:

"No one can charge that the civil law was powerless in Missouri, or that its officers were derelict in their duties, and yet military occupation and military rule have been resorted to."

Again:

"Mark it and remember it. If the downward tendency which has distinguished the history of political affairs of this country during the last two months shall pass by, no earthly power can save the Northern portion of this country from wildest anarchy or direst despotism. One or the other is sure to result from the present state and tendency of things as that any consequent follows its antecedent. Mark that!"

We also find the following in the same article, with reference to those who call his sheet a secession paper :

"As some of you well know, he [the editor] has not said one word in favor of the secession of Missouri; nor has he said one word against it."

He further on adds:

"We soberly advise you to one of two courses; either stop your pious whining and groaning, and leave off your affectation of sanctity, or else quit your lying and slander. You know you have no right to call this a secession paper, and whether the editor is a secessionist or Unionist is more than you can tell from any thing he has ever published in the paper."

A few selections from the St. Louis Christian Advocate will show the animus of its editor toward the Methodist Episcopal Church :

"To carry on the operations of the Church North in slave territory is next to impossible. And now mark the following particulars: 1. There is no abatement of the abolition feeling in the Church North, nor is there likely to be any. 2. Men laboring in slave States, in connection with the Church whose organs these papers are, must be more or less liable to the charge of abolitionism. The public mind will look upon them in their relations, and form, to some extent, its judgment of them by the company they keep." [3]

"Notwithstanding such repeated declarations from a number of these missionaries, that they were not abolitionists, and were not interfering with the institutions of the country, still the opinion seems to prevail that these devoted, *self-sacrificing* missionaries are laboring with might and main to pull down the strongholds of slavery, and give freedom to all the race." [4]

[3] St. Louis Christian Advocate, August 12, 1852.   [4] Idem, March 1, 1855.

Speaking of the mobbing of our preachers, the editor says:

"Deeds of violence, which mistaken, misguided, and imprudent men have brought upon themselves." [5]

"They are unwilling to have their preachers in slave territory unless they will array themselves in open hostility to the institution of slavery. . . . Array themselves against the laws of the land. Stir up strife." [6]

"They were organized in direct violation of a solemn agreement. . . . And where the North covenanted they should never be. . . . They certainly can not expect a large share of the confidence or respect of honorable men, and when that direct legislation comes upon them, they will pass away unwept and unsung. Let them go."

"Honorable, God-fearing men keep covenants, dishonorable men break them. . . . They can never do much good here." [7]

Quotations from the St. Louis Christian Advocate could be given in a continuous chain to the present time—October, 1864—the purport of which would be the same thing that Bishop Pierce uttered in 1860, namely, that the Methodist Episcopal Church ought not to be tolerated in slave territory.

The neutrality of Dr. M'Anally and Rev. Andrew Monroe is identical with the most outspoken treason of the Southern Methodist press. The St. Louis Christian Advocate has the imprimatur of the Charleston, Richmond, Nashville, and Texas Christian Advocates.

Bishop Andrew writes, at this time, in the Southern Christian Advocate, as follows:

"The women of the South, during the Revolution, were proverbial for their patriotic devotion to their country's

---

[5] St. Louis Christian Advocate, August 28, 1856.
[6] Idem, June 7, 1855.   [7] Idem, January 14, 1848.

weal. I am perfectly satisfied that their daughters have inherited, in full measure, the same spirit. Our people intend to fight to the death for their homes and their altars, and even should it so turn out that Lincoln's Government should succeed in 'crushing' or 'whipping out' the South— which seem to be the pet phrases now so freely used by our enemies in reference to us—it will have been a costly struggle, and their victory will ruin them. But I have little fear of their success. 1. Because our cause is righteous. 2. The people of the South—thanks to Lincoln's folly and perfidy— are now very nearly a unit. 3. We are fighting *at* home and *for* home. We ask only to be permitted to govern ourselves. We wish to relieve our late associates from all participation in the sin which has so sorely troubled their conscience. 4. We have soldiers enough—an army made up of the very best material, and commanded by officers second to none on earth ; and, *finally, and above all*, we look up for God's direction and blessing. Thousands of our soldiers are Christian men, who are not ashamed to confess Christ in the camps, and every day thousands of prayers go up to God, invoking his presence and aid. In many of our churches, prayer meetings are being constantly held in behalf of the country, and our sons, and husbands, and brothers on the tented fields—and will not God hear and answer?"

The Nashville Christian Advocate, early in June, in answer to loyal letters from Kentucky, remonstrating against its secession character, says :

"We are for the Confederate States and their success in this war. Call you that secession? By that or any other name you like—disunion, rebellion, revolution. But you have all along been holding that our pulpits and presses should not interfere in politics. We hold that yet, and are consistent. Neutrality in politics is one thing; neutrality in war is another, and very different."

24

"That the people of Tennessee, on the 8th of June, at the ballot-box, unite as one man, and give their unanimous indorsement to the action of our Legislature, declaring our noble State independent, forever, of the United States Government, now in the hands of abolitionists, and usurpers, who have subverted the very principles of liberty for which our fathers fought. And we recommend further, that in view of every consideration of present protection and of future interest and honor, the people of Tennessee vote unanimously, on the 8th of June, to ratify the action of our Legislature, cut loose from the North forever, and adopt the Constitution of the Confederate States." [*]

This is the *neutrality* that prevailed in the Church South, and varies little, if any, from the spirit which underlies the ambiguous mutterings of Mr. Monroe and Dr. M'Anally, and is but the counterpart of Bishop Andrew's hostility to the Union.

5. We devote this paragraph to the case of Rev. J. E. Gardner, a very worthy preacher of the Missouri Conference of the Methodist Episcopal Church, and on Utica circuit, Livingston county, Mo., during the occurrence of the events here noted. In 1860 he had been the object of various threats from the secessionists, especially from some of the Southern Methodists. A committee of three called at Mr. Gardner's house, informing him that he was charged with being an abolitionist, and with tampering with negroes. After considerable parleying, by the committee, he received the following notice:

"UTICA, Mo., *December* 20, 1860.

"MR. GARDNER—*Sir:* At a meeting of the citizens of Livingston county, Mo., it was unanimously resolved, that notice be given you that your longer residence in our county is not desired by our citizens, and that you be required to

---

[*] Central Christian Advocate, June 20, 1861.

leave this county within three days from this date." Signed
by Charles Cooper, and thirty-seven other names. Of these
four at least were members of the Methodist Episcopal
Church South.

After considerable interchange of sentiments, it was
thought best not to exact immediate obedience to their demand. But, January 3, 1861, while Mr. and Mrs. Gardner
were busy with their domestic concerns, a friend came and
informed them that the mob was collecting. They soon
came to the house, armed with rifles, shot-guns, revolvers,
and knives. Mr. Gardner hastened to the house, bolted the
door, and stood in a position to defend himself. Some
cried, "Burst in the door," others vociferated, "Break in
the windows." One Cooper gave Mr. Gardner ten minutes,
by his watch, to decide to leave the county within twenty-
four hours, or to have the house burned over his head, and
he ordered a bunch of hay to be brought for kindling the
fire. However, as the mob could not agree among themselves, the fulfillment of the threat was not then put into
execution.

In the afternoon Mr. Gardner had occasion to go to
Utica, to adjust his affairs, as he purposed leaving as soon
as possible, under the instruction of the Savior, "When
they persecute you in one city, flee to another." As he
was conversing in a store, one Austin, a Southern Methodist, slipped out and informed the mob where he was. Before he was aware of it, he was surrounded by the mob,
insulted and abused, and preparations were made to take
him. Mr. Gardner, seeing no chance to defend himself,
went out of the store through the back way. He was there
immediately surrounded by the rabble, who came upon him
with drawn revolvers. He was immediately seized, a "Lincoln rail" was ordered, upon which they violently forced
him, and proceeded to ride him on the rail. They shrieked

like fiends, and shouted tumultuously, "Northern preacher," "Lincolnite," "Nigger thief;" while some were clamorous for tar and feathers, others shouted for a rope.

Mr. Gardner, as they carried him along, commenced exhorting them to flee the wrath to come, and preached Christ to them. Afterward he sung, with animation:

"Children of the Heavenly King,
As we journey let us sing," etc.

Some tried to mock. One Schafer swore "he would make him shut his mouth," at the same time striking him with a large piece of ice on the shoulder-blade, crippling him for the time being. They then called a halt, and let Mr. Gardner down, to consider what further measures they would take.

About this time Mrs. Gardner left her sick daughter Allie with a lady friend, and made her way, through snow eight inches deep, into town, in order to do what she could to relieve her husband. She walked boldly into their midst, through horrid oaths and threats, and demanded the deliverance of her husband, informing them that she would have him released or die with him. Through the interposition of two men, John Harper and William Wells, he was permitted to go home, accompanied by them. They advised him to leave as soon as possible, as it would be unsafe for him to stay. Mr. Gardner giving assurance to these gentlemen, to carry to the rabble, that he would go away, he was left unmolested for the night. Friday, January 4th, Mr. Gardner and family left Utica and went to the country.

Mr. Gardner afterward commenced a suit, in Chillicothe, against the leaders of this gang of outlaws, but a mob was collected, and compelled Squire Hughes, before whom the case was to be tried, to burn the papers. Thus there was no law, in Utica or Chillicothe, to protect persons belonging to the Methodist Episcopal Church.

Dr. M'Anally, in his paper of April, called in question

the facts narrated in this case, and some three anonymous writers in his columns joined in the denunciation of Mr. Gardner. These anonymous letters, in themselves, showed they were truly apocryphal, and the editor of the St. Louis Christian Advocate declined giving the names of the authors, although he published their misrepresentations. Mrs. Gardner, in her reply to Mr. M'Anally, showed that these barbarities would not have been perpetrated "had it not been for Rev. J. Austin, of the Church South, who came to Utica and taunted the rabble, and spared no argument to provoke them to madness, all of which the reverend gentleman did not pretend to deny when called upon in the presence of witnesses." [9]

6. Paul, writing to the Galatians, exclaimed, "O, foolish Galatians, who hath bewitched you?" Gal. iii, 1. He then asks: "Are ye so foolish? Having begun in the Spirit are ye now made perfect by the flesh?" The Greek word $Βασκαίνω$, rendered *bewitched*, occurs only in this place in the New Testament. Greenfield defines it *to deceive by magic arts, bewitch with the eye, fascinate, mislead by delusive pretenses.* It may mean to *deceive* or *mislead* by any means or in any way.

The word *foolish*, $ἀνόητοι$, means a want of intellectual culture or exercise. See Luke xxiv, 25; Romans i, 14; 1 Tim. vi, 9; Titus iii, 3.

"A little leaven leaveneth the whole lump." Gal. v, 9.

---

[9] Thus, in a controversy between our preachers and a vicious, infuriated, persecuting mob, we always know where to find these unpolitical apostles of a pseudo-Methodism. Invariably their divine visages shine out from the midst of those who shriek and howl, and carry the tar, the ropes, bludgeons, bowie-knives, revolvers, and other like civilizing implements; and any of this spiritual fraternity who find it inconvenient to be present on these gala days take pleasure in their studios in either, 1. Indorsing and approving the mob; or, 2. Showing the just provocations of the mobocrats, bringing forward circumstances palliative of their outrages, and, with pastoral affection, apologizing for the playful didos of their herds; or, 3. They flatly deny the statements made by the persecuted or their friends as to the shameful abuses suffered.—EDITOR.

With the Galatians there was a gradual work of deteri-
oration. It began small, proceeded gradually and imper-
ceptibly, but the final effect was a total infection of the
man. The Galatians, beginning in the Spirit, ended in the
flesh.

So it was with the Southern States and Churches. Beginning in liberty, professedly, they ended in oppression.
The civil power led the way, and the Southern Churches followed. The State commanded, the Churches obeyed. Politicians said, "You must not meddle with politics." The
ministers agreed to it. This non-interference with politics
meant simply a cessation from discussing the moral phases
of civil or public affairs. Applied to "the peculiar institution" of the South it meant the abandonment of at least
three of God's commandments, as "Thou shalt not steal,"
"Thou shalt not commit adultery," "Honor thy father and
thy mother," etc. Slavery steals from the slave his liberty,
his self-control, *the use of himself*. No true marriage can
exist among the 4,000,000 American slaves. But the
Churches in the South were *voluntarily silent* on these
great sins; Church and State united in the monstrous immorality. Death to the individual was the Bible penalty
for man-stealing. Political and ecclesiastical death smote
the State and the Church for the same crime. Hence a
terrible scourge, if not, indeed, the destruction of Southern
political and ecclesiastical corporations, is now pending,
while we write, October, 1864.

7. The Missouri State Journal, edited by a Southern
Methodist local preacher, a native of South Carolina, by
the name of Tucker, pleaded the cause of the rebels with
much zeal. Among a thousand other falsehoods he says:

" Observe, a war of extermination is waged against sovereign States, for no other reason than that they have
chosen, for solemn cause, to exercise that original right

of self-government—the right to modify, change, or abolish their form of government at pleasure."

This deluded man seems to have gone so far in vice as to have lost from his being the sense or test of it, and so believed he was right. The evil leaven of error had so leavened his intellect, moral feelings, and passions, that he seemed already past cure. We account for his condition on a principle in the philosophy of mind, which explains the nature of disordered intellectual, pathematic, and moral operations. John Brown was similarly affected, but on the opposite side of the question, which shattered Mr. Tucker. In New England, at one time, they put "witches" to death. Devout Catholics tortured the lives out of Protestants as a religious duty. In the South, Calhoun's political mania ruled the hour, and drove Southern Methodists, and most other Churches, into similar mental aberrations and moral obliquities.

This Joseph W. Tucker went so far in instigating and defending rebellion that, on the 14th of June, he was arrested by Deputy United States Marshal Tunnecliff, upon warrant of United States Commissioner Hickman, issued on the affidavit of John D. Stevenson, for treasonably giving aid and comfort to the enemy by writing and publishing articles in their interest, and hostile to the American Government. He gave $10,000 bail to answer before the proper court. His friends, however, fell into spasms of grief and rage because he could not be at liberty to use all his powers openly for the destruction of that benign Government which protected his graceless neck, had from his birth sheltered him with its certain safeguards, and blessed him with its liberal citizenship and social immunities.

CHAPTER XIV.

JULY TO OCTOBER, 1861.

1. AFTER the 6th of November, 1860, persecution was renewed against our ministry and people. Surveying the various districts in the Missouri Conference, we saw multiplied desolations made in our spiritual field by unjust invasions of our rights as citizens of the United States and of Missouri.

The St. Louis district may first be noticed. There was no molestation in St. Louis. Some of our people, however, left in anticipation of disturbance. Others were out of employ, and in consequence of the rebellion could scarcely support themselves. But in other portions of the St. Louis district our religious services were for the most part suspended. The presiding elder, Rev. Samuel Huffman, in this exigency, took a chaplaincy in the Sixth Regiment of Missouri volunteers, under Colonel Bland, and was of great service in the army, in the south-eastern part of the State, a region included in his district.

On De Soto circuit, Rev. F. S. Beggs, for three months prévious to this time—July, 1861—was prevented from holding meetings, except occasionally at De Soto.

Rev. J. Linan was driven from Jackson circuit, with the necessity of leaving his family there alone for several months. He returned only when under the protection of United States troops, but even then he could hold no meetings.

Rev. J. E. Baker was driven away from Fredericktown circuit. Rev. W. A. Pile, who was stationed at the Boatman's chapel, entered the army as chaplain, and continued to do eminent service, rose on his own merits to the grade of General, and now heads Missouri's Congressmen.

On Jefferson City district religious services were almost entirely discontinued. The presiding elder, Rev. N. Shumate, was pursued and often waylaid, but by great skill, energy, and bravery escaped with his life. A survey of his case is given elsewhere.

In short, at this time, religious services could be kept up in our Church in very few places. The details can scarcely be given in our limited pages.[1]

Under date of July 10, 1861, in detailing these persecutions, we penned the following paragraphs, which we now—December 21, 1864—reproduce:

"Let our friends write to us, and let us know how our affairs in Missouri are. The experience of the past has taught the persecutors that the plan of killing people is neither safe to themselves nor reputable to their cause. Hence, as cowards and unprincipled men, they have had recourse to the dastardly mode of rail-riding, warning to leave and the like, and threats of death. If this does not intimidate men it does women and children, and many have left Missouri to preserve the peace of their families. We advise our friends in Missouri to join and get arms from the United States authorities, or procure them as best they can. Our brethren who have done this have been able to keep their ground. We instance the case of brothers Shumate, Lee, and Huffman, who have armed themselves; and we hope, while they pray and preach they will keep their powder dry. Let them carry their arms with them, if need be, to their appointments, and use them when necessary.

[1] See Central Christian Advocate, July 10, 1861.

If the United States are too slow, let them go on the score of self-defense, the first law of nature, and therefore the first law of God. We hope our refugee Union men, preachers as well as others, who have left the State will return and occupy their former positions. Let each bring with him a revolver and double-barreled rifle, practice well loading and shooting, and stand up for his rights. As there is just now no civil protection before the courts in Missouri, or as it is evaded by mob-law, our own right hands must meet the mobs. Let all be done without malice or revenge. Let the protection of our persons, our wives, children, and the weak be our solemn purpose and work; and if the self-protecting act involves the death of a murderous assaulter, let the example of our civil judges, where law is in exercise, be our guide. While he pronounces the sentence of death, he utters the prayer, MAY GOD HAVE MERCY ON YOUR SOUL! Go and do likewise!"

2. The disloyal press of Missouri, in July, was very persistent in favor of the rising Confederacy.

The Missouri Republican occupied both sides as usual, but fully prepared, as a matter of choice, to be the avowed pleader for the rebels whenever any prospect of success for their cause might appear.

The St. Louis Christian Advocate followed the dicta of the South Carolina political school, which was founded on an ideal military despotism. In its columns the Southern rebels are praised without stint. When the United States Government passes its editorial telescope, all is disorder, confusion, and tending to certain ruin. Great defeats are observed to have just taken place, or discerned as about to happen.

He played into the hand of the editor of the Missouri State Journal, with whom he was manifestly, though covertly, a confederate, in political and religious works and affinities, both being members of the Southern Methodist Church.

In his selections, Dr. M'Anally was quite ready to report Governor Jackson's proclamation, the pretended official acts of the Southern Confederacy, and oftentimes, without self-committal to any thing, by his clippings taught that rebellion was for liberty instead of despotism, for right instead of wrong.

There could be detected in the editorials of the St. Louis Christian Advocate various indications of intellectual bewitchment, a thing more common in the world than many suppose. This bewitchment or deceptive influence may be found in most if not all sects of religion, in all the schools of philosophy, whether of mind or matter, and runs through the adherents of the various political systems. Such anomalies as yet exist in connection with religion, politics, and philosophy. They only who follow after truth and right, under Divine guidance, will escape the errors to which we here refer.

The Missouri State Journal at this time vapored away, throwing nonsense, sense, religion, secession, and rebellion into a ludicrous conglomerate. 'Mr. J. W. Tucker, the editor, was noticed in a previous page as a man partially insane on the subject on which he wrote. It was not to be doubted, therefore, that his frothy and treacherous extravagance would ere long lead to a catastrophe in his editorial career. Accordingly, about four o'clock, A. M., of July 12th, a company of the Home Guards, of Colonel M'Neil's regiment, marched to the office of the State Journal, on Pine, between Third and Fourth streets, and seized the weekly and daily forms of the paper. They took away the numbers printed and carried them to the Arsenal. The order from Colonel M'Neil, by order of General Lyon, authorized at Washington, stated " that the Journal gave aid and comfort to those who are in active rebellion against the authority of the Government of the United States, by its encouraging them to take up arms against the authority of the United States, in publishing false intelligence, by urging citizens to overt acts of treason." For months this course was pursued by the Journal, with a manifest purpose of building up the Confederacy. Therefore, its suppression was a necessity, as a sober measure to protect the Government of the United States.

These secession sheets and their friends claimed, under the guarantee of freedom of speech and of the press, a right to utter falsehood and slander without restraint. But this wantonness is well met by Chancellor Kent, in the following paragraph on the subject:

"That this amendment was intended to secure to every citizen an absolute right to speak, or write, or print whatever he might please, without any responsibility, public or private, therefor, is a supposition too wild to be indulged in by any rational man. This would be to allow to every citizen a right to destroy, at his pleasure, the reputation, the peace, the property, and the personal safety of every other citizen. . A man might, out of mere malice and revenge, accuse another of the most infamous crimes; might excite against him the indignation of all his fellow-citizens by the most atrocious calumnies; might disturb, nay, overturn, all his domestic peace, and imbitter his parental relations; might prejudice all a man's civil, and political, and private rights; and might stir up sedition, rebellion, and treason, even against the Government itself, in the wantonness of his passions, or the corruption of his heart. Civil society could not go on under such circumstances. Men would then be obliged to resort to private vengeance to make up for the deficiencies of the law; and assassinations and savage cruelties would be perpetrated with all the frequency belonging to barbarous and brutal communities. It is plain, then, that the language of this amendment imports no more than that every man has a right to speak, write his opinions upon any subject whatever, without any prior restraint, so always that he does not injure any other person in his rights, person, property, and reputation, so always that he does not thereby disturb the public peace, or attempt to subvert the Government."

This grave opinion of Chancellor Kent affords a just and sufficient reason for the suppression of the St. Louis Christian Advocate and the Missouri State Journal as papers giving unlawful aid and comfort to the enemies of the Union.

After the suppression of his paper we find Mr. Tucker in Columbia, and other secession regions of Missouri, raving against the Government and liberty, and pleading for rebellion and its evil acts. The excessive leniency shown to his case in St. Louis seems to have given him great encouragement to scatter firebrands, arrows, and death elsewhere.

If any doubt should be entertained of Mr. Tucker's treason, this must be dissipated by his violent address of December 18, 1861, in the Missouri Argus extra, issued to hail General Price and his rebellious army. We can give only specimens of the rebel's excessive zeal for rebellion. Hear him:

"CITIZENS OF NORTH MISSOURI! Hail to the chieftain and his hosts who come to wrest you from a tyrant's grasp! Hail! thrice hail, my countrymen oppressed! The day of your deliverance dawns! Freemen of North Missouri, who ne'er can bend the supple knee or crouch at the tyrant's power, who have vowed to your God, your country, and your families that you will have liberty or death, while I am writing this 9,000 valiant brothers from your chieftain's swelling camp are crossing your noble river in three divisions, with a force on foot behind just strong enough to overwhelm all resistance."

Referring to the troops of Price, Mr. Tucker represents them as coming to punish the loyal Germans, whom he calls *dogs* and *devils*.

"They come to purge the land accursed by the God-forsaken followers of John Brown, and by the Hessian dogs whose fathers, for ten cents per day, sought to bury freedom by shedding the blood of our Revolutionary sires, and by the Union-shrieking, Home-Guard murderers, cowards, traitors, and tyrants, blind to reason, tories to country and traitors to God, dogs in principle and cut-throat devils in practice, associate with slaves, and drag angels down to their own base level."

Take another specimen from Tucker:

"The subject must hereafter be treated according to its *nature;* as a hog is unfit for a parlor or sitting-room, so is a Federal soldier for the treatment of a gentleman, or even of a human being."

Our Confederate partisan concludes his battle-cry with the following poetic effusion:

> "To arms! to arms! your chieftain calls;
> To arms! brave boys, the tyrant falls;
> Awaken now, both sire and son,
> And ere you sleep the work is done."

After the suppression of Tucker's rebel sheet his subscribers very generally took the St. Louis Christian Advocate as a substitute in the cause of rebellion, and Mr. Tucker, in 1864, published a high eulogy on Mr. M'Anally, in the Southern Christian Advocate, in which he represented him as always true to the interests of rebels.

3. Many events transpired in the course of the month of July which show how terribly the cause of our Church was suffering under the influence of secession.

Rev. E. Mudge, writing from Independence, Missouri, describes the state of things there after the capture of Camp Jackson. From his communication of June 21, 1861, we learn he found the Union men at that time in the majority, except in Kansas City; but the Union men, then under the military control of conservative leaders put in power through the influence of Governor Gamble and his conservative associates, were compelled to keep still. These conservatives, otherwise secessionists and rebels, used their utmost efforts to send Union men from the country. Some who rented them grounds, if they succeeded in driving away the Union men, could obtain the growing crops for their own use. Others drove Union men away that they might thus possess their lands, recently bought and paid for by cash put in the hands of these robbers. Stealing was the favorite courtesy of secessionists toward loyalists. Others would have the members of our Church driven out that they might make a gain of it. Whole families often were driven out by intimidation. Yet for one Union man thus driven out ten would be expatriated should the rebels succeed in their schemes. Such is the picture drawn by Mr. Mudge, than whom no one could be more reliable for veracity and rectitude.

Rev. S. S. Wood, of Sugar Creek circuit, Missouri Conference, under date of July 9, 1861, wrote the following, which appeared in the Central Christian Advocate of July 17th:

"BROTHER ELLIOTT,—For some time before the arrival of the troops at Rolla there was an activity exerted by Jackson and his dupes which, had not the Government interposed, would have run out or have so intimidated all Union men as to have placed that entire part of the country in the hands of the secessionists. Guns and ammunition were being sent and deposited in various parts of the country. Companies were enlisting and drilling every day. Pamphlets and blanks were being sent to county officers from the Governor, for the purpose of compelling Union men to take an oath to support his treasonable movements. Two mule-teams, six to a wagon, went through Vienna loaded with guns and ammunition. Seven cannon were found buried in the graveyard at Rolla, and taken up by the soldiers after their arrival at that place. All the time these preparations were being made Union men were threatened, warned to leave, and that, too, at the very shortest possible notice, giving no time to them to adjust their affairs. In one case one of the ringleaders drove off a poor fellow who had bought some property from him, and then bought back the same property for half what he first sold it for. In another neighborhood some fifteen or eighteen families were driven off at once, leaving behind them between seventy-five and one hundred thousand dollars' worth of good property, their crops, gardens, orchards having just been set. Mobs professing to be under the Governor came upon others, demanding of and taking from them all they had, and then sent them off, homeless, houseless, and friendless. A German Union man living on the Osage, who had a quantity of good bacon, was called upon by a gang of these scamps, who said the Governor sent them, and after taking all his bacon, and every thing else, they ordered him to leave the country. Others had to lie out in the woods, and hide themselves about their dwellings, and run and dodge, day and night, to save themselves, and that, too, while the mob was prowling around their houses. No law was put in force in favor of Union men, nor any against disunion men. Union men could be insulted, abused, in person and property, and no attention was paid to it. But a disunion man could and *did commit murder without being interrupted!*

"But, thank God, there is a change. That which we could not do by argument, and even tears, the Lord has done for us by the appearance of the bayonet among us. Well, they will have it so, and now it is their turn to run or behave themselves. May God hasten the time when wars shall cease, and restore unto us that peace and prosperity we once enjoyed as a people!"

4. Brother Wood reached our office July 8th, on his way to Illinois to see his friends and get supplies. He had only twenty-five cents in his pocket. Our office inmates made a little collection to pay his fare. He slept in the woods several nights in order to evade his pursuers. We provided a bed for him in our office, where he slept soundly, and we had the pleasure of furnishing him with supper and breakfast at our regular eating-house. As soon as he made his visit in Illinois he returned to his field of labor, holding meetings wherever he could.

5. At the close of July, Rev. Joseph Brooks, preacher in charge at Ebenezer, St. Louis, became Chaplain to a regiment. The official members of the charge requested us, in his absence, to take the pastoral oversight of the congregation. This, under the circumstances, we consented to do. In a few weeks, as there was eight hundred dollars of ground rent on the church, due to a Southern Methodist, the church was shut by him for want of payment. This broke up the congregation. The one at Hedding was also about dissolved in consequence of the times. And Simpson Chapel was the only place of worship open for the Methodist Episcopal Church in St. Louis, up to March, 1862. The year 1861 was a year of desolation for the Methodist Episcopal Church in St. Louis.

The rebel flag had been hoisted early in January, 1861, at the head-quarters of the minute-men, on the corner of Fifth and Pine streets, and was continued there up to the middle of May. In many parts of the State the rebel flag floated insultingly in the face of a benign Government. In St. Louis, very few National flags were to be seen at any time. The insignia of rebeldom, however, were worn by great numbers of the citizens, and, indeed, insolently exhibited. We felt desolate and lonely contemplating the displacement of the old Stripes and Stars by the disloyal Palmetto emblems. Hence, on the evening of July third, we went to a loyal store, and purchased a small Federal flag, with thirty-four stars, that we might display the ensign of the Republic, according to our custom for nearly fifty years, on the morning of the glorious FOURTH OF JULY. With a large needle and strong thread we fastened it to a small staff of five feet, and thrust it out of the window in the third story, and this we did regularly every morning. It was a real feast after witnessing defiant Palmetto rags for six months. When Captain M'Ginnis and brother Huffman visited our office, they took a fancy to our flag, and bore it away to their camp. But brother Shumate immediately purchased another for us, as we purposed to have the old flag about our premises, till we are buried under its wavings. In a few days the boys in the printing-office made up a purse of eight dollars, with which was purchased a very respectable flag, which was thrust out of the window, in the morning, daily, while our office was continued in the secesh Southern Methodist Book-Room building.

As a business expedient the Book Agents rented for our office the third story of this house, corner of Fifth and Pine streets, just opposite the head-quarters of the "minute-men." The flag, when hung out from our window, floated over the sign of the St. Louis Christian Advocate, whose office was in the second story. Passers-by were wont to observe that our flag was a protection to the secession editor, over whose sign it waved. The truth is, there was no reference in any way to this, as it was barely a symbol of our own allegiance, and that of our Church, to the lawful Government of the United States. Our two flags, first used, were, however, only forerunners of that beautiful one provided for us by the liberality and loyalty of the Illinois preachers, of which more on a future page.

6. We have gleaned information of many and varied events transpiring in Missouri, which we will narrate, as far as we can, in chronological order.

At Hannibal, some members of the Church, who read the Baltimore Advocate, misled by its pro-slavery mania, became secessionists in Church and State. Many of the citizens were compelled to leave the city in order to procure a living. In consequence, the livelihood of Rev. William Hanley, their preacher, became very precarious. Providence, however, provided, the tide began to turn, and to the Methodist Episcopal Church there appeared a sign of liberty of conscience. For wherever, at this time, in Missouri, the rebel flag waved, there was proscription and banishment for the old Methodist Church, which first planted Methodism in the State. The presence of the rebel flag was also a pledge of victory and privilege for the Methodist Episcopal Church South.

Rev. N. Shumate took a trip, in August, to Indiana, where his family had fled for protection. He delivered many lectures, and enlisted two companies for the regiment of which he was Chaplain. This was the more needful, as Union men were entirely under ban in Missouri, except where United States troops or Home-Guards were quartered.

Many fugitives were constantly leaving Missouri to avoid death or the spoiling of their goods. In the eastern part of the State, the emmigration was soon checked. But in the South-West, where the secessionists were in the ascendency, many Union men were constantly being driven out.

Many left their all behind them. Few, however, were killed
at this time, as the rebels feared retribution. But constant
intimidation renders families so uneasy, that most fathers
preferred leaving to having their families in constant terror.
Some were compelled to sleep in the woods to avoid death,
or personal assaults. We instance the father-in-law of
brother M'Donald, whose house was visited by thirteen
armed secessionists, and searched for him. He anticipated
the assault and retreated to the woods. The rebels left the
house, and went after, but could not find him.

The Missouri Conference of the Methodist Episcopal
Church South was to sit this year in Hannibal. But the
Southern Methodists were afraid to meet there, and changed
the seat of the Conference. As Bishop Pierce was to preside, his people seemed to be conscience-stricken. They
could but remember how he had breathed out slaughter
against all "NORTHERN METHODISTS" in Southern territory, and, doubtless, felt that such a persecutor of the
brethren could not escape being whipped of justice, if
necessary, by the very stones of the street rising up in
vengeance against him. A guilty conscience is its own accuser. A Southern Methodist wrote to us at this time as
follows: "I shall endeavor to advance the circulation of the
Central. I have no Christian fellowship with traitors and
treason. Dr. M'Anally has ruined the Church in this
country, and I hope to see the time when a loyal Church
shall occupy the entire ground."

7. August, of this year, was an eventful month.

The fallen state of many Southern Methodists is graphically represented, by a Methodist preacher, a native of
South Carolina, in a letter to Bishop Andrew, published in
the California Christian Advocate, as follows:

"Your prominent preachers are generally slaveholders.
He who does not own house servants is thought to be rather

shabby and plebeian. Talented young ministers do not find it difficult to get a few negroes by marriage. Having itinerated a few years in the South, I speak from personal knowledge. One of my first presiding elders was a talented young man—poor, but ambitious. In casting around him for a helpmeet, his eyes rested on a young lady who possessed a number of slaves; but she was an imbecile in body and mind. He soon felt it proper to locate and take care of his wife, and make his slaves profitable. Another preacher, of the same Conference, bought one slave child, rudely breaking the holiest and tenderest ties that unite child and mother. The same preacher said to my colleague, 'Brother, you ought to purchase a nigger.' 'Why?' 'To convince the people you are not an abolitionist.' In an adjoining Conference, a young preacher, with burning zeal and soul on fire to preach the Gospel to sinners, sold a child eight years old, as he needed money for an outfit for the itinerancy. Such are not extreme cases, but of frequent occurrence. Bishops, elders, preachers, stewards, exhorters, leaders, and members are alike implicated. All give the weight of their influence to rivet the manacles, and forge the chains which shall hold their fellow-men in servile bondage to the end of the world. They traffic with impunity, rudely breaking the holiest and tenderest ties ordained of the Creator."

How fallen! this race of Methodist preachers is a mockery compared with those who labored in the South at an early day!

On the 10th of August, the battle of Wilson Creek was fought, eventuating in the death of General Lyon. He was gallantly leading his host in a charge upon the flying foe, had just grasped victory with a resolute hand, when chieftain and charger, smitten by the same leaden volley, both fell in glorious death. With the heroic General, the

courage, hope, and strength of his devoted soldiery seemed
to expire.   The enemy, by force of numbers, turned and
wrested victory from the true conquerors, bowing, paralyzed
with grief, over their dying commander.   Lyon was greatly
loved and confided in by the Union people of Missouri, and
his death, at this critical juncture, filled them with grief
and consternation.   To-day, they pronounce his name with
accents of veneration and love.

Rev. J. E. Baker, of Fredericktown circuit, Missouri
Conference, and Rev. Thomas Reed, of the Arkansas Conference, were driven from their work and their homes, and
made their way to Benton, Illinois.   Mr. Baker was so for-
tunate as to have his wife with him.   Mr. Reed was compelled to leave his wife in Arkansas, and was forbidden to
see his family under penalty of death.   Such is the freedom of the South, a freedom to drive good men from their
homes and families, because they are for the Government
that guarantees political and religious liberty.

Rev. S. S. Wood, under date of August 17th, wrote to
us as follows, from Millersburg, Bond county, Illinois:
"We have the fourth company organized, in Bond county,
reported, and received, and ready to march to Springfield,
Thursday next.   This may serve to answer the question
why I did not return to Rolla, and join Rev. S. Ing's company.   As we have succeeded so well I will remain with
this company, unless brother Ing's boys think they can 't
do without me; then my company say they will give me a
transfer.   I have no commission in this company, do n't
expect any.   It is commission enough for me for my children to know that their father fought to sustain the Government that their grandsires bled and died to establish.
It is enough for me to know, when I am dead and gone,
my children will have the same Stars and Stripes waving
over their homes that my father gave me to wave over and

protect mine. Let my children have the same country, the same Constitution, the same banner, and the same liberties that I have had and enjoyed, especially when I know it is the best the world ever knew.

"The death of General Lyon has created a deep feeling among the people here. I do hope our Government will let no more of our men be killed for want of reënforcements. We have the men, means, and cause, why can 't we bring them into action? I am afraid we depend too much on our strength, without properly laying that strength out. Our clerks, students, and merchants are not sufficient to contend with the farmers of the South, especially when they outnumber us in every engagement. Our hardy peasants must turn out, and that to a man. I am almost satisfied that they have spies all over our country, and know our strength and movements as well as we do, and they intend to whip us before they are ready to fight; hence they have pressed every one into the service that can bear arms, and if we will all turn out that can go, and make no frivolous excuse about our business, etc., we will whip them right out, and drive them down to the Gulf of Mexico, and make them knock under or take water. We have four Methodist preachers in our company—Rev. G. U. Keever, Captain; Rev. T. L. Vest, of Southern Illinois Conference, First Lieutenant; Rev. James N. Maxey, private; and myself, Third Corporal."[2]

8. The editor of the St. Louis Christian Advocate employed all his powers of sophistry to evade every charge of disloyalty to the Government. When he was likely to be arrested for his aid and comfort to treason, he addressed to Major M'Kinstry, Provost Marshal, August 24, 1865, a letter, in which, among other things, he says:

"That the paper belonged to the Church of which he

[2] Central Christian Advocate, August 28th, p. 140.

was a member, and that as editor he had charge of its columns, offering the Marshal a copy to peruse." He also states, "I violate no law, civil or military, human or divine, if I know it. The opposition to the paper I edit, originated and is kept up among bigoted religious sectarians, and is religious, not political."

To this Mr. M'Kinstry, on the 25th, answered, that

"In these times of political excitement, and heated discussion, and civil war, it would be more becoming, as well as more consistent, that a public newspaper belonging to and advocating the doctrines and principles of the Church of Christ, should abstain from publishing articles of a political character calculated to inflame the passions of men, and evidently hostile to the Government of the country. You say, sir, that the opposition to your paper 'originated and is kept up among bigoted religious sectarians, and is religious, not political.' Permit me to inquire how, if this be the fact, the opposition to your paper arises among all true patriots, whether members of your own Church or in any way interested in it or not? I have read and perused the paper heretofore, and am aware of the nature of its contents.

"You say you violate no law if you know it. Did it never occur to you that patriotism is enjoined in the Bible, and that the publication of seditious and treasonable language, particularly when cloaked in the garb of religion, is one of the most heinous and aggravated forms of violation of Divine law?"

The Marshal then exhorts him to confine himself to the proper sphere of a religious paper, and should he do so, it would never come under the discipline of his department.

On this occasion we penned the following paragraphs:

"That the St. Louis Christian Advocate is a secession paper we believe, for the following reasons: 1. It is the

organ of a Church which has lent all its influence to promote
the rebellion by the approbation of nearly all its leading
members and its press. 2. The Southern Methodist papers
have indorsed the St. Louis paper as true to the interest of
secession. 3. Its version of the events of the last ten
months has been on the side of rebellion, and against the
Government of the United States. 4. The members of the
Methodist Episcopal Church South, who are Union men,
pronounce the paper a secession sheet. 5. And the secessionists of the Southern Church recognize it as on their side
of the question. 6. As far as I have learned, all impartial
persons consider the paper in question as hostile to the
Government of the United States, and affiliating with its
enemies.

"Mr. M'Anally says he violates no law if he knows
it. This is a favorite figure of speech with him, as his
studied style seems to be to use words in such a sense as
to avoid being detected in what he does say. We are
really at a loss to know how any man now can attempt to
take a *neutral course*, except in view of destroying the Government of the United States. All who are not for it, at
this time, are against it. Therefore, to declare *neutrality*
is, in fact, to practice hostility. So we believe all honest
men, not bewildered with mystification, consider this to be
the case. And in this light the Marshal considers the subject. The Twenty-Third Article of religion, both of the
Methodist Episcopal Church and of the Methodist Episcopal Church South, places this in a very clear light. It requires all to support and submit to the civil government
under which they live.

"We can not at this time utter any uncertain sound
while the enemies of our country are engaged in destroying
the best Government in the world. The aim is to *destroy
liberty* and promote a *military despotism* of the worst sort.

26

It commences with secession, that is, the disintegration of the parts of the country necessary to support the whole. The next step is actual rebellion, and this effected by *treason;* and treason comprises perjury, theft, murder, and all lawless violence. To us, indecision looks like neutrality, as to whether it is right or wrong to lie, steal, deceive, commit perjury, murder, and all acts of violence.

"We exhort Dr. M'Anally to consider his ways, cease to lend his aid to the enemies of the country by his indecision, as well as in any other way. It is a scandal to any one, bearing the name of Methodist or Christian, to be found breaking down the Government of the United States, which has proved so great a blessing to the people of this country, and promises so much good to the whole human family."

We are not alone in our judgment of the disloyal character of the St. Louis Christian Advocate. The Missouri Democrat, on the occasion of the correspondence between its editor and the Marshal, says : "The St. Louis Christian Advocate has been doing all it could in a quiet way to benefit the rebels." This accords with the judgment of the Marshal, as expressed in the correspondence. In short, this paper has been considered by all loyal men, and even disloyal persons, as a supporter of the Confederate Government and an opponent of the National Union. A long list of quotations could be adduced on this point.

9. Rev. D. David, whose circuit was in Northern Missouri, partly in Holt and partly in Nodaway county, preached with great earnestness on his circuit, without saying any thing about slavery. But as he belonged to the Methodist Episcopal Church, that was crime enough. While his congregation was assembling, some forty secessionists were discovered on their way to assault him. The preacher had just time to retreat, and ran into a corn-field near at hand. They had arms and a rope, and came swearing that they

would hang him. But he happened upon a hollow stump, around which some sprouts had grown up; into this he sprang and hid himself. In his further retreat, as he was crossing a narrow prairie, his pursuers after him, he came up to a Union man who was riding a mule, which the generous man let him have, and leaping upon it, and putting the animal to its full speed, he escaped the cut-throats and arrived safe at *White Cloud*, where he found protection. This zealous brother received one dollar and fifteen cents .on his circuit up to that time, a period of some six months.

Macon City had some fifteen hundred citizens at the close of 1860; in August, 1861, the population was reduced to about three hundred. Our Methodist brethren, who had a small Church there, with other Union men, were dispersed, some going to Iowa, some to Illinois, and others to Kansas. This is merely a specimen of what occurred in most other places in Missouri.

10. The following letter from Rev. N. Shumate gives, as far as it goes, a correct view of things at the State capital:

"BROTHER ELLIOTT,—I reached this city on the 5th inst., and found every thing quiet and orderly, so far as the surface is concerned; but there is manifestly a deep undercurrent of sympathy with the great secession movement of the South, but it is held in check by the presence of United States troops, who are continually on the look-out for the sccesh.

"On Saturday last I visited our little chapel, and preached twice to the little remnant of members, and found them glad to see one of their ministers among them again. The church-house shows unmistakable signs of the violence of Governor Jackson's mob. The windows were literally mashed to bits, the panels of the door were broken in, the window-blinds completely demolished, and several of the lamps broken, and the wall and frames scarred and dented by the rocks and other missiles which they threw against it, leaving traces of their vandalism which will remain till the church molders into ruins. The citizens of Jefferson City have, at their own expense, repaired the house, and I found it in good condition. Our valuable brother Hyatt was holding his Sabbath school in the church, and seems intent on keeping it up at all hazards. I shall not soon forget my feelings while sitting in this sacred place during the exercises of the school. I thought of the late pastor, Rev. Z. S. Weller, who stood at his post amidst threats of violence, and even death itself, from the armed minions of the arch-traitor Jackson till his church was demolished, and I said, Lord, has the like ever been known before? If so, when? Certainly not in this land of boasted religious liberty and toleration. No, verily; to find the like one must travel back to the darker ages when it was said, 'They have thrown down thine altars, and slain thy prophets with the sword, and I, even I only am left, and they seek my life to take it away.'

"But the little brick chapel is not the only object upon which this band of. Goths and Vandals spent their fury. Railroad bridges, telegraph wires, station-houses, steamboats, and whatever else they can lay their vile hands upon, the ruin of which would in any manner cripple and injure the country, they seize and reduce to destruction.

"I have just had a conversation with a gentleman who was moving from the immediate vicinity of the Carthage battle-ground. He says that fifteen hundred horses were killed in that battle, and not less than twelve hundred rebels! He says that several gentlemen who helped to bury the killed estimated the number at *two thousand*. Dead bodies were found all over the woods and in the oat-fields for weeks after the battle. Some were found several days after the fight who were still living, though so badly wounded as not to be able to crawl even, but died soon after being found. This statement I give just as I got it from my informant.

"I hear of nothing being done in religious matters any where. The clergy of this city have all, or nearly all, suspended operations. Only one Protestant Church besides ours is holding meetings at present. The reason I know not. I am still of the opinion that my place is on the battle-field, and unless things look more encouraging than at present I shall join the army by and by.

"JEFFERSON CITY, *August* 15, 1861."

11. Rev. John H. Cox, August 28, 1861, wrote us that in the early part of June the Union men of Clark, Scotland, and Lewis counties, North East Missouri, were organized as Home-Guards, under General Lyon. Some fifteen hundred rebels attempted to overwhelm the Union camp at Athens, Mo., but failed. We quote in full the rest of the letter. Brother Cox is a noble young preacher of the Missouri Conference, whose patriotic letter, in a paragraph further on, reads as follows:

"I have been compelled to abandon my circuit in consequence of the rebels, who are now ravaging the country, under the command of the Greens. 'Jim' is General, 'Mart' is Major, and I suppose 'Ab' is Brigadier-General. We have taken 'old Hallam,' the meanest man in this country, a prisoner, and sent him to St. Louis. He was in league with those fellows who went to brother Davis's—father-in-law to brother M'Donald—with arms and rope, either to shoot or hang the good man, but he made his escape by lying in the brush seven days. They have threatened that, if I attempt to preach again, they will take me out and attend to my case, but I have sent them notice that as soon as the civil law can put down mob-law *I will preach*, for I was sent here by the Lord and Bishop Morris to preach the

Gospel, and by the grace of God and Colt's arguments I 'll
try to fill the bill.

"Doctor, I wish you would advise, through the Central,
what course the preachers in the Missouri Conference should
pursue till the war is over. I have not seen my presiding
elder this year; in fact, I do n't know that I have one. I
shall never quit Missouri till the Church so orders, for I
feel that it is a privilege to suffer persecution for righteous-
ness' sake, and I can most heartily adopt the language of
Melville Cox when he said, just before his death, 'Though
a thousand fall, let not Africa be given up.' I say, Though
ten thousand fall, let not Missouri be given up.

"Brother Elliott, I have traveled my circuit on foot for
three months, and have received but twenty-five cents, and
that all in cash. Yet I love the Missouri Conference; my
heart has its home here. I 've shed my tears with my
brethren here in the brush, and lain with them in the corn-
fields.

"But I learn that our brethren in the free States complain
because our membership remains in this mobocratic State.
Let me say to them that a majority of our ten thousand
Methodists took their existence here; all they have of a
temporal character is here, and they can not dispose of it.
Then, we have all been anxious to reëstablish our mother
Church, and it will be replanted as surely as God is its author. I love it dearly, for she is my birthright, and now
that war is waged against her I do and will fight for her.
Again, beside our streams and on our plains lie sleeping
those who taught us life's first lessons; there, too, are the
old oaks, the groves, the camp-grounds, and rude school-
houses where many of them were converted. I am sure
you can not wonder we do n't leave Missouri.

"P. S. This regiment marched to *Camp Desert*—Green's—
known as *Sulphur Springs*, the place where the notorious

Harris, of Palmyra notoriety, rendezvoused his men, but Green had gone out. I there learned that thirty-seven Southern Methodist preachers had been in that camp. I got a squint at one, Paxton, a tool of M'Anally's. If I ever meet any of these men in heaven I'll look for Judas."

12. We alluded, in a previous paragraph, to the origin of our flag. The one originating in our office gave ordinary expression as it hung out from our window in the third story of the Southern Methodist Book-Room, where strange circumstances placed our office facing the head-quarters of the rebel minute-men. On the second floor was the office of Dr. M'Anally, who never deigned to give us the ordinary salute of a citizen, although we entered the same front door in going to our respective offices, and passed each other sometimes on the common stairway. On the same second floor, too, was the office of the WAR BULLETIN, the successor of the condemned rebel sheet, the *Missouri State Journal*. The matter was aggravated, also, by the large capital letters stretching all along the second story, from end to end—THE ST. LOUIS CHRISTIAN ADVOCATE.

Although our second small flag was a fair one, and sported gracefully and loyally on the face of the large rebel capitals, still it did not come up to our idea of the real thing. We wanted more *expression*. We wished to have in striking letters, connected with the flag or on it, "THE CENTRAL CHRISTIAN ADVOCATE *of the Methodist Episcopal Church, organized in* 1784 *by Mr. Wesley*." We wanted E PLURIBUS UNUM exhibited in a significant way, and we wanted on it Jackson's declaration, "THE UNION, THAT MUST STAND," and such other insignia of unity and liberty as would express more than words could say.

Accordingly, on our visit to the Illinois Conference, sitting, September 11th, we were presenting our ideas of the matter to our well-tried friend Dr. Cartwright, and two or three other brethren, when, presently, a motion was carried unanimously, appointing a committee of one from each dis-trict to make a collection. The result was that, in a few moments, they put in our hands *fifty dollars* for this pur-pose. We gave then, and we now—December 26, 1864—give them thanks for their gift. But the spirit and patriot-ism of every member of the Conference were such as far exceed the money value of the flag. It was on their part a tribute to liberty and patriotism, and the National Gov-ernment—THE UNION.

On our arrival in Missouri again, we selected five excel-lent Union, Christian, Methodist ladies to be the makers of the proposed flag. These were: Mrs. H. Kennedy, Mrs. General C. B. Fisk, Mrs. S. Rich, Mrs. Cummins, and a fifth. They bought the material, and put it together with their own loyal hands. Our study was not a large flag, but one of medium size, with proper devices. In devising our plan we examined all the flags we had access to. After fixing on the size, the ladies purchased the best silk mate-rials to be had in the city. A gentleman made them a present of a constellation of stars. An artist, a good loyal Methodist brother, skillfully proportioned the size of the letters for the mottoes. The outline was as follows:

E PLURIBUS UNUM, that is, one government from all the States. This was placed on a broad blue silk ribbon, and attached as a pendant, since there was not room for it around the constellation of bright stars.

GOD AND LIBERTY. This was on one side of the flag, as an avowal of liberty, under the immediate recognition of God as its author.

SUSTAIN THE UNION was on the other side, as a Chris-tian utterance of patriotism, alluding to Jackson's motto, THE UNION—IT MUST STAND. The meaning intended was that as Christians we should support the Union, and if the commandment is not observed, then, under the military, loyal authority the sword must do its lawful work of destruction to evil-doers.

THE CENTRAL CHRISTIAN ADVOCATE OF THE METHODIST EPISCOPAL CHURCH OF 1784. This motto was placed at the foot of the flag, a little abridged. This motto went to say, that the present Methodist Episcopal Church was the same antislavery Church that it was at its organization in 1784, with one unvarying testimony and protest against the moral wrongs inherently and incurably embraced in the system of American slavery.

The letters of the mottoes were wrought in superb needlework, with blue silk. This splendid embroidery, paid for at the usual rates, would have cost little, if any, less than a hundred dollars.

We carried this flag to several Conferences, among them, the General Conference at Philadelphia, May, 1864. We purpose to use it on special occasions, and, finally, to leave it, with other mementoes, to our children and grandchildren. And we wish it to wave as we are carried to our grave, and over our grave, when the words, *clay to clay*, *ashes to ashes*, are uttered by the officiating minister. What, indeed, is so fitting as that the flag which has been the emblem of liberty in life should still wave over the grave of its friends!

So much of the material for the flag was donated, that after purchasing all that was necessary, some twenty dollars of the fifty remained. This sum we left in the hands of the ladies, to be devoted to some Church purpose. Instead of that, however, Mrs. Kennedy, soon after, brought to my office a remarkably fine morning-gown, the material of which was purchased with this money. Of course, we accepted the beautiful garment from their hands, and we propose to wear it while it or we endure.

27

13. Early in September of this year the system of passes was established at St. Louis, and no one could leave the city without one. Nor could any one obtain a ticket on the cars without a pass. Before crossing the river on the ferry-boats, tickets must be presented. The same was required on all steamboat packets.

The pass-office was on Fourth-street and corner of Washington-Avenue. The crowd of applicants was so great for a number of days that it was difficult to obtain one. He was lucky who could succeed in the course of a day. On Fourth-street, some dozen or more soldiers, with drawn swords, and pistols at their belts, stood sentinel to preserve order and to guard the access. The doors were also guarded, and some soldiers were posted in the room where the passes were issued.

Having proposed to meet Bishop Simpson at Lebanon, on Wednesday, 4th, we must, of course, procure a pass. On Monday, 2d, the press was so great that we made no attempt to obtain one. On Tuesday, we were on the spot at seven, A. M., but when the office was open the crowd was such that we gave up the attempt. Happily for us, Chaplain Davis, of Alton, came to our office, and kindly offered his services. He got us inside the outward inclosure of sol-diers, but we were not allowed to enter the hall. The CAPTAIN, however, as the guard called the Chaplain, might enter. So he went in, and after a little time the gentle-man giving the passes came out, received us politely, and immediately executed our pass. We found in him an old acquaintance, who had read the Western Christian Ad-vocate when we edited it.

Some of our readers may be interested in a description of our pass. It is on a piece of thick paper, about seven inches by five. On one side, printed across the paper, is the DESCRIPTION OF PERSON. On the other side is printed the certificate, the lines running so as to cross those on the opposite side.

Description of Person.

Name—CHARLES ELLIOTT.

Age—Sixty-nine.

Hight—Five feet, ten inches.

Color of Eyes—Blue.

Color of Hair—White.

Peculiarities—Patriarchal.

It is understood that the within-named and subscriber accepts this pass on his word of honor, that he is and ever will remain loyal to the United States; and if hereafter found in arms against the Union, or in any way aiding its enemies, the penalty is DEATH.

CHARLES ELLIOTT.

OTHER SIDE.

OFFICE PROVOST MARSHAL, }
St. Louis, Mo., September 3, 1861. }

Permission is granted to REV. CHARLES ELLIOTT to pass beyond the limits of the city and county of St. Louis, to go to Lebanon, Alton, etc., to attend Conference at pleasure.

J. M'KINSTRY,

Major U. S. A., Provost Marshal.

Such is the pass. Death was the penalty of taking up arms against the United States or in any way aiding her enemies. This was a most righteous decision in reference to every citizen of the United States, or any enjoying its protection.

14. We here present an editorial we wrote for our paper about this time, which contains statements pertinent to the period :

"This poor, incombustible plant—the Methodist Episcopal Church, in the South-West—has been more than once apparently consumed, but like Moses' 'burning bush' it has continued to this day a living existence.

"And we are confident that the days of its consuming will come to an end, and it will flourish like the tree planted by the rivers of water. After instigations to murder our laborers in the South-West manifestly worked disrepute to the instigators, a safer policy was adopted. It was to rid Missouri of our people, improperly and falsely called 'Northern Methodists.' The process of mob law was enforced by inflaming the low rabble for the work, while the undertakers of the business, as is usual with 'contractors,' stood at a respectful and respectable distance from the performance of the vile 'drudgery.' All sorts of annoyances were resorted to. Warnings to leave, threats of violence, the erection of gallows, the presentation of ropes, intimidations to women and children, the mad-dog cry of 'abolitionist,' 'Black Republican,' 'Northern men,' and a thousand and one other modes of harassment were in requisition to rid the country of Union men and 'Northern Methodists.' The process was but too successful, and eventuated in multiplied expatriations.

"Hence, since the first of May, the religious services of our Church have been so far suspended as to break up the regular appointments on the circuits, and few quarterly meetings have been held for four months. At this time our circuits and districts. are mostly broken up. Some of the preachers have gone where life and persons are safe. Others remain with the remnants of their now dispersed flocks, who can render them very little for family support.

"Some may conclude from this that the Methodist Episcopal Church is about to become extinct in Missouri. It is true, were the State to become one of the Confederate States, liberty of conscience could not exist for the Methodist Episcopal Church. The Southern Methodist would be the State Church, with such like-minded Presbyterians, Cumberland Presbyterians, Baptists, and others as would 'never say any thing against political measures, however corrupt they might be. The preachers would be dictated to in such matters by the politicians, as all true Southern ministers never 'preach politics,' but the 'Gospel alone.'

"But as Missouri is in the Union, and will be in it, the Methodist Episcopal Church, as soon as the laws displace mob law, which has ruled here for several years past, will begin to assume the place and rank it occupied before 1844. 'Southern Methodists' are beginning to see how they were misled by the cotton States' influence in 1844 and since. Many of them, what proportion we say not, are for the Union, and reject the teachings of the St. Louis Christian Advocate, which they consider a secession journal. We have this information direct from various members of the Church South, and we can rely on it. We have recently conversed with many army chaplains who have been in different parts of the State, and they confirm the same.

"As soon as the State becomes settled, and our ministers can resume their labors, there must, of necessity, be a reconstruction of our stations, circuits, and districts. Some of our banished and persecuted people will return. Many will never seek homes and altars in Missouri again. But others will supply their places at no distant time. We shall have full access to the people of the State out of whom to form Churches. Reconstruction and reorganization must be the order of the day. It will be a time like the return of the captive Jews after their captivity and their restoration. The cxxxiii Psalm will be a grand National hymn to be sung when the divided Methodists of Missouri in many places will unite in this UNION HYMN, when schism in the Church and rebellion in the State shall have been cast away and forgotten among the cantos of Union. This will be an era in the history of the Methodist

Episcopal Church in Missouri. We can say for one, we were never so much encouraged for Missouri Methodism as now. The field is open and white for the harvest."

15. Several Conferences gave utterance to strong sympathy for the brethren in Missouri. One in Western New York, among other resolutions, passed the following:

"That our loyal brethren in the border States are deserving of our profound sympathies; that the Church should warmly cherish her interest in the border Conferences, and should make liberal appropriations of men and money for the maintenance in these regions of a loyal Methodism; and that as insurrection and treason, warmly supported by the Methodist Episcopal Church South, are backward driven, the line of our Annual Conferences should be extended till the banners of our Church as well as the flag of our Union shall once more wave in the breezes of the Mexican gulf."

The Illinois Conference passed resolutions expressing their sympathy and proffering aid to their suffering brethren in Missouri. The expressions from every portion of the Methodist Episcopal Church greatly encouraged our persecuted people in these regions.

16. At the request of many we wrote an address to the suffering preachers and members of our Church in Missouri, September 18th, and published it in the Central Christian Advocate as the best mode of reaching them. We now reproduce it as the best way of presenting the historic reminiscences of the times:

"Beloved Brethren,—We have no formal ecclesiastical authority to address a letter to you, but as you are now greatly scattered and separated from the usual sources of information, and as some ask us, 'What shall we do?' we deem it proper to furnish a few words of exhortation to meet the present distress.

"We therefore entreat all the preachers to remain, if possible, in the State and do what they can to be near the field of their pastoral labors. This is important in order to exhibit a true Christian courage as well as to manifest a readiness to do whatever can be done where little, at least for the present, is possible. The first preachers of our holy religion had much to suffer in planting the infant Churches of Christianity. Let us, therefore, be followers of those who, by patience and perseverance, served their God and his people. Let us compare our circumstances with theirs, and from the comparison let us learn to be sufferers, and to be steadfast and immovable, knowing that our labors shall not be in vain in the Lord.

"To our persecuted people we would say, as far as lieth in you, remain in Missouri, and cleave to your homes to the last in the use of prudent and lawful means of protection. It is your privilege as Christians and as citizens of Missouri to protect yourselves with fire-arms and other weapons of defense from the assaults of mobs or traitors to the country as the last resort, when the civil power can not or will not protect you.

"When this dernier resort must be used, beware of every wrong temper and every wrong act. Here will be need for the wisdom of the serpent, the harmlessness of the dove, and the courage of the lion. Unite these and use them. Let forbearance be used as far as it may justly go. But forbearance toward assassins long continued ceases to be a virtue—it is a crime. Do not commit it. Beware of being driven away by empty bravado and intimidating threats. It is time now to have recourse to the civil and military arm for help wherever these can be had. Treat your neighbors with civil and Christian kindness up to the point when nothing but your arms of protection will sustain you. Persecute no one; injure no one. Pray for your enemies; but you are bound to protect your own lives. And if you or the assassin must fall, let his blood be on his own head. You have delivered your own soul when you resort to this as the *last* mode of protection. It is God's provision. Use it as such from the hand of your Heavenly Father, who protects his obedient children, even at the peril of the guilty.

"Allow us to say to our preachers and people, your re-; demption draweth nigh. The State will soon be completely under the broad shield of the General Government. The State, too, we must believe, will soon be able to exercise its lawful State rights, and will, therefore, supersede mobs and violence. The days of expatriation are now, or soon will be, gone. Your Churches will shortly be reorganized, and your civil and religious privileges secured. Have such meetings as you can; use largely family and private prayer; read the Holy Scriptures; sing the songs of Zion; meet for social prayer where only two or three can meet together; let any brother or sister deliver the word of exhortation on the occasion as the Spirit giveth them utterance. Consider how long the Jews were in Babylon with their harps hung unstrung on the willows. At last Zion became vocal with these harps, set to the words of the cxxxiii Psalm—'Behold, how good and how pleasant it is for brethren to dwell together in unity,' etc.

"One word more. Our brethren of the Methodist Episcopal Church South have been misled and deceived by Southern politicians, and are thus in their present sad dilemma. Many of them are now true to the Union in Missouri to our knowledge. Many of those misled will soon see how they have been deceived. Let any past acts of theirs that have pressed on you be forgotten, and exercise yourselves unto prayer on their behalf, that God would turn their captivity and bring them into a large place.

"We purpose, with God's help, to remain at our post to the last extremity, sending forth our weekly issues to you, accompanied with our prayers. And we trust that the time is at hand when Missouri will be settled in the same civil and religious quiet which prevailed before its peace and prosperity was disturbed by this invasion of principles, theories, and forces."

17. The following reflections were published as an editorial in the Central Christian Advocate of September 11, 1861, and were the best utterances we could then make. And even now—December 26, 1864—we record them anew, as testimonials of the *state of the country:*

"We see the General Government bestirring itself with unremitting energy. We are not disposed to censure, although we can not overlook grave mistakes which have cost us, in Missouri, many lives, and have been followed with great public loss. Errors are inseparable from the highest trusts confided to our best men. Yet we are bound to use all possible means to remedy these errors in future. When General Lyon was just ready to seize, at the same moment, the traitorous Frost and Jackson, and their immediate aids, General Harney was put in command, and the Harney-Price truce was concocted as if the conspirators were to be aided in maturing and promoting their rebellion. And while the Southern Confederacy was pouring in its devastating troops, in order to seize St. Louis and the seat of government, General Lyon and our cause was again sacrificed for want of some two or three regiments, that were almost within gunshot of the enemies who threatened the life of the State. Traitors in our midst meanwhile were preparing their flags to be raised in their expected triumphal rejoicings over the destruction of liberty in Missouri.

"We have reliable information that the President was very restless over the peril of Lyon. We do not, however,

accuse General Fremont of intentional neglect, nor yet Mr.
Cameron. The exposure of General Lyon was not believed
to be imminent by these officials, nor by Lyon himself in
time to avert it. We are supporters of the powers that be,
and not mere censors, although we intensely feel the result
of unintentional error.

"But the General Government is now acting in earnest,
and perhaps could not do so sooner. Several incendiary
papers in the North, in the pay or interest of the rebellion,
have been suppressed or warned to desist; although we
still hear of some of them claiming the right to subvert
the liberties of the country, under the plea of liberty of
the press, which with them means liberty to destroy peace
and the Government. Their demand is for the right to lie,
perjure themselves, rob, and murder. Hypocrisy aside, this
is its meaning.

"Several unprincipled women—the Jezebels and Ath-
aliahs of the day—have been restrained also. It is to be
hoped they will not be allowed to aid in murdering millions
of men and making thousands of widows, simply because
they are women. Such leniency, that is, guilty encouragement to murder, would be but poorly concealed under the
hypocritical cant of gallantry, or the like.

"The arrest and detention of sympathizers, that is, co-
partners with the rebels, seems now to be assuming a serious character.

"As our news department shows, and we had not room
for a tithe of it, the Southern, Northern, and Western por-
'tions of this State have been ravaged by the rebels, and
the Union men generally robbed of every thing movable.
Nothing remained but martial law, and this is now come.
Its sentence is—and this is the decision of God's justice—
DEATH TO ALL WHO TAKE UP ARMS AGAINST THE STATE,
OR THOSE WHO IN ANY WAY AID THEM. This is the only

way to have peace, even under the God of grace and peace. It is the unchangeable law of Heaven. Angels in heaven who sinned had to be excluded. And the punishment of hell is the only allotment which the Son of God, who died for man, can make to impenitent sinners rejecting his mercy and grace. Every civil court acts on this principle. And when the civil power is prevented by anarchy from punishing the guilty, the resort is then, in justice, to martial law.

"Let us just note the retribution of Heaven here. Missouri, in her days of border-ruffianism, invaded Kansas at the instigation of men in Cottondom; now those disturbers of the peace have left her to her fate, to suffer tenfold of all Kansas ever suffered. Kentucky has been neutral, namely, untrue to her National faith, and now the very confederates of her disloyalty are about to visit her altars and hearths with desolation. Eastern Virginia has disloyally entered into the ranks of wickedness, and her desolation must follow, and what awaits the cotton regions we are at no loss, from the analogy of God's government, to understand, and we shall see it, if spared, when the time comes. What the Northern States may suffer for their sins time will also unfold. But LIBERTY, in the end, will flourish in these thirty-four loyalized United States in spite of all the malice and wickedness of men. What Providence may have in store, by way of correction, for the loyal States in consequence of our sins we know not; but we are sure the righteous God will not sustain the military despotism of the Southern Confederacy. Its days must be short and inglorious, should it even be recognized, *de facto*, by the United States Government, and by all the governments of the Old World. Had England at first offered to the United States the service of her army and navy to put down the rebellion, it would have been in keeping with what the United States ought to do for England in like case. England and France can not afford, however, to sustain the cotton king. Were these Governments to do so, their people would lose faith in even the good Victoria and the far-seeing Napoleon, and allegiance to the people would soon supplant allegiance to the Queen and Emperor. In any event, the tools and diplomatists of European medieval aristocracy, cousin german to the new cotton-military despotism, will be crowded to their urns by the destiny of the nineteenth century. Let the sons of liberty rejoice, for God reigns, and liberty will triumph!"

CHAPTER XV.

THE CHRISTIAN SOLDIER.

THE following is from the pen of Rev. N. Shumate, whose adventures similar to those contained in this brief letter, were they all collected, would, of themselves, make a considerable volume. Of such a possible book this may be taken as a sample chapter, and will speak for itself of the address and courage of one who has faithfully defended true Methodism in the South-West through many stormy years:

St. Louis, Mo., *December 26, 1862.*

DR. ELLIOTT,—You requested me, when I last saw you, to furnish you a narrative of my last quarterly meeting on the Jefferson City district, together with any other incidents of itinerant life in Missouri known to me. I take pleasure in granting your request, and if my statement will subserve your purposes you are at liberty to use it as you may judge proper.

My last quarterly meeting for Leesburg circuit was held at the house of the Hon. Benjamin Harrison, in Crawford county, late in March, 1861. The public mind, at that time, was much excited on the secession question, and those favoring that measure sought every opportunity for giving currency to the belief that the ministers of the Methodist Episcopal Church in Missouri were the principal promoters of the troubles which they saw approaching them. They said by the agitation of the slavery question the peace of the State was destroyed; the Northern-Methodists are the agitators of that question, and they ought to be crushed out.

Under this conclusion mob after mob was formed to drive us from our homes, and the graves of our families and friends.

Two weeks before the quarterly meeting in question a mob had met brother Early, preacher on the circuit, at the village of Leesburg, and chased him, with guns, hatchets, and bludgeons, from the town, he saving his life only by having a fleeter horse than his pursuers.

The secession rabble, having succeeded in expelling the unprotected Early from the field, boasted that the quarterly meeting at Harrison's should not be held, and accordingly they fixed for giving us a grand rally if we undertook to hold said meeting. But a few wide-awake friends got in possession of their plans and met me at Leesburg depot, and gave me full details of the movements of the mob. The brother who gave me the information said if I concluded to go to the place of holding the quarterly meeting I should have all the protection possible in the case. Accordingly, arms were furnished me, and a number of brethren armed themselves and accompanied me to the place. We found quite a number of persons assembled at the house, among them some of the leaders of the mob. When the hour arrived for the services to begin, I took my place at a table and commenced singing,

> "Though troubles assail
> And dangers affright,
> Though friends should all fail
> And foes all unite."

Perfect stillness reigned, and at the close of the hymn we bowed in humble prayer. When I rose from my knees I saw several of the mob look at each other and smile; otherwise they were orderly. I announced as my text, "Let every soul be subject unto the higher powers," etc: "We have come to this place to-day," said I, "simply, in the discharge of our religious duty, to worship God. In the enjoyment of this right we are protected by the Constitution of the United States and by the Constitution of the State of Missouri. This we hold to be an *inalienable* right, and we intend to have it, *peaceably* if we can, *forcibly* if we must; and if we have to fight or be mobbed, we are ready to fight, and the privilege of holding this meeting I shall only yield with my life."

I did not know but this last remark might be construed into a banter, nor did I care much if it was, though I only meant to give them notice that we were ready for them if they were for war.

Nothing was done, however, during the sermon to disturb the peace of the meeting; but after we adjourned the mob got together and held a consultation, and concluded to defer action till night.

We, too, held a council of war, and full arrangements were made to meet them on whatever ground they might take. When the people began to assemble for night-meeting a picket-guard was placed out to watch their movements. One man was placed in the garden behind the currant-bushes to guard the lane, which ran immediately by the garden fence. This proved to be an important outpost, for the mob assembled in the lane and directly behind the garden, and consequently within a few paces of our concealed pickets, who heard all they said. They organized and agreed on the mode of attack, but as a prudential measure they sent a spy into the house in order to find out our strength and report before they brought on an engagement. They selected one whom they supposed would not be liable to suspicion, and charged him to watch "old Ben"—the man of the house—"for," said the leader, "he's as sharp as a hawk." We had made all the arrangements for an attack; the children had been sent up stairs, the guns stacked in a convenient place, and the axes and bludgeons put where they could be made available any moment. I took my stand by the table, with my revolver where I could put my hand on it instantaneously, and with these *essential* preliminaries all arranged, I again notified them of our readiness to preach or fight, just as they might elect. The spy remained inside long enough to count our numbers, and get a glimpse of our guns, and hear the children walking over the upper floor, whom he took to be our reserves, and then left and reported the results of his observations. His report was in substance as follows: "As well as I can ascertain they are about forty strong and well armed. I saw lots of guns and several axes in the corner, and I could hear a crowd of them walking round up stairs."

"Who is preaching?" said one.

"Shumate," said the spy, "and he said he was ready to preach or fight, 'ary one,' and I believe him, too, for he hain't got all them guns for nothing."

"Yes," said another, "old Ben Harrison's been out all over the neighborhood getting guns to-day, and they'll fight like h—l."

Here a long consultation ensued, when it was finally agreed they would not be safe with their present numbers to make the attack. Our picket then came in and reported the enemy retreating in good order, thus leaving us to enjoy a bloodless victory.

While this almost fearful tragedy was going on at the scene of my last quarterly meeting, another mob in the town of Rolla was in full blast within seven miles of my family residence, before which my name, with those of others who have stood up for the Government of the United States, was brought, and we were denounced and threatened with death by hanging unless we left the county within ten days.

This latter mob in Rolla placed my case in the hands of one John King, who was appointed to notify me to quit the country or take the consequences. Fortunately, however, this Mr. King had cause to remember me, and his recollections of a rencounter with me at a camp meeting, only a year before, served to protect me from harm from that quarter. Although I sent him word that I was ready for him to serve the aforesaid notice on me, he did not come, for I took occasion at the same time to notify him that I had picked my flint and put in a fresh charge, and that he had better make his *will* beforehand.

The fearful storm which had long been gathering now began to break around us. One after another of the preachers were forced by the rebels to quit their fields of labor and fly for life. First, I received a letter from Rev. Z. S. Weller, preacher in Jefferson City, that his life was in jeopardy, and that the rebel soldiers, under the traitor Governor Jackson, had stoned and demolished his church; next, and soon after, Rev. Robert R. Witten was driven at midnight from Rolla, and fled to my house; then Rev. Wm. Sellers was hunted like a stricken deer by blood-hounds, and then Rev. Stanford Ing, who for so long a time met and foiled the rabble in many a contest, at last had to fly for life. Thus they gradually closed in upon us, till by midsummer there was but one preacher of my district who could remain in his charge, namely, Rev. J. M'Knight.

I could go no place without encountering the mob. So I staid at home till they destroyed and stole all my property, except what I was forced to sell at a great sacrifice, mostly on time, to persons who have since turned traitors, gone into the rebel army, and will never pay me. I can truly say I escaped with my life only. After scraping up about fifty dollars to bear the expenses of my family to Indiana, I had not twenty left out of nearly two thousand

28

in available property. As soon as I could get my family started from the scene of strife to a place of safety, I took a horse and started toward Fort Scott, determined to find out what the rebels were doing in the South-West. To avoid detection I had to leave the road and travel through the woods, lying out at night, and fasting till I got beyond the bounds of my acquaintance—then I officiated in the capacity of a stock buyer, but always found cattle too high to buy any.

CHAPTER XVI.

EVENTS OF OCTOBER, 1861.

1. A POLITICAL counteracting control over the Church is one of the most dangerous evils that ever beset her. The true status is the independency of the Church, and also the independency of the State; the one in spiritual, the other in political affairs. Yet both are closely allied, as the body and the spirit. In the same person is to be found the Church member and the citizen; and all are bound to obey the civil power within its proper sphere. But it is easy to pass over the lines of demarkation here. This is instanced in the history of the Church, from the days of Constantine down to the present, in those countries where the civil power controls the spiritual. It has been fearfully exemplified also in the case of the spiritual power of popes overruling civil affairs.

It would seem as if this catastrophe might have been avoided in the United States, but it has not. When the Calhoun politicians in 1832 saw they could not accomplish their object by political measures, they had recourse to the moral influence of Churches. The Churches, other than the Methodist, were not committed by any special antislavery principles in their Disciplines. The Methodist Discipline, however, was antislavery from the first, as was the Mosaic law and the New Testament. Hence the political game in 1844 to induce Southern Methodists to secede. Then a political card was played, to lead them to interpret the General Rule on slavery as meaning nothing; then to teach that the Bible sustained slavery; after this, to take every thing out of the Methodist Discipline against slavery, then secession comes on, and with it treason, rebellion, and every evil work.

The Methodists in the South, with ordinary exceptions, were good men in 1844. They have been deteriorating ever since they prohibited ministers from preaching against breaches of the ten commandments, or, in other words, against theft, robbery, man-stealing, disobedience to parents, adultery, and murder, all of which are involved in the accursed system of slavery. But with conscious hypocrisy they called preaching against such iniquities "preaching politics;" and this last phrase worked like a charm, and succeeded for the time, with all the Churches in the South.

Rev. Joseph Boyle, of the Methodist Episcopal Church South, and presiding elder of the St. Louis district, in a communication to the Missouri Republican of October 29th, among other things, says:

"I am compelled to concur with you in the opinion that Northern *preachers* have done more to bring upon us the present catastrophe than any other agency, or indeed than all other agencies combined. Had ministers of the Gospel confined their pulpit ministrations to the legitimate topics of the sanctuary, instead of prostituting the temple of God with abolition lectures, we would not now be witnessing the horrors of this fratricidal war."

He further says:

"As a Church we form no alliance with any political party. We take no partisan position; nor do we, as the manner of some is, get on the house-top to make ostentatious proclamation of our loyalty. We do neither, because we deem both to be outside the proper functions of the Church of God."

Thus Mr. Boyle marches under the wing of the Confederacy, and joins hands with those who work treason. A Northern man, with Northern teaching, he now uses the very language of prejudice and misrepresentation employed by Southern ministers generally, at the dictation of the politicians. He is also implicated in all the gross misrepresentations and the treasonable and inflammatory utterances of the St. Louis Christian Advocate, as he was one of its publishers.

His son, a traveling preacher in Missouri, went into the rebel army, it is said, by the advice of his father, was captured by the Federals at the battle of Booneville, and was released on his parole, but afterward he returned to the rebel army. It is no very remarkable exhibition of immaculate modesty, supernal piety, nor yet of worldly wisdom and address, that Mr. Boyle does not take his Church to the house-top to make ostentatious proclamation of its loyalty. Not exactly. It would not cut a very interesting figure in that peculiar attitude. Mr. Boyle would doubtless wish to be excused from officiating in such a ceremony before these people, hard a check as he can command in a doubtful cause.

We are grieved that Mr. Boyle has got into this snare. Truly, "evil communications corrupt good manners." When we were presiding elder in Western Pennsylvania, he received through our hands his first license to preach. We remember, also, when he called in our office in Cincinnati, in the Fall of 1844, urging us to resist secession in our paper, for he was instructed by the Methodists of St. Louis to resist it. He made a similar call on Bishop Hamline, at the same time, asking his influence against the secession of the Southern Methodists. But after hearing at the Louisville Convention, for three weeks, the speeches of the Southern preachers, he forgot all his instructions and the

principles of his better days. But he was not alone; there
were the principal leaders of the Church secession, Bishop
Soule, Dr. Bascom, and others—Northern men—in this
same dilemma.

Missouri was considered by the Southern rebels as a
necessary part of their territory, as also was Kentucky.
Bishop, now General, Polk may be considered as pleading
for both when he uses such language as the following in
the Memphis Appeal: "The State policy of Kentucky can
only have one of two alternatives—resistance or submission
to abolition dominion. Should it be the first, our assistance
will be solicited to break up the Lincoln encampments and
drive the Federal forces from her limits. If the second,
we can but rank Kentucky among the enemies of the
South, and invade her soil as a measure of self-preservation
from the odious despotism which oppresses them. Kentucky
may bend her knee at present to the Baal of abolitionism,
but the strong arm of our National power will rescue her
from the possession of the enemy before the termination
of this war. The South needs her territory, and must
have it, though at the price of blood and conquest."

Such was the language of Mr. Polk, the same in spirit
as that urged by his fellow-traitors in Missouri, and this
always bore heavily on our Church, as it was far above
any other in the State loyal to the Union.

2. The preachers of the Methodist Episcopal Church in
Missouri at this time occupied prominent places in supporting the Government, of which we give a few specimens out
of the many that might be adduced:

Rev. Mr. Ing, October 2d, came to our office in full
uniform, and stature of six feet high, looking as if he
could leap over a wall and run through a troop with perfect ease. We mentioned in a former page his great
bravery at Rolla, which he exercised to the last, till he

could engage again in the ministerial work. Nor was he singular in this contest against rebellion. Others of our preachers entered the ranks and fought either as privates or officers.

Chaplain Huffman, of the Sixth Missouri Regiment, wrought manfully in his own peculiar sphere, and did much to cheer the sturdy combatants and to promote the moral strength of the Union cause. His affectionate care, doubtless, saved many valuable lives.

Rev. W. Hanley, in charge of Hannibal station and the district in which it was included, maintained his cause with great effect. He preached a sermon on the wickedness of rebellion and the justice of the American Government for the instruction of his people in their duties as citizens. After the sermon he read "The General Rules," and also the article of religion on the duty to the civil Government, and the note appended to it. He gave all to understand that if there were any rebels in the Church, he would deem it his duty to have them expelled according to the Discipline. One only had withdrawn from the Church, but this man had three sons in the rebel army, and was himself a rank secessionist. In short, every Union man then in Missouri, whether clergyman or layman, felt now called upon, from a sense of duty, to use all reasonable means to defend the National Government and to put down this wicked rebellion.

Rev. G. W. Keener, after being run off from Pilot Knob, and refused the privilege of instructing his little flock, decided that if he could not have the liberty of preaching, he ought to take the liberty of fighting to protect the country and its liberties. So he went back to Bond county, Illinois, and raised a company numbering ninety-six men. Rev. S. S. Wood was of this company, and was chosen fife-major. Incidents innumerable of like sort might be furnished. The foregoing, however, will suffice.

3. The Methodists of Louisiana, Missouri, in 1844, were, by their circumstances, led into the Southern Church, although much against their will. At a meeting of the members, September 30, 1861, they expressed their views in a preamble and resolutions, which appeared in the Central Christian Advocate of October 23d. After decided measures of loyalty to the Government, they expressed themselves very plainly in reference to Church matters. We select the following resolutions:

"That in our opinion the position of our Church, as indicated by the action, teachings, and influence of our bishops, editors of our Church journals, and the great body of our traveling preachers, according to the best information we have, is that of hostility to the General Government and in favor of the rebellion, and therefore, so far as that influence goes, it meets with our unqualified condemnation.

"That in our opinion, based on actual reading and examination of its contents, besides numerous other facts within our knowledge, the St. Louis Christian Advocate, as conducted by Rev. Dr. M'Anally through the last eight or nine months, notwithstanding the oft-repeated declarations of the editor that he has taken no side in favor of disunion and rebellion, has exerted a most sinister and injurious influence in favor of the rebellion, and to its insidious, but false and jesuitical teachings, is to be attributed mainly the fact of so many of our Church members being carried away in thought and in action in favor of the wild, delusive, and wicked fallacy of secession.

"That the failure of our late Annual Conference to condemn the course of the St. Louis Christian Advocate in respect to the rebellion, or to condemn the rebellion raging all through our borders, as well as from the known and acknowledged fact of so many, said to be nearly all our traveling preachers, sympathizing with the rebellion, is an indirect indorsement of the rebellion itself."

Under these circumstances the Southern Methodists in Louisiana prepared to leave the Southern Church in a body, and to reunite with the Methodist Episcopal Church.

4. The St. Louis Christian Advocate was very zealous, during this Fall, in supporting the rebellion, of which we gave many specimens in the Central Christian Advocate of October 16th. The Kansas and Missouri Conferences of Southern Methodists supported it to the utmost.

Their Kansas Conference, which met at Atchison, September 5th, passed the following resolutions:

"1. That we highly recommend the consistent, dignified, and Christian course that the editor of the St. Louis Christian Advocate has taken during the present existing difficulties in the country.

"2. That we, as a Conference, respectfully request the next General Conference to reëlect Rev. D. R. M'Anally editor of the St. Louis Christian Advocate.

"3. That we will be more diligent in extending its circulation."

The Missouri Conference of the Methodist Episcopal Church South, which sat in Waverly, Mo., September 28th, took the following action:

"The St. Louis Christian Advocate, our official organ, has continued to grow in interest and in favor with the people, both among our people and the public at large. It is now looked upon as the most reliable medium of public news known to the people within the limits of its circulation.

"*Resolved*, That the St. Louis Christian Advocate is worthy of our fullest confidence, and should be sustained by our Church, through these troublous times, as indispensable to the best interests of the country and the cause of religion."

29

The resolutions of both these Conferences were nothing less than an open indorsement of the rebellion, and a denunciation of the Federal Government.

5. The desolations of the war and of our Church are well presented, in a letter to the Central Christian Advocate of October 20th, by that uncompromising Methodist patriot, Ellis G. Evans, written from Steelville, Mo. He states that their preacher, Rev. S. Ing, was long since forced to leave his circuit, or rather was driven from his country. He entered the army as captain of cavalry, moving toward Springfield with General Wyman. The Central Christian Advocate, through irregularity of the mails, did not reach them, and they could not hear from their friends. He says to the preachers:

"Speak, brethren, for the sake of the rest of us. We have spoken out often from this place in days gone by, and it is hardly necessary to repeat that we still intend to stand by the Discipline, by the Church of our fathers, by our native State, and by our nation.

"As to this war, some of us have been in it for sixteen years. We have been fighting against a tyranny that refused us and our children civil rights granted to others; for instance, remember 'Ebenezer High-School,' 'Jackson Seminary,' and 'Jefferson City University.' We first had legislation directed against our children as the offspring of Methodists; but last Winter the same power extended the legislation against all the children of the State. For a long time our little band was nearly alone in the fight, but now we find the whole people who love their State rising up in defense of their children, born and unborn.

"We feel somewhat lonesome out here at present, but we were once deprived of our Church for several years, say from 1845 to 1848, when the General Conference heard our petitions.

"But we are told we are without a Union, and, to quote Dr. M'Anally, 'There is no Union.' Well, our fathers were for a long time in the same fix, and we used to read about their fighting seven dreary years to create a Union; so now, if they did not pay more than a Union is worth, how long should we strive for National existence and independence."

These are brave words, and true and honest as brave.

6. As to the state of the Methodist Episcopal Church in Missouri in October, we published, in the Central Christian Advocate, an account of it, on the 30th, which we here transcribe, for we can not now mend it, except in the tense of the verbs, and other minor points:

"Our friends at a distance may desire to hear of our affairs in Missouri. Indeed, our own preachers and people are so scattered that half of them do not know how the other half fare. Our post-offices are deranged in some two-thirds of the State. Some of our preachers are, of necessity, out of the State for the present; others of them are in the army, and away from the avenues of communication; others are in such places of safety as they can best provide. We will, however, descend to particulars.

"No quarterly meetings have been held in our Churches in Missouri since the first of May last. Three of the presiding elders, Messrs. May, Smith, and Lathrop, were compelled, as a matter of safety, to leave the State. Brother Smith is in Iowa, as he could hold no quarterly meetings in his district, which includes Kansas City and the South-West.. Brother Lathrop, in Northern Missouri, had to fol-low the Scripture, 'When they persecute you in one city, flee to another;' he is now in Iowa or Nebraska. Brother May is in Hamilton, Ill. He expected to take work in the Central Illinois Conference, but there was no room for him, so he is now without means of support or pastoral charge. Brother Hanley is in his place, as brother May had concluded to labor in Illinois. Presiding elders Huffman, Oyler, and Shumate are chaplains in the army, and, of course, must follow their regiments, and can hold no quarterly meetings. Brother Hanley, now presiding elder of Hannibal district, is also preacher in charge at Hannibal. He can fill his station, and hold some quarterly meetings, when any are possible. Three of our stationed preachers, brother Brooks, of Ebenezer, brother Pile, of the Boatman's Chapel, and brother M'Donald, of Hedding, are chaplains. Brother Beggs, who traveled De Soto circuit, is now at Jefferson City, preaching to large congregations. We have no information as to the locality of many preachers of the Conference. We earnestly request them to let us know where they are, that our brethren may learn the true state of things. Several of our preachers are in the army, in various relations, some as officers, others as privates.

"Great destitution is at this time the lot of most, or, at least, many preachers of the Missouri Conference. Brother Linan is here in the city, with his wife and family, without any means of support or employ. During the Summer he was forced to quit his circuit, and left his family among the rebels. He afterward, however, succeeded in getting them to the city, at the risk of his life.

"Professor Mudge, who was stationed at Independence, and was five times warned to leave, is now at Quindaro, Kansas. This devoted man, in a letter to brother Stewart, of this city, describes his condition. We are permitted to copy it. From the letter our readers will learn the temper of this good man, who purposes to renew his labors as soon as an opportunity offers. He says:

"'I am here, off and on, but expect next week to be in Manhattan, Kansas. Matters have been greatly stirred up in Independence since Price gained his advantage at Lexington, thirty miles distant. It is in some degree safe to what it has been, and soon will be quite so. But I must leave for want of support. Our people need pastoral aid. They need also food and clothing. My board would be far more than they could pay. I have received for six or eight months' labor from the people six or seven dollars; $37.50 missionary money at Conference, none since. So, by the advice of the Bishop, I go to Manhattan to fill out the year. I do not take a transfer. I can not bear to see the work in Missouri forsaken, and if I had a support I should certainly stay. I hold myself ready to return in the Spring, if it is judged best. No people need pastoral care more than the flock in Missouri. With all the war troubles I have never enjoyed a year better than the past. If the rest of the year is as pleasant and profitable I am content. It has been a wonderful Providence that has been over me, keeping me from the dangers that have been all around. My health is first-rate. Milton is perfectly well. I know of no one on all the Kansas City district who is now at work. I believe I am the last. Brother Gaither is at Baldwin City; brother Mitchell at Independence.'

"Take another specimen of the distress of one of our preachers. He is now at Oskaloosa, Kansas, and writes, October 10th, he was compelled to leave his work some two weeks previous. He has been sick since he went to that place. He wants his quarterly installment of missionary money sent him, amounting to $25. This was drawn by the presiding elder, who is now chaplain in the army, and has to follow his regiment. The presiding elder does not know where the preacher is, and the preacher does not know where the presiding elder is. The preacher's goods are at Leavenworth with $25 charges on them; he can not get them without money, and yet he has none. The poor preacher asks us this question: 'Brother Elliott, do you think that the missionary appropriation to the circuit will be paid to the preachers when they were compelled to leave their works?'

"Such is the statement of this case; it is similar to many now occurring in Missouri. About half of our members have been compelled to leave the State, and there are few left to support the preachers; the little missionary supply seems to be the only resource. This will not apply to preachers who serve the army, because the army supports them. Our brothers who are isolated and can not hear as to others, want to know the state of things.

"Although the preachers of the Methodist Episcopal Church South in Missouri are mostly secessionists, yet there are exceptions. One of them is a loyal chaplain in Col. Wright's Regiment of Missouri Volunteers. Another preacher of this Church is in the army at Rolla, and there are several others of whom we have heard, but we need not detail. Brother Shumate and brother Huffman's families are now in St. Louis as a place of safety from the assaults of rebels to which they have been exposed, the one at Rolla and the other at De Soto.

"In this city our three German Churches are in a healthy state, true to their God and true to their adopted country. The state of our three English Churches is as follows: *Hedding* has a very small congregation, if congregation it may be called; but there is a good Sunday school. At *Simpson Chapel* we have a good Sunday school, and a promising state of things in the congregation. At *Ebenezer* services are suspended, as the rent on the lot not being paid, the landlord closed the house. Nevertheless, there is much inquiry now after the Methodist Episcopal Church of 1784, and its fallen altars, we are persuaded, will be reërected in St. Louis. Of this we will give some notice after a short time.

" We conclude this article by stating that in our judgment the Methodist Episcopal Church will have a prosperous future in this State. Its unfaltering loyalty throughout the United States wherever it exists gives it a prestige
which will command the respect of all men. In Missouri
the day of its depression will soon be over. Loyal citizens will see where it has stood and. is likely to stand.
Those who have been entangled in the meshes of secession, after they are cured of their delusion, will find a
desirable ecclesiastical asylum within its pale. As soon
as the rebellion is crushed out in this State our work
will commence anew. One or more of our bishops and
other brethren will commence the work of reconstruction
in all the places now desolate. *A Central or Metropolitan
Methodist Episcopal Church* will rise up like a phenix in
the midst of St. Louis. O, we wish we could reach all
our scattered and peeled friends who are now in the State,
or who have been temporarily driven out of it! We would
utter words of encouragement to them. We would say to
them, 'Your God liveth, your captivity is ended.'"·

CHAPTER XVII.

EVENTS OF NOVEMBER, 1861.

1. In the Fall of 1861 there was a double stampede of inhabitants from Missouri. The first was that of Union people flying from the State before the scourges inflicted upon them by secessionists. At the close of October it was supposed that two hundred thousand loyal citizens had abandoned the State from force or fear. The other departures from the State were of slaveholders, who, to save their slaves, either emigrated permanently with them to the South, or went there temporarily in charge of them, to await the issue of the war. There was not at this time, perhaps, more than one-fourth as many slaves in the State as had been in it twelve months prior.

2. The sufferings of our preachers and people in Missouri at this time were very great indeed.

Rev. A. J. Gaither was in the region of Springfield, on Mt. Vernon circuit. He joined a company of the "Missouri Home-Guards," but they failed to get arms. So when the Government troops retreated from that locality he had to leave. With his one-horse buggy he made out to reach Kansas, leaving his furniture and goods behind him. Here he was without business or any resources for a livelihood, and with his sick wife; he had a time of sore trial and suffering indeed. He received a small missionary appropriation for the first quarter of the year, but as he and his presiding elder were separated he could get no more.

Rev. Henry Martin, on the Shelbyville circuit, was greatly

annoyed by rebel interferences. But he nobly stood his ground.

Rev. A. H. Powell, of the Methodist Episcopal Church South, who traveled their Springfield circuit, left the Southern Church and became chaplain in one of the Missouri regiments, and having done good service to the Union cause in that relation, finally united with the Methodist Episcopal Church, in whose communion he is now, doing praiseworthy service.

Another Southern Methodist preacher, Rev. Mr. Reah, who conducted an academy in Springfield, Mo., and was the pastor of the Southern Methodist Church there, made his way to Iowa, having realized that the man who does not favor secession and maintain slavery is not qualified to preach in the Southern Church.

Rev. F. S. Beggs writes, November 6th, from Jefferson City, that when he arrived there he found all in excitement and bustle. Soldiers were arriving and departing with great rapidity, all destined for the seat of war. Yet he says things have changed for the better, and concludes his letter with the following cheerful view: "We feel like the day will soon be ours. After a short time our Church in Missouri will spread her wings and overshadow the whole State. Then 'the wilderness and the solitary place shall be glad for them, and the desert shall rejoice and blossom as the rose.'"

Rev. Mr. Lyon, a chaplain of our army, who was in the State of Missouri during Price's war upon it, and who knew well the calamities of our people, gives the following sketch of their condition. In an article in the North-Western Christian Advocate, after referring to our own privations, he says:

"His *co-sufferers* are our brethren of the Missouri and Arkansas Conference. These moral heroes have main-

tained their integrity, and they have kept their posts till
driven away at the point of the bayonet. Nearly sixty of
them have been driven from the work assigned them by the
Bishop. They had been nearly half starved before the war
broke out, and now they are left entirely destitute—many
of them with families on their hands. A few of them have
been appointed chaplains in the army, but about fifty of
them—as noble and self-sacrificing men, and as heroic patriots as there are in the land, who are now unable to get
work—are now penniless and in a suffering condition.
They belong to the Church—can nothing be done to relieve their present distress?"

3. The following account of the Kansas City district,
comprising the south-western tiers of counties from the
Missouri River to the Arkansas line, corresponds to the accounts already given. Rev. J. C. Smith was presiding elder
on the district. We publish entire his truthful account, as
given at Agency City, Iowa, November 10, 1861:

"BROTHER ELLIOTT,—Below I give you a few items concerning the ministers of the Kansas City district, Missouri
Conference. The interruption of the mails and the frequent
changes occurring in our residences and circumstances, have
rendered it impossible to keep posted as to each other's
situation.

"But for these difficulties I would have written sooner.
Rev. W. S. Wentz, who was stationed in Kansas City, is
supplying the Atchison station, Kansas Conference. He
has been there since the early part of Summer. I learn he
is doing a good work, but is in feeble health.

"Rev. T. H. Mudge, who had charge of the Independence
station and circuit, was able to remain at his post till about
the time of the fall of Lexington, when he found it necessary to leave, at least for a time. There being no means
available for his support, he found it difficult to continue

his work. He is now in charge of the Manhattan station, Kansas Conference, where he will, in all probability, remain to the end of the Conference year. Rev. O. H. Mitchell has spent the most of the Summer in Independence and its vicinity, where he is at present. He has been unable to do any thing on his circuit since Conference.

"Rev. C. E. Carpenter was driven from his circuit early in May, after encountering the pro-slavery mobs. His circuit included Papensville, where a battle has been fought. He went to Kansas, where he spent a few months, and then removed to Iowa. He now resides in Fairfield.

"Rev. T. C. Babcock—of this good brother I have no knowledge. When I last heard of him he was captain of a company of Home-Guards, whose avowed object was to protect themselves from the rebels, who resolved to mob the 'Northern Methodist preacher, Babcock.' How they succeeded in that, under the leadership of the 'Northern preacher,' I know not. I have written him several times, but got no tidings from him.

"Rev. A. J. Gaither, of the Mt. Vernon circuit, remained at his work till the battle of 'Wilson's Creek,' which was within the bounds of his charge. He was then obliged to leave the country, or fall into the hands of the rebels. He is at Baldwin City, Kansas.

"Rev. G. W. Fisher was obliged to leave his work and flee to Kansas. At last accounts he was at Mound City, and his family in South-Western Missouri. He dare not return to them. I understand he is supplying a circuit in the Kansas Conference.

"Rev. B. Hall was in South-Western Kansas when last heard from. He left his work early in the Summer.

"Rev. P. H. Early was obliged, early in the Spring, to leave his circuit. He spent most of the Summer in Kansas, but finding there was no hope of being able to resume his work in Missouri, he removed to Iowa, and is now stopping near Newton, Jasper county.

"Rev. J. H. Vaughan, surrounded by peril, remained at his post till it was impossible for him to get out of the country. He then joined the 'Home-Guards,' and has been in the service of his country for some three months or more. He was at Jefferson City when I heard from him last, but is doubtless now with the army, in the South-Western part of Missouri.

"As to myself, your readers know my whereabouts. I had no work on my district; I therefore thought it best to spend the Summer in Iowa, where I could provide for my family. The continuation of the war in Missouri precludes the idea of resuming our work there this Fall; I therefore resolved to spend the Winter in Iowa. I am teaching school, and preaching when opportunity offers. I shall return to the South-West in the Spring.

"If this should fall under the eyes of brothers Vaughan, Babcock, and Hall, will they please write me, at Agency City, Iowa, and give me their post-office addresses, or the nearest point where 'express' agencies can reach them? I will send them the missionary money due them.

"Our work, in the bounds of the Kansas City district, will have to be reorganized when the war is over. Our laymen are, generally, driven out of the country. They have suffered greatly in property and feeling. So far as I know, the ministers of the district all expect to return to their work as soon as it is practicable to do so. Let the Church remember them in prayer."

4. As to the general state of the Methodist Episcopal Church, we reproduce the view we took of it, on the spot, November 27, 1861:

"Our brethren at a distance are desirous of knowing how our religious concerns are in this State. Both preachers and people wish to know the whereabouts and doings of each other, but their requests can not be met. Some of our preachers are in the army either as chaplains, officers, or privates; others have left the State for safety, or for the purpose of providing for themselves and their families in the best way they can; while others are confined to one place on their circuits; and up to this time the principal risk of life has been in traveling from one place to another. The pinching want of most of our preachers for the commonest necessities of life has been very great indeed. Our Church members have been scattered; perhaps one-half or more were driven from the State as early as August last. The remnants have been concealed or have escaped by various stratagems since that time. The rebel wars and robberies have stripped our people of what yet remained. Some individuals here and there, preachers and people, ask us where are the others of our fellow-sufferers, and what are they doing? Alas! we can not give the information, except in a very limited way indeed.

"Well, we will begin and report ourself. We. are in better health since we came to Missouri than we have had since our early manhood, when we jumped in the bogs, bathed in the river, and studied our lessons in *hic, hæc, hoc*, with buoyant hopes of the future. We sleep in our office, eat at an eating-house, and receive daily visits from patriotic chaplains, officers, and soldiers. Our spirits were never better, and our hopes never so strong for religion and the Union. We expect to change our office this month from the upper story of Dr. M'Anally's premises to Locust-street, between Fourth and Fifth. The public say our old flag has been a safeguard to editor M'Anally, and saved him from suspension by its daily graceful waving over his secession sheet. As he is now safe from the proscription which he earned and courted but could not secure, we change of choice, not of necessity, our place of issuing our paper, lest we should give aid and comfort to secession. As our old flag has done its work of protection at No. 78 Pine-street, third story, we will raise our new sign and flag at No. 101 Locust-street, north side, between Fourth and Fifth. Now as to the Missouri Conference.

"KANSAS CITY DISTRICT is fully described by the presiding elder, Rev. J. C. Smith, who is teaching school for an honest living in Agency City, Iowa.

"ST. LOUIS DISTRICT. The presiding elder, Rev. S. Huffman, is a soldier in the army doing noble service. Brothers Brooks, of Ebenezer, and Pile, of Boatman's Chapel, and M'Donald, of Hedding, are chaplains. Brother Linan has escaped with his life, and is in the city. Simpson Chapel is our only English Church in the city with regular services, with brother Stewart as pastor. Other parts of this district are without religious services. Our friends in this city are arranging for a new move.

"JEFFERSON CITY DISTRICT. Elder Shumate is chaplain with the army, doing earnest service for God and his country. Brother F. S. Beggs is now in Jefferson City, with large congregations of citizens and soldiers. Brother Ing is captain of a cavalry company, and brother Wood is private in the same. No preacher in this district has regular services except the one at Jefferson City.

"HANNIBAL DISTRICT. Brother Hanley, as stationed preacher, has kept his ground and maintained his cause admirably. He has recently been at Louisiana, looking after our interests there. He will act as presiding elder and preacher in charge till reorganization takes place.

"We have no recent information from the other districts. Our confidence is strong that our Church in Missouri will soon recover what it has lost by persecution and rebellion with vast increase. Our people here were never in such good spirits as now."

5. The great expected battle passed away without any fighting in Missouri. The rebel army under Price and M'Culloch went to Arkansas. The United States troops left Springfield and came north to Sedalia, Jefferson City, and St. Louis. Garrisons of considerable force were placed at Pilot Knob, Rolla, and most other places in Missouri. As Union men were suffering the loss of all things, they were leaving in great numbers with our army. Many of the rebels left with the army of Price, and the country became nearly desolate in many parts. The tide, however, began to set in in favor of the Union, with manifest indications of success to its cause; and, although our Church was very much scattered and weakened, those who remained were very much encouraged in contemplating the future of Methodism in Missouri. They saw the curses of their enemies and persecutors come home to roost on their own heads. They saw the majesty of the National Government driving its thundering cannon-wheels over and crushing into the mire the very iniquities which they had denounced for years, but for the denunciation of which they had suffered the loss of all things. They were now marching in the wake of victory. They saw the raging storm and heard its deep-toned threatening mutterings with a feeling not altogether of terror. There was something of wondering admiration and even love about it, for they knew that God was in the storm. Amid the rush of the tempest they heard the rending of lashes, the breaking of yokes, the snapping of fetters, the falling of chains, and the hoarse, dying cry of the human auctioneer. But beyond and above all these they heard the triumphant halleluiahs of four million, four thousand, four hundred and four of God's poor. And they saw this peeled people lift itself

from its long-inflicted and grievous thralldom and stand upright in the image of God, with its face toward heaven as it were the face of a man. And our people echoed back the halleluiahs.

6. The St. Louis Christian Advocate, in an address on *personal matters*, occupying more than one-half of his first page of November 14th, says:

"These slanderous pens and tongues, whose name is legion, confined mostly, however, to Northern Methodists, led on by their papers and army chaplains, which have pursued me for months, and sought to excite against me and this paper the officers of the law, may expect to receive all proper and due attention. Hitherto I have shown up their false double-dealing, their bad faith, and their prevarications only in part; the remainder is yet to come. For months and years past they have pursued me with a venom they have exhibited to no one else, and now I hope to be with them in six troubles, and not to forsake them in the seventh; but I will be with them in no unchristian spirit, and will meet their falsehoods with truth, their fallacies with facts, and their bald assumptions with sober reason."

His paper of the 21st abounded with mournings over the loyal Methodists of the Methodist Episcopal Church. Of the recent *Beaufort* affair he sneers in these words:

"At first the Federal fleet had taken the place, and then it had n't; then again it had, and the last *had* stands as yet."

This is a specimen of his dealing with every act of the General Government.

CHAPTER XVIII.

EVENTS OF DECEMBER, 1861.

1. In the month of December, and previous, the rebel General Price, with a considerable army, was endeavoring to conquer Missouri to the South. Most of the Southern Methodist preachers and many of their members were co-laborers with the General in this treasonable work. In the case of Rev. R. J. White, we have a specimen of the prevailing habit of the times.

Mr. White had been a member of the Pittsburg Conference, and subsequently of the Illinois Conference. The climate not suiting his health, he moved to Missouri, and here united with the Methodist Episcopal Church South, and was stationed in Lexington for the second year. Suspicions and prejudices arose against him because he came from Chicago. These were much strengthened when it was known that he was the friend of Mr. Lincoln at and after his election in November, 1860. He was violently assailed by two secession old maids, members of his Church, and they were industrious in spreading the news of his being an abolitionist. After this, two of his congregation met on the street, and the following dialogue ensued: "Well, brother E., did you know that our preacher is a Black Republican?" "No, I did not, and I think you must be mistaken." "I can not be mistaken, for the information has come to me very direct—from a lady who heard him sustain the Administration."

On Monday, the post-office brought the following note:

"LAFAYETTE COUNTY, Mo., *May* 11, 1861.

"REV. MR. WHITE,—You are believed to be an abolition-ist of the deepest dye and opposed to the institution of slavery. It would be well for you to leave Missouri imme-diately, as you are aware the war of extermination has commenced in the State. Your wife is also known to be abolition from birth. It is believed by many of your con-gregation that you have no religion, and are nothing more than an abolition fanatic, and imposed yourself on us falsely."

Mr. White was met in all directions with the charge of being an abolitionist, and so intense was the feeling that he concluded to leave at once, without his goods; the con-gregation owing him $500 of arrears, which, we presume, he never received. But he got away with his life, which was a very fortunate event under the circumstances.

2. Rev. James Lee, formerly a member of the Missouri Conference, but now a local preacher near Kansas City, at-tending his farm and preaching the Gospel to his neighbors with great fidelity, wrote us from Auburn, Kansas, Decem-ber 12, 1861:

"DEAR BROTHER ELLIOTT,—By the superintending prov-idence of my Heavenly Father, I am safe amid kind friends in the State of Kansas, having barely escaped from the rebels' grasp in Missouri. But my dear family are still there if they have permitted them to live. On the 8th November, three armed men came in the night, called us up, and demanded two horses, which they took away. They requested that I should come out, as they wanted to shoot me; and, not making my appearance, they de-clared the first sight they got of me they would shoot me down. After consultation and prayer I determined in the morning to leave home and all that was dear to me in the world and flee to Kansas City, as a place of safety, supposing when I was gone my family might remain unmolested, and I be near to render assistance if necessary. On the day after I left home, ten ruffians, all armed, surrounded my dwelling, entered my house, and made a diligent search for me in all the premises. They returned the following day for the same purpose, but I was in Kansas City, twenty miles away. On the 23d of November several of my neighbors were compelled to leave their homes and come to Kansas City with Jennison's command, and several of them are members of the Methodist Episcopal Church." From Auburn, Kansas, he continues: " Here I am in a state of suspense, one hundred miles from my dear wife and children, and not permitted to return, except at the risk of life. All this because I am a minister of the Methodist Episcopal Church, and love the laws and Constitution of the United States. My dear Doctor, if I can get my family out here safe, I can say, farewell farm, house, stock, and crop. All is nothing if wife and children are safe.

" A good brother, a local preacher, of the name of L. Steward, on the Independence circuit, was murdered in November last, in our neighborhood. His body has not yet been found ; but the rebels who committed the dark deed are known, yet there is no justice enforced. Murder can be committed with impunity by the rebels, and there appears to be but little protection from the Federal forces for Union men. They are driving them out of the State. Such is the State of affairs in Jackson county, and the border counties generally. A more vigorous and rigid course will have to be pursued ere Missouri is at peace."

3. While Rev. N. Shumate was on his journey as chaplain in the army, on its march from Jefferson City to Springfield, through Boonville and Sedalia, in June, 1861, several

incidents of a curious character occurred. This region was comprised in his district. While at Boonville he called to see a local preacher of the Methodist Episcopal Church, when the following interview ensued:[1]

"I chanced to make some noise at the gate, which brought my friend to the door, and, on seeing a man in blue, and buttoned up to the chin, he raised his hands and eyes in holy horror, and exclaimed, 'Is it possible you are here among these men?' 'O, yes, brother H., I am here among these men. Does it disturb your nerves to see a Federal soldier?' said I. 'Ah,' said he, 'I am sorry to see a minister of Christ among these invaders of the sacred rights of a sovereign State.' 'Is it possible,' said I, 'you have turned traitor to the Government, and are among those who are trying to ruin the State of Missouri? I am astonished.' A few words more passed between us, when he asked for his certificate of membership in the Methodist Episcopal Church, but I declined, on the ground that all traitors ought to be hung, and that a man who ought to be hanged could not be an acceptable member of the Methodist Episcopal Church. This is the only member of the Methodist Episcopal Church I found among the secessionists."

While on march toward Springfield our chaplain was on General Kelton's staff, and had not yet appeared in uniform; but on the march he put on his uniform, and rode out in front of the regiment, with the other field officers, encouraging the men, who vociferously cheered their officers, and proceeded on their march with renewed alacrity.

4. At the close of the year 1861 the following sentiments were uttered, in an editorial, December 25th. The expulsion of Union men from the State was carried on by a variety of expedients. Bishop Pierce was a prime counselor in this business of expatriation, and many Southern Methodists

[1] Central Christian Advocate, p. 201, col. 5.

were active and efficient coöperatives. Our utterances then were:

"O that we could reach our scattered and peeled people with a word of comfort! We have to say, Your God reigneth in Missouri. This State is now ravaged as she attempted to ravage Kansas, thus to establish oppression in Kansas, in the hope of continuing it in Missouri. In the fifteen months of your persecution since the martyrdom of Bewley, our Stephen, one-third of the slaves of Missouri have been taken from the State by flight, sale, or otherwise. Kansas is free. The power of slavery and persecution is broken in Missouri. The State is in the Union, and will remain there. Bishop Simpson, in a few days from now—December 20th—will commence the work of reconstruction of the Methodist Episcopal Church in Missouri. Pray for your enemies, persecutors, and slanderers. Our cause will soon commence in this loyal State. If some of the persecuted ones never return, thousands will come in their places, ten to one. Rebellion, and the entails of murder, robbery, and perjury, will soon be totally crushed out of this State.

"Brethren, prepare your banners. We are preparing ours. This day we thrust out our old flag from our window. Our sign is in the artist's hand, namely, the Central Christian Advocate of the Methodist Episcopal Church, organized in 1784—not 1844. There it is. Our new flag will soon be in readiness with its insignia, not only of stripes, and thirty-four stars, but also of GOD AND LIBERTY, E PLURIBUS UNUM, PRESERVE THE UNION, etc. Let each refugee from Missouri procure a little flag and hold it up wherever he may be. Stick one on your horse's head; fix it to your wagon; hold it in your hand.

"What a time we expect to have in St. Louis when our next Conference meets! We may then, like the primitive Christians, rehearse the names and sufferings of the martyrs of the South-West. In the mean time, let the dispersed ones remember Missouri, as the Israelites remembered Jerusalem and Zion, while their harps remained unstrung during the seventy years of captivity.

"Our Conference love-feast must be protracted several times in order to give utterance to the pent-up emotions of the Conference year 1861–62. We would be glad to have Messrs. Haven, of Boston; M'Clintock, of Paris; Thomson, Wise, and Whedon, of New York; Eddy, of Chicago; Kingsley, Clark, and Nast, of Cincinnati; and some from Baltimore, Philadelphia, and Peter Cartwright and Dr. Akers, there to witness and join in the *Io triumphe;* and then we should want all to unite in some good Union Psalm, such as '*Hail Columbia*,' or '*The Star-Spangled Banner*.' Friends, prepare for the occasion."

CHAPTER XIX.

EVENTS OF 1862.

1. DR. M'ANALLY commenced editorially, in the year of grace 1862, an elaborate defense of slavery. In his paper of January 9th, and four successive numbers, he pleaded earnestly for this iniquitous system. He maintains the doctrine of his Church in the following words:

"She [the Methodist Episcopal Church South] believes that the *relation* of master and servant is recognized by the Holy Scriptures, *and so it is.* She believes that *with that relation,* she, *as a Church,* has nothing to do. Neither did the blessed Savior, nor his apostles, nor the primitive Church interfere with the relation, although it existed all around them."

He then states the subject as follows:

"1. Was slavery sanctioned by the Almighty in the patriarchal ages, or was it not?

"2. Was, or was it not, incorporated into the only National Constitution which ever came from God to man?

"3. Was, or was not, its lawfulness recognized and its moral duties regulated by Christ and his inspired apostles?

"4. Considered *as an institution of society,* is it one of cruelty or of mercy?"

The Doctor, in his five long editorials, attempts to show that slavery was sanctioned by God among the patriarchs; that it was incorporated by him in the Jewish law; that Christ and his apostles sanctioned it; and that it was an institution of mercy.

On the 5th of February we addressed ourself, in the Central Christian Advocate, to the false reasonings of Dr. M'Anally in the following language:

"PLEAS FOR MAN-STEALING.—Our late neighbor of the St. Louis Christian Advocate, between whom and ourself now three squares intervene, has in his last three numbers come out in favor of stealing men, women, and children. The Spartans, to be sure, taught their children to steal; but Dr. M'Anally declares that the Almighty teaches certain men to steal, that his laws approve even theft of human bodies and souls, although it might be wrong to take another's money. It is true God formerly enacted the express prohibition, 'Thou shalt not steal.' He also declares, 'He that stealeth a man and selleth him, or if he be found in his hand, he shall surely be put to death.' This is repeated by Moses and recognized as God's law by Paul, who classes the man-stealer with the murderer of parents and the perjurer. Dr. M'Anally insists, however, that God, in the only government instituted by him, authorized slavery, and therefore theft; for every slave is a stolen man, and every one that holds or keeps a slave, except to free him, is a man-stealer. Our former neighbor brings Jesus Christ and his apostles into the slave shambles, and has them engaged in this thievish traffic, as if it were the most holy thing in the world to sell human beings or breed slaves. Editor M'Anally, however, and those of his stripe, contend that it is hugely wrong for abolitionists to steal negroes. But abolitionists when they do steal, as some of them do, commit the theft that they may restore the object stolen to its proper owner, that is, to himself. But our friend Mac. contends for the right of stealing when the stolen property is never to be restored to its rightful owner, but to be thievishly held by the robber while he sanctimoniously quotes Scripture to palliate and justify a larceny, the violence of which is reprobated by the moral impulses of every ingenuous, unbiased nature," etc.

The foregoing, we allow, was no very unctuous retort, but when a minister, calling himself a Methodist, became a special pleader against the Government, and for rebellion and slavery, we believed then, as we do now, that sharp reproof was called for, especially so since at that very time Missouri was in peril of being transferred to the Southern Confederacy, of which slavery was proclaimed to be the corner-stone.

2. On January first of this year we made a plea in behalf of the Central Christian Advocate, directing our appeal to the Book Agents, Bishops, Annual Conferences, and the Book Committees, but more especially to the patronizing Conferences. This plea appeared in the first number of the year. The wants of the South-West were urgently set forth. The war and persecutions had deprived us of almost all our patronage from Missouri, Arkansas, and Kansas. With the view of saving its life, the Central Christian Advocate was diminished in size, while the other two papers, circulating in the same region, were enlarged. All these pressures seemed to conspire to crowd the Central Christian Advocate out of existence, notwithstanding its great importance to the religious interests of the South-West.

3. The vicissitudes experienced by Rev. John Linan about this time constitute a mournful case. He had been stationed on Jackson circuit, in the vicinity of Cape Girardeau, surrounded with secessionists. He was formally notified to leave the country, on pain of being maltreated as one worthy of any punishment, however extreme, and for no other assignable cause than that he was a preacher of the Methodist Episcopal Church. After enduring much hardness as a good soldier, he, at last, quit that region, leaving

his wife and children there by necessity for several months, he himself becoming a wanderer, without home, business, or support. After much delay, he got his family in safety to St. Louis, and there for some time, without pastoral charge or employ of any sort, and, hence, without income, he brooked all the cold privations of poverty. In the year 1864, by Price's second invasion, he was again forced to flee to St. Louis as a place of safety. But this good man bore all these afflictions with a spirit of martyrdom that would have done credit to the times of primitive Christianity.

4. It has often been stated by *Conservatives* in Missouri, as they were called, in February, 1862, that after Price was driven from the State, secession was entirely crushed out in Missouri. A writer from Kansas City, February 2d, gives a very different view of this subject, and adduces facts to the contrary. His statements are reliable. Here are some of the deeds perpetrated: The raising of the rebel flag in Kansas City by some fifteen hundred secessionists; the robbing of the Liberty Arsenal of a large amount of United States arms and ammunition by the citizens of Independence, Westport, and Kansas City; the firing into Union men's houses, by men who were once or are now in Price's army; in August, 1861, driving all the Union men who dared to speak their sentiments from their homes, robbing them of their stock, and threatening their lives; going, in September, in vast numbers to Lexington, and participating in that battle, furnishing food and clothing to the enemy, and insulting Federal prisoners on their way home, refusing them water, food, etc.; in October, waylaying our troops; in November, burning a train of Government wagons, and driving away all the cattle, after having sold the cattle to the Government; in December, firing into Union men's houses in Independence, tearing down the

American flag, robbing the mail and seizing the stages and
horses; in January, killing a disabled Federal soldier, and
robbing the mail and express.

These are mere sample deeds of the lawlessness prevailing in Missouri, especially in the two tiers of counties along
the Kansas line. And these acts were done by the very
men, who, when Federal troops were in their vicinity, were
loudest in their protestations of loyalty to the country.
These were forward in procuring safeguards from our officers
by sycophantic conduct, and knowingly and willingly perjured themselves by taking the oath of allegiance to the
United States as a mask of protection in their acts of rebellion. Besides, these perjured men calling themselves
"loyal Missourians," permitted Hays, Quantril, and others
of that sort, to come into their towns and neighborhoods,
to commit depredations on Union men, giving them aid and
comfort in their fiendish ravages. Of such there was a
very large number in the Spring of 1862, who had studied
various plans to deceive the Government, and succeeded to
a perilous extent in undoing what the General Government
had done. This class of men, as a matter of course, afforded
all possible aid and comfort to General Price, in invading
Missouri in the Fall of 1864, rendering him all the assistance they could in ravaging the country anew.

5. The Southern Methodist preachers of Missouri were
almost a unit on the side of the rebels. At this time, however, two or three, who were from the first on the side of
the Union, declared their protest against their disloyal
Church, and were only waiting for an opportunity to unite
with the Methodist Episcopal Church.

Several Southern Methodist preachers were put in jail
in St. Louis and elsewhere. Van Cockerel, who had en-
camped with five hundred men near Columbus, was captured
by Jemison, and this ministerial traitor was then, it is said,

lodged in the military prison. Rev. Mr. Caples, of the Missouri Conference, Methodist Episcopal Church South, was put in close confinement for lecturing other prisoners in favor of rebellion. He was General Price's chaplain, as Price had been class-leader under Caples. Two other Southern Methodist preachers were also in jail here. After some time Mr. Caples was sent to the Alton prison, and was subsequently let out on parole. He figured very prominently at his Conference, in Missouri, and tenaciously sustained his own and his Church's secession proclivities. The following paragraphs are taken from the St. Joseph Herald, as there reported:

"PIOUS BLASPHEMY PUNISHED.—Dr. Caples, a former chaplain in the rebel army, and latterly a citizen of Glasgow, having charge of the Methodist Church South in that place, whom General Fisk, under a heavy penalty, required to superintend the keeping of the telegraph in order in his district, was advised by the Union officers to keep out of the way of rebel shells. He replied that God had put a·band of iron around him, and the shells of his friends, the 'Confederates,' would never harm him; but, shortly after uttering this exclamation, a shell came screaming through the air and carried away one of his legs·close to the body, and he died in a few hours."

"MAJOR PORTER AND THE REVEREND REBEL, MR. CAPLES, OF GLASGOW.—During the late battle of the Forty-Third, at Glasgow, Major Porter, who is surgeon on General Fisk's staff, had charge of the hospital, and, while busily engaged in attending wounded soldiers, received notice that Rev. Mr. Caples was wounded, and desired his immediate attention. The Major sent word that he was engaged, but if they would send Rev. Mr. Caples to the hospital he would see that he had every attention. The family returned word that 'they would never consent to Mr. Caples entering a

Federal hospital, and the doctor must visit the house.' The
Major returned word that, if the reverend gentleman died
and went to hell, he would not neglect wounded Federal
soldiers to attend on a rebel. This Rev. Mr. Caples was
formerly chaplain on Price's staff, and sneaked into the
Federal lines, took the oath, and gave bond, and was a star
preacher in the Southern Methodist Church. We would
like to have some one furnish the names of a half dozen
loyal preachers in that Church."

6. At the opening of 1862 we penned an editorial for our
paper, the Central Christian Advocate, from which the following is an extract:

"Several meetings of our leading brethren, the bishop,
Dr. Clark, and Rev. Henry Cox have been held in reference
to our spiritual affairs in St. Louis. The chief question
considered was a reorganization of our Church, and the formation of a central congregation around which our friends
may now rally. Union and disunion now divide the Protestant Churches generally in St. Louis, except our own,
which is one, and Union only, without any disunion element
whatever. Our members, whom the times have dispersed
among other Churches of the city, are now inquiring most
earnestly after the ordinances and communion of their spiritual *alma mater*. The neglected harps which, during years
of captivity, have hung unstrung, are now taken down and
being put in tune for such songs as the one hundred and
thirty-third Psalm. At a concluding meeting, held in our
office, on the 2d inst., by a few brethren, utterances were
made and prospects presented which truly refreshed all
present. We may say, in general terms, we have no doubt
but the Methodist Episcopal Church will rise in this city
with the same vigor which characterizes it in Northern
cities. We make these statements for the gratification of
our friends throughout the State and the entire country.

We are quite sure we do not overstate the matter, and that time not far distant will verify our declarations.

"In conclusion we would say, the Methodist Episcopal Church will have a glorious future in Missouri. Its loyalty and stability will recommend it to citizens of the State, because it has stood as a unit for the country at large, and has never been the tool of nor mixed itself with party politics, nor encouraged lawlessness in any form whatever."

7. Union Church, in St. Louis, forms the pleasing topic of discussion in this paragraph. This magnificent structure, corner of Eleventh and Locust streets, was built by the Presbyterians, in 1850, at a cost of $90,000, including parsonage and furniture. It was purchased, March 14, 1862, for the Methodist Episcopal Church of St. Louis, and although the cost—$37,300—was small compared with its actual value, yet it required men of faith and courage to assume its payment at such a time. The edifice is one hundred and twenty feet on Locust by eighty-one on Eleventh-street. The hight of the main tower is one hundred and sixty feet, that of the other one hundred and four feet.

The purchase of this church was greatly promoted by the untiring zeal and labors of Rev. Henry Cox. He had great skill and much experience in such enterprises, having been principal in building a large and beautiful church in Newark, New Jersey, and having, also, just emancipated Wabash Avenue Church, in Chicago, from a debt of $25,000 or $30,000, besides several other achievements of like kind. The brethren in St. Louis greatly coveted his services as pastor. To meet this case Dr. Cox, with a committee from St. Louis, attended a meeting of the bishops, at Springfield, Ohio, where the committee's request had a favorable hearing. He next visited St. Louis, and raised one thousand dollars among our people, with which to close a written contract for the church. He then speedily raised five thousand

UNION METHODIST EPISCOPAL CHURCH,

Corner of Eleventh and Locust Streets,

ST. LOUIS, MO.

dollars in St. Louis, which secured us the occupancy of the building for the Missouri Conference, opening February 26, 1862. The following Summer he went eastward and collected six thousand dollars, which was applied on the remaining debt. While the Doctor was pressing these financial measures with remarkable activity, the spiritual interests of his charge were husbanded with like perseverance and success. We question whether the success of this enterprise has a parallel in the Union. Three years from the day of its purchase this noble temple was wholly paid for. Its congregation was, during these years, the largest Protestant one in the city. The membership had grown to over four hundred, and the Sunday school reached about the same number.

8. The session of the Missouri Conference, commencing February 26, 1862, was an important event in Missouri Methodism. Our entire white membership in St. Louis did not exceed eighty-two, thirty-two of whom belonged at *Simpson Chapel*, and the rest were the remnants of *Ebenezer* and *Hedding* charges. In addition to these we had a small colored congregation, but their existence hung upon a very slender thread. Their church might be closed any hour by the rebels, following the precedent of their violent expulsion from their Church by Southern Methodists after their secession.

The process of proscription and expatriation had been most assiduously plied in St. Louis as well as abroad in the State. The fell curse visited on our cause was made so exhaustive that we were almost without a people. For over six months our fragmentary charges had been without pastors, they being driven into the army for personal safety, as well as through the double pressure of duty to their country and their families.

When we were unexpectedly sent to St. Louis to edit the

Central Christian Advocate, Dr. M'Anally twitted brothers Shumate, Huffman, and others, and proclaimed aloud that he would soon prostrate Dr. Elliott, "the abolitionist of terrible dimensions," as Dr. Longstreet had christened us in the dozen letters he wrote against us for the South Carolina Advocate, 1845, and which were copied in most of the other Southern Methodist papers. We count this cognomen conferred upon us as peculiar and special honor, and, although little given to vanity, were we to glory in any thing about ourself, we would make this the theme of exultation.

Although Dr. M'Anally plied the work of prostrating us with special relish, he was doomed to succeed little better than in his labored efforts to destroy his country and found his ideal Confederacy.

At the appointed time, more members of the scattered Conference were present to respond to roll-call than might reasonably have been expected, and the Spirit animating them may justly be characterized as apostolic.

We copy a report of the occasion prepared for The Methodist of March 8, 1862, by AN OLD WESTERN PIONEER, St. Louis, March 1st:

"THE MISSOURI CONFERENCE.—*Interesting proceedings—The Oath of allegiance taken by the entire Conference.* The Missouri Conference of the Methodist Episcopal Church opened its session in St. Louis, February 26th, Bishop Simpson presiding. His health is now poor, but is somewhat improved. The session was held in the Union Presbyterian Church, corner of Locust and Eleventh streets. This church was recently purchased by the members of the Methodist Episcopal Church of St. Louis, and possession is to be given on the 14th of March. The Conference, on the first day of the session, passed a resolution requesting the Provost Marshal to come to the church and administer the oath of allegiance to the entire Conference. The hour was set for Friday, at ten o'clock, A. M. The names of the Conference were called, and all stood up in a circle, with the Bishop at their head, and Doctors Elliott and Poe. After the oath was administered, each man signed his name to the paper. This being done, several speeches were delivered.

"It should be mentioned that Dr. Elliott's flag had for the first time been exhibited on the occasion, with its expressive mottoes in beautiful embroidered letters, which presented a flag, in many respects, different from all others. After the ceremonies of the oath had been performed, without any previous programme, several persons were called, and short speeches were delivered, of which the following is a brief outline. The Provost Marshal, General Farrar, was called on, and addressed the Conference, and the visitors, who had increased to a respectable congregation :

."The Provost Marshal rose to a general call, and briefly said it had been his pleasant duty to be present at the meeting of the Conference, and he viewed their proceedings with much interest. It was refreshing to find such an exhibition of voluntary obedience affirmed to the Constitution and laws of our glorious Union. When he remembered the number of secessionists who had come to his office since the fall of Forts Henry and Donelson, and our recent victories elsewhere, he could but contrast their action with that of the present assembly, and question the existence of a loyalty so slow of development and uncertain in tenure. The damnable heresy of secession had so dried up the fountains of his faith in, he regretted to say, many of his fellow-countrymen and citizens of Missouri, that it became to him a most pleasant duty to turn away from them and fraternize with men who had been always loyal. The meeting and the occasion afforded him much gratification, and he predicted a prosperous future for all as a result of their harmonious and patriotic action. The General was loudly cheered in many parts of his address, of which we give but a brief synopsis, doing feeble justice to the effort.

"Rev. A. Poe, of Cincinnati, on call, rose, saying, as he was a preacher, he preferred, in speaking or in preaching, to take a text, and by consent would now take one—the Twenty-Third Article of Religion of the Methodist Episcopal Church. He then read as follows: 'The President, the Congress, the General Assemblies, the Governors, and Councils of State, *as the delegates of the people*, are the rulers of the United States of America, according to the division of power made to them by the Constitution of the United States, and by the Constitutions of their respective States. And the said States are a SOVEREIGN and INDEPENDENT NATION, and ought not to be subject to any foreign jurisdiction.' He remarked, the Provost Marshal has just commended us for being always loyal. He thought no credit was due to them for this, as they would be heretics if they were not loyal, according to their own book. Let it be borne in mind, that the Methodist minister who does not sustain the Government of the United States is a heretic. Formerly, heretics were burned, but as a more merciful punishment, he would suggest that they be no more than hanged. Our brethren of the Methodist Episcopal Church South have the same articles, but they proposed at their General Conference in May next—he doubted if they would get there—to change this article to read, 'Rulers of the Confederate States of America.' He had the good fortune to be born in Ohio. It was a good State, not only to be born in and emigrate from, but to stay in. They all were loyal, and therefore no necessity for administering the oath there. But he regarded this article of religion with special interest, as being equivalent to the oath of allegiance to all Methodist ministers.

"Rev. Dr. Elliott, editor of the Central Christian Advocate, was called out and said, he would call attention to a beautiful silk embroidered flag which hung before the audience. He would speak of it historically and expositorially. About a year ago, it will be remembered there was hung out in the center of the city a rebel flag. He so hated it that he never looked at it to ascertain what were its symbols, but heard people say there was a rattlesnake on it. Could not vouch for the truth of it. He remembered many stories about snakes, big and little. There was one well authenticated, about a snake in the garden of Eden. Most of us know the trouble and woe that snake caused. It was the old Apollyon himself. The story goes that after that time it was only his apprentices that were sent out to deceive the people, but he believed that now, in this rebellion, it was demonstrated that the old fellow had come out again in *propria persona*. Last Fourth of July he invested twenty-five cents in a little Union flag, and hung it out gloriously from the third story on Pine-street, over the head of brother M'Anally, and believes it had been of considerable use to the Doctor in the way of protection. This was a small flag, but we got up a better one, aided by the boys. On attending the Illinois Conference last Fall, the brethren there subscribed fifty dollars to purchase a handsome one, and here it is. See the elegant embroidery; examine it; done by the hands of noble Union ladies in this city. What fine texts for speeches are on it: 'GOD AND LIBERTY!' These are the principles of the Methodist Episcopal Church, from which the Methodist Episcopal Church South has apostatized, or, rather, been bewitched and misled. On the other border we read, 'Sustain the Union!' This as a Church we do, not with the sword, but we so teach the people. And if they will not, then we must hand them over to those whose business it is to handle the sword.

He said he would take this flag to every Conference he attended, and hoped to gather up his feet, and lie down with joy under its folds when this rebellion is crushed out, and E Pluribus Unum waves over a united people.

" Rev. H. Cox, being called out, said, he felt it to be a privilege to express his opinion and defend his position with reference to that flag. He was a comparative stranger. It gave him deep satisfaction to be present and take the oath of allegiance with his brethren on his entrance upon the work here. He was born in England, and for thirty years owed allegiance to the British Government. He came to Canada as a Wesleyan missionary, but from associations began to feel aspirations to mingle with his brethren in the United States, and in due time took the oath of allegiance. That oath he regarded as indicative of a government. He never dreamed that within the United States there could be found a man so vile as to lift his hand against the General Government. He regarded that oath as binding him to sustain that Government against all interference, domestic or foreign; even though Great Britain herself should rise against us, he was pledged to the Stars and Stripes.

" When, however, men talk to him of the possibility of British intervention, he maintained that the body of the English people would never allow any such intervention in favor of the so-called Southern Confederacy. Never did the fire so burn within him as when he read the demand of the great British Government for those contemptible fellows Mason and Slidell. Had war come, he must have stood by his adopted country. So do I stand to-day, and never will I cease to wage war and battle till the flag of our Union floats in every State, and over every foot of land within the borders of our Republic. A stain will always rest upon that man, that Church, or that community which has faltered in this day of trial.

"Bishop Simpson being loudly called for, spoke of his visit to the Missouri Conference, seven years ago; of his journey on through Jefferson City, Springfield, etc., to the Conference in Bonham, Texas, in company with the late, lamented martyr, A. Bewley; of their being threatened to be mobbed on the way, and other incidents, and said the present Conference had a right to stand around her altars, and declare her unalterable attachment to our glorious Union, so beautifully represented in the flag before us; a flag cut with angels' hands from the blue above—a flag upon which no lion could spring, and to which no eagle can soar—a flag gazed at with their eagle eyes from their blest abode. And yet there is a higher symbol than this flag; it is the cross—the ground of our hope—higher than the stars. The cross first, our country next. Let us, by its benign influences, cultivate love to our enemies, while we love our country and our God.

"It is impossible to do justice to the speech of the Bishop. His feeble health prevented a fuller display of his powers.

"In conclusion, Dr. Porter was called up, and felt willing to mingle with his Methodist brethren in their rejoicings. He would have joined them in taking the oath, but had taken it a few days previously. He had a question to propose: Have you, as a Church, a right to be patriotic? Here is a great political problem in process of being solved. He believed it to be the duty of the Church to be patriotic. It was as clearly taught in the thirteenth of Romans as in the Twenty-Third Article of Religion in the Methodist Discipline. It is also taught in the fifth commandment. The first government was patriarchal. God delegates his authority to man. Our fathers are but the delegates of their fathers. The Presbyterian Church is bound by a thousand obligations, as the Methodist Episcopal Church, to be loyal. Had the Church done her duty, the rebellion would not have happened. The Church has been silent too long, and her silence may have been termed criminal. Let us wipe it from her record. It is not for us to ask, what is treason? It is well defined, and can not be misunderstood. 'The powers that be are ordained of God.' Let the Church awake to her duty and her responsibility in the premises.

"The occasion was one of vast interest to Methodism in Missouri, which almost for the first time since the Southern secession has been brought before the public of St. Louis. As the Conference is yet in session, I content myself with this account of the proceedings in advance. After adjournment, you shall hear from me again."

9. As secession, on the opening of 1862, seemed to be effectually strangled in Missouri, the following lamentations were uttered by the editor of the St. Louis Christian Advocate, and it seems that pungency was added to the mourning, because the Union Church was about to be organized, and the cause of the *abolitionist, Elliott*, seemed to have gained the day. Hear him, when the National victories were so triumphant in the country:

"What a scourge is upon it! [the country.] What chastisements it is undergoing! Who that really loves it can reflect upon its present condition, without feelings of bitterest anguish! Distracted, disrupted, torn, and bleeding! Its material interests all marred—its social relations almost broken up—its educational and religious interests all languishing! And the prospects for the future more dark, if possible, than the aspects of the present! Think of the bitterness of feeling—the blood-thirstiness and cruelty which are being manifested—the hatred and vindictiveness of one part of the people toward the other! Who, twelve months ago, would have believed the people of this country could ever have been led to indulge the feelings they have recently manifested? How total, in many instances, has been the disregard to private rights, private interests, and property! Think of the destruction of homes—the waste of towns and villages, and the desolations of whole tracts of country that have occurred—the thousands of innocent women and children who have been rendered houseless and homeless—and the tens of thousands of sober, industrious men, made desperate by the sufferings and privations they have endured!"

The editor of The Methodist, after quoting the foregoing, March 8, 1862, justly remarks:

"All this is sternly true, but what is the guilty cause? It is the Southern treason against a righteous and Constitutionally administered Government. All this woe comes from the men with whom the Advocate has been in tacit alliance. Why does it not turn its doleful admonitions toward them? The article from which we quote has no allusion to the reprobate culprits who inflict this misery on the country. Such is the maneuver of this Western editor. Why does he not treat with the retreating foes of his country?"

The same number of The Methodist has the following: "Bishop Early, of the Methodist Episcopal Church South, opened with prayer the fourth day's session of the rebel Congress."

10. The following, written to Dr. Thomson, we produce, as it appeared in the Christian Advocate and Journal, preface and all:

"LETTER FROM REV. DR. ELLIOTT.

"Our old friend Dr. Elliott, whom we have long admired and revered, gives us the following letter, which is far better than any thing we can write:

"THE UNION METHODIST EPISCOPAL CHURCH IN ST. LOUIS.

"'MY DEAR THOMSON,—Allow me to renew the pleasant acquaintance of former years, as well as to convey to you

32

intelligence that will gladden you and your readers. Last
week the scattered remnants of the Church of 1784, after
several primary meetings, paid in the sum of $5,000, which
secured to them a deed with a mortgage of the Union Presbyterian Church on Locust and Eleventh streets. This
gave us the occupancy of the church. A programme of
the exercises for Sunday, 16th, was struck, and scattered
among the seats. The services were announced in the daily
papers of Saturday preceding.

"'The love-feast in the vestry, at nine o'clock on Sunday
morning, was one of great interest, and even novelty. Our
people who had been in our church here since its reconstruction in 1848—the remnants—were there. Their old
church, Ebenezer, has been shut up for some seven months,
and they have been homeless, as sheep without a shepherd.
The small fragments of *Hedding Chapel* were there. The
few left of the dispersions of *Simpson Chapel* were present.
The whole force of political influence, of social disownment,
of commercial domination, and the contempt of nearly all
the Protestant and Catholic Churches of the city, had nearly
buried our feeble flocks. These had various utterances to
express their joy, and such as reminded me of the exulta-
tions of the Jews after returning from their seventy years'
captivity.

"'Here were several refugees, who had been driven from
their homes and Churches during the last year, and were
now returning to their former abodes, purposing to collect
what remained of their dispersed Church, begin the world
anew, like Job, and raise the standard of the Methodism of
1784 in all its original purity—antislavery, pure, operative,
and dauntless. Their brief declarations spoke volumes.

"'And then there were here those who had been of our
Church before their arrival. Some had united with the
Methodist Episcopal Church South, as the best they could

do in their judgment; others had temporarily worshiped in other Churches; others had been looking out for homes. These expressed, in language too emotional to be penned, their joy at again being housed in their cherished Zion. All these were just prepared, after the close of love-feast, to enter the church while the choir and organ sang, 'Long-loved Zion,' with its admirable chorus—

> "We 're thronging home, we 're thronging home,
> Home to long-loved Zion,
> We 're thronging home, we 're thronging home,
> Home to long-loved Zion."

The preacher, Rev. H. Cox, delivered an admirable sermon on the sower, at the close of which the fine old National psalm, 'America,' was sung by the choir and the large congregation with the justly allied shout of devotion and religious patriotism. O how cheery was it to hear sung—

> "My country, 't is of thee,
> Sweet land of liberty,
> Of thee I sing!"

And the concluding line,

> "Great God, our King,"

reminded me of the song of Moses, and the children of Israel, and of the one hundred and thirty-third Psalm. But a higher scene followed. The pastor, just as this hymn closed, stepped down from the pulpit and gave an opportunity for persons to unite with the Church. He invited the members of Ebenezer to assume their membership in the Union Church; also those from other Churches who had certificates of membership, or if these were not within reach, their Christian character would be the standard, and those having no certificates might join on trial. Here was a touching spectacle. The remnants of the shattered Churches presented themselves with no common emotions, while the zealous pastor gave them, in hearty style, the

right hand of fellowship. Many members of the Methodist
Episcopal Church South presented their certificates, which
were read aloud; others, who had temporarily been without Church privileges, manifested no ordinary interest.
Brother Rich and family, recently from Boston, and who
have been so active in bringing this day to pass, were
among the exultants. Brother Leonard, also, very active
in this good work, with his good wife was of the number.
Brother Fisk, formerly of Michigan, another leader in this
work, with his whole family, was among those who stood
up by the flag of his beloved Church and country; and his
little son Charles—a promising boy—said he was from 'Old
Ebenezer,' and claimed membership. This Charles, I trust,
will do good service in the Church and in the world. The
readers of your paper can scarcely be aware of the interest
we have felt in this occasion. Now in St. Louis, where the
full influence of politics, of society, of commerce, and of
business, and other Churches was against our Church, we
have the prestige of unswerving loyalty to speak for us in
the gate.

" ' We will have our proportion, too, of social and commercial influence. Of those who united with us all are
loyal. Mr. Cox distinctly stated that no disloyal person,
either by certification or by probation, should have a place
in our Church; and this is as it ought to be till the person sees his error, confesses it, and manifests true loyalty.
This, according to our Articles of Religion, is a term of
membership in the Methodist Episcopal Church in Missouri.
The congregation, morning and night, filled the spacious
church.

" ' Here is a fair beginning, and only a beginning. It
will require time, an able ministry, and much labor to
replant, build up, and establish the Methodist Episcopal
Church in Missouri. The door now, for the first time, is

open in St. Louis. Up till this period our Church has labored under difficulties entirely insurmountable by any means that could be employed to counteract them. But now God has opened the door, and we have the privilege of entering this great harvest-field with good prospects of success. Thanks be to God!

"'Your brother in the patience and tribulation of Jesus Christ.

"'St. Louis, *March* 17, 1862.''

11. We had purposed to leave the St. Louis Christian Advocate to its own chosen way, as far as we were concerned. But the loyal press felt called on to take some notice of it.

The Missouri Democrat refers to it in the following words:

"The St. Louis Christian Advocate, D. R. M'Anally. editor, blends piety and secession politics in curious fashion. The number for this week, though cautious and guarded, evinces its adherence to the cause of rebellion about as clearly as the paper did before the Rev. editor took the oath of allegiance. Nearly every article, except a brief leader on *The Church*, is pervaded by a most evident desire for rebel success, more offensive from the affectation of candor. Men who profess religion and practice crime, who pray and commit perjury, contrive robbery, bloodshed, and treason on their knees, and stir up wicked men to deeds of wickedness, in Scripture phrases, must find this an acceptable and comforting family journal."

The Evening News of St. Louis, after quoting the above, remarks:

"It is a mortification to the loyal Methodists of Missouri that a paper, which assumes to be the organ of their sect, should have degenerated into an organ of secession. We have published several complaints against the Christian Advocate from members of the Methodist Church in the interior of the State, and we know that the course of that paper is the subject of the severest condemnation among the loyal Methodists. It not only seeks to injure the cause of the Union, but it brings shame upon the cause of religion by sympathizing with, and advocating, with whatever boldness it dares assume, a revolt which is as wicked as it was causeless. The Christian Advocate has done much evil by nurturing and encouraging the spirit of disloyalty in this State. It has no right thus to abuse the leniency of the Government to which it is indebted for protection; and it will be worth while for the military authorities to consider the propriety of suppressing it if its glaring hostility to the Union is persisted in."

12. We see at this time the double spectacle of the Methodist Episcopal Church South, on the one hand flying from their strongholds, and on the other hand attempting to extend their cause into the Northern States.

A Nashville contributor to the Central Christian Advocate says:

"All the Southern Methodists are skulking rebels. The whole Book Concern is corrupt. M'Ferrin fled to Alabama as a rebel—left home and Book Concern. Dr. M'Tyeire, the editor, has fled to New Orleans. Huston is here as an evil spirit among the secesh. Dr. Summers, being formerly of the Alabama Conference, is supposed to have returned thither. Dr. Green is skulking around here, preaching secession and rebellion against the existing military power. He figured in the secession of 1844, and has two sons and a son-in-law in the rebel army."

April 18th and 19th, the Southern Methodists held a bogus Conference at Atlanta, Ga. Bishops Andrew, Pierce, and Early were there; also, Drs. Green, M'Ferrin, and M'Tyeire, Revs. W. J. Parks, W. J. Scott, M'Donnell, Huston, and Joseph Wheeless, Esq.

It was thought impracticable to have a General Conference before April, 1863, but it was left with the bishops to convene one if they thought it feasible.

The publishing-house in Nashville was left in charge of the General Book Agent and Publishing Committee, to be managed as best they could.

The support of their bishops was distributed as follows: Bishop Soule was to be supported by the Tennessee and Memphis Conferences; Bishop Andrew by the Alabama, Louisiana, and Florida; Bishop Paine by the Mississippi, Texas, East Texas, Washita, and Arkansas; Bishop Pierce by Georgia and South Carolina; Bishop Early by Virginia, North Carolina, and Holston; Bishop Kavanaugh by Missouri, St. Louis, Kentucky, Louisville, and Western Virginia.

The Nashville and the South Carolina Advocates were to be united, and published at Atlanta, Ga., under the supervision of their former editors, Messrs. M'Tyeire and Myers.

Their whole work was distributed into five Episcopal districts. Profoundly disloyal, and passionately devoted to the so-called Confederacy, they nevertheless planned to continue and extend their rebellious Church over loyal territory. Hence the district of Bishop Kavanaugh embraced Missouri Conference, September 3d; Kansas Conference, September 11th; St. Louis Conference, October 1st; Indian Mission Conference, October 22d; Arkansas Conference, November 5th. This occupancy of loyal territory by rebel Conferences can only be understood as a deliberate purpose and effort to establish and perpetuate an ecclesiastical organization in avowed opposition to the Government, and in sworn allegiance with its enemies.

13. A correspondent of the St. Louis Republican, while in General Curtis's army, writes as follows from Salem, Arkansas, May 5th:

"Among the noble Union men of this county—Fulton—

is Rev. Joshua Richardson, an old resident, originally from Massachusetts, and a man of spotless integrity and uprightness of character. Several months before the rebellion he became convinced that the Methodist Church South, with which he was connected, was thoroughly disloyal, and he arose in the Conference and publicly withdrew from the body, alleging his reasons, and exposing their tendencies. Since then it has been proved that the entire Methodist Church South, both clergy and laity, is utterly treasonable, and has aided and abetted the rebellion to the extent of its power. Soon after the rebellion had got fairly under way Mr. Richardson was arrested, at the Union camp-ground in this county, a place devoted to Methodist camp meetings, and was afterward hurried to Little Rock, and kept a prisoner there for two months. During his imprisonment, out of four hundred prisoners arrested as Union men, only fifteen had the fortitude and courage to hold out to the end. Of these he was the animating spirit, and they determined to stand their trial for treason to the new Confederacy, even though it should result in their execution. All the others joined the Confederate army rather than stand the test. A grand jury, composed of persons from each county in the State, ultimately failed to find any thing against them, since they had committed no overt act, having merely refused to deny their attachment and adherence to the Union, and they were discharged; but emissaries were sent out to stimulate rebel parties on their route home to murder them. They, however, arrived home in safety, and have survived the tyranny of the rebel Government up to the present time. Many times Mr. Richardson has been informed that the rope was already prepared with which to hang him, but he has steadily held to the Union faith, and refused, at all times and under all circumstances, to deny his principles. His brother and three of his sons were compelled to flee for their lives, and the latter have been active soldiers in the Union army, under Colonel Phelps, of Missouri, and fought bravely at the battle of Pea Ridge. Their names are Franklin and Alexander. One of them was the guide of our army to Batesville. These young men are devoted to the cause of their country. Since the army has been here the old gentleman has been in to offer whatever he had left to the Union cause, and invited the soldiers to visit him freely and partake of his hospitality. The force of his Christian character has protected him through the reign of terror."[1]

14. The system of passes was at this time in vogue in St. Louis, and having to attend, during the Summer, several Conferences as well as the Commencement Exercises of the college at Mt. Pleasant, we took occasion to procure a pass, nor did we ever find it irksome to be at any pains necessary to fully conform to and support the rigorous policies employed for the protection of the innocent and detection of the guilty.

15. On the occasion of the final suppression of the St. Louis Christian Advocate we wrote the following as an editorial for the Central Christian Advocate of May 8, 1862:

"It is a matter of much grief to us that there was reason and necessity for this severe measure. For some time we have contented ourselves with barely reporting in our columns the protests against the course of this paper, and, could we now consistently relieve the editor and his paper of the decision against them, we would cordially do so. But we can not give *aid* and *comfort* to rebellion, much less can we be *neutral*, when the very life of our nation is not only threatened, but assailed, attacked, and, with murderous design, every means used to destroy it, as well as to establish in its place the most wicked and oppressive

---

[1] See The Methodist for 1862, p. 156.

33

despotism that ever cursed the world. We have read carefully the St. Louis Christian Advocate since June, 1860. In regard to it we now make the following statements, which we believe we can prove by testimony that would pass for true before any impartial jury or court in the United States:

"1. It is the organ of a Church which avowedly has sanctioned and aided rebellion, and has thrown all its influence against the National Government. On this Church the leaders of the rebellion have imposed silence, requiring them not to meddle with their conspiracies, but to acquiesce in them, and give them all the sanction of their professed religious sanctity. Their Church has been used as the tool of rebels. It has been bewitched and deceived, misled and controlled by the rebel leaders.

"2. Those ministers and laymen of the Methodist Episcopal Church South who are truly loyal—and we rejoice that some of them are so—have pronounced the St. Louis Christian Advocate a supporter of the rebellion.

"3. The disloyal members and preachers of the Methodist Episcopal Church South have approved and patronized this paper.

"4. Disloyal citizens and members of other Churches in Missouri, whether Catholic, Protestant, Presbyterian, Baptist, etc., have become its patrons and subscribers as a means of supporting their rebellious career.

"5. This paper has been recognized as the successor, de facto, of the treasonable Missouri State Journal, edited by J. W. Tucker. The Missouri War Bulletin was published in its office, printed on its press, often edited in its buildings, and was fraternally treated.

"6. The political rebel press has recognized this paper as on their side of the question.

"7. The religious rebel press has had full fellowship with it

"8. The loyal political press has placed this paper in opposition to their cause.

"9. The loyal religious press has, without exception, put the paper on the side of rebellion.

"10. Hence, by its influence, a large portion of the professors of religion and inhabitants of Missouri have been alienated from the Government, the sanctity of oaths invaded, many lives lost, much property destroyed, and all under the profession of truth and right.

"From the columns of the St. Louis Christian Advocate we draw the following *internal proofs* of its disloyal character:

"1. It has made constant weekly selections from the hostile rebellious or apologetical press.

"The foreign press has been drawn upon in republishing selections, either disparaging to the Government of the United States, or eulogistic of the cause of the rebels.

"The Southern press has been resorted to to support the cause of rebellion, and to depreciate our Government.

"The patrons of the Northern press having Southern affinities, and uttering disparagement to our Government, have been quoted or cited frequently by this paper.

"The apologists of the rebel cause in the North have been cited with approbation in its columns.

"2. The St. Louis Christian Advocate has colored the course of the South favorably to its cause, and eulogized its principles and measures.

"3. It has also depreciated and discolored the course of our Government, so as to prejudice its cause.

"4. It has largely fabricated current news to correspond to its theories. It has generally discredited the issues of the telegraph and other sources of weekly news, misrepresenting them. And it has published principally, not the authentic news, but its own version, and by this means has substituted its own disloyal theories for the authentic facts and principles of the reliable press.

"5. All this has been done under the profession and sanctity of religion, by this means sapping the foundations of public and private morals, and leading many to abhor the religion which teaches that such moral and political monstrosities are consistent with Christianity.

"The editor of this paper, some five or six months ago, had been warned of his danger, and exhorted by the Provost Marshal to change his course. He even subsequently took the oath of allegiance *as a citizen;* and now the presumption is, that he felt himself justified in doing acts as a Christian and editor which he abjured as a citizen.

"He and others seem to be so far deluded as to believe they are doing God service by such acts. But this is only an aggravation of the sin, as it argues a want of just intellectual views and moral feelings, allowing persons to break every commandment of the decalogue, under the plea of serving God.

"We beseech Almighty God to open the eyes of the understanding of these men, lead them to acknowledge and forsake their horrible sins; and may God have mercy on their souls!"

After the suppression of the St. Louis Christian Advocate, the editor himself was put in prison in St. Louis, in consequence of his editorial course. About a month after his imprisonment we were traveling in the cars to our office from the western part of the city. Three, gentlemen in the cars, Southern Methodists, approached and addressed us in behalf of Dr. M'Anally. One of them hinted that I might petition for his release, as I had been the cause of his arrest; but he immediately recalled, or, at least, did not persist in this statement. It was stated by them that Mr. M'Anally, in consequence of his confinement, must soon die unless released. The question was then put to us, "Would you petition for his release?" I told them I would, on certain principles. It was then agreed that they would meet me at my office next day at ten o'clock, and I would then accompany them to the Marshal's office. With this agreement, we parted.

In the mean time I drew up the following address to the Marshal, on the score of mercy to a culprit:

OFFICE CENTRAL CHRISTIAN ADVOCATE, }
101 *Locust-street, St. Louis, Mo., May* 10, 1862. }

PROVOST MARSHAL GENERAL FARRAR:

DEAR SIR,—I respectfully petition you to release the Rev. Dr. M'Anally from prison, under such restrictions as your patriotism, humanity, the public safety, and your official obligations will admit.

In making this request, I do not intimate, nor do I believe that injustice has been done him or his friends, in the suppression of his paper, as my editorial remarks on the subject will show in the Central of May 8th, a copy of which I send you.

In presenting this petition, I am not to be understood as making any apology for his errors or as indorsing any of them. Nor can I recall or apologize for my editorial course in reference to the St. Louis Christian Advocate or its editor.

I am an unconditional Union man, and stand by my country whether it is right or wrong. If it be right, to keep it right in a constitutional way. If it be wrong, to put it right according to the Constitution; but not to destroy it.

Very respectfully,　　　CHARLES ELLIOTT,
Editor Central Christian Advocate.

None of these gentlemen, however, appeared at my office the following morning. For what reason they declined to meet me according to appointment I can not tell, nor did I inquire. By some means, however, they succeeded in having their friend released from prison, and we did not think proper to make any inquiries about the business.

16. Toward the close of May of this year our people, who had been driven to Kansas or elsewhere, began returning. Many loyal persons of the Southern Methodist Church were waiting anxiously for the services of the Methodist Episcopal Church. Many loyalists of other disloyal Churches as well as citizens were looking earnestly for the ministrations of our denomination, the only undividedly loyal Church in Missouri.

In Kansas City, Sedalia, Booneville, Lexington, Independence, Tipton, and Springfield, the services of our Church were called for.

Near Cape Girardeau, where secession had hitherto reigned supreme, the tide seemed turning.

At Rolla, where much disturbance had prevailed, the people appeared to be coming back to sobriety.

On the whole, the door, so long shut, opening with encouraging prospects, yet on the threshold were many hinderances.

June 4th we wrote the following to our esteemed brother, Dr. Thomson, which was published in the Advocate and Journal of June 12th:

"It is not usual for one editor to write for the columns of another, but the close alliance between you and myself for many years may allow an exception. Besides, I think an article now from me will give you more reliable information about Missouri than could be easily obtained from another source occupying the same space in your columns. Furthermore, the present Missouri Conference year is the beginning of a new era in this State.

"Allow me, then, to glance at the past in a few words.

After the great Church secession in 1844–45, our Church in this State was superseded by the Methodist Episcopal Church South. When, after 1848, owing to the non-compliance of the Southern Methodists with the terms of a regular organization, our Church resumed its former status in Missouri, the new, or Southern Church, used every means to prevent our success in the South-West. Political, social, and business influences were all arrayed against our people throughout the State. Violence was resorted to, embracing murder, riding on rails, intimidations, threats, and expatriation. These means were so effectual that, at our last Conference, one-half of our six thousand English-speaking members in Missouri had been driven out of the State.

"In this city these influences, in connection with the war, were so powerful as to reduce the number of our members to a mere handful. The members of our Church emigrating to this city, finding their Church in this condition, considered it too unpromising for permanency or efficiency, joined other Protestant Churches, or remained isolated from all Churches. These Protestant Churches were mostly of the secession stripe, ours being the only entirely loyal Church in the State.

"But when the lines between loyalty and rebellion were fully drawn, all loyal men saw the predicament of belonging to a disloyal Church, and having their disloyal preachers. Hence they ceased to attend the ministrations of the rebel ministers. On looking around they saw no Church in Missouri fully loyal but the despised, rejected, and persecuted Methodist Episcopal Church, with its loyal antecedents, accompaniments, and prospective character. Hence in our Union Church we have now nearly two hundred members, a Sunday school of over three hundred scholars, and large congregations. And could we pay off the debt of our Church at once, our people in this city would then be enabled to proceed in the work of church building to great advantage, and at no distant time our Church here would bear such a relative proportion to population, as it does in Cincinnati, Pittsburg, Chicago, or other Western cities. My best information from the State goes to say that in most of the Southern Methodist Churches there are more or less members who have ceased to attend the ministrations of their Church, and are anxiously waiting an opportunity to unite with our Church. To a limited extent, the same is true of members of other Churches, and loyal citizens are looking to our Church for spiritual instruction.

"I inclose a brief editorial of mine on the subject from the Central Christian Advocate:

"'Besides, the work of emancipation is sure to proceed to completion in the State, and then hundreds of thousands will emigrate from the free States to Missouri, whom we should meet with open arms, and enroll many thousands of them on our Church books.

"'Our Central is a necessity for the South-West. But for the war, I am persuaded it would be more than self-supporting, and would never need to draw the appropriation made for its support. As it is, the appropriation of $4,000 will be exhausted with this volume. Our enterprising Agents, who are strictly forbidden to exceed that sum, are now making vigorous efforts to sustain the paper till May, 1864. To aid them I put myself on half rations from January 1, 1862, to June 1, 1864; unless the grave should receive my remains, in which the earthly man will need no more supplies than the angels in heaven. And as a dernier resort, if all other means fail, I purpose, in *behalf of the General Conference*, to become publisher and editor, if life and health are spared, should the issue be only once a month, quarter, or year, and no larger than a handbreadth. This I am, with God's help, determined on. There is just as much need and as much support, also, for our paper here as there is in Boston, New York, Cincinnati, or Chicago. And this is not left to the option of General Conference or the Methodist Episcopal Church, except temporarily, as the genuine and loyal Methodists of the South-West, if need be, will see that this is done. Of this I have no doubt, and therefore write with perfect confidence.'

"I have never enjoyed better health and spirits than I have in going through the Missouri wars. During some seven months after January 1, 1861, we looked that any week might array about one-half of St. Louis in deadly and close battle against the other half. In about half an hour's reflection I meditated on the differences between being shot through the head, hung like a dog as was Bewley, or cut to pieces with dirks and swords. This over, I became indifferent as to how this might be, slept soundly and unarmed in my own office, never losing an hour's sleep, and lived without fear, but in full hope of the blessed future. And now, brother Thomson, my sheet is full, and I send up this prayer, may God bless you and your family!"

17. In June of this year Rev. H. Cox was deputed to visit the East to obtain aid in paying for Union Church, St. Louis. Bishop Morris, at Springfield, Ohio, June 16th, gave him the following introductory letter. We copy it to show the decided and just position of the Bishop, as well as to give a fair survey of the true Methodistic interests of Missouri:

"Yours of June 10th is received; I reply promptly. I am in favor of the Union as it came from Washington, and of Methodism as it came from Asbury. Our free institutions are a power for good, and unadulterated Methodism is also a power for good. The decided manner in which our ministers and members generally have come to the aid of the Government in its efforts to put down rebellion, will increase our influence as a denomination, especially in the border slave States. Hence the importance of the great work in which you are directly engaged, that of restoring and reorganizing Methodism in Missouri on its original basis. Missouri is one of the largest and most fertile of our Western States, and would have been greatly in the ascendant only for its connection with the 'peculiar institution.' It is destined soon to be numbered among the free States. This is as certain as that effect follows cause; and when relieved from the shackles of slavery its population will double in seven years, and in wealth will more than double in the same period. So I think. St. Louis is the head and heart of the State of Missouri; and the Union Church, of which you are pastor, is in the center of that city. This is beginning at the right time and in the right place to operate on an extensive scale. Hence the importance of success in that enterprise. If we fail there the pitcher will be broken at the fountain, and the wheel will be broken at the cistern. But if this central Union Church can be released from debt and sustained, it will send forth a current of life through a thousand arteries into every part of Missouri; to be returned through a thousand veins, and keep up a healthy action in the body-ecclesiastic. Let every Christian, every patriot, and every philanthropist unlock his safe, bring out his treasure, and rally to the rescue. May your mission to the East be-a success; may you obtain favor in the sight of God and the people, and return with a telling report!"

18. Lieutenant Kennett, of the United States Army, Superintendent of the Ordnance Department at Nashville, in the discharge of his duty, had occasion to visit the Southern Methodist Publishing-House. On examining the basement, where machinery had been placed for manufacturing certain parts of Confederate ordnance, Rev. Mr. M'Tyeire, the editor, commenced explaining that certain bolts and screws

were used in stereotyping, with other implements in the printing business, going through quite a list of articles. After hearing him through, the Lieutenant remarked, that every sentence he uttered was a falsehood. The Lieutenant remarked that he had been educated for the ordnance department, and knew where every one of these bolts, nuts, and screws belonged on a gun carriage.

The Nashville clergy about this time were quite nonplused. Rev. C. D. Howel and Rev. Ford, of the Baptist Church; Rev. C. D. Elliott and E. W. Sehon, of the Southern Methodist Church, were brought before the Governor, who required them to take the oath of allegiance to the United States Government or suffer the consequences. They begged for time to consider; one day was asked. This was granted. Next they asked a few days more, which were also given. Such hesitation, under the circumstances, showed these men to be lost to the moral sentiments of genuine patriotism. Surely a strong delusion had taken possession of these clergymen.

The editor of the California Christian Advocate learns that Dr. Carnes, of the Methodist Episcopal Church South, and editor of the Texas Christian Advocate, was in command of a rebel regiment, made up mostly of Southern Methodists, preachers and members.

19. The contrast, between July 4, 1862, and that of 1861, was very striking indeed to those who resided in St. Louis. Early in 1861 traitorous officials were scheming night and day to subvert the State Government and to overthrow the municipal authorities in St. Louis, and thousands of citizens were boastfully promoting these menacing conspiracies. A succession of plots led Price to an army, and put that treacherous host in battle array against the National Government and the State of Missouri. St. Louis was viciously threatened, and Union men appointed to the alternatives of

exile from the State, or loss of property, imprisonment, and death. Union men were gathering about them every available weapon of defense for their lives, Government, homes, and property. On the FOURTH, few Federal flags were to be seen in all the city. It was to us a dreary day; yet, trusting in God while the earthquake threatened from beneath, we dared to put our colors on the tainted air.

How changed from this was July 4, 1862! The former secession Chamber of Commerce was nearly extinct, and the new Union one was flourishing. The Mercantile Library Association was revolutionized, and the old Stars and Stripes floated over its halls. The Union element was rising in the Churches. The Fourth was celebrated and observed as in former years, without any outward expression for rebellion.

We visited Benton Barracks, where eight hundred soldiers were feasted by loyal people. Speeches were delivered, to which we could utter a hearty AMEN. Toward the conclusion we were called to offer prayer. We prayed for the sick soldiers, and also for our deluded enemies, that they might see their sins and forsake them, by laying down their arms, and returning to their allegiance. We thanked God for our victories, and prayed that he would soon give us peace by subduing our enemies; and should European intermeddlers send their ships and their men to destroy our liberties, under the hypocritical cant of *intervention*, that *our God*, by his waves, his winds, his storms, and newly created maelstroms, would swallow them up as he did Pharaoh and his host, to which all the people, as was right, said AMEN AND AMEN! But we did not forget to tell the *boys* that, were it of any use, we would 'march on with them, and when we fell they might bury us, if they HAD TIME to do so. General Fisk made a short speech, just such as only he could.

20. The desolation of the Southern Methodist Church in New Orleans is thus described by an army chaplain, under date of June 5th:

"Yesterday I visited the office of the New Orleans Christian Advocate, and Southern Methodist Book Depository, situated on Camp-street, a few squares south of Canal-street, and found the whole establishment closed, and as desolate in appearance as though a pestilence had passed over it. A business man in the next door—and a member of their Church—told me the Advocate suspended for want of paper, and the Depository for want of purchasers; and that all the business men of the establishment, from the highest to the lowest, were in Beauregard's army at Shiloh, in some official capacity, the last he knew of them. So that in New Orleans, no less than in Nashville, the Methodist Episcopal Church South has left its moral, intellectual, and religious operations to languish and die. Their churches are, most of them, without pastors or preachers, except what the local ministry supply, and prayer and class meetings are generally suspended."

21. At a meeting of the loyal members of the Methodist Episcopal Church South, of Montgomery county, Mo., held at Danville, July 16, 1862, a preamble and resolutions were unanimously adopted. The preamble went to lament that the Conferences, bishops, preachers, and editors of the Methodist Episcopal Church South had been misled so as to be ranked among rebels. The resolutions, five in number, expressed their loyalty to the country in plain but decided terms.[2]

Methodism in Missouri at this time was undergoing a process of transformation. The enterprise of *Union Church* opened an era of success to the Methodist Episcopal Church in the State, through the energy of Rev. H. Cox. There

---

[2] Central Christian Advocate, July 31, 1862.

was a call now for loyal preachers, notwithstanding the
many hinderances yet in the way.   The Church South
was in a disorganized state, and there is little reason to believe it will soon, if ever, recover from its demoralization
and anarchy.   A portion of its members, several of its local
preachers, and a very few of its traveling preachers have
kept themselves unspotted from the great sins of slavery
and rebellion.   The Methodist Episcopal Church, however,
after its many and long sufferings, from 1844 to 1862, a
space of eighteen years, having passed through fire and
water, is now prepared to occupy the whole State, and
gather up the broken fragments of its own people, and also
the misled and houseless members of the Methodist Episcopal Church South, without any afflicting criminations for
the past.

CHAPTER XX.

THE HEROIC MAJOR.

THE following narrative, from the **pen of** Rev. Thomas J. Babcoke, formerly of the **Missouri** Conference, Methodist Episcopal Church, will be read with interest by every Christian and patriot. It is difficult to decide which excels, his Christian **character**, his pure patriotism, or his masterly generalship. He is worthy to command a regiment, and yet he was deprived of his Major's commission by Governor Gamble just because he was a radical, or uncompromising Union man, and a member and minister of the Methodist Episcopal Church; for, according to the ideas of Governor Gamble and his conservative, or secession, allies, any one of these characteristics was sufficient ground for degrading him from office. It was a dark day for Missouri when President Lincoln, honest man that he was, was misled by the so-called conservatives of Missouri. Although Mr. Babcoke lost his commission because he voted for Mr. Lincoln, was a "Northern Methodist," etc., he was, nevertheless, first to take arms again to repel the invasion of the traitor Price. But let Mr. Babcoke speak for himself:

"BROTHER ELLIOTT,—I take this opportunity to pen you a few items of my history in Missouri. In December, 1859, I arrived in Shelby county, and tarried a short time in Shelbyville, the county seat. I there became acquainted with the Methodist Episcopal Church South. They politely offered me that station for the rest of the year. I declined, and started, with my effects, for the Osage country, where

I landed in January, 1860. I purchased a small farm in
Miller county for our home. The people seemed kind and
accommodating till I inquired for the Methodist Episcopal
Church; then the inquiry arose, 'Does he belong to the
South or *North* Church?' I informed them I belonged to
neither, but was a member of the Methodist Episcopal
Church. Learning brother M'Knight had an appointment
three miles distant, I attended and gave in my letter. The
news flew like wild-fire. Then commenced the cry, 'He is
an old abolitionist, and has come here to steal our negroes.'
I strove to counteract the report, but all in vain; the
Southern preachers strove to give it publicity from the desk.
They declared the Methodist Episcopal Church was an abolition Church employed by the North to steal and run off
negroes. Then they began their persecution, threatening to
tar and feather and drive me from the country, and even
threatening my life. They frequently met me at my appointments, and ordered me to leave and not return. I still
attended to my duties and filled my appointments, notwithstanding their threats. At length I resolved to meet their
charges publicly. I appointed a day for that purpose. I
tried to show our position. For a few days things were
quiet. This was against the 'Church South.' They lost
ground unless they kept the people inflamed with a spirit
of persecution. For the purpose of kindling the public
mind against us, Rev. John D. Read, a Southern Methodist
of Miller county, announced a lecture at one of my preach-
ing-places, and requested me to meet him. I went. He
brought a Rev. Mr. Marcus with him. They refused to let
me reply, and their general treatment of me was such as
one might have expected at a country groggery. Read tried,
by insults and low-bred slang, to wound me and excite the
people against me. They lectured six hours to prove we
were all abolitionists. They quoted largely from the North-

ern Independent, and told the people that paper was published by the Methodist Episcopal Church. This they stated some twenty times. They also read several resolutions passed by the abolitionists, and declared they were passed by the Methodist Episcopal Church. Their sole purpose was to fire the people against us, and force us to leave the country. While making his false charges against us, Mr. Read, pausing, asked, 'What ought to be done with such people?' An old Mr. Wilks spoke out, 'They ought to be served as Ray was,' alluding to a man hung by a mob. Such was my treatment at the commencement of my labors in Missouri. The preachers above alluded to were both from the North. They were acquainted with the Methodist Episcopal Church, therefore, and knew their statements were false. I was compelled to hear their falsehoods, without the privilege of correcting a single error. Gross insults were heaped upon me during the lecture. At the close I rose and told the people that fully two-thirds of the charges made against us were base falsehoods, and, denied the privilege of replying there, I would meet them in four weeks, and try to correct public sentiment in reference to the Church. I met the people on the day appointed, and endeavored to show them our position on the slavery question. Such experiences and events filled up the first two years of my life in Missouri. Every falsehood and insult that could be invented was heaped upon the Church. Several times they met to mob me, but the providence of God preserved me. In Johnson county a mob, headed by a Baptist doctor, was coming in sight of me, when some of my friends informed and advised me to leave. This was so contrary to my disposition that I resolved to meet them and defend myself, at all risks, but a lawyer of the place prevailed on the mob to disperse. It would require a volume to detail all the insults of which I was the subject on account of my connection with the Church they loathed. When the rebellion broke out they redoubled their persecution. I was abused in every assembly. It was publicly declared I should die. A Southern Methodist preacher said to one of my neighbors, 'He can never escape; they are determined to kill him.' It was a trying moment. I looked in all directions for a friend, and, for some time, thought myself alone. I visited a family by the name of Duncan, who had been friends to me indeed. I shall never forget the day they said to me, 'We are still your friends.' Some of them wept, and said, 'I can see no chance for you; they are determined to kill you.' For a moment all looked dark, but, quick as thought, this came to my mind, 'I will shield thy head in the hour of battle.'

"I returned home, not knowing what course to pursue. My family became alarmed, and urged me to leave the State. This was impossible. I was without money. They had a consultation, and resolved to take my life. A tree was selected for my gallows. About this time I was employed to drill a company, which was said to be for mutual protection. I hoped by so doing to receive protection; but in this I was disappointed. A friend informed me they had resolved to reject me; for said they, 'He will be killed, and we want true Southern men to command us.' This took me by surprise. But as another expedient we resolved to make an effort to raise a Union company. At this juncture, Captain Johnson, a rebel chief, sent twenty men to take me. But when they came I was not at home. Drill-day came for the first company. I informed them I had learned of all their plans, and would save them any further trouble. I spoke in favor of the Union, and warned them to be careful what they did. When I closed, a Mr. Bliss called for Union volunteers. I stood still. To my astonishment forty enrolled for the Government. I was called upon to command them. We prepared as fast as possible for defense. Our second meeting was in Tuscumbia, Miller county. That day we captured two pieces of artillery, concealed in a rebel's hay-mow. The rebels then banded together to attack us. I met them in person, gave them my reasons for enlisting, and told them of their abusive conduct. Some of them swore I should not leave alive. I warned them of the consequences. Returning home the next day, I was informed that they had resolved anew to take my life, and were then on the way to execute their threat. I then determined to engage in the war in earnest. I told my family not to look for me till they saw me coming. I started to Jefferson City to make some arrangements for our defense. I stopped at a blacksmith's shop, near Hickory Hill, to get a horseshoe set. The shop-bench was covered with gun-locks and other fragments of fire-arms. The smith inquired, 'Where are you from?' My answer was evasive: 'I am from the South-West.' 'Do you know of any companies being raised out there for the Union?' 'I believe I do.' 'What are the names of the commanders?' I paused as if to study. He then asked, 'Is there one called Babcoke?' I paused a moment, and answered, 'O yes, he is called a hard case.' 'Yes,' he said, 'but we will stop his career soon.' I encouraged him to do so. He then said, 'We are making up a company to take him as he passes down to Jefferson.' I told him to be very careful whom he told this to, for we did not know whom we might be talking to. 'Ah!' said he, 'I know whom to trust.' He gave me the names of the leaders of the gang, which were Peter Taylor, of Morgan county; James M'Kinsey, of Cole, and Dr. Waters, of Miller. I learned their whole plan, and then left him ignorant of whom he was talking to. After making the necessary arrangement, I started with my command for Jefferson City. We got through without harm, though we were waylaid by Taylor and his gang. Failing in this attempt, two hundred of them leagued together to take us on our return. The commander at Jefferson City, learning this, ordered Colonel Mulligan to accompany us with a part of the Irish brigade. While passing Hickory Hill we were fired upon by a small gang of skulking rebels, but without effect. We then marched to Mt. Pleasant, Miller co., and found it evacuated. The next day we found all kinds of goods in almost all kinds of places. We sent teams and gathered them in. There were dry goods, groceries, hardware, boots and shoes, caps and hats, provisions and medicines, all boxed up and hid out in hollows and thickets. Only two Union men were living in the place. It was a rallying point for rebels. A Southern Methodist Church was there, and their meetings were frequently improved by prayers and lectures in favor of the South. Wm. P. Dickson, of this place, was a leading rebel and a Southern Methodist. It was this Dickson who said, 'These Northern Methodists are all negro thieves, and ought to be driven from the State.' He is the man, also, who solemnly affirmed before God, there were no contraband goods on his premises, and in less than two hours we dug up one hundred and fifty pounds of powder buried in his stable. When found, he acknowledged he put it there. He it was, too, who took the oath of allegiance, and solemnly swore to reveal every thing coming to his knowledge of a treasonable character. And still he kept this powder concealed with which to kill Union men. This raid into Miller county was all placed to my charge. If I was before the object of their hate, I was now much more so. They now sought my life with redoubled energy. My family was insulted by both males and females. They would pass my house, using the most abusive language possible. The cries of 'old abolitionist,' 'negro equality,' and the like, fell upon the ears of my wife daily. They destroyed my farming utensils and all other articles of value they could get hold of. A short time after this a choice pack of seven chivalrous men came to my house in my absence and ordered my wife to leave, under penalty of death. I give the names for the benefit of their posterity; namely, Berry Taylor, Preston Taylor, jr., 'Brit' Taylor, Elijah Spence, one Hilman, and one Hase, all members of a professed Christian Church! After this gentlemanly act they concealed themselves in the brush, and Calvin Tindal, another Baptist, cooked provision, and with his wife carried it to them. The abuse daily heaped upon my family occasioned me to move them to Jefferson City for protection. I remained there during the Winter. The dangers and uncertainties of war-times had prevented me from making any thing during the year for support. Living in the city soon reduced my little stock to a very small pittance. My family again beset me to leave the State. But where should we go, and what should we have when we got there? were questions of no small import. In fact, there was no alternative but to stay and fight it out. I resolved at once to move back to my farm.

"Contrary to the advice of my friends and entreaties of my family I started, arriving in March, 1862, with my goods on my own premises. Immediately the word came that the rebels had determined to kill me or force me to leave. I was informed of their council at Judge Wilks's, and of their decision to attack my house at a given time. I immediately prepared my house for defense. I procured fire-arms enough to have given them twelve shots. With these I resolved to stand my ground. They learned of my preparation, and so did not come. But the most horrid threats and bitter oaths human depravity could invent were daily fulminated against me. Still God was near to deliver.

Notwithstanding all their menaces we planted a small crop of corn, and, for a time, tilled it; but before we 'laid it by' the guerrillas were prowling through the whole State.

"In the Spring of 1862, the Conference appointed me to the Otterville circuit. I made several attempts to reach the circuit, but was as often intercepted by bands of guerrillas. I seemed more than any one else in all the country the object of their hate. They sought my life with zeal worthy of a better cause. Failing in all efforts to reach my field of labor I at last abandoned the idea of trying to do the work of a circuit preacher. I devoted myself, as far as possible, therefore, to my farm, working and watching by day, and sleeping at night, with two double-barreled shot-guns, two pistols, and an ax so near my bed that I could lay my hands on them any moment. Thus I lived till the time above mentioned, when the guerrillas commenced their work of plunder and death. Then I entered the service again in the militia. Scouting and fighting occupied us till cold weather came. And though our fighting was not as severe as that experienced in many places, we saw enough to learn the horrors of war. Cold weather setting in, the guerrillas disbanded or went South, and we were called to Jefferson City, where we remained till March 1, 1863. Then we were furloughed home to report for duty at a moment's call. During all this time we had received nothing for our services. I served five months in the Home-Guards, and seven in the militia, living upon my own limited means. Many of our families were in a most destitute condition. Undergoing every privation ourselves, the horrifying intelligence almost daily reached us of peaceable Union citizens being shot down in their doors or in their fields. Others were attacked and robbed of coats, hats, shoes, jackets, and some were stripped of their pants and socks. Houses were often robbed of the last vestige of wearing apparel, and even bed clothes were taken, and bedticks emptied to make rebel shirts. Women and children were driven from their houses, and the houses burned before their eyes. I have seen family after family fleeing for safety, their feet bound up with rags to keep them from freezing. I have listened to accounts of suffering, and the weeping of mothers and children till my heart grew sick. In the midst of all this desolation, speech after speech was made in the North reprobating the Government, and eulogizing the South. These reached us, and aggravated our sufferings. Such men will have their reward. They will be hated on earth, excluded from heaven, and loathed even in hell.

"Notwithstanding the fiery trials of these times, we had some manifestations of the goodness of God in the outpouring of his Spirit. We had some excellent meetings. In the Fall of 1860 we held a camp meeting on Proctor, in Morgan county, near the residence of Rev. B. F. Wilson. It will long be remembered. About one hundred conversions were witnessed. Many promising young men were of the number, some of whom are gone to their reward. When the war broke out these young men flew to their country's aid. While I write, my soul rejoices at the remembrance of the happy prayer meetings of those young converts, in their tents or in some secret spot outside the army encampment. But where are they all now? Some have fallen in battle, others by slow but fatal disease. One of the number, a brother Wilson, was accidentally shot, and we found him only in time to see him die. The rest are still filling their places in the Union army. May God preserve them and our country! I am still in the service of the State, and probably will be till the war closes.

"I have not been able to note one circumstance in a hundred, but I have given the outline of the whole

"ROCKY MOUNT, MILLER COUNTY, Mo., *April* 18, 1863."

The following appeared in the Missouri Democrat of October 21, 1864, toward the close of Price's last raid into. Missouri. The writer, from Jefferson City, makes the following statement as prefatory to the article: "The hero, Captain Babcoke, was a Major in the Home-Guards, at the commencement of the war; and afterward a Major in the E. M. M., from which position he was removed by Governor Gamble, through the influence of Colonel Flesh, commanding the regiment, for being a Radical. He is, besides being a worthy and most reliable citizen, a man of great decision of character, courage, and self-reliance, and he possesses in a peculiar degree the quality recommended by Danton, *audace, audace, toujours audace.*" Thus in English, *bold, bold,* ALWAYS BOLD.

"On the 7th instant, April, 1864, Captain T. J. Babcoke, being in command of a militia company, organized under Order 107, was returning from Rolla to Jefferson City, with thirty men, mounted, having been sent to the former place with dispatches from General Brown to General M'Neil. About twelve miles from Jefferson City he came upon a rebel picket-guard of thirteen men, including a Captain and Lieutenant, at a farm-house, part of the party being inside the house. Thinking a bold course the better one under the circumstances, he rode up to the sentinel in the road with the greatest coolness, and when the sentinel halted him, he said, in a commanding tone, 'Halt yourself!' and assumed such an authoritative air, that the rebels supposed him to be one of the officers of their own army, making the grand rounds. It must be remembered that Price's rebels are sometimes clothed by whole companies in Federal uniform. The rebels, thus thrown off their guard, permitted Captain Babcoke and his men to ride into the yard. As soon as the house was surrounded, Captain Babcoke told the whole party of rebels to surrender, in such tones as told them they were sold. He had men that he could rely upon, and he ordered them to shoot down any rebel that attempted to move or use his gun. The rebels outside of the house dropped their guns, and those inside, seeing the house surrounded, surrendered at discretion. The horses of the rebels were hitched at some distance in the woods; these the Captain sent for, and mounting his prisoners—two officers and eleven men—started for Jefferson City.

"This capture was within one mile of Price's main column, and Captain Babcoke soon found himself like the man who won the elephant in a raffle. He had 'got a good thing;' the point was to 'keep it.' But the mind that conceived the capture of the rebel outpost was fertile in expedients. He placed his prisoners in the front, and started to go around the rebel army, which lay between him and Jefferson City. He crossed the Osage several times, and made a number of narrow escapes from running directly into the rebel lines. He was tangled in the bends of the Osage like Mr. Raymond in the 'elbows of the Mincio,' at the battle of Solferino, but he knew the country, and succeeded in effectually dodging the whole rebel army.

"On the next day after the capture of his prisoners, while riding down a hill, he saw a rebel company descending a hill opposite, and coming toward him. He conceived that his safety lay in boldness, and, with his thirty men and thirteen prisoners, he charged on the rebel company with a yell, and drove them back. Each prisoner had two or more men especially to look after him, as well as after the enemy in front, and the captured rebs, instead of being an incumbrance, were an advantage, as they helped to swell the numbers of Captain Babcoke's force, and make it appear more formidable. No sooner had he got the rebs in front of him on the skedaddle than he made a sudden detour by

35

a by-path, and got into the brush. It was afterward ascertained that the skedaddlers reported to Price that the Federals were advancing in force in their rear, and he had his army drawn up in line of battle to meet them.

"The rebels were hunting for Captain Babcoke for six days, knowing he could not have reached the Federal forces at Jefferson City. The brave men of his company had a tedious time camping out nights, and, between guarding their prisoners and keeping a watch-out for the enemy, they had little time for sleep. Six days and six nights were thus passed, when Captain Babcoke and his faithful band safely arrived in Jefferson City, and delivered to General Brown their thirteen prisoners, who are now safely confined here."

CHAPTER XXI.

EVENTS OF 1863.

1. JANUARY 1, 1863, was made a day of National celebrity by the Proclamation of liberty to all slaves in rebel States. It was announced September 22, 1862, that this event would take place in every State remaining in rebellion on January 1st. Every true Methodist had special cause of thanksgiving, as the elementary principles of his Church called for the extirpation of slavery, and our bishops in their address to the General Conference officially recommended that no more slaveholders should be allowed to enter the Methodist Episcopal Church. Hence the decision of the General Conference of 1784, requiring freedom in all cases, but which the civil power had suspended for eighty years, could now be carried out to the letter by the General Conference without any vote from Annual Conferences. It was deemed prudent, however, to have the votes of all the Conferences in recognition of this providential deliverance which God himself effected by his servant, Abraham Lincoln, through a military necessity, in conformity with the Constitution and the principles of justice and Christianity.

2. The providence of God seems especially manifest now in numberless instances.

Rev. John Moorhead, writing from Chillicothe, Mo., January 2d, says: "The President's Proclamation will doubtless occasion some little agitation. But the people are becoming reconciled to emancipation, as they see it is inevitable. I mean by the people in the above, the secessionists, as they are the stronger party in this country. The Union men have been reconciled to the measure all the time. Let me inform brother and sister Gardner that old Charley Cooper, the leader in brother Gardner's rail-riding expedition, was shot and killed in his own house, a few weeks ago, by parties unknown. Truly 'the way of transgressors is hard.' 'Vengeance is mine, I will repay, saith the Lord.'" This Cooper was leader in the mobbing and riding Mr. Gardner on a rail, of which we spoke in a previous chapter.

Through Rev. Mark Robertson, we learned this month that two Methodist preachers were murdered in Arkansas; these were James Murray, traveling, and Charles Cavender, a local preacher. Mr. Robertson, the fellow-laborer of Mr. Bewley several years in Arkansas, was finally compelled to leave. Were the murders and banishments of our ministers and members in the South-West enumerated, they would form a lengthy list. But there they stand recorded in God's Book of Remembrance, and they will shine forth with splendor in the world's trial-hour.

Many loyal Methodists of the Church South were deeply mortified by the course of that denomination. This was expressed with true Christian feeling and dignity, January 16, 1863, by Edwin Draper, Esq., a man of ability and prominence in the Church in Louisiana, Mo. He remarks:

"I will say in brief, I long since discovered, and was perfectly satisfied that the Methodist Church South was not only bowing its neck willingly to the yoke of the slave power of the South, but that it exerted a powerful, if not a preponderating influence in favor of the rebellion. Many of our members have been satisfied of the same fact, and more especially since the developed treachery of the Church organ at St. Louis. The Union members, and a few of the preachers, as soon as we became fully convinced of these facts, commenced our opposition to the malign influence of

the paper by protesting against its course and teachings and
the influence of the preachers directed against the Union
and the Government."

According to the analogies of God's providence in the
history of the world, both sacred and profane, we now see
the principal seats and perpetrators of wrong-doing especially visited with the scourge. The war so rages over old
Virginia, and portions of Georgia, and South Carolina, that
the strongholds of their former and confirmed iniquities
are likely to be utterly broken up. Several monstrously
criminal measures render this a justly deserved retribution.
1. They voted in 1797 to make the North-Western Territory free, that they might have the monopoly of slave growing, although such a vote was, in itself, right. 2. For a
similar reason, they favored the suppression of the African
slave-trade. 3. They raised for the South-West able-bodied
laborers for money, many of them sons of their own free
white citizens. 4. They selected their female breeders to
provide the markets of the South-West with a new supply.
5. They raised white concubines in great numbers and sold
them at high prices to vicious men further South. 6. By
their atrocious laws and pro-slavery morals, they banished
thousands of their best citizens to Southern Ohio, Indiana,
and Illinois, where they sought free communities, and these
localities are now sending back thousands of soldiers to
visit their iniquities with stripes, and to maintain the Government established by Washington. 7. They neglected
the education of the white masses, while they prohibited
that of the colored people. Thus a just and holy God is
visiting these iniquities in as signal a manner as he did
those of the antediluvians, the Sodomites, the Egyptians,
and other impenitent and wicked nations.

But in all the free States there is peace and plenty, as to
all the conveniences of life. Crops have been good, business

brisk, and none are wanting the supplies necessary for comfort. The principal cause of grief with them is the cutting down of the heads or members of many families by the slaveholders' war. But as complicity with moral wrong has been our great sin, we must expiate it by the blood of our citizens and payment of the war expenses. The retribution of the free States, however, is one of great mercy, though justice must strike the tempered blow.

3. During February and March many pressing calls in various parts of Missouri were made for our preachers, by members of the Methodist Episcopal Church South.

Mr. M. Y. Graham, a loyal Methodist of Westport, Mo., wrote to us:

"If ever there was a time when a holy religion was needed, now is that time, for verily wickedness stalks abroad at noonday. There are other considerations I will mention. This portion of country will be occupied by some religious denominations, and it appears to me altogether proper for our Church to lead the van, as it is well known to be the pioneer Church of the age. The ministers of the Methodist Episcopal Church South are so universally disloyal that their Church is nearly numbered with the things that have been, while a portion of the lay members are loyal. I believe this portion would gladly unite with a loyal Church. I further believe that a first-class minister would be liberally supported by the two towns—Kansas City and Westport—which places are only four miles apart, with a good M'Adamized road between them. Now, Mr. Editor, can not something be done to accomplish so desirable an object?"

From many other places in the State similar earnest and urgent requests came for the ministry of the Methodist Episcopal Church.

4. The President's Proclamation of liberty to the slaves of rebels began as early as the last of February to work out

its appropriate results. None of the predicted insurrections took place. In Missouri the sentiment became general that the system was hopelessly ruined. The slaves, too, were disposed to bide their time, as they considered deliverance near at hand. Thus public sentiment was gravitating toward the status of the Methodist Episcopal Church, which, from the first, testified and acted against slavery with a view to its final extirpation. The Church maintaining this stern position never, however, infringed the civil law, unjust as it was, considering that moral means constituted her great weapon. But the rebellion had annulled the Fugitive-Slave law, and the Almighty himself seemed to be ushering in the great jubilee of deliverance for four millions of enslaved men, women, and children.

5. The successful prosecution of the war by the United States Government toward the close of February, 1863, seemed to be life from the dead to the Union men of the South-West, especially to the scattered fragments of the Methodist Episcopal Church yet left in Missouri. With such thoughts as the following, we occupied the columns of the Central Christian Advocate, as a sober reason for the encouragement of these dispersed and peeled Methodists:

"Of the fifteen slave States, the rebels have thirteen under their control and in their alliance. Missouri would have been added had it not been for the influence of Kansas, Iowa, and Illinois. Delaware, Maryland, and Kentucky were divided in their allegiance. With these exceptions, the fifteen slave States were identified with the rebellion They swayed the entire South, the Mississippi included They possessed the military arsenal of Harper's Ferry, and the vast naval yards at Norfolk and Pensacola. They held the eastern shore of the Chesapeake Bay, which gave them the control of that bay to the ocean.

"They have lost during the war, up to this date, the

eastern shore of Chesapeake Bay and the command of the
Potomac, the city of Norfolk and its arsenals and dock-yards,
and the neighboring country and the dock-yards of Pensacola; they have lost all Virginia west of the Alleghanies,
Missouri, Arkansas, and part of Tennessee, comprising Nashville, the civil capital, and Memphis, the commercial capital;
they have lost Hatteras, Hilton Head, New Orleans, the
Mississippi, from its mouth to its junction with the Ohio,
and many other places. The insurgents do not now hold a
foot of ground which they did not hold early in the war.
Their armies have been driven from an area of more than
one hundred thousand square miles, while the flag of the
Union floats in every slave State save one.

"None of the loyal States have been the seat of war—for
the raids on Pennsylvania, Indiana, and Ohio are scarcely
worth mentioning—while general prosperity has prevailed
in the free States.

"The steps in the progress of National justice have been
numerous and marked in the free States. No more slaves
are to be admitted into the Territories; the District is now
free; the pirate Gibson has been hanged; there has been a
treaty with England to suppress the slave-trade; Hayti and
Liberia have been recognized; Missouri is in process of becoming a free State; the Confiscation bill, as an act of justice, confiscates the slaves of all rebels. The Proclamation
of the President does no more than carry out or execute
the law of the land; for, as slaves are property, and the
property of rebels is confiscated, therefore the slaves of all
rebels, according to all just laws, are confiscated.

"The hand and providence of God seem manifest in the
present state of events. The unjust platforms of political
parties are now broken. The Republicans bound themselves
to proceed no further than to stop the extension of slavery,
although, in general, they acknowledged it to be wrong.

The Democrats turned their eyes from its wrongs, and were intent on the preservation of their party, but their wrong purposes led to their division and confusion. The *Union party* is now the only one, and its counterpart is made up of *neutrals*, sympathizers, and rebels, or traitors, while, at the same time, God has sustained the cause of primitive and Scriptural democracy among those who vote, sustain, and fight for the *unity of the United States*, which is only another name for liberty, the Constitution, and the laws.

"God, in his providence, has baffled technical political parties. He has raised the National party to support the American system of free Government. He is also bringing defeats and confusion to the advocates and aiders of oppression, as truly as he did to Pharaoh and his hosts and nation."

The foregoing survey, recounting the doings of the Almighty, so encouraged our people in Missouri that, not with dejection, but with hope, they looked toward the future.

6. In a letter from Arkansas, early in March, by Hiram Ward, a private member, we learned that Mr. Bewley preached his last sermon at the parsonage of Bentonville mission, Arkansas. "His text was—2 Cor. iv, 5—'For we preach not ourselves,' etc. In a few days afterward he was caught, and carried back to Texas and murdered. Methodist preachers were notified to stop preaching, or they would share the same fate. We dared not assemble to worship in any way in the name of Methodists and Union men. Some of the members escaped from the hand of the rebels, and found homes in Indiana, Illinois, Missouri, and Kansas. Part succeeded in getting some property away, and others lost all. Some are still trying to stay in Arkansas, under all their trials, and some of us are still hanging to the old ship."

Rev. J. R. West, who had been greatly harassed, made

his way to Kansas. Rev. C. Baker was then in Arkansas. Three laymen, R. V. Hoback, Wallace True, and Hiram Ward, made out to reach Tecumseh, Kansas. Very few of our members or preachers were left in all the State.

7. At this time there was a clear outspoken testimony from many of the Southern Methodists against the rebellious and pro-slavery character of the ministers of the Methodist Episcopal Church South.

Rev. Alfred H. Powell sent us a letter from Springfield, Missouri, March 1st. We gather from this that he was born and raised on slave soil, and joined the Methodist Episcopal Church when only fourteen years of age. As a matter of course he went with others, in 1845, into the Methodist Episcopal Church South, and was a traveling preacher among them from 1850 to 1861. During the last-mentioned year he located, in consequence of the disloyal character of the Southern Methodist Church. He then became a chaplain in the loyal army, and served till December, 1862, when he resigned. He stated that many Southern preachers, in response to objections to the Fugitive-Slave law of 1850, argued that obedience to the powers that be was the duty of Christians. But on the election of Mr. Lincoln in 1860, this was considered criminal, even in the face of the Twenty-Third Article of Religion. He therefore concluded, for just reasons, to leave the Southern Church and unite with the Church in which he was born and baptized. He was always loyal to the Government of the United States. He refers to several Southern Methodist preachers who were loyal men; namely, Foster, Williams, and Myers; also to several local preachers, as A. C. Mitchell, Dr. Wm. Denby, Isaac Routh, and R. B. Rogers. Such was the honest course of this noble man, who has since that time done good service in the Methodist Episcopal Church.

Rev. N. Shumate and Rev. Wm. Hanley spent several days, embracing Sabbath, March 19th, in Louisiana, preaching to and visiting the people of that city, who received them with great cordiality. Most of the Southern Methodists there were loyal, and disposed to unite with the Methodist Episcopal Church. It was also reported that some two thousand loyal Southern Methodists in that region would soon leave the disloyal organization and unite with the Methodist Episcopal Church. Similar statements could be made of numerous other places in Missouri.

8. The Missouri Conference sat this year at Hannibal, March 4th, Bishop Ames presiding. The Conference of 1861 made its missionary appropriations on the usual basis, supposing the missionaries would be permitted to prosecute their work. On the contrary, they were very much interrupted. Preachers were driven from their work, and people driven from their homes. Some preachers, dependent principally on the missionary appropriation for support, in consequence, were in great straits. The Conference decided that when preachers received remuneration from Government or other sources, they should not receive missionary money. This was all very right, but it did not meet the difficulty of several sent to fields of labor who were to be supported partly by the missionary grant and partly by their circuits. Several of these could not labor on the fields assigned them, our people having left the country, and the preachers, on account of the war, could find no hearers. These, in the general chaos, unable to secure any business or position of profit, had no means of support from any source. When such were cut off from their missionary appropriation, it was felt to be a cool severity, easier in theory than in practice. Thus, about one thousand dollars of the appropriation allowed in 1861 were refunded to the Missionary Society. This anomaly formed part of the

sufferings undergone by the Missouri preachers that year, and was such as never occurred before, and may never occur again.

We here present the statistics of the Missouri and Arkansas Conference for several years back as follows:

1859...8,341 members.
1860...7,764   "
1861...5,129   "
1862...2,141   "
1863..4,387   "

In 1863 there were three districts and thirty-two circuits and stations, requiring thirty-five efficient preachers to fill them, and of these there were five appointments to be supplied. And where there were three districts south of the Missouri River, in former years, there was then only one of twelve appointments. All the territory west of Rolla and Sedalia, and south of De Soto and Rolla, had no preachers. The rest of our preachers and people in Arkansas and Texas were either driven out of these States or left for California, Oregon, and Kansas. Missouri lost many from the same causes and in the same way.

But notwithstanding all these disadvantages, the door formerly shut was now open to our preachers to an encouraging extent. No pro-slavery or unpatriotic stain was upon our people or preachers in Missouri.

One of the preachers of our Church was appointed to preach in the Southern Methodist Church in Hannibal, on the Sabbath of Conference. On his way to the church, in a crowd, they were stopped by a company coming from the church, one of whom remarked, "I think there won't be much of a meeting at our church; there is to be a preacher from Ohio." One of the company asked, "Will he preach politics?" The preacher remarked, "If it is the Ohio man, he will preach Christ, he will not preach politics." "Well,

I will go and hear him, and if he does, I will get up and leave the house." The minister preached as usual for him, and left the people weeping. The next morning, one of the members said, "I liked the sermon well enough, but I did not like his praying for the President; it is the first time such a prayer has been heard in our church for two years." This incident had much significance.

9. About the close of March, 1863, the affairs of the Methodist Episcopal Church began to assume a more favorable condition than for the two previous years, although the impediments were still numerous, and such as time alone could remedy.

The *Tories*, who uttered blasphemy in calling themselves Democrats, seemed pretty well used up, during March. In the West they were urged on by the Chicago Times and the Cincinnati Enquirer, as principals, and the Quincy Herald and Missouri Republican, as seconds, to say nothing of some other sheets of less importance. But these did not represent the great Democratic body, the reliable men of which were then rallying around the Union Government.

The Union armies in old Virginia, South Carolina, and Georgia were treading out the wine-press of the iniquities of these devoted regions.

At the beginning of 1862 the enemy was intrenched on the Mississippi, and holding it from its mouth to Cairo, and from New Madrid and Columbus, and extended to Forts Henry, Donelson, and Bowling Green. At this time we hold the great river, and with it Forts Henry, Donelson, Bowling Green, New Madrid, Nashville, Memphis, New Orleans, Baton Rouge, etc.

For nearly two years hostile armies marched over Missouri, desolating fields and firesides. Roving bands of robbers and murderers triumphantly rioted in once peaceful homes. Many of our citizens were murdered, others robbed, and still others driven from the country.

The President's Proclamation was working wonders in favor of the Union and liberty.

The colored troops, too, important auxiliaries to our armies, are being marshaled to complete the war force.

The loyal States also were in great prosperity and comfort, with the exception of the valuable lives lost in the war.

The mighty hand of God at this time was manifestly pleading the cause of justice and liberty, and punishing transgression.

10. Rev. A. H. Powell, of whom we formerly made favorable mention, was anxious to have the loyal Southern Methodists unite with the Methodist Episcopal Church. In a letter dated April 6th, in the Central Christian Advocate of April 16th, he argues that as the Southern Methodist Church as a whole was disloyal, the only course for her loyal members was to unite with the Methodist Episcopal Church. They could not consistently remain where they were, to form a new Church would be unavailable, and to meet the exigency, there was nothing left but to join the old Church. Several letters were addressed by him to his brethren in the Southern Church, and published in the Central Christian Advocate.

11. A marvelous change has taken place in Missouri on the great question of slavery. When the Convention, in the Spring of 1861, was called, Governor Gamble spoke as follows :

"No countenance will be afforded to any scheme or to any conduct calculated in any degree to interfere with the institution of slavery existing in the State. To the very utmost extent of executive power that institution will be protected."

In calling the Convention in April, 1863, Governor Gamble stated that it might " consult and act on the subject of the emancipation of slaves."

Thus the work of emancipation was progressing in Missouri. The providence of God was overruling and controlling the adjustments of political parties according to the righteous judgment of God. The old Garrisonian party would dash to pieces the Constitution, divide the Union, or any thing else short of fighting, in order to free the slaves. Now all is changed. The Republican platform avowed no more interference with slavery than merely to stop its extension. The technical Democrats would allow it to extend every-where. The Garrisonians, diminished in numbers, were hurrahing for the Union. The recent Tories almost ceased to exist. Congress, in 1862, would have given ten millions to Missouri for freeing her slaves; but the pro-slavery men wanted twenty millions. This demand not being met, the rapid movement in favor of freedom in the issue overturned forever the greed of being paid for theft and robbery. If justice were to have full sway, every slaveholder should be compelled to give to his emancipated slaves from one hundred to one thousand dollars, or more, for the oppression inflicted on them while they were slaves.

12. The loyal members and ministers of the Methodist Episcopal Church South, of Pike and Montgomery counties, few in number, however, had a meeting to repudiate the doings of the Missouri Conference, held in Glasgow, in 1861, and also to consider what was to be done for their relief. One of them, in the Central Christian Advocate of April 30, 1863, gives the following outline of the case:

" The disunion preachers and members are the seceders from the Methodist Episcopal Church South, in the United States, because their new Church was *the Church* of the Confederate States ; and, therefore, the Union preachers and members compose the Methodist Episcopal Church South. The Twenty-Third Article of Faith of the Southern Church is the same with that of the Methodist Episcopal Church, and recognized the United States Government. The Missouri Conference at St. Charles, in 1860, appointed Hannibal for its seat in September, 1861. In the mean time the rebellion broke out, and some of the preachers removed the Conference to Glasgow, being afraid of the Unionism of Hannibal, and thus the Conference threw itself into the arms of the rebel, Mart. Green. At this session, the rebel, Rev. W. G. Caples, was chosen President, no Bishop being present. If Mr. Caples claimed to be a citizen of the Southern Confederacy, he was a foreign enemy. If he claimed to be a citizen of the United States, he was a domestic traitor. By electing him, the Conference indorsed him; they announced themselves as a body of traitors. In every place where the rebel army had control, the Southern Conferences met. The Holston Conference, Bishop Early presiding, held at Athens, Tenn., October, 1862, suspended all its Union preachers. The Missouri Conference uttered no disapprobation. The following incident would illustrate the case of Southern Methodist preachers generally in Missouri: A Southern preacher applied to the Provost Marshal for a permit to go into the country to hunt. After receiving it, he remarked to the officer, ' Well, Colonel, this pass will protect me among the Federals, but what shall I do if the bushwhackers get hold of me?' ' Do?' said the Colonel, ' why, just tell them you are a Southern Methodist preacher, and the name will carry you safe through rebeldom.' Another Southern Methodist said, '.The Southern Church is strong enough to take the State out of the Union, and if she does her duty she will take it out.' Thus far the Southern Methodist."

13. The loyal Methodists of Kansas City, Weston, and

vicinity, early in May, addressed Bishop Ames, asking for
a preacher. They declared themselves in favor of a permanent Methodist Church in Kansas City; that religious as
well as civil affairs had been with them in an unsettled
condition, owing to the rebellion, and now they needed the
molding influences of religion in their midst. Some of
them were members of the Southern Methodist Episcopal
Church, but the day of usefulness for that Church was now
past, and their only hope was in the Methodist Episcopal
Church, which has never swerved from its allegiance to the
Government, whose flag has been and is the emblem of
light and Christian civilization the world over. They then
earnestly petition for an able, loyal minister of the Methodist Episcopal Church.

Rev. Samuel Huffman, who had labored eight years in
Missouri, knew the whole State, and who had nobly served
a successful term as chaplain in a Missouri regiment, speaks
as follows, in the Central Christian Advocate of May 7th:

"In this region, where we have been so long proscribed and
maltreated, I think we have now cause 'to thank God and
take courage.' We can preach almost every-where now
without serious molestation, unless it may be in some localities where treason is in the ascendency. In such places
our intense loyalty, now read and known of all men, prevents our being heard, but these places are getting few and
far between. Thank God and our good Government for it!
The door is opening, and the field is large and white unto
the harvest, but the laborers are few. O how much we
need help here on this vast field, so singularly and so won-
derfully being opened for our occupancy!"

A former Southern Methodist at this time exhorts his
brethren thus: "My advice would be to unite at once with
the old Methodist Church. It has always been loyal, and
I expect it always will be. This is the plan we have

adopted in this neighborhood—Cahoka, Clark county, Mo. Last July I withdrew from the Southern Church, for no other reason than simply because I regarded the Church as disloyal. A few week's after I withdrew we organized a class of old-fashioned Methodists in Cahoka; now it numbers about fifty members," etc.

14. Up even to this time the Churches in Missouri, the Methodist Episcopal excepted, were, in their majorities, on the side of rebellion. The Old School Presbyterian General Assembly, in May, 1862, decided, by a two-thirds majority, against rebellion; but, in Missouri, the majority are still for secession. The Presbytery of St. Louis, May 16, 1863, in the case of the notorious traitor, Dr. M'Pheters, decided in his favor by a majority of fifteen to four, and this gave about their proportions throughout the State. The same status prevailed among the Episcopalians, Baptists, Cumberland Presbyterians, and Campbellites; but the Presbyterians were, even then, in process of attaining a more loyal condition.

Dr. M'Anally, who had been sentenced, a short time before, to banishment to Dixie, was relieved from the sentence, May 13th, by Provost Marshal General F. A. Dick, on the representation of a Mr. Stafford, who professed to be loyal— so loyal as to esteem rebels to be loyal. The Democrat of thé 21st remarked on the occasion: "His [M'Anally's] paper, the Advocate, was a viper concern, and, while permitted by the military authorities to exist, did more, in an insidious way, to poison the public mind of Missouri toward the Government than almost any other treasonable agency among us." At this time a new order of things was commenced, through the conservatives, one effect of which was the dismission of General Curtis from the command in Missouri. Governor Gamble, Mr. Henderson, and others of like sort, at that time, were among those who were foremost in

the removal of General Curtis. This proved very injurious
to the peace of Missouri; for, when the new dynasty was
initiated, loyal men, especially loyal Methodists, came under
its displeasure almost as much as rebels themselves. It
seemed difficult for these quasi-loyal authorities to desist
from their former habitual abuse of these parties.

15. The progress of the war was now such as to give encouragement to our beleaguered Church in Missouri; for,
while more or less disaster occurred to our armies, on the
whole, the good cause of the Union was on the advance.
This animated our people very much, while it dismayed
those who had opposed and persecuted them.

Although, as was right, the Government of the United
States did not purpose, in going to war, to destroy slavery,
but to preserve the Union, yet Providence ordered otherwise. The slave system converts men into *property*. The
laws of nations, natural law, the dictates of reason, and
Scripture decide that the *property* of rebels should be confiscated to the State. Congress acted constitutionally in declaring that slave property, as well as any other property
of rebels, should be confiscated, and the President's Proclamation only published what Congress had authorized. Thus
slavery contained the very elements of self-destruction, in
spite of all the civil laws that could be enacted. National
rights, as the Roman law long since decided, overturn, necessarily, these decisions of civil law. Laws to authorize theft,
robbery, murder, arson, assault and battery must be self-de-
structive, and so with the slave laws, guards, compacts, etc.

Divine Providence, in the exercise of justice, overruled
our movements for the purpose of treading down and crushing out rebellion against law and liberty. The vengeance
of the Almighty fell specially on the regions most guilty.
Putting the sword into the hands of the downtrodden
colored people has infused into them a , new courage and

consciousness of manhood. Thousands of colored soldiers have been marshaled on the fields of battle. Their race, in America, is now free, never to be enslaved again. This is the Lord's doings, and is marvelous in our eyes.

16. The door of usefulness, amid many hinderances, began to open to the Methodist Episcopal Church in all quarters of the State.

Rev. J. H. Hopkins, writing from Kansas City, May 4th, says: "I have organized a Church in this city of about forty members; the most of them are from the Methodist Episcopal Church South. In Independence there are thirteen, in West Point about twenty, and they are very anxious for a preacher. There is nothing to prevent the Methodist Episcopal Church from taking possession of the entire ground in this part of the State."

The southern part of the State for two years prior had been very much disturbed, and recent rebel raids in the South-East, at Cape Girardeau, Fredericksburg, Pilot Knob, etc., renewed the disturbance. In the South-West the prevalence of bushwhackers prevented any successful occupancy at that time. On the Missouri, from Kansas City downward, the guerrillas were so very troublesome, that the preachers were confined to towns where soldiers were stationed. In Kansas City and Independence Chaplain J. H. Hopkins labored several months till relieved by Rev. A. H. Powell. Presiding elder Smith, visiting that city, had to go by way of St. Joseph by railroad, as traveling on the river was eminently dangerous for a preacher of the Methodist Episcopal Church.

To meet the wants of Missouri and Arkansas, our Missionary Society appropriated $7,000 for the neediest portions, besides $3,000 as a contingent fund. Our Church began with the county seats, and principal towns, and cities, and as dangers and perils abated, has since penetrated to every nook and corner of the land.   The following observations were made at that time:

The day of controversy between the Methodist Episcopal Church and the Methodist Episcopal Church South is now over.   The lines were drawn.   The Methodist Episcopal Church South is on the side of rebellion, *as a Church*, and the Methodist Episcopal Church, *as a Church*, is for the Government of the United States, and is antislavery in principle and practice.   This is now well known.

The Methodist Episcopal Church is called upon to promote, in the South-West, education in all its grades, from the highest collegiate to the primary or common school. And hence it will be necessary to introduce teachers in great numbers.

When the days of bushwhacking are over, the Methodist Episcopal Church will occupy all Missouri.   A loyal antislavery Church is needed, and such is the Methodist Episcopal Church, without a speck of disunion or pro-slavery tinge.   The few pro-slavery disunionists in the Virginia part of the Baltimore Conference, and a few in Western Virginia, were not of the Methodist Episcopal Church, and their own errors and missteps separated them from the body on which they were unnatural parasites.

17. We note here several items, showing the condition of the religious element in Missouri:

Rev. A. H. Powell addressed, through the Central Christian Advocate of June 18th, a letter to Southern Methodists, in which he says he was raised in a slave State, and might formerly have been considered as in favor of slavery. But now he was in favor of emancipation, because slavery repudiates the marital rights; it invades the ballot-box, invades conscience, and destroys the freedom of speech and the press; it fosters ignorance, and prevents the exercise of the ministerial office.   In view of these facts, he asks

his loyal Southern brethren if it is not their duty, as Methodists, to return at once to the old Church, and as citizens
to remain firm in the Union.

Rev. W. S. Wentz, presiding elder of St. Joseph district, wrote as follows: "Scarcely a week passes but we
receive either written or verbal requests to furnish preaching. Send us a LOYAL MINISTER is the CRY on all hands."
This call came from all quarters of the State.

Emancipation became the leading topic of the times.
That element of the Constitution, which was on its adoption a legal fiction, seemed now to have given place to the
higher constitutional principle of *justice* and the general
good. As slave laws made man *property*, justice confiscates
this property when held by traitors. The rising indignation of Missouri called for the vengeance of total destruction to the whole system. The day for remunerating
slaveholders for emancipation of slaves had passed away,
never to return.

In the Central Christian Advocate of June 11th, Rev. J.
C. Smith and the editor published a circular, urging farmers, mechanics, miners, teachers, merchants, local preachers,
itinerants, of unquestionable loyalty, to come to Missouri,
as the way was then, or shortly would be, open for them
to enjoy life in peace and protection and unbounded
prosperity.

18. While it is true many places were now opening to
our ministry, bushwhackers still infested many places in
the State. Our preachers could not travel in the South
and South-West without imminent peril, nor could the people be collected for worship. Notwithstanding the cry for
loyal preachers from many quarters, there was much more
difficulty in occupying Missouri than these favorable indi-
-cations would seem to indicate. There might be many
favorable omens and much improvement on the past, and

yet the fortune of our ministers and people be a hard and dangerous one.

Besides, the fifty thousand Southern Methodists, and their two hundred preachers, though now disorganized and demoralized, as a whole, had a very strong antipathy to the Methodist Episcopal Church. Yet we must provide for the loyal ones, or as many as would cleave to the Church of their fathers. Presbyterians, Baptists, Campbellites, Cumberlands, Episcopalians, were most generally rebels or sympathizers, and had no friendly bearing toward the loyal Methodist Episcopal Church. And then our people had been so thinned as to leave us scarcely a moiety of what we were some three years previous. Under these circumstances, we penned the following exhortation for the Central Christian Advocate of June 11, 1863:

" We hope and urge, as we have frequently done, that our religious brethren, where two or more can meet, will hold prayer meetings, hear exhortations and preaching where there is a preacher. This means will provide temporary spiritual assistance and comfort, and lead the way to a more thorough organization. Most of the Methodist Churches in America commenced in this way. Come, brethren, organize, *organize*, ORGANIZE, or meet to pray, hear exhortation, sermon-reading, or preaching, as the case may be. This done, you are a Church, if only two or three meet in this way. Let us hear from you. Choose your own leader. Select your sermon-reader. If you have not sermons, read Christ's sermon on the mount for one full year, every Sunday, and you will be greatly blessed. Start a Sunday school. Gather the children on Sabbath day; *talk* to them, *read* to them, and *pray* with them, and the work is done. This will lay the foundation for a large Church. We have seen this done in hundreds of places. If there are no Christian brethren, there may be sisters.

Come, sisters, call your neighbors together, and call on the men to read, and if they will not read or pray, read, pray, exhort, preach yourselves till God revives his work. One zealous woman thus introduced Methodism into France. Mrs. Wesley read sermons and prayers to the parishioners of her husband. Three negro slave women thus labored in the island of Antigua, from 1764, after the death of their master, Mr. Gilbert, till they obtained a missionary from London. This was the precursor of West India evangelization, and that of emancipation."

19. In Missouri, this year, a marvelous movement was in progress. Emancipation, resisted by the conservatives, was urged by the antislavery men with great vigor. The President of the United States, misled by these conservatives, lent his authority to the temporary humiliation of the genuine Union men. While all these commotions were in progress the opponents of the Methodist Episcopal Church were checked, and our remaining ministers and people were encouraged to labor on, as they saw their redemption drawing near.

The body of the Methodist Episcopal Church South in Louisiana, Mo., late in June, made a solemn protest against and a renunciation of the communion of the Methodist Episcopal Church South, and declared their adherence to the Methodist Episcopal Church. In regard to the division of the Church in 1845, and other questions, they say: "This division was consummated against our judgment, in the hope that peace might be promoted by submission. In this hope we have been sorely disappointed, and when rebellion culminated in open hostilities we had the mortification to see, not only in the seceded States, but in our own State, all the official powers and authorities of our Church, with a very few honorable exceptions, arrayed against the Government with all their influence and power. Many of the ministers not only refused to utter or to tolerate the utterance by others of the usual prayers for the authorities and officers of the Government, but, on the contrary, *openly and publicly* prayed for the success of traitors *in arms against it;* publicly urged, by speeches and otherwise, the young men of the country to commit the crime of treason against the Government; urged them to kill, burn, and destroy—to *"wade to their knees in blood"* to destroy that Government framed by Washington, Adams, Jefferson, Franklin, and their compeers. We further find the Conference of our Church in Missouri, so far from rebuking this conduct in their ministers, pass their characters unimpeached. Not only 'so, but we find our own Conference, in the absence of the bishop, elect in his stead, as their presiding officer, one of the most able, active, and efficient of these preachers of treason. . . . We are unwilling to be made to bow down and worship an institution as a divine inheritance which had its origin in a cruelty and barbarity without a parallel in the history of the world as the *price* of our Church relations and Christian privileges.

"We hereby declare our relations as members of the Methodist Episcopal Church South forever severed—severed by the treasonable acts and conduct of that official body which should have been the guardian of our rights and of the purity of our Church; therefore,

"*Resolved,* That we hereby recommend to the members of this Church, as a body, to apply to the proper authorities of the Methodist Episcopal Church for connection with that ecclesiastical organization."

Eighty-five signatures were appended, and many more were added afterward.

A brother wrote us the following:

"These are truly trying times. I live in what *was* called the St. Catherine circuit, but we have been by some means, as it were, *left out in the cold.* St. Catherine lies on the Hannibal and St. Joseph Railroad. I live twenty miles north-west of there. Our preachers have not been around on this circuit for two or three years. We get to see no Church paper; do not know whether the Central is alive yet or not; would hardly know a preacher if we should see one. We will not let the rebels preach under the flag. There is a good opening here to form a lay class, if we had preaching. If the Central is alive yet, and if there has been a Conference this Spring, will you send me a copy of the paper of the last issue, and the one containing the list of appointments for the present year?"

July 4th Rev. W. Hanley, of Hannibal district, informed us of a prosperity in his district hitherto unknown. The long night had passed away, and was succeeded by the light of day. Many who had regarded our ministers and members as their worst enemies, were then of a different mind. He had visited Louisiana, the third Sabbath in June, and received the loyal Southern Methodists of that city into the Methodist Episcopal Church of 1784. Here he met Rev. H. Cox, of Union Church, St. Louis, and Rev. J. C. Smith, presiding elder of St. Louis district. After this meeting, Bishop Ames appointed Rev. N. Shumate to a district lying along the Mississippi River, and between the Hannibal and St. Joseph Railroad and the Missouri River, including the towns on its south bank, except Jefferson City. This new field was called the Louisiana district.

In the Central Christian Advocate, July 9, 1863, we spoke thus: "Many Churches are to be organized in the South-West as soon as possible. And we assure our friends that brother Shumate is fully prepared to do the work. No man is more peaceable than he; but as he will carry with him his two revolvers, and other Gospel accompaniments needful for teaching bushwhackers, we expect he will travel through the country with little molestation. We advise him to 'say his prayers and keep his powder dry.' This is a fitting Gospel advice for him in Missouri, and we earnestly utter it with a good conscience."

20. In July it was announced that Bishop Kavanaugh would hold three Conferences of the Methodist Episcopal Church South, in the Fall—one in Kansas, one in Northern Missouri, and the St. Louis Conference. The Missouri Conference was to be held at Fulton, Callaway county. It was said there were not a dozen loyal citizens in this whole county. No place was fixed for the St. Louis nor for the Kansas Conference. These appointments had the aspect of renewing the rebel raids on Missouri, and encouraging a fresh invasion. The Bishop himself was the representative of a rebel Church, and acting officially for it, and whatever his private views were, he could not be considered as a messenger of peace, but of rebellion. Kansas viewed the movement on her territory as the precursor of a clandestine assault. Such an assembly did not differ remotely from the *Knights of the Golden Circle.* How this would end, it was difficult to say; but the indications were any thing but promising to the cause of the Union or religion.

The Southern General Conference was to meet in New Orleans, November 1, 1862. But the members, conscious of their Confederate complicity, declined to meet. All the authorities of the Methodist Episcopal Church South were on the side of rebellion. Very few of her two hundred traveling preachers in Missouri made any pretensions to loyalty. Many were in the rebel army, many were in the most notoriously rebel communities, some led guerrilla bands, and a valiant few went where the "darkies" went. before the war, namely, to Canada. These last, self-reputed non-political saints, have since returned to apologize for every enormity perpetrated by traitors, and to insult to its face the

Government they dishonored abroad and refused to obey at home.

21. The arrest of Rev. T. B. Bratton, presiding elder of St. Joseph district, and of Mr. Harbaugh, the editor of the Chillicothe Constitution, occurred in July. Mr. Harbaugh was also a Methodist. Mr. Bratton's services in the Union cause in North-West Missouri were very considerable. To raise troops, and maintain the laws of the United States, he spent more than his last dollar. His principal sin was that he was a minister of the Methodist Episcopal Church. After arrest, the prisoners were told to shut their mouths, were placed under a heavy guard, and denied the privilege of communicating with their friends, either by mail or telegraph. On Sunday, July 12th, while Mr. Bratton was singing a hymn, he was abruptly commanded to desist, and after Sabbath both prisoners were hurried to Macon City, and there confined. Among many other things, the editor of the Copperhead sheet in Chillicothe said, " It would be better the gates of hell were opened on Missouri than that the Northern Methodists should occupy the State."

22. After the administration of General Curtis had been suspended by the President, and General Schofield put in his place, Missouri affairs became very much confused. As we had sufficient opportunity to know the state of public matters, we could not avoid making some observations on the course of the President. August 5th we penned the following:

"It was then a sad mistake in President Lincoln to declare that there were two factions in Missouri—at the head of one was Governor Gamble, and at the head of the other was General Curtis—and, as he could not remove the Governor, he must remove the General. Now, it is an utter mistake to say that Mr. Curtis was at the head of a faction, unless it is factious to be an uncompromising Union man, and it is, when weighed, an unjust charge to bring against men who have, from the first, been Union, and, in Missouri, have stemmed the tide of rebellion; and they still do the same thing that President Lincoln is endeavoring to do with the aid of the entire army, navy, and purse of the United States. If Missouri uncompromising Union men are to constitute a *faction*, then the President himself is the sovereign head of that faction, and not General Curtis, or any other man than President Lincoln himself.

"Another remark. It is certain that, while we award loyalty to the professions of Governor Gamble—for he has done many noble acts as Governor—yet it is true to the letter that many who have been disloyal, if not rebels, and now favor the rebel cause, belong to his party, or, as the President says, his *faction*. To his party belong some now who have been in the rebel army, others who have favored secession from the first, and deem it proper to oppose unconditional Union men with all their might.

"The one faction, to use the words of the President, are for the Union and the President's administration, to support it with their lives, their fortunes, and their honor, yet grieved on account of any errors the President may commit. The other faction, as the President calls it, is made up of professed loyal men, of strong pro-slavery men, of men who have been in the rebel army, and, in short, of leaders who make it a part of their business to arrest and imprison Union men, and set disloyal men at liberty, even when taken as bushwhackers.

"Now, let us look at the results of this administration of affairs in Missouri:

"The other day a preacher of the Methodist Episcopal Church, Rev. Mr. Bratton, was arrested, imprisoned, and retained in prison several days, just because he was a Union man, and for nothing else; but when his case was brought before General Schofield he was unconditionally set free, no charges being sustained. Mr. Harbaugh, an editor and a lay Methodist, was also arrested at the same time, treated in the same way, and released because there was nothing to be proved against him.

"The captain who arrested them commanded loyal ladies to fold up their flag and not exhibit it, because they pleaded to learn why the arrests were made. Judge M'Farren, a leader in this, on another occasion ordered the United States flag to be taken down because it was demanded by rebels. · The leading secessionists in this Chillicothe occurrence some two or three years ago rode Rev. Mr. Gardner on a rail because he was a minister of the Methodist Episcopal Church, and for *nothing else*, except an allegation known to be false.

"Since these events several Union men have been arrested, on Mr. Guitar's district, for being Union men, and nothing else.

"It has been, till recently, a crime, in the view of the governing powers of the South-West, to be a member or a minister of the Methodist Episcopal Church, or, as they call it, the *Northern Methodist Church*. The party—call it faction or what you please—that is operating with Governor Gamble has renewed this proscriptive judgment and practice in the arrest of Mr. Harbaugh and Rev. Mr. Bratton. Is this to go on under the party that our misled President calls a *faction?* If so, it is time this was known to the most numerous and most loyal Church in the United States, which, with their adherents, number several millions of loyal citizens, with scarcely a disloyal minister or layman among them.

"We ask President Lincoln, Are the many thousand preachers of the Methodist Episcopal Church to be arrested, imprisoned, and tyrannized over by such upstart captains as he of Chillicothe, and put and kept in jail for many days, because they are loyal, and supporters of your administration and the Union which you maintain? Is this so, Mr. Lincoln? If so, let us know. it, that we may all, millions of loyalists as we are, EXPOSTULATE with you for this GREAT ERROR of your administration before we take up arms to defend the Union, which, by this ill-advised course, you would deliver up to Jeff. Davis.

"Many such questions might be asked, but we stop just at the threshold of our inquiries. Some false representations have surely misled our beloved President Lincoln. We hope he will review this affair of Missouri's oppression, worse in its *results* than the attacks of our expelled rebel Governor, Jackson.

"We would say to all, of the Methodist Episcopal Church in Missouri or elsewhere, be slow to believe evil of the ruler of our people. Honest Abe is our lawful ruler. We must support him to the last. He will surely relieve Missouri from this ill-advised course."

An editorial in the Central Christian Advocate of August 13th, one week later, reads thus:

"We are bound by the Decalogue to speak well of and support the ruler of our people. Hence, we support the President in the discharge of his onerous duties. And to notice his mistakes, when plainly such, and dissent from them too, is one branch of the duty of supporting him. Such are the counsels of friends, and not the attacks of enemies.

"We are also bound to submit to the lawful control of the Governor of the State, Mr. Gamble, and to observe the laws of the State of Missouri. But it is our right, on moral principles, to disapprove of misgoverning acts.

"We are also bound to submit to the military power now exercised over us in Missouri. And while we deplored the mistake of removing General Curtis, our allegiance is due to his successor, General Schofield, for whom we entertain a high opinion, and expect from him a salutary administration. He checked at once the unjust acts under General Guitar in arresting and imprisoning loyal men, such as Mr. Bratton and Mr. Harbaugh. We look for much from General Schofield's administration, and expect it will, on the whole, be salutary and entirely safe.

"There are also some great principles and National measures which we feel ourselves bound to recognize on moral, patriotic, and Scriptural principles; such as that these United States form one Supreme Government, and that no one State, of its own accord, can secede from the Union; that the Union should be maintained at any cost, and the war prosecuted in view of entirely subjugating the rebellion; that the South, without cause, commenced this war, and were, and are now, the aggressors; that the Confiscation law of Congress, confiscating the property of all rebels, and that the Proclamation of the President, authorized by this law, is a just retribution, and in accordance with the laws of all nations, which authorize the forfeiture of the property of rebels, as slaves are property. Arming the negroes, too, is sound policy; it is just and National, and the protection of negro soldiers can not be called in question. The resistance to the Conscription law is wrong, and those who resist it, oppose, or discourage it, are more than disloyal, as they are hostile to the Government. Finally, to be *neutral*, or so concealed in using words and acts as to give no public assurance of our loyalty, is to be in opposition to the Government. These points, to our mind, are very plain, and it is only necessary to state them. With this we are content, without further explanation."

When the news of the arrest of Messrs. Bratton, Harbaugh, and others reached us in St. Louis, a meeting of the

male members of the Methodist Episcopal Church was
called, and held in Union Church, to deliberate what was
best to be done for preserving our rights as citizens and
religious men. The aspects of things threatened a new
persecution in Missouri against our lives, our liberties, our
honor, and religious privileges. For if things went on so,
the Central Christian Advocate must soon be suppressed,
our churches confiscated, and nothing be left us but to
escape for our lives to other States. A very pointed address
was drawn up to all Methodists and loyal citizens of the
United States; but it was judged prudent to send, next day,
a deputation to Mr. Schofield, then in the city, to secure
to us the rights of citizens. The committee consisted of
Generals Fisk and Pile, and Rev. H. Cox. The matter
was fully laid before Mr. Schofield next day, who at once
set at liberty the prisoners on the mere representation of
the committee.

Hear a little episode in this connection. A committee,
consisting of Bishop Ames, Drs. Peck, Cummings, Colonel
Moody, and myself, was sent, during the session of our
General Conference, in May, to Washington, to express the
high esteem the Conference entertained of the President's
administration, and to assure him of the loyalty of the
Methodist Episcopal Church. After all had been introduced, our address presented and read, and every thing disposed of according to the usual diplomacy, the President
and the Committee being in the most pleasant mood, I
undertook, as an incidental matter, to remark about as
follows:

That we, in Missouri, felt aggrieved that some of our
preachers and people should be imprisoned, as a principal
charge, because we belonged to the Methodist Episcopal
Church, and, next, because we were uncompromisingly
Union; that we were unwavering supporters of his general

administration, had voted for him, and intended to vote for him again—we thought it hard to be put in jail for these reasons; that our oppressors were generally disloyal men, opposed to the Union and his administration. And now, we said, we trust this case will not occur again. The President heard our brief statement courteously, and all passed off pleasantly and with great cordiality.

23. Political movements in the State were all astir now, the old pro-slavery party striving to preserve its fast-declining influence, while the Radicals, as they were called, were sharply using every advantage to carry their purposes. In Colonel Guitar's district, where Mr. Bratton was arrested, there was much activity among loyalists. At St. Joseph the Conservatives were worsted. At Palmyra, where a meeting of Conservatives was called, the Radicals rushed in, in crowds, and passed Radical resolutions. Mr. Henderson, who was there, took a new turn, and called his former political friend, Governor Gamble, by an ugly name. In the Senate, Mr. Henderson introduced a bill to pay the slaveholders of Missouri twenty millions for their slaves. This killed the House bill, granting ten millions, finally failed itself, and Missouri got nothing, while the Convention of 1865, almost with one voice, proclaimed emancipation. Mr. Schofield very handsomely snubbed Mr. Guitar and his subservient Captain, at once setting Bratton and Harbaugh at liberty, thus apologizing in the most satisfactory manner for their unjust arrest.

The south-eastern part of the State, under the charge of General Fisk, appointed by General Curtis, and continued by General Schofield, was pretty well pacified. This was to be expected from General Fisk's energy, his unswerving Unionism, now and always, as well as his high moral and religious character.

West of Jefferson City the returned rebels were at work,

recruited, encouraged, and reënforced by their friends in the middle of the State, and in Guitar's command.

We can but respect General Schofield as a very worthy man. But the ruling power in Missouri at that time trammeled him. His associations threw a sort of bewildering influence over him, and former commitments from specious connections presented stumbling blocks in his way.

24. The Methodist Episcopal Church was quite prosperous in August, although much of the State could not be occupied by our ministry. A few notes on some places will illustrate the whole.

In St. Louis our cause was rapidly advancing under the untiring pastoral labors of Rev. Henry Cox and Rev. L. M. Vernon. Almost daily additions were made to our membership, and there was a constant growth in moral power and social influence. Our pastors were courteously recognized by other city ministers, pulpits were exchanged, and we found openings for usefulness and indications of encouragement on every hand.

The loyal Southern Methodists, of Jones' Chapel, almost all united with the Methodist Episcopal Church, and equally repudiated rebellion and the disloyal Church South. "*Constitutional Union men*," became a phrase to designate secessionists or rebels.

Mr. E. G. Evans, of Rolla, informs us that "the enemies of the Union are also the enemies of the Methodist Episcopal Church, because antislaveryism and loyalty now go hand in hand, as well as pro-slaveryism and treason; that loyal people every-where sympathized with the persecuted Methodists."

Elder Shumate had formed the following new charges, namely: Bowling Green, Danville, Mexico and Middletown, and Kansas City. Four brethren from the Church South, truly loyal men, entered on these charges as ministers in the Methodist Episcopal Church. Clarksville, also, was occupied in connection with Louisiana.

Rev. Isaac Martin, Edina circuit, received forty-eight into Church fellowship, of whom thirty-four were from the Southern Methodist Church.

Rev. W. S. Wentz, of St. Joseph district, wrote: "Two weeks ago I had the privilege of preaching at a meeting-house in Platte county, called Moore's Chapel. Two years since a pro-slavery mob broke up the house and so scattered the flock, that many thought our cause lost in that part of the country." Referring to emigrants, he said, "Let none but Union men come, as the people up here are in earnest in their devotion to the Union, and will smoke *out* every traitor. I have never known a government so heartily despised as the Gamble, Henderson, and Hall provisional government, so-called. Deacon Gamble made a grand mistake when he concluded to sacrifice his domestic happiness in order to secure peace; that is, to conserve the institution of slavery."

As much controversy had existed between the Church South and our Church, and as Providence seemed plainly pleading our cause, we wrote in August the following paragraph by way of caution: "Let the Southern Methodist Church alone. The day of controversial warfare is over. Let them reconstruct their Church in their own way, as far as the Methodist Episcopal Church is concerned. And as we hold out our hands to all loyal Methodists who see proper to unite with us, let us not afflict them by the reminiscence of the past. It is mortifying enough to them that their preachers have misled them, and that their preachers have been deceived by Southern politicians. These afflictions are enough. Let us not spend our time in a warfare with those who see fit to remain in the Southern Church. Let them, as far as we are concerned, pursue their own way."

Rev. N. Shumate, in a letter to us about the same time, drops the following paragraph : "Let us leave the Church South to manage her own troubles, and content ourselves with doing our duty to God and the country, and we have no fears as to what will become of the loyal element of the State."

25. In September two new political parties were forming. After the removal of General Curtis, the peace of Missouri was greatly disturbed. One party embraced the uncompromising Union men, or Radicals; the other consisted of the Conservatives, the opponents of President Lincoln at his election, pro-slavery men, returned rebels, and others.

The latter succeeded in removing Generals Loan, Blunt, and others who acted with General Curtis.

The Radicals, for the most part, were laboring for the majority on moral principles, adopted from the first. The Conservatives were endeavoring to overthrow the Confiscation bill, the President's Emancipation Proclamation, the arming of negroes, etc.

Such were the leading characteristics of the parties in process of formation in Missouri.

The state of religion at this time was greatly affected for good or evil by the absence or presence of bushwhackers. They principally controlled the Missouri above Jefferson City, and the region south along the Kansas line to Arkansas. Dr. Denby, a local preacher, however, formed a society in Dade county, and was preaching to the people as best he could amid the general peril. But almost all the southern part of the State was destitute of our preachers, and, indeed, of ministers of any Church; yet Rev. J. H. Vaughan was laboring on Buffalo Mission, and received seventy-four members, mostly from the Southern Methodist Church.

A Southern Methodist, from Plattsburg, Clinton county, Mo., writing to us September 24th, says: "The Union ministers do not think it incompatible with religion to pray for the Government, but the Southern preachers are dumb on this subject."

26. In October, Missouri State affairs became very precarious. The two parties, Radical and Conservative, were now formally organized. The latter was largely managed by Mr. Bates, Montgomery Blair, Frank P. Blair, Mr. Henderson, Ex-Governor King, and a few others, who procured the removal of General Curtis. After that event the Conservatives seemed to be Lincoln men in a certain sense. It was soon manifest that among the consequences of removing Curtis were, the burning of Lawrence, the imprisonment of loyal men, the disturbance of the State, and such encouragement to rebels as seriously damaged the cause of the Union.

The Radical party sent a deputation to Washington to expostulate with the President on this state of affairs. In their address they stated they had "a unanimous and confiding faith in his patriotism, generosity, and integrity, and his readiness to do right whenever he was fully advised concerning the affairs of the State." The final result was, the President sent an order to General Schofield that "no person who had borne arms against the United States, or had given aid and comfort to its enemies, was qualified to vote, or be judge of elections." This was really a deathblow to the Conservative party in Missouri, as it largely consisted of those who were disfranchised by this order, those willing to use all kinds of disloyalists for party ends, and those *now* Union men through mere policy.

At this time Union men were very much harassed, in many places, in various ways, as if it were a crime to be unflinching supporters of the National Government, and to avow their adherence to President Lincoln's Administration. Governor Gamble, at this time, seems to have forgotten his proper place when he called Union men *conspirators*, or, in other words, TRAITORS, and this he did as Governor in one of his messages.

Rebel raids now reached several places occupied by the Methodist Episcopal Church, preventing their occupancy as formerly, while the regions not visited by our ministry were almost entirely in possession of the disloyal party. Our case may be stated thus: Just in proportion as the Conservatives gained ascendency, our Church was depressed and hindered in its proper work, and *vice versa*. The Methodist Episcopal Church was so identified with the National Government that it must, in the South-West, rise or fall with it.

The General Conference of the Methodist Episcopal Church South was to be held, November 1, 1862, in New Orleans, anticipating this city would then be in possession of the rebels. But the city was taken by the loyal army, and the contemplated session, for some reason, failed. The Southern Methodist Missouri Conference met at Glasgow in the Fall of 1861, under the protection of the rebel, Martin Green, to whom the Conference paid its respects. But when the Federals reached that place, Green made his escape, and the Conference dispersed.

The Southern Christian Advocate, of July 23, 1863, informed us that Bishop Paine had appointed Rev. Dr. Kavanaugh, brother to Bishop K., as missionary to Price's army, and Rev. E. M. Marvin, missionary to any rebel army west of the Mississippi. Mr. Marvin was pastor of Centenary Church, St. Louis, previous to the Spring of 1862, Dr. Boyle being presiding elder. Mr. M. was a delegate to the General Conference that was to meet in New Orleans, November 1, 1862. . He declined taking the oath of allegiance in St. Louis, and could not get a pass to leave the city. Prior to April, however, he escaped clandestinely, without a pass, and proceeded to Jackson, Mississippi. Before July, 1863, Dr. Kavanaugh and Mr. Marvin were sent mission-

.aries to the rebel army in Missouri. These appointments were ominous, and one can not avoid considering them as *coincident* with the rebel movements in the South-West. The Southern Bishops sent out or recalled their rebel preachers in the South-West, according to the varying fortunes and movements of Price's army.

Mr. Marvin's rebel notoriety, in their last General Conference, promoted him to the Episcopacy in preference to men of far greater intellectual and moral worth. Surviving his "lost cause," because traitors are not hung, Bishop Marvin is evidently determined that the embers of rebel prejudice, passion, and hate shall burn as long as possible. His Episcopal labors and residence in Missouri augur little good to the growing spirit of National patriotism, or to our free institutions and civilization.

The resolutions and pastoral address of the *Missouri Conference*, Methodist Episcopal Church South, October 20th, at Fulton, Mo., were published in the Missouri Republican, October 23, 1863. In their resolutions they assert their Church, in its organization, claimed the world for its field. They talk of submission to the powers that be, and quote Rom. xiii, 1–8, and, also, the Twenty-Third Article of Religion as binding. The Pastoral Address, a studied evasion of the case in hand, is followed by the appointments, and Rev. Wm. G. Caples, Price's former chaplain, is placed at Glasgow. The whole taken together is a mere shift to evade, as best they can, their proper character as devotees to rebellion.[1]

27. The rest of the year, November and December, 1863, was a period of gradual advancement in both Church and State. It was a kind of truce between the discordant elements and the growing movement in the right direction.

In politics, the Radicals became victorious over opposing

---

[1] Central Christian Advocate, October 29, 1863.

combinations, supported by the President, misguided by the advisements of Mr. Bates and the Blairs. In Missouri, the influence of the National Government was, for some time, very soothing, and even auxiliary to rebels and sympathizers. Faithful men were thus tried to the utmost. Regarding the President as greatly mistaken, they also believed he would soon clearly perceive his error.

After July, many advances were made on the side of liberty. The Chattanooga region was cleared out. East Tennessee was relieved from rebels. The Mississippi was opened. Over 100,000 able-bodied negroes, Americans by birth, were in the army of the Union; while 100,000 more were on the way to join them. All this without insurrections. Among anomalies, we find the Missouri Conservatives in Congress going against the President, who patronized them so fully; while the Radicals of the State supported him, although he displaced them from the State offices. Our armies and navies increased to adequate power, our finances were equal to our wants, and there is gold enough in our own territory to redeem the greenbacks as soon as necessary.

This is the work of God. Our nation has received the just stripes due to the sins of robbing and oppressing a weak and innocent people. Old Virginia, Georgia, South Carolina, and North Carolina have been providentially chastised, instructed, and subdued by the two great armies operating in those regions. We here quote the acclamations of the elders in heaven, as suitable to this great work on earth: "We give thee thanks, O Lord God Almighty, which art, and wast, and art to come; because thou hast taken to thee thy great power, and hast reigned." Rev. xi, 17.

28. The retrospect at the close of 1863 suggested the following reflections:

"The year 1863 has been an auspicious year for the

United States. The absurd teachings of politicians are being thrown to the winds. The preachers who followed them are being confounded with their errors and their sycophancy. The Almighty is carrying on this great work of giving victory to truth and justice. So that these two will in the end dominate over error and wrong.

"We see in this stupendous movement the repetition, or rather the continuance, of the jubilee instituted in the books of Moses. The bond service of the Jews was so restricted by the Almighty as to prevent its running into slavery. The periods of this service, from five years up to the year of jubilee, were all, without exception, to be terminated by the jubilee. The following is its instituted law: 'And ye shall hallow the fiftieth year, and proclaim liberty throughout all the land unto all the inhabitants thereof; it shall be a jubilee unto thee.' Lev. xxv, 10. This is reiterated—Isa. lxi, 2, and lxiii, 4; Jer. xxxiv, 8, 15, 17, and Luke iv, 19. This law was instituted 1491 years before Christ.

"Isaiah, 698 years before Christ, repeated the jubilee of Moses, and prophesied that Christ would carry it out. It is said of Christ that God 'sent him to bind up the brokenhearted; to proclaim liberty to the captives, and the opening the prison to them that are bound; to proclaim the acceptable year of our Lord, and the day of vengeance of our God.' Isa. lxi, 1, 2.

"Jeremiah repeats the jubilee law as in full force 591 years before Christ, 'to proclaim liberty to the people'—Jer. xxxiv, 8—and he pronounces the following malediction for disobeying this law, as follows: 'Ye have not hearkened unto me in proclaiming liberty, every man to his brother, and every man to his neighbor; behold, I proclaim liberty to you, saith the Lord, to the sword, to the pestilence, to the famine.' Jer. xxxiv, 17.

"Our blessed Savior, in opening his mission, makes the

proclamation that, along with spiritual blessing, to all he has come to preach 'deliverance to the captives, and to set at liberty them that are bruised, to preach the acceptable year of the Lord.' Luke iv, 19, 20.

"And now, in the year of grace 1863, we have thirty free States and five slave States, and their jubilee celebration is not far distant.

"Even the Popish nations are partially turning their attention to the teachings of Protestants and of Scripture, and leaning toward liberty, in a sort of defiance of the Papal bulls that tolerated it; and even Catholics in America are now, inconsistently enough we allow, claiming that these semi-pro-slavery bulls are genuine, unadulterated antislavery anathemas.

"We would now say to the members of our Church, let us all praise God for his deliverance. Although there is much in the past to make us blush as a people, yet God has enabled us, in some degree, up to this day, to maintain the principles of 1780 and 1784. Our Church preferred purity to unity in not making concessions, in 1844, to our erring brethren of the South. We have been providentially saved from the adoption of the various new rules that would vitiate our original principles. We shall have, in 1864, the very platform adopted in 1784, of eighty years' continuance. Our protest remained, all along, against the civil legislation which prevented us, as well as the Quakers, from carrying out our principles of moral right. Our Church has resisted, all along, the Garrisonian scheme, which, in brief, may be thus expressed: 1. It was an infidel scheme. 2. It purposed to make the Church a tool to carry out mere political action. 3. It was a disunion scheme. Our principles were stronger against slavery than those of the Garrisonians. Our Church suffered, we allow, in refusing the teaching of the extremes. The result was, a secession in the South, and another in the

North. But, thank God, the Methodist Episcopal Church is now a unit as to slavery and the Union.

"The slavery contest, blessed be God, is now terminated; our periodicals will need to say but little about it. Our great work is to spread Scriptural holiness over these lands. Angels might covet to engage in it. Let us all remember our Christian vocation as Methodists and Christians.

"As editor, being now relieved from this slavery discussion, we purpose to commence the next volume without the controversial troubles of the heretofore knotty question of slavery."

29. On looking forward to the future, the following historical observations were presented, at the close of 1863:

"1863—THE YEAR OF JUBILEE.—One hundred and twenty-four years ago, or in 1739, John Wesley, on his return from America to London, reported to the London Board, whose missionary he was, a plan of Christianizing the negroes, namely: To purchase a number of them, keep them, as slaves, on a farm, in view of their Christian instruction, and finally free them. Mr. Whitefield pursued the same plan in South Carolina or Georgia, we forget which. Several gentlemen in the West Indies, in after years, did the same. But all this amounted to nothing. Mr. Wesley, in his correspondence with the distinguished Presbyterian preacher of Virginia, Rev. Samuel Davies, from 1755 to 1757, made no mention of the state of the colored people, as slaves, but they both agreed in the great work of evangelizing them as ignorant and degraded human beings. When Mr. Gilbert, from Antigua, Speaker of the Legislature of that island, and his two slave women were converted, in 1758, through the preaching of Mr. Wesley, nothing was said or done by him in regard to their state as slaves, but barely as ignorant and degraded human beings, similar to the free colliers around Kingswood. Thus, up to

1772, Mr. Wesley seems to have spent no thoughts about the negroes as slaves, but as ignorant and needy sinners, like his colliers in England.

"But, in 1772, Mr. Wesley read the book of Anthony Benezet, a Hollander by birth, but a long time an inhabitant of Philadelphia, and a Quaker, or Friend. On reading this book, a copy of which we possess, Mr. Wesley saw the enormity of slavery proper for the first time, and pronounced it the 'sum of all villainies.' In 1774 he wrote and published his powerful essay against slavery, and sowed it broadcast over Great Britain and America. The rising Methodist societies in America caught up at once the strong doctrine from Mr. Wesley's tract, and in 1780 the Baltimore Conference, and in 1784 the General Conference, decided what, in substance, we may express as follows: That slavery was contrary to natural law, to the Divine law, and to justice. And subsequently it became the settled principle and Discipline of the Methodist Episcopal Church, and remains so to this day, that there should be no purchase or sale of human beings allowed, except to free them, and emancipation was required in all cases of inheriting slaves, if the laws permitted this to be done. But the Southern States forbade emancipation, and thus the Methodist Episcopal Church was hemmed in in exercising this moral Discipline, and had to content itself in ameliorating the condition of the slaves as best it could, and could only *protest* against the injustice of the laws, although the Church felt it to be its duty not to resist the laws against which they protested; and the principles of the Methodist Episcopal Church were formed and adopted while the thirteen original States were all slave States.

"In 1776 the signers of the Declaration of Independence borrowed from the old Roman law and from Scripture the great moral truth that all men are born free, and their natural inherent rights entitle them to life, liberty, and the pursuit of happiness. The result that followed this assertion and the Wesleyan teaching was, that before twenty years elapsed, or before the close of the eighteenth century, seven, out of the thirteen slave States that composed the United States, became free States, some of them by immediate and others by gradual emancipation. And some of these seven were made free by judicial decisions, and others by legislative enactments. Thus the work of freedom had been progressing till the 31st day of December, 1862, so that on January 1, 1863, thirty out of the thirty-five States of the Union became emancipated, and there are no slaves in them. Nearly four millions of freedmen have been metamorphosed out of four millions of slaves.

"And now the Church is freed from the impediment with which the civil power bound her, so that she can exercise that stringent discipline which the Bible and the Church demanded, the slave laws sinking with the system which gave them their binding nature.

"While we thus see the power of truth and justice in Church and State, we can also see the influence of error."

CHAPTER XXII.

EVENTS OF 1864.

1. BEFORE we survey the Methodist Episcopal Church in the South-West, at the beginning of the year 1864, a few preliminary items will be in place.

In January, Rev. S. Ing, of Otterville circuit, gathered up the fragments of our Church to the number of one hundred and thirty or forty. He also took into his Church about one hundred Southern Methodists, comprising all that were loyal among them in that locality.

The collected remnants of Simpson and Hedding Chapels, St. Louis, numbered only thirty-three at the Conference of 1862; but now there were one hundred and forty-nine members at the former charge. In Ebenezer, previous to March, 1862, the number was reduced to fifty-two. In January, 1864, there were four hundred and eleven members in Union Church.

The pressure on our Church was still very great. In the Southern and South-Western parts of the State we had no regular Church organizations at the commencement of 1864. We had then only a few fragments of a small previous remnant. Our people, however, had their principles, and had good hope of no more being driven from the country as in former days. No tinge of pro-slaveryism or disloyalty adhered to them. They were, therefore, of good courage and trusted in God.

We here present the statistics of the Missouri Conference

from 1848 to 1864 inclusive, adding those of the Arkansas during the years of their combination:

A. D.	Members.	Traveling Preachers.	Local Preachers.
1848	1,538	26	24
1849	3,591	41	61
1850	5,249	51	86
1851	5,528	63	80
1852	5,742	68	69
1853	6,276	82	93
1854	7,472	75	107
1855	8,190	79	114
1856	6,602	60	82
1857	6,431	38	91
1858	7,532	85	121
1859	8,341	85	121
1860	7,764	85	103
1861	6,245	72	117
1862	2,141	32	39
1863	4,387	37	66
1864	7,697	57	130

The foregoing is an accurate statistical survey of the Methodist Episcopal Church in Missouri and Arkansas from 1849 to 1864 inclusive. The number of preachers and members in 1848 was the mere fragment that survived the secession of 1845, at which time the body of Methodists in these States were decoyed into the Methodist Episcopal Church South.

The irregular labors of Rev. Messrs. Henry, Bewley, Dr. Akers, and others, from 1844 to 1848, preserved to us in the South-West 1,538 lay members, 26 traveling preachers, and 24 local preachers; and this number, though small, was the seed of the purified Methodist Episcopal Church.

From 1849 to 1855 inclusive, a period of seven years, there was a moderate increase from 1,538 members to 8,190. Border-ruffianism at this time began to operate so adversely as to diminish the number of our members and adherents. In 1859 the previously organized opposition developed into an exterminating process. Hence, from 1859 to 1862 our membership was reduced to 2,141, and our traveling preachers from 85 to 32.

The great crime charged upon our Church was that of abolitionism. Nearly all our male members were adjudged unpardonably guilty because they voted for Fremont and Lincoln. Every true Southron, saintly or otherwise, felt himself charged by Heaven with uncommon vengeance to scourge these vile opinions out of the impious *Northerners*. Thus by special entreaties, with prophetic maledictions in the background, our members moving to Missouri were generally seduced into the Southern Methodist Church.

In October, 1860, Bewley was murdered, and there seemed a prevailing appetite for our blood. Certainly not less than 20,000 of Methodist population were driven from the State after 1859, to say nothing of the thousands who were prevented from emigrating to Missouri. All this took place principally before the war commenced. Thus by Conference time, 1862, our people in Missouri and Arkansas were nearly extirpated.

The following are the statistics of Arkansas:

A. D.	Members.	'Traveling Preachers.	Local Preachers.
1848	......	...	...
1849	568	5	10
1850	848	5	9
1851	547	8	11
1852	1,285	8	10
1853	1,777	36	30
1854	2,041	26	39
1855	2,545	21	41
1856	1,738	20	22
1857	1,262	19	29
1858	1,262	20	21
1859	1,257	20	21
1860	1,145	16	24
1861		5	...

The above is a carefully collated view of the Methodist Episcopal Church in Arkansas, embracing a few in Kansas.

There were no returns of membership after 1860. Thus the Methodist Episcopal Church was driven from Arkansas and Texas by mob violence. Such is its history in these two States from 1848 to 1860, when it became extinct with the martyrdom of Bewley.

2. The Missouri and Arkansas Conference of 1861 appointed five preachers to Arkansas; namely, J. R. West, J. W. Murray, T. Reed, H. Hess, and C. Baker. In 1862 no account was received from them, and they were reappointed without any designated fields of labor. At the Conferences of 1863 and 1864 nothing was heard from these preachers, and it was supposed they had fallen victims to the fury of rebels. Rev. Leroy M. Vernon, presiding elder of Springfield district, in a letter dated August 8, 1864, and published in the Central Christian Advocate of August 31st, gives an account of two of them; namely, Rev. Hiram Hess and Rev. James W. Murray, from which we glean the following :

"In the Spring' of 1861 Mr. Hess labored on the North Fork circuit, lying between White River, the North Fork, and Gainsville, in Missouri. This charge had eighty members, and was without missionary appropriation. By the time he made one round on his circuit, the State seceded. On his second round he was met by three different mobs, who threatened him with death should he return. He next went to Jasper circuit, which he formerly traveled, and where his family still lived, the preacher appointed not having come. A band of guerrillas, driven from Missouri, came into his vicinity, and commenced plundering and murdering. After this he remained quietly at home. Finally, a band of rebels, in January, 1863, came to his home and robbed him of all his money, horses, and all the clothing of the family except what they then had on their persons, and every article of furniture they found. After this, he and some thirty others lay concealed in the mountains for some time. After Mr. Hess had been compelled to leave his family on the circuit, they suffered much from the guerrillas. The family carried grain upon their own shoulders two miles to the mill, and often before they could carry it home, the guerrillas seized it. The oldest daughter, near seventeen years of age, cut and carried all the wood they used, which hardship brought on a distressing rheumatism. At last, after many other privations and hardships, he and his family, by aid of the army, escaped and reached Springfield, Missouri, in great destitution, where Mr. Vernon met and relieved him.

"The record of Rev. James W. Murray is a sad and brief one. He was traveling a hundred and thirty miles below brother Hess. There he was charged with being an abolitionist and a Northern Methodist. The rebels, thirsting for his blood, came to his house, and took him away, saying they were going to try him, prove he was an abolitionist, and deal with him according to Southern law, which meant to hang him. Having gone only a few hundred yards from his own house, they shot him to pieces with demoniac rage. Surely the South-West is made sacred by the blood of martyrs."

3. The secular affairs of Missouri were in a transition state, but there was a marked progress toward a better condition, notwithstanding the schemes of pro-slavery conservatives, and the disabilities of the truly loyal men occasioned by the opposition of the Gamble regimen, and the want of backbone in General Schofield to counteract the doings of Broadhead, Guitar, and others. Messrs. Loan, M'Clung, Boyd, and Blow, members of Congress in opposition to the preferment of General Schofield, declared his administration in Missouri a failure—that he permitted Porter, in the Summer of 1862, to muster, in Northern Missouri, five or six

thousand men, to ravage the country, and murder and harass loyal men. Poindexter, in the central part of the State, north of the Missouri River, was allowed to do the same. When General Curtis was in command things were different. On his removal a great change took place. Under General Schofield the power was intrusted to those in sympathy with rebellion, to the almost entire exclusion of those of known loyalty. From this arose guerrilla depredations, the burning of Lawrence, and other atrocities.

Six members of Congress from Iowa informed the Senate that those returned from the rebel army were furnished with arms by General Schofield and Governor Gamble, and, organized into companies in counties near Iowa, were putting the peace of Iowa in jeopardy.

A change occurred, however, in spite of the Gamble Government and the easy course of General Schofield. The cause of law and liberty was advancing. The Legislature passed an act allowing militia to choose their own officers. This was vetoed by Governor Gamble, but the Legislature reënacted it over his veto, and it became a law. The Governor could no longer put such men as Guitar in office, who would glory in putting loyal men in prison, and disloyalists in position.

Fraudulent elections gave the conservative candidates for Supreme Judges seven hundred majority, whereas, there would have been a Radical majority of two thousand had not the soldiers' vote been rejected. Notwithstanding these and various other subterfuges, the cause of liberty gained. The revolution in Missouri went on triumphantly till law and order assumed the mastery over pro-slavery despotism.

4. The Missouri Conference met March 2, 1864, in Jefferson City, in the hall of the House of Representatives, Bishop Baker presiding. Here was a strange thing, indeed. The Bishop sat in the Speaker's chair; the Secretaries of the

Conference occupied the table of the Secretary of the Legislature. Bishop Ames, a few years preceding, was refused the privilege of preaching in this hall. The Legislature, in this same hall, refused to charter a seminary for the Methodist Episcopal Church, and also a university, to be erected in that city. The members of our Church and their minister had been warned to leave, on pain of severe punishment, or even death. But now the Conference of the Methodist Episcopal Church meets and deliberates here, and none make them afraid. These, the Lord's doings, are marvelous in our eyes.

At Conference were several preachers who had been mobbed from their work, but they were now ready to resume it; here Shumate, Huffman, Smith, Caughlin, Ing, Sellers, Hopkins, Gardner, and many other heroes tried as by fire, who had been violently driven from their charges, and had wandered for days in by-paths to escape the murderous hands of their pursuers.

Going from St. Louis to the seat of Conference, several reminiscences were called up to our mind. We saw the charred remains of the bridge which the rebel Jackson ordered to be burned the night of May 10, 1861, when General Lyon captured General Frost and his rebel army, near St. Louis. Passing the State mansion, we were reminded of the Governor's flurry when he heard of the capture of Camp Jackson, and came near being drowned in a cistern in the confusion of his fright. At Jefferson City, ascending the river bank, we were shown the stump of the pole which floated the rebel flag at the capital.

The whole number of members and probationers, in 1863, was 4,387. The number now, in 1864, was 6,697, making a handsome increase; besides, there were over 2,000 German Methodists in the State not included in the above.

Some four preachers from the Southern Methodists joined

our Church, and one was received into the traveling ministry. Between one and two thousand members of the Southern Church also united with us during the Conference year 1863—4.

The Methodist Episcopal Church, having maintained the occupancy of Missouri during the fiery ordeal of the last twenty years, now stood, redeemed and victorious, on the field of her struggles and sufferings. The land, providentially delivered from mob-rule and violence, and blessed with sure guarantees of freedom of speech, opinion, and conscience, spread out beautifully before us. The fields were white unto the harvest, and never did laborers go forth to their toil with more hearty good-will and animating hope than the preachers who belonged to this Conference.

5. In accordance with the law of nations, the property of rebels is forfeited to the use of the Government against which they rebel; and as the Southern Churches, as corporations, aided the rebellion, their property was liable to confiscation. The Union army, advancing southward, seized the churches of the South, and, in many cases, opened them to loyal people of the same religious creed. The order for the occupancy of churches by loyal congregations was issued by Mr. Stanton, Secretary of War.

The first of these orders, as far as we can learn, was given to Bishop Ames, November 30, 1863. It was directed to the Generals commanding the departments of *the Missouri, the Tennessee,* and *the Gulf.* The commanders were ordered "to place at the disposal of Bishop Ames all houses of worship belonging to the Methodist Episcopal Church South in which a loyal minister, who has been appointed by a loyal bishop of said Church, does not now officiate." They were also required to give the Bishop all the aid, countenance, and support practicable in the execution of his important

mission.   Other bishops of the Methodist Episcopal Church
received similar orders.

December 23d, Brigadier General Veatch, in obedience to
this order, placed *Wesley Chapel*, Memphis, Tenn., at the
disposal of Bishop Ames.

January 14, 1864, a similar order was given to the "American Home Baptist Society," in reference to churches of disloyal Baptists in the South.

Mr. Stanton, in the authority given to Bishop Ames, declared, with great truth, "that Christian ministers should,
by example and precept, support and foster the loyal sentiment of the people." He also declared that all the churches
of the Methodist Episcopal Church South were confiscated,
for the time, in which "a loyal minister, appointed by a
loyal bishop, did not officiate." This statement seemed to
indicate that loyal ministers and members of the Methodist
Episcopal Church South might retain their churches, provided there was a *loyal bishop* to make the appointments.
But no such bishop could be found in the Southern Methodist Church, as their bishops were either openly avowed
rebels, as Andrew, Paine, Pierce, and Early, or *neutral*, as
Soule and Kavanaugh were represented to be.

In the order relating to Baptist churches, Mr. Stanton
said: "It is a matter of great importance to the Government, in its efforts to restore tranquillity to the community
and peace to the Nation, that Christian ministers should, by
precept and example, support and foster the loyal sentiment
of the people." The order stated that "all houses of worship belonging to the Baptist Churches South in which a
loyal minister of said Church does not now officiate are
placed at the disposal of the American Baptist Home Mission Society."

The Missouri Republican jumped into this question without understanding it; and as a sympathizer with and patron of disloyal Southern Methodists, it raves at random against the Methodist Episcopal Church for seizing the property of their neighbors. Similar statements were made by most of the disloyal sheets in the North. The Republican, however, depended much on the disloyal Methodists of St. Louis and Missouri, and, therefore, as on all other occasions, he pleaded their cause, whether right or wrong, with great earnestness.

Although power was vested in Bishop Ames to occupy churches belonging to disloyal Southern Methodists in Missouri, he declined exercising his authority. Of the same mind were our preachers and members. At the Conference in Jefferson City, a committee, of which Rev. H. Cox was chairman, presented a report adverse to any occupancy of such churches. The preamble stated, that many of the Southern Methodists had already united with the Methodist Episcopal Church, and others were preparing to do likewise; that there was no need of our people occupying such churches. The following resolution was unanimously adopted:

"*Resolved*, by the Missouri Annual Conference of the Methodist Episcopal Church,

"1. That, as a Conference, we feel highly gratified by this exhibition of the unbounded confidence of the Government and the people in the loyalty, patriotism, and religious power of the Methodist Episcopal Church.

"2. That we fully approve of the course pursued by Bishop Ames in this State in not acting under the power conferred on him by the War Department last November.

"3. That we most earnestly recommend to our Bishops a continuance of the same course, inasmuch as *we* do not desire either the occupancy or the possession of any property to which we have not a legal title, but that, relying upon the blessing of Almighty God, we will preach a pure religion,

and an unconditional loyalty as essential to the restoration
of peace and National unity."

6. The status of the Methodist Episcopal Church South
during the Presidency of Mr. Lincoln deserves historical
attention at this point.

The leading officials and prominent men of this Church
manifestly gave their full influence to the measures of the
rebellious conspiracy from the first.

Nothing is more to the point, in proof of this, than the
Confederate Almanac, issued at Nashville, November, 1861.
A copy of this Almanac, now before us, presents the fol-
lowing particulars:

The title-page reads, " The Confederate States Almanac,
for the year of our Lord 1862. Edited by T. O. Summers, D. D., Nashville, Tenn.: Southern Methodist Publishing House. Entered, according to act of Congress, in
the year 1861, by J. B. M'Ferrin, Agent, in the office of
the District Court for the Middle District of Tennessee."

The second page is headed, " Government of the Confederate States," and has two parts.

The first is occupied by a doggerel poem, headed, "Stars
and Bars," which eulogizes the Confederacy without stint,
and denounces in similar mode the United States Government.

The second portion of page second contains the names
of the Southern political officials. Under date of November
25, 1861, it says, the rebel legislature, by a unanimous vote
of twenty-three in the upper house, and seventy-seven in
the lower house, at Neosho, took Missouri out of the Union.
In the catalogue of books published we find the "Confederate Primer," the " First Confederate Speller," and the
" Second Confederate Speller." The Moral Philosophy and
Mental Philosophy of Dr. Rivers, duly Southernized, are
also published.

Thus the rebel Government, as early as November 26, 1861, is duly acknowledged among the official publications of the Methodist Episcopal Church South. Among the *memorabilia* of the Almanac, we also find several items of secret history. Mention is made, October 31st, of an alliance between the Confederate States and Missouri. And under November 2d is a record of the bogus Missouri Legislature, which met at Neosho, under the traitor Claib. Jackson.

The poem alluded to declares "The old Union is gone," and was "the badge of tyranny and wrong." Listen, however, to its opening stanza, which is a type of the rest:

> "'T is sixty-two, and sixty-one,
> With the old Union, now is gone,
> Reeking with bloody wars—
> Gone with that ensign, once so prized,
> The Stars and Stripes, now so despised,
> Struck for the Stars and Bars." [1]

The Methodist Episcopal Church South, at the beginning of 1864, seemed almost in a state of transition; yet confused by previous entanglements. In St. Louis, advertising pews for rent or sale in one of their churches, they called it " The Methodist Episcopal Church," omitting the postfix, *South*, as if they would abjure it. In St. Joseph and elsewhere they used the same expedient of omitting the word *South* from their name. One of their preachers, near Otterville, inviting members to join, used the designation, " The Church to which I belong."

The Kentucky Conference of Southern Methodists, this year, passed a report asserting its independence of the other Conferences of the Church South, disavowing its complicity with the resolutions of other Conferences or the rulings of their bishops, and reasserting its loyalty to the Government of the United States. The Conference also took the

---

[1] Central Christian Advocate, for 1864, p. 48.

necessary steps to organize itself as a corporate body, under the laws of the State of Kentucky.

7. A volume would scarcely contain the records of loyal citizens, especially loyal Methodists, murdered by rebel bushwhackers. The following is one case of a thousand of like kind. It appeared in the Central Christian Advocate, and was republished by the North-Western Christian Advocate of October 5, 1864:

"On the 10th day of July—being Sabbath—the rebels, numbering thirty-two, headed by the notorious guerrilla, Captain Taylor, came into the neighborhood of brother Morris, and took dinner with a rebel sympathizer, Lewis Williams, after which they marched down to brother Morris's house, and, surrounding it, ordered him to surrender. This he refused to do, saying he knew how they treated prisoners. They then commenced firing on him from all sides, the balls passing through the house and among the family, which consisted of sister Morris and two little girls. Brother Morris now commenced firing out of the doors and windows at the fiends, with a revolver, and succeeded in killing two of them, and seriously wounded a third. The house was now fired in four or five places, while sister Morris implored them, as they intended to murder her supporter and protector, to spare her the only shelter she had in the world; but no attention was paid to her entreaties. She was driven away to the barn by two fiends in men's garbs, who cursed and abused her, brandished their pistols in her face, and threatened to shoot her if she attempted to come back. The little girls in the mean time having bid farewell to their father, and received his dying blessing, joined their mother and moved away to a place of greater safety. The flames had now reached the ceiling, and the rafters had commenced falling in on the second floor, when brother Morris stepped out at the front door and walked toward the gate. Scarcely had he stepped a dozen paces when he fell, pierced by four bullets, which killed him instantly. The house was entirely consumed, and with it all the family possessed in the world. Sister Morris did not even save a bonnet for herself or little daughters."

8. Conclusion. The world has hardly witnessed two decades of more heroic suffering and labor on the part of any Christian body than those through which we have thus imperfectly followed the Methodist Episcopal Church. "The half has not been told."

But how like burnished gold from the crucible does our beloved Church shine as she stands victorious and manifestly vindicated at the close of 1864! The year was one of steady material and spiritual prosperity and growth in popular favor. Old reproaches were wiped away, and the Church, strong in her conscious fidelity, and rectitude, and rejoicing in abundant omens of heavenly mercy and blessing, "came up out of the wilderness leaning upon the arm of her beloved, fair as the moon, bright as the sun, and terrible as an army with banners."

From the close of 1864 to this present—February, 1868—Providence has made us glad in the South-West with unabated progress. The circulation of our books and periodical literature has been vastly increased. The work of education has been heartily espoused and liberal incipient agencies have been devised for giving a just permanence and success to this great cause. Churches are building in all quarters, and new societies and congregations are forming on every hand. "In the wilderness waters are breaking out, and streams in the desert. And the parched ground is becoming a pool, and the thirsty land springs of water."

The Missouri and Arkansas Conference now embraces, in round numbers, about 20,000 members, and 200 ministerial laborers, members of Conference and "supplies" taken together.   Nor has the Church any where a more loyal and devoted membership or a more self-sacrificing, consecrated, and laborious ministry.

And while we learn with profound satisfaction that the whole Church has made a Centenary contribution of EIGHT MILLION DOLLARS, we are equally pleased and surprised to know that this Conference, so lately a mere handful of scarred veterans with a territory spoiled and pillaged by contending armies, should have raised $157,243 of that amount.

To the South-West the future is full of hope and promise, and could this pen resume its work a score of years hence its task would doubtless be far happier than that which is here finished.

THE END.